Human and Divine

Human and Divine

*An Introduction to the Philosophy
of Religious Experience*

Gwen Griffith-Dickson

Duckworth

First published in 2000 by
Gerald Duckworth & Co. Ltd.
61 Frith Street, London W1D 3JL
Tel: 020 7434 4242
Fax: 020 7434 4420
Email: enquiries@duckworth-publishers.co.uk
www.ducknet.co.uk

A catalogue record for this book is available
from the British Library

ISBN 0 7156 3053 9

Typeset by
Derek Doyle & Associates, Liverpool
Printed in Great Britain by
Biddles Limited, www.biddles.co.uk

Contents

Contents

Acknowledgements

This book was formed and shaped in dialogue. My students over the years have questioned, challenged, and contributed to these reflections on philosophy of religion. The maturity, breadth of background and richness of life experiences that Birkbeck students bring to their study – and their teaching of me – has enriched me, and left me humbled and grateful – and exhilarated.

Birkbeck College and the Faculty of Continuing Education in particular have supported this work through generous research grants to make possible its completion – which at times seemed impossible. I would like to record my thanks to my colleagues here. Particular thanks must go to Victoria Harrison, for her patience, thoroughness and good critical judgement in assisting the research.

The most intense support came from my family and friends. Without practical help from my mother, Joan Griffith, my husband and Louise Lambe, the book would still consist of illegible notes. I am indebted also to my father, Richard Griffith, for his unfailing support and to Malie, who contributed the wonderful photograph on the cover. My husband Andrew, my sister Mary Weston, and dear friends Michael Barnes, Norman Ballantyne and Jenny Goodman all read and re-read texts, offering critique, agreement and disagreement, and encouragement; while my mother yet again demonstrated her incomparable theological, critical and editorial skills. My two children, Andrew and Alexander, made work slower and much more complicated – but enriched and deepened my philosophy and reflection in a way that no other relationship can do.

June 2000   Gwen Griffith-Dickson

For Andrew Maxwell Dickson

E ala ke aloha ma ka hikina
Ka pi'ina a ka la
Ha'eha'e ke aloha ma ka hanohano

Ku'u hoapili o ka ua
O ka waiwai iho lā no ia o ke aloha
O ka'u mea no ia e malama nei

*

Where we will we find tranquillity?
In the ascending pathway of deep longing
Tell the story
In the name of Hi'iaka.[1]

[1] From the chant, *'Aia la 'O Pele i Hawai'i'* (There is Pele in Hawai'i), a chant in honour of Hi'iaka.

Invocation

The taboo-markers fluttered just now;
And now, you have extinguished them.
The hills in the taro patch are shared out,
They parcel out the clumps of taro in the ditches:
The land goes free, the children protected;
Sacred is the whole people; the waters run free ...

In peace I go forth from your presence;
I came to you in my nakedness.
　　Profound reverence upon me![1]

This conclusion of a hymn in praise of the Hawaiian goddess Pele alludes to the elaborate taboo system (*kapu*) in ancient Hawaii, where places, species, people were marked off as forbidden, protected, sacred. But it also announces the overthrow of the kapu: now all the land is free, to be shared out, now all the people, above all the children, are sacred and to be protected from harm. The chant encapsulates everything I find most beautiful and moving about religious feelings, thoughts, desires: reverence and wonder in the face of the awesome; the courage to strip oneself bare to confront and be confronted by ultimate truth; the deep peace resulting from such extraordinary encounters; the aspirations for liberation; the vision of a spirituality that is at home in the world, a vision which imagines the result of religious and ethical righteousness as peace between human creatures and peace between humanity and the land – and the self-transcendent, self-subverting capacity of religions which can deconstruct the rigid structures which they themselves have given rise to, suggesting a deity who saves the people from their own religiosity.

But religion has an ambivalent power, which it shares perhaps only with sexuality and other love relationships, to bring tremendous joy and transformation – or to generate tremendous oppression and destruction. At the head of this book I could have placed texts which set out codes and laws which disenfranchise or anathematise part of humanity, which place the sacred taboo on a chosen few rather than proclaiming the sanctity of all humanity. I could have provided accounts of children, not protected by a reverence that keeps them from harm, but abused by those who exploit the taboo to protect themselves from examination or criticism. There are texts aplenty which provide a religious justification for the exploitation, abuse, or even murder of certain castes, races, women, or

1

tribes; or which interpret creation accounts as legitimising the misuse and defile-
ment of the parts of creation which enjoy the privilege of not being human.

Religions with their beliefs and practices are not decorative garnishes that can
be left on the side of the plate by those who do not wish to partake of them.
People do things on the basis of these beliefs; indeed, the behaviour they seek to
control is not just their own, but also other peoples'. So we are immediately
affected by other peoples' religious beliefs, practices, and experiences, even if
we have no religious interests of our own. If you want to observe restrictions to
your diet, to your activities, to your pleasures, that needn't worry me. But often,
you insist that *I* must dress differently, or that *I* cannot do certain things, because
of *your* religious beliefs. Then the legitimacy of *your* religious claims suddenly
becomes of importance to *me*.

Of course I may find my own beliefs the object of scrutiny. What lies behind
my impulses to say 'I believe in that' or 'That's wrong'? And how well do my
claims hold up in conversation? And why don't people always agree with my
own eminently sensible beliefs?

The best way to get to grips with what you believe is to study it and reflect
on it in an analytical, often critical way. This is also the best way to get to grips
with what you don't believe, or what you would like to leave behind. Above all,
it is the best way of coping with other people's beliefs. Philosophy of religion is
as important for atheists and agnostics as for believers.

Archimedes was famed for inventing the lever. So intoxicated was he with his
discovery, and its powers and potential, that he claimed that with a lever he
could move the earth. 'I just need to find the right place to stand ... Give me a
place to put my foot outside the world, and I can move the earth.' What is the
right standpoint to find, from which we can survey the terrain of religion? If we
can identify it, the right philosophical method or principles, it will give us the
necessary foothold outside the world in order to have the authoritative, objective
overview of the world and human existence within it.

The Hawaiian demi-god Mau'i wanted to unite all the islands of Hawaii[2] into
one single landmass, and determined to do so by means of his marvellous
strength (and a stout rope and hook). The problem was finding the right foothold
to brace himself as he hooked each island in turn and pulled them all together.
The place he chose was Ka'ena Point, the westernmost point on the island of
O'ahu, one of the central islands in the chain. This extraordinary spot is also the
jumping-off place for the Hawaiian's spirit when departing the dead body. So the
right foothold allows you more than the best view: it also allows your unencumbered spirit to unite complexity, diversity, and multiplicity into an
all-embracing unity, a vision of the whole.

Procrustes, a dwarf, had a dwarf-sized bed in his guest-room. This caused
visitors some discomfort, but when they emerged, complaining, from their room,
Procrustes would explain patiently that there was nothing at all the matter with
his bed, as he followed them back into the room. When the disgruntled guest

climbed into the bed to demonstrate its inadequacy – 'You see, my arm is hanging over the side ... my feet are dangling off the end of the bed ...' – Procrustes could demonstrate that this was not the case at all. He produced an axe and removed all the bits of the visitor that did not fit into his bed, to show how they did in fact fit perfectly within it. So with the right tools, as well as the right starting-point, you can also reduce an awkward and bulky phenomenon to a more appropriate size and shape.

The medieval Jewish thinker Maimonides, considering how one might go about studying religion, distinguished the 'quest for truth' from the 'defence of the faith'. The right standpoint and the right tools could equip you for a quest for what is really true, even if it means relinquishing opinions previously held. You can discover the truth, even if it is unwelcome; not just defend what you believe, right or wrong.

Mau'i's hook, when cast into the island of Kaua'i and pulled, tore off the great boulder of Pōhaku o Kaua'i into the sea where it still sits, visibly, off the western coast of O'ahu – creating yet *another* island.

In this book, we will focus on human experience: how different religious traditions have reflected on it philosophically, and how different philosophical traditions have reflected on it religiously. Philosophy of religion, as the majority of books practise it in the West, tends not only to focus exclusively on Christianity, or something called 'Judeo-Christianity', but also to work within a certain philosophical style. 'Analytical' philosophy is more popular in English-speaking countries than the styles of philosophy found on the European Continent (let alone other Continents – or islands).[3]

There are a number of challenges and difficulties in departing from this well-trodden path of discussing a single religion within only one philosophical stance. The greater the number of different cultures and their ideas that one speaks with, the easier it is to make a fool of oneself; worse, the easier it is to offend without realising it.

But I didn't grow up in a culture in which one religion, race or ethnicity was predominant; I grew up in Hawaii with a variety of cultures interacting sometimes harmoniously, sometimes explosively; eating each other's foods, visiting each other's temples, sleeping with one another and beating one another up, speaking a pidgin which mingled and mangled everyone's language. So I aspire to the philosophical virtue of making a fool of oneself gracefully and the theological virtue of being wrong graciously.

However, I apologise to those religious traditions with which I am less familiar. It was irresistible to engage with your ideas, even if I have sometimes lured them out of their original frameworks and into mine. I have been fascinated not only to find the great differences that exist in the thinking of other traditions, but also by the fact that arguments and ideas that look very familiar have popped up in unfamiliar contexts. Still more interesting is the fact that one often finds agreement between people of different faiths over against their coreligionists. For example, if one put Jewish, Christian and Muslim philosophers together in a room to debate the nature of God's power, we would not find three camps: one Jewish, one Christian, one Muslim. We would find *two* opposed groups. One would be composed of Maimonides, Aquinas and Ibn Rushd, that is, a Jew, Christian and Muslim, all insisting together that God cannot do what is logically impossible. The other camp would likewise contain Jews, Christians (Descartes, for example) and Muslims (al-Ghazālī would be one such), all in agreement that God *can*. Many issues in religious philosophy do not represent irreconcilable dogmatic disputes between different faiths, so much as differences in philosophical faith and outlook – a sort of temperamental difference that divides persons, not religious traditions.

However, I am sorry if I have misinterpreted some of your religious traditions. The philosophical traditions in which I am less at home may be less forgiving of any errors on my part; but I confess I am less repentant on this front.

The danger for the reader is of course a certain philosophical jet lag as one hops from one culture to another. It has not been feasible to set each idea carefully within the context of the history and theology of its home culture. You will not have a thorough understanding of any of the religious traditions from reading this book. It will not be like visiting a country and experiencing it in all its concrete detail; it will be like attending an international conference, where no one is on their home ground, and everyone has gathered to discuss a single topic together, despite the differences in their backgrounds. To counteract the potential confusion for the reader, there is a Glossary at the end of the book giving brief background information on the most famous or influential thinkers, schools, or ideas of the different religious cultures, as well as explaining certain terms which may be unfamiliar.

Although I hope to introduce you to some of the issues in Philosophy of Religion, and survey some of the literature on the subject, the fundamental aim of this book is to encourage you to think for yourself on these matters.

The book's aim is to introduce the reader to the practice of philosophy of religion: not just certain topics and issues, but also an activity and a community of people who engage in it. So you will meet some of its jobs, interests, hobbies; some of its main characters and practitioners. But I hope also to encourage you to join them actively, not passively: to invite you to think critically on these matters. This means that sometimes I have hinted and suggested at possibilities, rather than spelling everything out. The reader can unpack these as she likes.

I hope this can go forward despite the absence of studied neutrality in this book. People who write on these issues have strong opinions about them. My opinion is usually, 'I don't know.' (But I know what I like.) A neutral, objective style is supposed to efface the writer's opinions and avoid prejudicing the reader. My own feeling is, the more neutral and objective the style is, the less likely you are to realise that this is *one person's view*, which you can discard without undue anxiety. The more of the author's personality you meet, the easier it is to engage critically with her and sharpen your own wits against hers.

Since the intention is that the enquiry range across a number of different religions, and different styles of philosophy, the task of surveying *all* the topics of philosophy of religion proved to be too long for single convenient volume. Consequently some of the material, that which deals with conceptions and images of the divine and some of the arguments for the existence of God, will appear later in a companion volume.

The gender of pronouns used for people in general, and for God, is a problem. I have cut the Gordian knot: I refer to God as 'She' or 'He' in alternate parts of the book. Correspondingly, human beings are referred to as the opposite gender to make it clearer which sort of being is under discussion. To aid clarity further, God's pronouns are capitalised.

Philosophy of religion is often said to be a critique of religious ideas and beliefs. But in order to do this, surely we need a 'meta-critique' – a critique of critique itself? Consequently this book begins in Part I with a look at some of the 'metacritical issues' involved in contemporary philosophy of religion – questions of reason, belief, and language. The question of knowledge about the divine recurs throughout this book, but will feature more prominently in the companion volume. These metacritical issues are often thought to comprise the 'foundations' of the discipline, which is why they appear first here. 'Foundations' could be that which you have to build first before you can build anything else. However, 'foundations' are also that which you find last in an excavation, having dug up everything else first. These chapters are also arguably the most difficult. Some readers, therefore, might prefer to leave them until last and go on to Part II.

The earth, other people, love, birth inspire religious awe. Evil, suffering, and death may make it impossible to believe. Spiritual experience encompasses both ecstasy and intense suffering. A philosophical examination of the issues and questions of religion could profitably begin with human existence and how the divine seems to be entangled in it. Religious experience and the problems raised by evil and suffering are the aspects of religious existence that affect our beliefs most powerfully, so they are the subject of this book. Part II considers one side of the coin of human experience: particular spiritual experiences as prisms for the more diffuse experience of acting or seeing life in a religious way. Part III deals with the other side of the coin: the experience of evil and suffering, and whether these proscribe every religious outlook or can be part of religious experience and insight.

Are you the heart or the heart-throb? The soul or the soul's beloved?
– I don't know.
You are all Existence; whether this or that,
– I don't know.
Except you, any other soul's beloved in the universe,
– I don't know.
I find nothing in my heart other than the tumult of your Love,
Other than the mad passion of joining you in my soul,
– I don't know.
What can I offer? The heart is not worthy.
What can I sacrifice? The soul is not deserving.

All I had was a bleeding heart, and that I lost too,
Where is that madman now?
– I don't know.
Every moment you pour sufferings upon my heart and soul,
What do you want from this wretched wanderer?
– I don't know.
If your intention is life, then show your face and take my life,
But if you have other intentions, this or that,
– I don't know.
I have an agreement with you, you have a covenant with me,
Have you broken the covenant? Are you keeping the agreement?
– I don't know.

Since you are manifest in the eye of every atom,
Why are you so hidden from this bewildered being?
– I don't know.
I do not find you in my heart, nor in the world, nor the universe,
Oh … where shall I seek you, I am bewildered,
– I don't know.
Even more strange, is that though I see your radiant Beauty, yet,
I don't know what I perceive, so ignorant am I,
– I don't know.
All I know, is that the world is bright, day and night, from your Face,
but are you the sun or the iridescent moon?
– I don't know.

Fettered am I in Eraqi, a prisoner of your separation,
will I be released from this captivity?
– I don't know.[4]

PART I

Metacritical Issues

1. All at Sea

Rationality and belief

The insane man jumped into their midst and transfixed them with his glances. 'Where is God gone?' he called out. 'I mean to tell you! We have killed him, you and I! We are all his murderers! But how have we done it? How were we able to drink up the sea?'[1]

The island of truth

In his *Critique of Pure Reason*, Kant speaks of the territory of pure understanding as an island, 'the land of truth – enchanting name! – surrounded by a wide and stormy ocean, the native home of illusion, where many a fog bank and many a swiftly melting iceberg give the deceptive appearance of farther shores, deluding the adventurous seafarer'. Characteristically, Kant does not want to venture onto the sea in such a dangerous undertaking until he has explored it in all directions and 'obtained assurances', as well as consulting maps of the land he is about to leave.[2]

This nautical metaphor expresses Kant's desire to attain to pure understanding, and the undisputed truth. In so doing, however, there are many potential dangers; these largely consist in errors of unreason and irrationality. Kant's underlying belief is that the correct use of reason is what ensures success in the journey to truth.

Kant's work hardened the distinction between reason and faith, both in their methods and their territory. There are certain fields in which reason alone may not attain knowledge, and knowledge of a transcendent God is one of them. The relationship between reason and faith, he suggested, was that philosophy could 'make room for faith'; but it does so largely by preventing theology from making unwarranted claims to knowledge by the use of reason.

This is a development of a process that had been evolving in Western European reflection. John Smith suggests that the problem of the relation of faith and reason exists in Christianity from the start, because unlike some Eastern religions, philosophy was encountered as autonomous from religion, as an inheritance from the Greeks (whose religion Christianity did not share).[3] Three polar tensions developed, in his view. The first is the tension between the assertion that there is a *continuity* between rationality and the content of faith, as we see in Augustine and Anselm, who describe their quest as 'faith seeking under-

standing'; and the assertion that there is a *discontinuity* between religious insight
and all forms of rational mediation, such as we find in Tertullian, who 'believes
because it is absurd'. For the first group, understanding illuminates and supports
but does not create faith. But the latter group insist on the uniqueness, even the
absurdity of faith, for two reasons: because the ultimate mystery of religion
defies articulation, and because adjusting faith to rational demands results in
either a distortion or a subordination of faith to secular thought, or self-deception.

Secondly, he suggests that there is a tension between the *conative* side of faith
(the personal relations of trust, dependence, commitment, devotion) and the
cognitive side of faith (concepts, truths about God, etc.) Each of these attitudes
stands in a critical relation to the other. Faith understood as a relationship stands
opposed to faith as a 'propositional attitude'; while the other viewpoint maintains that the conceptual content of faith is essential; without it faith is blind and
lacks rational foundations.[4]

Finally, he suggests that there is a third tension, between a new, secular standard of rationality and what we find in the (Christian) religious tradition. The
modern standard for what is rational is influenced by three factors: by the norms
operative in experimental science, by a logic which purports to be entirely
formal and thus independent of particular philosophical commitments, and by
reason which is conceived in a technical and instrumental way, as distinct from
reflective and speculative reason.

In the Indian subcontinent, however, styles of more philosophical reflection
grew up alongside scriptures recording hymns, legends, myths; in Buddhism it
is very difficult, if not impossible, to make a distinction between 'philosophical'
reflection and pragmatic discussion of how one attains salvation. In Hinduism,
attaining salvation by the 'way of knowledge' (*jñāna-marga*) might be distinguished from the 'way of devotion' (*bhakti-marga*) and the 'way of action'
(*karma-marga*), but dividing 'knowledge' up into 'philosophy' and 'theology'
seems misconceived. In the Far East, we do not find the same tendency to divide
the sources of knowledge, such as 'revelation' vs. 'reason'; so the underpinning
that facilitates the opposition of philosophy and theology, or reason and faith,
does not exist.

On the other hand, the distinction between 'philosophers' and 'theologians'
became marked in Islam after the appearance of the first thinkers to self-
consciously describe themselves as 'philosophers' in medieval times, largely
galvanised by discovering the (pagan) philosophy of Aristotle, whom they introduced to the medieval Christians. In the history of Islamic thought, the
difference between logical and reasoned reflection and the exposition of sacred
writings and teachings was highly contentious. What could be known through
philosophical reflection as opposed to what was revealed in the Qur'an was a
matter of passionate dispute; a dispute which Jewish thinkers and eventually
Christian ones began to imbibe and reproduce.

In the Christian and post-Christian world in the West, philosophy of religion is now largely seen as that which can help us to see whether or not religious beliefs are worthy of acceptance. The idea here is that philosophers can single out particular religious beliefs and ask questions such as 'Is this belief rationally defensible?' or 'Can this belief be supported by argument or appeal to evidence?' Lying behind such questions is the assumption that religious beliefs are either true or false and that their truth or falsity can be settled or discussed at an intellectual level.[5]

Thus in the post-Enlightenment West, we have a discipline called 'philosophy of religion' whose task is either to ground religious beliefs and statements in rational argument or to deny that they can be so grounded.[6]

This represents a shift in emphasis from previous centuries and other philo-sophical and religious cultures. A fundamental philosophical-religious preoccupation for many cultures has been the question of *knowledge*: how best to *know* the divine and the ultimate possibilities for humanity. More sceptically, the question has been whether such knowledge is possible. In 'philosophy of religion', however, it seems as if the battle for the possibilities of knowledge has been tacitly conceded since the eighteenth-century Enlightenment during which Kant was writing. After the challenges and critiques of the possibility of knowledge made by various schools and developments in analytical philo-sophy, the debate in the English-speaking world has largely shifted from the question of *how it is possible to know* the object of our religious longing, to the question of *whether it is rational to believe*, apparently in the absence of 'real' knowledge.

Scylla and Charybdis

The image of a sea voyage is one that recurs frequently throughout the history of philosophy as a metaphor for the quest for truth or knowledge.[7] Hans Blumenberg unpacks some of the ideas that lie behind the image. One is that the land is the natural, and usual, boundary of our human activity. Leaving behind solid land to undertake a sea voyage suggests something arduous and extraordi-nary. Secondly, the image often involves the demonisation of the sea as unpredictable, lawless, incalculable, which can confound our attempts at orien-teering.[8] It is a symbol of the arbitrariness of violence, the difficulties and delays of the homeward journey, and of shipwrecks, in which the reliability of the cosmos becomes questionable.

Pamela Sue Anderson is uncomfortable with Kant's image, because of the frequent association of the sea with the feminine. This makes the land of truth and rationality into the territory of the male; leaving the feminine (and real women) as the irrational, threatening, unreliable sea.[9] This is all in keeping, I feel, with the tendency of Western thinking to divide things into pairs and oppose them. It is expressed in a legend of another seafarer, bolder than Kant, whose dualisms were even more threatening than the opposition between reason and faith, the senses and the understanding, mind and body:

' "Two ways will lie before you, and you must choose between them as you see fit, though I will tell you both. The higher rock rears its sharp peak up to the very sky. It is the home of the monster Scylla. No crew can boast that they ever sailed their ship past Scylla without loss. The other of the two rocks is lower. A great fig-tree with luxuriant foliage grows upon the crag, its roots far away down below, and it is below this that dread Charybdis sucks the dark waters down. Heaven keep you from the spot when she is at her work."

"Yes, Circe, but could I not somehow steer clear of the terrors of Charybdis, yet tackle Scylla when she comes at my crew?"

But the goddess only cried out at me as an obstinate fool, always spoiling for a fight and welcoming trouble.'[10]

Circe warns Odysseus (Ulysses) of the dangers of two extremes between which he must find his way. Western philosophy has also described 'two ways' to sail to the island of truth and knowledge – or two ways to prove that you are rational. One aspires to soar to the heavens unencumbered; the other to root itself solidly in the depths of the earth. One trusts pure reason and regards the fallible human senses with suspicion; the other distrusts the human capacity for self-deception in the very act of reasoning itself, claiming instead that it is the senses which tell us what is really true.[11]

These differences in philosophical temperament can be seen in certain fundamental affinities and aversions. Do you fundamentally place your faith in what you can see, hear, handle? Does it settle the matter beyond dispute if you can point to an object or to evidence in the laboratory? Then you are probably an 'empiricist'. The empiricist believes that what knowledge we can have comes from experience. In most moderate forms, this means 'most factual knowledge': what the world is like and what exists. Moderate empiricists will make an exception for the truths of logic, or logical relations between concepts. A stronger form of empiricism is called 'positivism' when applied to the possibility of knowing. 'We can only know what we can perceive with the senses.' When applied to the question of what exists, it is called 'materialism': nothing immaterial or non-physical exists. The positivist believes that all genuine human knowledge falls within the bounds of human experience, that is, within the bounds of science; whatever questions we have that cannot be answered by science cannot legitimately be answered.

On the other hand, you might be inclined to trust reasoning. You may be able to doubt what you see – after all there can be optical illusions, tricks of the light, defects of vision – but you could never really doubt that $1 + 1 = 2$, for that is not a matter of one individual's perception. You might, then, be a 'rationalist'.[12] The rationalist believes that by the use of reason alone it is possible to attain knowledge of reality and what exists, and its nature. It usually follows that such thinkers believe that knowledge will form a single rational system; that this will be deductive, and that in principle everything can be known and brought into this one all-encompassing system. For the rationalist, things that are beyond human experience are not necessarily beyond human knowledge; one can sometimes make logical inferences about them.

You might be happy with neither of these positions. You might believe that religious doctrines or truths cannot be grasped or proven by reason but must be accepted by acts of faith. You might hold that reason and faith have some areas of overlap but are also different spheres proper to themselves. Or, if you are as provocative as Tertullian, you might not only reject the suggestion that you should cease to believe because the Christian religion is absurd; you might indeed claim, as he did, 'I believe *because* it is absurd.' If so, you would be labelled a 'fideist'.

You may have noticed that I have consistently used the word 'believe' in relation to these philosophical stances. That is because I think that ultimately these philosophical views all rest on a kind of choosing and believing, not on proof. A saying from Thomas Aquinas is often taken to be the empiricist's manifesto: 'There is nothing in our minds that was not first in our senses.' But this fundamental claim of empiricism is nowhere empirically given. There is nothing one can see under a microscope, or test in a laboratory, to ground this particular 'empiricist' claim that knowledge can only come through the senses; it is a sheer assertion of faith. Reliance on reason and rationality is also a fundamental question of faith and doubt in different activities that we perform under different conditions.

Nevertheless, these options move within the sphere of a common question. Once this question was: how do we know things? By reason, or by the senses? Now, the question is: what justifies us as rational people? Being logical, or being scientific?

It is also possible that none of these positions fits you well. You might want to know why you cannot have faith in your senses, *and* in your reasoned reflection, *and* still be able to believe things in the absence of sensory or rational proof. Why force them to compete for the highest honours if in practice they are all geared up to work cooperatively?

'All through the night I was swept along, and at sunrise found myself for the second time at Scylla's rock and that appalling whirlpool, Charybdis. Charybdis was beginning to suck the salt water down. But as she did so, I was flung right up to the great fig-tree, on which I got a tight grip and clung like a bat.'[13]

Seaworthy ships?

Odysseus avoided both alternatives of the Either/Or and saved himself from destruction by grabbing for the roots of the great fig-tree. Most Western philosophers are inclined to think that such adventures and wrecks are signs of failure that should have been avoided in the first place.

W. Clifford made use of the seafaring metaphor to defend his assertion that it is wrong, positively unethical, to believe something in the absence of sufficient evidence.

> A shipowner was about to send to sea an emigrant-ship. He knew that she was old, and not over-well built at the first; that she had seen many seas and climes, and often had needed repairs. Doubts had been suggested to him that possibly she was not seaworthy. These doubts preyed upon his mind, and made him unhappy; he thought that perhaps he ought to have her thoroughly overhauled and refitted, even though this should put him to great expense. Before the ship sailed, however, he succeeded in over-coming these melancholy reflections .... In such ways he acquired a sincere and comfortable conviction that his vessel was thoroughly safe and seaworthy; he watched her departure with a light heart, and benevolent wishes for the success of the exiles in their strange new home that was to be; and he got his insurance-money when she went down in mid-ocean and told no tales.[14]

In Clifford's view, the sincerity of the man's belief was no defence, for he had no *right* to believe in such a situation, based on the evidence that was before him. Everyone, regardless of 'station' or 'simplicity of mind' has a universal duty to question what he or she believes. 'To sum up: it is wrong always, every-where, and for anyone, to believe anything upon insufficient evidence.'[15]

William James responded with an defence of the right to believe 'in spite of the fact that our merely logical intellect may not have been coerced'. He asserted 'the right to believe', not merely as a cognitive question, but as an issue affected by emotion and passion; 'In truths dependent on our personal action, then, faith based on desire is certainly a lawful and possibly an indispensable thing.'[16] He observed:

> To preach scepticism to us as a duty until 'sufficient evidence' for religion be found, is tantamount therefore to telling us ... that to yield to our fear of its being error is wiser and better than to yield to our hope that it may be true. It is not intellect against all passions, then; it is only intellect with one passion laying down its law. And by what, forsooth, is the supreme wisdom of this passion warranted? ...
>
> I, therefore, for one, cannot see my way to accepting the agnostic rules for truth-seeking, or wilfully agree to keep my willing nature out of the game. I cannot do so for this plain reason, that *a rule of thinking which would absolutely prevent me from acknowledging certain kinds of truth if those kinds of truth were really there, would be an irrational rule.*[17]

More than a century later, the debate over the rationality of religious belief is now the issue that dominates writing in Anglo-American philosophy of religion.

Most theistic philosophers who defend the right to believe, however, all but ignore James' campaign on behalf of the will and of passion. They tend to find ways of justifying religious belief within the usual confines of the game of rationality, engaging in a critique of the rules, rather than a metacritique of the game itself.

Must beliefs be rational, justified, grounded, based on evidence? Most, perhaps, say yes; one must have a well-constructed, watertight ship before one even thinks of setting out from the port. The differences then centre on whether or not the theist has any hope of building such a ship of their religious faith. For what counts as 'evidence' for one's religious beliefs?

How do you decide whether it is rational to believe whether or not something or someone exists? What questions do you ask? Has it been seen, heard, felt – by oneself or others? Have its traces or effects been experienced? For other sorts of entities – entities that have, as it were, a logical impact, like numbers perhaps – one can ask whether there are logical considerations that dictate or imply its existence.

So in philosophy of religion debates centre on whether there are appropriate categories of evidence for religious beliefs. Empirical evidence? Such evidence of incorporeal deities or entities is presumably hard to come by. Can one hope to find traces of divine activity or presence in the workings of the physical universe? Such claims are interpretations of the empirical data, and require complex justification and assertion. As such, they are subject to challenge and debate. Can one claim to experience an incorporeal deity in a non-material way? Can one accept the testimony of others to such experience or knowledge? In the absence of experiential evidence of one kind or another, are there logical arguments for the existence of religious truths?

These are the questions that underlie discussion of the rationality of religious belief, and discussion of them will occupy this book. The validity of each style of evidence, knowledge and justification – 'empirical', 'rational', etc. – are hotly disputed, as are their applications to the sphere of religious claims. Some might reject the application to religion of all these forms of justification a priori; some philosophers might accept all, and others might accept one mode but not the others.

In 'natural theology', the traditional form of philosophy of religion, rational arguments for the existence of God have been a principal focus of creativity and critique in Islam, Judaism, and Christianity. Such arguments are even older in Indian philosophy, as are the atheistic counter-arguments mounted by traditions of Cārvāka, Buddhism, and Jainism. Interest in the traditional arguments continues, but a growth area of philosophy of religion has been the use of religious experience as an argument for the existence of God. Philosophers have recently put forward arguments for the existence of God based on the phenomenon of religious experience. Often these arguments suggest that there is an analogy, or sometimes a parity, between religious and other forms of experience, such as that derived from the senses, which justifies the reliability of such evidence.[18]

Michael Scriven rejects all arguments for the existence of God, and claims that the absence of any empirical or other evidence means there is *no* likelihood that God exists. This is a complete justification for the claim that God does not exist. 'We need not have a proof that God does not exist in order to justify atheism. Atheism is obligatory in the absence of any evidence for God's existence. ... The proper alternative, where there is no evidence, is not mere suspension of belief, e.g., about Santa Claus; it is *disbelief*.'[19] Anthony Flew, among his many challenges to the viability of religious faith, calls attention to the *disconfirmation* in experience of a good and powerful God, such as the experience of suffering and evil.

However, some theistic philosophers have risen to the challenge to waterproof their ship of beliefs. Stephen Davis revives James' 'right to believe' doctrine, which he believes to be 'sound, if interpreted correctly'.[20] The 'right to believe' doctrine can give epistemological justification to religious faith if those beliefs are held with an open mind and are open to modification in the light of future evidence.[21] Central to his account, however, is his assertion that 'private evidence', personal experience, counts as evidence and is justified in some circumstances.

> ... where the truth of a belief cannot be settled on evidential grounds and where a person must choose either to accept or reject it, a rational person is justified in accepting for public or private reasons that belief which he finds most illuminating, which he is able to use to make the most positive significance for his life. This does not show that the belief is true – only that it is rational to accept it.[22]

One can, like Davis, suggest revaluation of one category of evidence which might improve the case religious faith can make. W. Donald Hudson is more ambitious; he provides a whole framework for justifying beliefs and defending them as 'rational'.[23] His criteria of rationality require that the belief in question must not be self-contradictory, that it must be supported by the relevant evidence, that the believer must be prepared to surrender it if given good reason, and that the belief in question must conform to the 'rational system of beliefs'. Considering how religious beliefs might fare under this regime, it is clear that they would enjoy sufficient tolerance to survive and conduct much of their business. A religious belief might reasonably aspire to the absence of self-contradiction; and if the evidence demanded is restricted to what is 'relevant', it can justifiably excuse itself from providing sensory data for non-material entities.[24] Hudson, then, proposes a framework that looks decently rational to other players, while accommodating religious beliefs.

However, the assumption that all knowledge and belief must be supported with solid evidence has been challenged by those who reject a view they characterise as 'foundationalism', as Phillips does here:

Foundationalism is the view that a belief is a rational belief only if it is related, in appropriate ways, to a set of propositions which constitute the foundations of what we believe. It assumes, from the outset, that belief in God is not among these foundational propositions. Belief in the existence of God, it is said, stands in need of justifications, grounds, reasons, foundations. We have to ask whether it is rational to believe in God. ... asking whether belief in God is rational quickly becomes a matter of seeking evidence for the existence of God. Such evidence, if it can be found, will constitute the foundation of the belief. If it cannot be found, it will have been shown that there is no good reason for believing in God.[25]

Alvin Plantinga observes that not every proposition or belief can be foundational. A foundational belief must be 'basic', self-evident, or incorrigible. But the assertion that 'only propositions that are self-evident and incorrigible are properly basic' is itself neither self-evident nor incorrigible; but nevertheless is 'basic' to the foundationalist. But why should *we* accept it, if it is neither self-evident nor incorrigible? Plantinga concludes that this requirement 'is no more than a bit of intellectual imperialism on the part of the foundationalist'.[26] One could add to Plantinga's points that the belief that one must 'either have evidence or not believe' is a belief for which no evidence can be provided – like many other essentially ethical beliefs.

Plantinga's alternative – to argue that belief in God is a 'basic belief' – we shall examine below. Here we will note that the mast and flag of his epistemological ship, a ship called 'Reformed Epistemology', is that Protestant Reformers such as Calvin[27] held that 'it is entirely right, rational, reasonable, and proper to believe in God without any evidence or argument at all; in this respect belief in God resembles belief in the past, in the existence of other persons, and in the existence of material objects'[28] – a direct rejection of Clifford's principle. The 'evidentialist objection to theistic belief' (that belief in God lacks evidence) is rooted in classical foundationalism, and is ultimately false and 'self-referentially incoherent'.[29]

Kelly James Clark maintains that the evidentialist objection is not just false but also irrelevant. 'The evidentialist objector assumes that belief in God is like belief in a scientific hypothesis. This assumption distorts our view of the rationality of religious belief. In actual fact, another analogy is more appropriate: Belief in God is more like the belief that persons have minds.'[30] As Plantinga has also argued,[31] just as belief in other minds doesn't require evidence to be rationally maintained, so too belief in God: we don't need *arguments* for either. If Christianity believes God is a person, then we should view belief in God in an analogous way to our beliefs in other persons. These are not based on evidence. 'The logic of scientific and mathematical discovery is perverse when applied to personal relations.'[32] It is the logic of belief in other persons that we should follow in assessing the rationality of theism.[33]

Norman Kretzmann has counter-argued that Plantinga misinterprets evidentialism. Plantinga's notion of evidence is too narrow. What evidentialism asks for is some kind of backing to one's claim; not just evidence that meets the most exacting criteria of indubitability. The 'circumstances', or 'warrant', or 'grounds' or 'justification' he claims for religious beliefs, such as immediate experience, is precisely what is included under the notion of 'evidence', rightly understood. But without this artificially narrow concept of evidence, Plantinga himself would not be an 'anti-evidentialist', Kretzmann suspects.[34] It is as if Plantinga interprets the need for a sound ship to mean that every plank used in its construction must be free of knots or flaws in the grain. But that is not what 'evidentialism' demands in its requirement for a well-built ship.

Perhaps, as David Burrell helpfully observes, the metaphor of 'foundations' itself is misleading. One has to lay the 'foundations' for a building first, as if God must *first* be shown to exist before we can engage in religious practice. The reality is the reverse, however. The search for 'foundations' is subsequent to the holding of belief and engagement in religious practice. 'Foundations' then suggests a two-way metaphor: the first is that of the builder, who lays a foundation before doing anything else. The second image, however, is of an archaeologist, who looks for the foundation as a goal of a lengthy dig.

> The logic of a search for foundations is more archaeological, whereas we retain some expectations from them more akin to a contractor. It is these latter expectations which make us want to assure ourselves of God's existence *before* we can responsibly undertake religious practice. Yet we have seen that presuppositions need not function like initial premises, and often cannot, for they are insufficiently determinate to do so.[35]

We are mistaken to handle the question of justification as if it is 'prospective' in character: as asking 'Why should I do this?' Rather, the justification of religious belief is not so much 'prospective' as 'retrospective': 'Why am I doing this?' We should shift our paradigm of justification to prioritise its retrospective character. It is more basic; and 'it makes more sense on reflection to see ourselves as attempting to understand the ways we find ourselves to be drawn'.[36]

Gareth Moore, in his Wittgensteinian investigation of Christian belief, observes that the grounds for believing in the existence of God are not like the grounds for believing in the existence of anything else. Providing 'evidence' for the existence of God is not the point:

> The Christian does not *fail* to produce God, where he might have succeeded. For the Christian *is* committed, upon pain of idolatry, to rejecting any and every candidate that might be presented as the discovered God. … So it is not that he fails in the task of producing God. Rather, in Christianity, there *is* no such task. For the Christian is committed to finding what the atheist too expects to find – *nothing*.[37]

Traditional epithets for God such as 'invisible, intangible' and so on are meant to say: 'There is no such thing as discovering God. Whatever you discover, is not God.'[38] The equator is an example of something that exists, and is invisible; but it would be foolish to say 'I believe in the equator, even though I can't see it', and then provide evidence for it. The equator is not a hypothesis, nor it is inferred, it is not an extra thing added to the other things on the earth that just happens to be invisible. A denial that the equator exists would have to imply a very different view of the earth than the one we have.

The case is similar with God, insofar as God is not an extra being in the universe that believers and atheists disagree about. It is a mistake then to offer evidence or arguments in support of God's existence; we have to describe the use of the word 'God' in our language and lives. Moore suggests three advantages to such an account: it avoids the usual difficulties about traditional 'arguments for the existence of God'; it shows that Christian belief is not a conclusion based on arguments; and it gives a much more positive role to God's 'absence': the absence of anything we can point to as 'God' is not a failed presence, but is essential to faith; a feature of the avoidance of idolatry.[39]

I suspect the real problem with 'evidentialism' isn't evidence as such. Moore too has a backing for his beliefs, or for why he has chosen to find a place for the word 'God' in his life. The problem is at the very least the narrowness of the evidence, as Kretzmann suggests, as well as the order of discovery of its foundations, as Burrell points out. More than that, the difficulty is created by the notion of rationality that is in operation. If the narrowness of what is allowed as 'evidence' is problematic enough, what about the narrowness of what is believed and supported? The obsession with the rationality of belief focuses almost entirely on the existence of a God, and spin-off issues about whether He or She is concerned with human beings or not. But the reason why we should be concerned with the 'rationality' of what we believe is not ultimately an issue of intellectual defensibility; it is a question of ethical responsibility. The demand for the support and grounds of belief which anti-evidentialists spurn is an urgent necessity once we leave the jousts and tournaments of seminar rooms, and encounter people with beliefs which not merely differ from ours, but may threaten us.

Shipbuilding

You want to go to sea. There is a dispute, as we have seen, over what tests you have to apply to the timbers of your ship, and whether your shipbuilding is up to the moral scrutiny you apparently should give it. But how do you build your ship in order to stay afloat?

You start with a framework. You must have a structure in order to construct a well-designed ship. This structure needs to be adequate to support whatever it is that you intend to do with your vessel. In a ship of any complexity, some timbers will be more important than others. They are weight-bearing, as well as conferring on the ship its shape and dimensions.

Systems of thought are similar. There are propositions or sentences or beliefs or bits of knowledge that are essentially trivial, and like planks on the deck or a foremast, they can be knocked off without sinking the ship. Other beliefs or assertions are like the mainmast: it would be crippling to lose it, but one might survive with some frantic repairs. Still others, if lost or irreparably damaged, would sink the ship completely with the loss of all hands.

We all have beliefs that are 'basic'; some are based on our perceptions, some on a kind of logic: unless I am a philosopher and therefore peculiar in this respect, I just believe that I exist, without troubling myself over evidence to prove it. I believe that things do not spontaneously cease to exist for no reason, so if my purse is missing, it must be somewhere and it is worth looking for it. A belief or assumption that things do not suddenly cease to exist for no reason is basic. A belief that *you stole* my purse would not be 'basic'; I would require evidence before I was justified in making such a claim.

These basic beliefs enjoy a kind of distinction comparable to the crucial spars and masts of a ship. They are essential, bear weight, support other planks, and cannot be dispensed with. I could not go through the day effectively disbelieving in my own existence and the basic reliability of material objects. Like the ship's framework and masts, these beliefs are also their own justification and support. They are not inferred from any other beliefs, but are 'rock-bottom', 'primary', 'fundamental'. They are the essential support of other planks, they do not require any further support than their own selves.

'Reformed Epistemologists' argue that, far from needing evidence and 'grounds', belief in God is 'properly basic' in this sort of way. As Nicholas Wolterstorff puts it,

> Deeply embedded in the Reformed tradition is the conviction that a person's belief that God exists may be a justified belief even though that person has not inferred that belief from others of his beliefs which provide good evidence for it. After all, not all the things we are justified in believing have been inferred from other beliefs. We have to start somewhere! And the Reformed tradition has insisted that the belief that God exists, that God is Creator, etc., may justifiably be found there in the foundation of our system of beliefs.[40]

Plantinga asks why belief in God must be one of the later, subsequent beliefs which can only be nailed onto the ship at a later stage? Why cannot belief in God be one of the basic beliefs, part of the framework itself? Why can only those beliefs and propositions meeting conditions of self-evidence, incorrigibility, or evidence to senses be accepted as 'properly basic'? This would make many propositions we all believe irrational, and for that matter this demand does not meet its own criteria for basicality or for evidence.[41]

This approach can be seen as a different kind of grounding. Plantinga stresses that basic beliefs are not *groundless* as such, but that specific conditions or circumstances provide the ground for the belief. 'I see a tree' – a basic belief when confronted by one – is not a 'groundless' belief, for the perceptual experience is the ground of the belief. Having the relevant experience plays a crucial role. But the belief is not inferred, or deduced, from the experience.[42]

The contention is that an experience of God can lead to a properly basic belief in the existence of God. Plantinga makes the point that the actual proposition 'God exists', which he calls high-level and general, is not itself basic but based on more directly experiential propositions such as: 'God is speaking to me', 'God has created all this', 'God disapproves of what I have done', 'God forgives me'. The analogy is with other basic beliefs such as: 'There are trees', 'There are other persons', 'The world has existed for more than five minutes', which are not properly basic either but are based on 'I see a tree', 'That person is pleased', 'I had breakfast more than an hour ago'.

By shifting the focus from logical proofs or arguments as evidence, to 'experience' as the vital factor in forming beliefs, this move gains ground for religious belief. While logical proofs for God's existence are highly controversial, the fact that many people claim to have religious experiences is hard to deny, even if you think these experiences delusory. So experience plays a crucial role in the formation and justification of these beliefs: they are (usually) derived from experience, we form beliefs on the basis of experience and perception. Pargetter speaks in terms of 'stimulus' and 'response'; that the experiences cause the belief, the formation of which we have no control over. The warrant for the belief is the experience; it is rational to believe on the basis of it.

> We shall consider those properly basic beliefs which are rational because they are grounded in experience. They are *basic* because they are not justified by, warranted by, or inferred from any other belief; they are *properly* basic because they are nonetheless appropriately grounded or warranted. Their warrant or grounding is in the experience or experiences of the person for who they are properly basic.[43]

This means that whether or not a belief is properly basic most often rests on the circumstances or situation of a particular individual. Plantinga gives the justification the form: 'In condition *C*, *S* is justified in taking *p* as basic.' Wolterstorff emphasises the person-specific nature not only of basic beliefs but all attempts at justification of religious belief: 'issues of rationality are always situation specific. Once the impact of that sinks in, then no longer is it of much interest to spend time pondering whether evidentialism is false. It seems highly likely that it is. But the interesting and important question has become whether some specific person' is rational; a question that cannot be tackled in the abstract.[44]

Can you believe *anything* and still be rational? Plantinga considers this issue under the heading, 'The Great Pumpkin Objection'. While accepting that watertight criteria for proper basicality are difficult to draft, he repudiates the notion that just *any* belief can be properly basic under his conception. Pargetter offers several criteria for whether a belief is properly basic or not. In addition to an origin in experience, there must be no 'defeaters'. A defeater is another basic belief which contradicts the new candidate. Agreement with other competent people or corroboration from others helps to establish the justification of a belief. But there can be situations where two people differ, reasonably, in the formation of a belief based on an experience. They might not have identical experiences. So perfect agreement cannot be laid down as a condition for rationality for beliefs grounded in experience. However is it important that a belief fits in with others in a person's belief system, and other desirable factors might be that the system is 'appropriately dynamic', i.e. 'responsive to change and to the addition of new beliefs', and lead to a better life, better adaptability to the environment, posses better survival potential.[45]

Whether the beliefs suggested are really 'basic', or whether 'basic beliefs' really possess the attributes claimed for them, has generated much debate. Some suggest that the religious beliefs proposed as 'basic' are really inferred from some yet more basic proposition; Stewart Goetz suggests that Plantinga's 'basic belief' 'God is speaking to me' should really be 'I am aware of God speaking to me'; and this requires prior knowledge of God's properties and the ability to differentiate God from voices in my head or what have you. But in that case it can't be 'basic'.[46] Robert Audi claims that 'basic beliefs' are still 'justificatorily dependent'. A belief that I ate breakfast may be 'immediate' and not supported by any evidence while I sit in my office, but it still rests on historical evidence. So even basic religious beliefs don't escape the demand for justification.[47]

It seems to me to be slightly perverse to call an immediate sensory experience a 'belief', 'a belief that I am having the experience that I am having'. The same can be said of a memory, *mutatis mutandis*. We can come to form 'beliefs' about experiences such as sense perception and memories, but that is a secondary activity. In ordinary communication, we report such things as 'I see a tree'. To re-cast this as a propositional belief is *derivative*, not 'basic'. If I form a belief on the basis of past experience, even if I do so immediately and suddenly and do not 'reason to' that belief, that just says something about the swiftness of the process; not the genetic status of it.

Either nothing is truly 'basic', or else even 'basic', perceptually-stimulated beliefs involve activity, agency, creativity on the part of the perceiver – above all, acts of interpretation and 'decisions' that if not conscious or volitional are certainly not inevitable. 'I see a tree' is an interpretation or judgement based on many other factors than immediate perception: we do not suppose a new-born baby seeing a tree for the first time would (if he could) think the proposition: 'I see a tree.' Experience and judgement are required to 'see a tree'. The fact that this takes place instantaneously and involuntarily should not blind us to the inevitable involvement of our subjective contribution. Kant emphasised the role that our own subjectivity plays even in constituting sense-perceptions – in shaping the myriad of sense-perceptions with categories and concepts such as quantity and causality. Continental phenomenologists, such as Edmund Husserl, have explored in detail the manner in which sense-perception is constructed.[48] In Husserl's thought experiments, the effort that must go into 'bracketing out' all our knowledge and beliefs about what we see in order to have a 'pure' perception tacitly demonstrates how much our ordinary perceptions are instantly, unconsciously shaped.

Judgements about God based upon experience show even more clearly the role of interpretation involved – yet it is hard to find a contributor to this debate who even mentions the word 'interpretation'. It would surely be better to say that belief in God which is based on experience involves a personal interpretation of our experience. The difficulty is that the tacit strength of 'basic beliefs' is that they seem to avoid that dangerously 'subjective' stage of 'input' or interpretation in the process of generating beliefs. It is that point of subjectivity that makes philosophers of certain persuasions feel uneasy about their absolute rightness and justification; it introduces the possibility of error, where 'basic beliefs' suggest instead self-evidence and incorrigibility.

Further questions centre on the claims that basic beliefs can somehow bypass the need for argument. Gary Gutting complains that Plantinga doesn't do justice to the fact that people can reasonably disagree on the question of God's existence. But the central problem is that when I claim that a belief is 'basic' for me because it seems obviously true to me, I must claim that I have a privileged access to its truth. But this is 'epistemological egoism'. Because many people do not share a believer's belief in God, believers do not have the right to maintain this belief without a justification. Antony Kenny insists that one cannot 'short-circuit the forbidding task of examining the arguments for and against the existence of God.' One can only rationally take belief in God's existence as basic if it is possible to provide arguments for God's existence (which Kenny believes fail).[49] Audi raises the spectre of a person having a basic belief in God on the basis of an apparent experience of God, but being aware of all the arguments that exist to disbelieve it. If they continue to believe, having countered these doubts, it is subsequent to argument. Does this mean that the same belief is no longer basic, because it relies now on argument and evidence?[50]

'Self-evident' as used by Plantinga is a fluid category. Things can become basic or nonbasic, and go back and forth: $21 \times 21 = 441$ may not be self-evident at first but then becomes so after I have learned it or calculated, and thereafter simply remember it. So not only is 'self-evidence' entirely relative to a self; it is also apparently not a fixed category of propositions for each self. One might wish the framework of one's ship to be a bit more consistent and rigid to perform its function of supporting other planks. The fundamentally obvious and evident truths that are necessary to make up an indispensable framework might benefit from being restricted to a more solid category: as 'analytic' or 'a priori' truth, for example, rather than the 'experientially obvious'. 'I see a tree' is not a belief that is fundamental to my world view. The belief on which it rests – 'My sense-perceptions are generally reliable, all things being equal' – is another matter. If that goes, my daily life becomes hazardous and unpredictable. We might do well to consider what job we want 'basic beliefs' to do. For the mass of beliefs that currently qualify are predominantly trivial (unlike belief in God, whether you approve of it or not).

The role of personal circumstances, which are various and individualised, makes it particularly difficult to expect widespread agreement in 'basic' beliefs. In cases of personal religious experience, the 'information' is not directly accessible to anyone else; in all other cases, one is still resting on one's own experience of the 'same' sense-data. Not only can these claims never be infallible or universal; it becomes difficult to see how they can ultimately even be shared. This can result in a situation where one has to say: 'it is reasonable for me to believe in God, but not for you.' *All* philosophical positions which base themselves ultimately on the perception of sense-data will have this paradoxically subjectivist, almost solipsistic result: sense-experiences are not infallibly transferable, in the way logic is supposed to be. But if basic beliefs are not universal, what then is the *social function* of claiming that belief in God is a basic belief? All the moral advantages in debate are lost. More importantly, this reliance on personal perceptions makes religion first and foremost a private affair; questions of shared belief, solidarity, common experience are problematised.

This social or indeed polemical inutility is worsened by the fact that basicality says nothing in itself about the truth of the belief, just about the manner in which a belief is acquired. Is that good enough? Yandell has argued that beliefs might be 'properly basic' but still 'unreasonable'. 'A belief that is not improperly basic is still such that one is irrational in having it unless one has grounds that epistemically favor it.'[51] Basicality would be no defence against the polemical atheist, who could say 'That belief may be basic for you, but it is still false.'

Nevertheless, taken as a critique of foundationalism or evidentialism, the account of basic beliefs suggests some important insights. Foundationalism or evidentialism cannot found itself infallibly on its own founding principle. It too is subject to substructural embarrassment, to justificatory gaps and lacks.

Secondly, some beliefs form a crucial role in our belief system, and it is misguided to demand evidence for them on the same basis as we do for other beliefs or else force them to walk the plank. The centrepiece of David Hume's epistemological masterwork is the deconstruction of the idea that 'reason' can in any way prove that there is such a thing as causality.[52] A 'cause', he insisted, is something that cannot be observed; we can at most 'believe' it, never 'prove' it empirically.[53] The lesson to learn from Hume's critique is that we have many 'structural' propositions – beliefs that are an indispensable part of our ship – for which we can provide no proof, or even evidence. But shall we therefore throw them overboard? If so, we shall go under.

Shipboard repairs

But doesn't the framework of a ship simply justify itself, as long as it keeps you afloat? One can reject the demands of foundationalism by rejecting the idea that all our beliefs require 'grounding' anyway. Like a ship's structure, our conceptual scheme or way of viewing the world has 'framework principles', fundamental elements of our thinking that may never be proven or provable, but are necessary parts of the structure or system of beliefs that we hold. This approach is inspired by the later work of Ludwig Wittgenstein: 'The difficulty is to realise the groundlessness of our believing.'[54] 'Wittgensteinian Fideists' (the name comes from Kai Nielsen, a critic) use this insight to argue that religious beliefs may have this role or function in a belief system, and that it is misguided to think they require justification in an evidentialist way. It differs in this from Reformed Epistemology, which insisted that it is specifically basic beliefs which are groundless. Those who embrace the groundlessness of belief make a virtue of this alleged fault.

Norman Malcolm[55] cites Wittgenstein's observation that children accept what they are told without asking for grounds. 'The child learns by believing the adult. Doubt comes *after* belief.'[56] We too accept, without evidence, much that shapes our lives and views. Malcolm suggests that

> the lives of educated, sophisticated adults are also formed by groundless beliefs. I do not mean eccentric beliefs that are out on the fringes of their lives, but fundamental beliefs. Take the belief that familiar material things (watches, shoes, chairs) do not cease to exist without some physical explanation. They don't 'vanish into thin air'. It is interesting that we do use that very expression. But this exclamation is hyperbole: we are not speaking in literal seriousness. I do not know of any adult who would consider, in all gravity, that the keys might have inexplicably ceased to exist.[57]

It is not that we consider it improbable, or even impossible, that this might happen – we do not even consider it in order to reject it as impossible. This attitude is part of the foundation of our thinking. We do not even try to support it with grounds or justify it with evidence; it belongs to the framework of our thinking about material things. These form a system; and Wittgenstein observes that all testing, providing of evidence, confirmation and disconfirmation take place *within* a system. It provides the boundaries in which we question and decide. But the framework principles of the system are not, and cannot be, put to the test or supported by evidence. 'This is what Wittgenstein means when he says: "Of course there is justification; but justification comes to an end";[58] ... and when he remarks that "whenever we test anything we are already presupposing something that is not tested".'[59] This is because it is essential that our inquiries and proofs stay within boundaries. Some steps in a calculation we might check, but other fundamental principles of mathematics we don't bother to test.

> We are taught, or we absorb, the systems within which we raise doubts, make inquiries, draw conclusions. We grow into a framework. We don't question it. We accept it trustingly. But this acceptance is not a conse-

quence of reflection. We do not *decide* to accept framework propositions. We do not decide that we live on the earth, any more than we decide to learn our native tongue. We do not come to adhere to a framework propo- sition, in the sense that it shapes the way we think. The framework propositions that we accept, grow into, are not idiosyncrasies but common ways of speaking and thinking that are pressed on us by our human community. For our acceptances to have been withheld would have meant that we had not learned how to count, to measure, to use names, to play games, or even *to talk*.[60]

Like Wittgenstein's notion of 'language-games', they are simply there; it is our life, it is what we do. Our belief in framework principles does not stand or fall on the basis of evidence; it is 'groundless'.

In this sense religion is groundless; and so is chemistry. Within each of these two systems of thought and action there is controversy and argument. Within each there are advances and recessions of insight into the secrets of nature or the spiritual condition of humankind and the demands of the Creator, Savior, Judge, Source. Within the framework of each system there is criticism, explanation, justification. But we should not expect that there might be some sort of rational justification of the framework itself.[61]

Testing and justification are carried out and are valid up to a point, but cannot go on endlessly. At some point, we come upon an answer that satisfies us and that is the point at which we stop. Anyone with small children in the 'Why?' phase will know that every explanation offered can have 'But why ...?' directed towards the explanation itself; the point at which the questioner finds the answer sufficiently self-evident is almost impossible to predict in advance. What Malcolm urges us to recognise is that there is no logical compulsion to stop at those particular points. 'We imagine that we have confronted the self-evident reason, the self-justifying explanation, the picture or symbol whose meaning cannot be questioned. This obscures from us the *human* aspect of our concepts – the fact that what we call "a reason," "evidence," "explanation," "justifica- tion," is what appeals to and satisfies *us*.'[62]

D.Z. Phillips employs these Wittgensteinian insights to argue that religious language and claims are answerable only to their own standards and framework. Religious belief should not have to satisfy criteria alien to it.

They say that religion must be rational if it is to be intelligible. Certainly, the distinction between the rational and the irrational must be central in any account one gives of meaning. But this is not to say that there is a para- digm of rationality to which all modes of discourse conform. A necessary prolegomenon to the philosophy of religion, then, is to show the diversity of criteria of rationality; to show that the distinction between the real and the unreal does not come to the same thing in every context. If this were observed, one would no longer wish to construe God's reality as being that of an existent among existents, an object among objects.[63]

Malcolm observes that the demand for a rational justification is particularly prominent in philosophy of religion. 'The obsessive concern with the proofs [for the existence of God] reveals the assumption that in order for religious belief to be intellectually respectable it *ought* to have a rational justification. *That* is the misunderstanding. It is like the idea that we are not justified in relying on memory until the memory has been proved reliable.'[64] Instead, he suggests, 'Religion is a form of life; it is language embedded in action – what Wittgenstein calls a "language-game". Science is another. Neither stands in need of justification, the one no more than the other.'[65]

Wittgensteinian Fideists reject the idea that believing in the existence of God is a question of 'fact'; they refuse to separate belief in God from an entire way of life, behaviour, or attitude towards one's own existence.[66] Phillips argues that coming to see that there is a God is not like realising there is another being that exists. This insight does not add a further fact to one's knowledge; it is a new meaning in one's life, a new understanding of what exists.[67] Malcolm makes a distinction between believing in the existence of God and believing in God. 'I do not comprehend this notion of belief in *the existence* of God which is thought to be distinct from belief *in* God. It seems to me to be an artificial construction of philosophy, another illustration of the craving for justification.'[68]

Should we give up the idea that empirical knowledge rests on any kind of a foundation? Michael Williams argued that foundationalism fails by its own standards. First of all, it leaves us unable to defend ourselves against the sceptical challenge that we do not really perceive the outside world and cannot know it at all. 'Once we accept the idea of a strict epistemological order, we cannot explain how a warranted inference to the existence of the physical world is possible.'[69] If beliefs must be taken in a strictly linear fashion, what is the supposed base on which they can rest? Secondly, Williams claims, 'no convincing account can be given of how there could be such things as intrinsically credible basic beliefs even though, according to the foundational view, without such beliefs nothing else can be justified.' On the other hand abandoning the foundational view leaves our knowledge of the physical world secure, with something like direct realism.[70]

Perhaps we cannot build a watertight ship from the ground up, before we embark, and expect it to remain shipshape for the entire journey. Otto Neurath suggested that philosophers were in the position of mariners who had to carry out shipboard repairs while sailing, without the possibility of putting in to harbour and putting the boat in dry dock and refitting it with the best supplies.[71] We still use and depend on our inadequate ship even while trying to rebuild it. In the same way, we cannot take our way of seeing and thinking about the world out of commission in order to fix it up, for we cannot do without it. We have to fix our conceptual scheme spar by spar, idea by idea, using it in the very act of repairing it.

Anderson is concerned that Neurath's image suggests a lone mariner, the work done by a man alone, which is not an image conducive to the formation of a feminist epistemology.[72] This need not be the case; we can imagine a crew frantically carrying out repairs co-operatively, for if they do not pull together, they will all sink. Williams suggests:

> Instead of the picture of knowledge as an edifice resting on fixed and immutable foundations, I want to offer the picture of human knowledge as an evolving social phenomenon. At any time, we will have a solid core of unquestioned perceptual reports, and the like, against which more marginal and less certain beliefs can be checked. But even this solid core may come in for drastic revision in the interests of deeper insight or theoretical advance. Any belief can be questioned, though not all at once. In this way, the pursuit of empirical knowledge can be seen as a rational pursuit not because empirical knowledge rests on a foundation but because … it is a self-correcting enterprise.[73]

Crossings

The Logical Positivist Neurath had language in mind when he unpacked his mariner metaphor. He was resisting the idea that the philosopher could construct an ideal language of pure atomic propositions; propositions which more accurately reflect the world as it is than our ordinary language, which, as Russell so memorably complained, still embodies the metaphysics of the Stone Age. ('The sun rises.') Rebuilding our ship at sea, without access to the best supplies, we have to put up with the knots and imperfections in the wood, and whatever minor flaws are there. This implies that we simply have to make do with the inadequate language we have to articulate our conceptual scheme and our perceptions of reality. 'Only metaphysics can completely disappear'[74] from our revisions of this world-view, not every little flaw and error that is embodied in our language (like the 'rising' sun). But even if 'metaphysics', any reference to a further, non-material reality or dimension of existence, is completely eradicated: we still cannot attain the absolute purity of beginning without preconceptions and presuppositions. The elimination of metaphysics is not accompanied by an elimination of the inaccuracy and imprecision of language, which carries with it, like a Trojan horse, an entire world-view.[75]

Paul Lorenzen adapts the seafaring metaphor to demonstrate his opposition to the Logical Positivists' view: he defends our natural language as a 'seaworthy ship'. As the later Wittgenstein and the 'Ordinary Language Philosophers' in Britain also argued, our ordinary, everyday language is a perfectly acceptable philosophical instrument.

If there is no solid land attainable, the ship must be build on the high sea; not by us, but by our predecessors. They could swim too and somehow, perhaps from driftwood, they built themselves a float, then continually improved it until today it has become such a comfortable ship that we no longer have the courage to jump in the water and start again from the beginning.[76]

As Blumenberg observes, 'the demiurgical desire' of these Robinson Crusoes of modernity is shown in the handiwork of the constructivists, who leave their home and heritage behind in order to 'ground' their life on the 'naked nothingness' of the ship they are building from scratch. But 'their artificial emergency on the sea', which requires this re-building, does not arise through a supposed decrepitude of their ship – the language and traditions of their culture. That has already reached a late stage of laborious building and rebuilding by one's predecessors. But obviously the ocean contains other material than that which has already been rebuilt; what else might the sea turn up? Perhaps the remnants left by previous shipwrecks?[77]

A new dimension has been introduced here with a passing consideration of the role of language in one's conceptual scheme; and with it another new idea as well. What are they doing here? Let's ask Johann Georg Hamann. 'Reason without experience seems as impossible as reason without language. Tradition and language are the true elements of reason.' So wrote Hamann to his friend, when engaged in reading their acquaintance Kant's *Critique of Pure Reason*.[78] When he came to write his own 'Metacritique of the Purism of Reason', a principal focus of his attack was on an alleged 'threefold purification of philosophy'. The first purification, 'partly misconceived, partly unsuccessful', is to purify philosophy from custom, tradition, and all belief in the latter. The second purification is to purify philosophy from experience; and the third purification concerns language. For Hamann, philosophy cannot be separated from tradition, experience, and language.

So reason, he tells us, (rationality in our current debate) is inseparable from language and tradition; language, he believes, is inseparable from experience and tradition. In Hamann's reckoning, we cannot therefore purify logic from experience, tradition, and language. So reason, rationality only operate *after* the priority of the social, the traditional, the experiential; above all, the use of language. Reason or rationality can never be 'pure'; the foundation it rests upon is not incorrigible, not self-evident, not logically necessary. We cannot reason or think, justify or use logic without absorbing the influences of our language, our culture, our social relations. If Hamann were a participant in the contemporary debates, he would no doubt tell us that these discussions of 'rationality' are pointless without a consideration of language; just as he told Kant that language was the crux of reason's 'misunderstanding with itself'.[79] 'Everything comes out of *tradition* in the end', he reminds his friend.[80]

To understand this argument, one must be clear on what 'Tradition' is. It is not an approved, tightly controlled canon of accepted doctrines and writings; this is far too narrow a conception, as we see from its use in Hamann's epistemology.

Hamann explains that reason and knowledge have a two-fold nature: we receive traditions from our community, which we appropriate and integrate; and we also conceive our own ideas and insights, which we in turn pass on in contribution to the tradition. The fruits of our reason 'are therefore in the truest sense *revelations* and *traditions* which we take for our own property', transform, and thus fulfil our vocation, to reveal and to transmit.[81] The gaps and lacks in our human nature fit us all the more for the enjoyment of nature through experiences and to enjoy our community through traditions. 'Our reason arises, at the very least, from this twofold lesson of sensuous revelations and human testimonies'.[82] In contrast to the views of Hamann's contemporaries, he does not see reason as distinct from experience or the senses and the body; still less is reason or rationality a 'given', something that is just there. On the contrary, 'reason' *arises*; it is created and instructed by experience and by the formative activities of others on us. This account of rationality and knowledge also makes it clear that reason and rationality are impossible without human relationships: people to teach us, people to whom to communicate our own revelations. Moreover, Hamann makes it clear that this state of affairs is less an epistemic conundrum than a question of *enjoyment*.

Consider a moment from the great epic of the goddess Hi'iaka's journey from Hawai'i across the entire chain of the Hawaiian islands to Kaua'i, to collect her sister's lover and bring him back. She and her travelling companion stand at Ka'ena Point, the place where Mau'i stood to try to unite the Hawaiian islands into one landmass,[83] when he tore the boulder Pōhaku-o-Kaua'i off of O'ahu and into the sea. Hi'iaka and her friend need to find a way from the island of O'ahu, across the sea to the island of Kaua'i. Hi'iaka recognises Pōhaku-o-Kaua'i as a sentient being, not as mere inanimate matter. Indeed, she acknowledges him as a kind of relation.[84] Pōhaku and Hi'iaka converse: she asks to borrow a canoe, but he has none; the only one he had was broken up in a storm. So she asks for a plank that he is using for a shelf, which he gladly sends over, along with other bits and pieces. Hi'iaka and her female companion lash these together to make a canoe, which they use successfully to make the voyage.

Hi'iaka' is bold enough to tackle the thirty-foot waves off Ka'ena Point in a makeshift canoe, and willing to accept imperfection and inadequacy rather than insisting on the perfect weather conditions and an absolutely watertight vessel before venturing forth. This stands out particularly against Kant's timidity. So too do the warm and cordial relations between the maiden and the rock, quite unlike Mau'i's vigorous determination to mould the material stuff of the islands to his will without consultation as to its opinions or wishes. The materials for canoe-building, even if salvaged from storm-wrecked predecessors, are provided by the kindliness and co-operation of another, and that is the only way she can make her journey. Hi'iaka has no material resources of her own on the shore – just her willingness to acknowledge and befriend a fellow being, whether animal, vegetable, or mineral.

Resolution and Discovery

'I am now aboard, on the wave of the world – full of resolution: to discover, to win, fight, fail, or blow myself up with all my cargo!' wrote Goethe in a letter to Lavater.[85]

We have embarked, Pascal tells us; living means being on the high sea without comforts and assurances of dry land. Nietzsche appropriates the image: 'We have left the land and have gone aboard ship! We have burnt our bridges behind us – nay, more, the land behind us! Well, little ship! look out! ... there is no "land" any longer!'[86] But as he later reflects: 'Philosophers! The moral earth also is round! The moral earth also has its antipodes! The antipodes also have their right to exist! There is still another world to discover – and more than one! Aboard ship! ye philosophers!'[87]

So when we set out on our voyage of discovery, full of resolution – what do we find?

Captain James Cook, with his two ships *Resolution* and *Discovery*, found the Hawaiian islands quite by accident – the Europeans had no idea of the existence of these islands or their people. Sometimes their encounters were friendly, courteous, generous:

The Hawaiian questions about the British departure had made [Lieutenant] King curious to know 'what opinion this people had formed of us.' He took some pains to find out, but all he could learn was they thought the British had come from some country where provisions had failed and they came to Hawaii to fill their bellies. Stroking the sides and stomachs of the now-fattened sailors, the Hawaiians told them 'partly by signs, and partly by words, that it was time for them to go; but if they would come again next breadfruit season, they should be better able to supply their wants'.[88]

Sometimes not:

A Canoe came to the Resolution ... in which were three men, they came almost within pistol shot of the Ship, then one of them stood up with Captn Cook's Hat on his head, he threw Stones at us, smacked his backside in Contempt of us, shewed us the Hat & in an insulting manner waved it over his head; we fired several muskets at him but they all got ashore unhurt.[89]

Sometimes the kindly intent was correctly interpreted, even if the symbolism was not:

These two now insist'd upon Cramming us with hog, but not till after the Kava; I had no objection to have the hog handled by Pareea, but the Captⁿ recollecting what offices Koah had officiated when he handled the Putrid hog could not get a Morsel down, not even when the old fellow very Politely chew'd it for him.[90]

Sometimes, despite the barriers of language and world-view, the conversation reached an impressive level of mutual openness and respect:

[Ka'eo was] very inquisitive about our Manners & Customs; the Questions that he ask'd would alone be proof that these people have a great Variety of Ideas, he ask'd after our King, our Numbers, how our Shipping was built, & our houses, the Produce of the Country, if we ever fought, Who was our God, & such like.[91]

When Cook and his men sailed forth with resolution, what they discovered was The Other.

The problem of how, or whether, one can ever hope to understand The Other, an issue that receives more attention in theology and in Continental than in Anglo-American philosophy, is a vast ocean of an issue and the sea traffic criss-crossing it too numerous to pursue. Here we will focus on a particular application of the problem, and the question it raises for philosophy of religion: the question of religious diversity, or 'religious pluralism'.

Let us imagine that Lt. King, in his conversation with Ka'eo, husband of the queen of Kaua'i, had the benefit of an education in twentieth-century European religious thought. He might be a follower of Karl Barth, for example. Scorning mere 'religion' in favour of Christian revelation from God, it would be clear to him that Ka'eo was a worshipper of a false god; led astray by 'religion' and deprived of revelation. Lt. King would be an 'exclusivist', as the position is now described (or a 'particularist'): one who believes that truth and salvation lie exclusively within the Christian religion (or whatever religion the exclusivist/particularist happens to adhere to).[92]

On the other hand, Lt. King might, like Karl Rahner, deem that Ka'eo, as an upright, moral, honest seeker for truth and the divine, deserves to be deemed an 'anonymous Christian'. This is one who, although not a believer in the religion, nevertheless can be counted as a kind of honorary member, due to sincerity and good will.[93]

But Lt. King might have found both the exclusivist and inclusivist positions patronising and offensive to those of other faiths, and he may have appropriated the work of John Hick with great enthusiasm. He would be a pluralist. He would start from a Kantian distinction between 'the Real' as it is in itself, and 'the Real' as we humans know it – which is precisely not as it is in itself. We experience The Real not as it 'really' is, but in the forms, concepts, images of our own religious culture – none of which adequately describe or exhaust the Real, which is itself ineffable.

This position allows Lt. King to do several things. He can suppose that Ka'eo is truly in touch with the divine, even though his beliefs and worship are so different from King's Anglicanism. Lt. King needn't become a missionary, then. He needn't become a convert either; he can remain an Anglican and consider *himself* in touch with the divine too, even though his beliefs and worship are so different from Ka'eo's. Neither need be 'wrong' in their religion. Nor need Ka'eo's religion be reduced to a second-class form of Christian revelation in order to harmonise their differing religious views. Their truth-claims do not conflict, because they are made about the specific forms of their own religious culture; not at the level of The Real itself.

Now, I say, if Lt. King is a Hickean pluralist, he must sail from the island of Kaua'i across the channel to O'ahu, to place his foot on Ka'ena Point. For he is following in the footsteps of Mau'i: he is striving to unite numerous and diverse islands, and he needs to find the right foothold.

Unfortunately, the right foothold cannot be found by a mortal being. For Lt. King must have a vantage point over all the religions of the world – outside the perspective any given religion in particular; and he must have an adequate insight into The Real As It Is In Itself in order to see that It is present to all these different religious traditions, despite their diverse cultures. So, like a dead Hawaiian, his soul must leap off Ka'ena Point, out of his bodily existence and into the next world. Lt. King must be not Mau'i but Archimedes, seeking his foothold *outside the world* in order to perform his task.

Do you suppose Lt. King can do this – just find himself a little foothold outside the world, in order to shift the rest of us off our orbit? If he *cannot*, then in the end – despite all his Hickean goodwill – he will be like our third role model in the Invocation, the dwarf Procrustes: cutting down others to his own size, whether it really fits them or not.

This point is well expressed by Michael Barnes:

The point is that there is no vantage-point 'above the action', as it were, which is not itself historically or culturally conditioned. This is where the apparent strength of the pluralist case masks real weakness; the assumption of the moral high ground can quickly become ideological. While it is not the case that pluralists hold that all religions are talking in different ways about the same thing, there is, nevertheless, a tendency to a certain sort of reductionist universalism. This determination to search out common values and essences tends almost inevitably to short-circuit the highly complex ways in which people of faith seek to identify themselves. Such a universalism fails to take seriously the variety of religions and the differences between them and turns out to be covertly élitist. In fact, on closer inspection what purports to be an objective, neutral and universal perspective looks suspiciously like a contradiction in terms. On the one

hand, each religion is given equal soteriological value; on the other, a privilege is assumed for the pluralist 'system' itself.[94]

But as Barnes points out, this drive for 'theoretical mastery' over the whole
domain of religions is sadly out of keeping with the spirit and ethic of inter-faith
dialogue itself. The Hickean position of religious pluralism is itself undergirded
with foundationalist presuppositions, he suggests. Analogous to the treatments
of rationality, we see here the drive to propel religious diversity towards a single
overarching truth, and the assumption of a neutral, value-free, 'view from
nowhere'. His conclusion: that despite its global aspirations, it remains the
product of Anglo-American empiricist rationality. In the end, ironically, it
doesn't take otherness seriously enough.

There are two dangers: the first is to assume, in a well-meaning and liberal
way, that 'we're all alike underneath'; that we are all trying to say 'the same
thing' in our different ways about the 'same' Ultimate or Divine Reality, and that
similar arguments, statements or claims *are* the same and serve the same function in their religion or system as they do in ours. This disregards the importance
of 'otherness'.

Suppose I now inform you that – contrary to the assumptions of Samwell
aboard the *Resolution*, who recorded the backside-smacking incident above –
the gestures of the three Hawaiians in the canoe were in fact signals of hospitality. To assume the clothing, like the Hat, of another and wave it, beckoning,
is a symbolic way of 'taking them on yourself', participating in their identity. It
is a gesture of great warmth. For the Hawaiian, moreover, to pat one's buttocks
is not a gesture of Contempt, as Samwell the Briton assumed, but a symbolic
invitation: 'everything I have and am, I offer you', expressing in a most striking
form the extraordinary breadth and depth of the famous Hawaiian hospitality: a
generosity that the more reserved Englishman could not even begin to fathom.
(Especially not in that form.) – If I explained this to you, you would see how
easy it is to completely misread a person from another culture, if one interprets
them from the basis of the symbols and customs of one's own.

However, if did I tell you this, I would be lying.

Samwell interpreted the backside-smacking all too accurately. There is
another mistaken view, then: that these cultural and religious differences are so
vast and intractable that we can never really understand people of other faiths or
cultures – that what an Englishman thinks of his backside and what a *kanaka*
associates with his *okole* might be so completely at variance that they have no
hope of mutual comprehension. This, in my view, leads in the end less to respect
for others than to an ultimate rejection of solidarity. I might then feel more
empathy and identification with a dog from my own culture than with a human
from a very different one. But I would be wrong to do that. There are indeed
several different things one can do with one's *okole* and therefore metonymically
associate with it; but the anatomical possibilities are finite and are relatively
stable around the planet. So too, then, are the semiotic possibilities. Of course

there is always a danger that we might assume we understand someone of a different faith and culture when we in fact we have misunderstood them. But this is something that happens all the time between husband and wife or two colleagues at work. It is a *human* problem, and not uniquely a *cultural* or *religious* problem. Cultural and religious differences add a different layer of potential for lack of understanding; but also contribute a new dimension for theological and philosophical insight, creativity, and 'Ideas'. How is *your* shipping built?

Nevertheless, this cross-cultural understanding is not a state of affairs that arises of itself, without courage, trust, openness and praxis. Captain Cook and his officers found themselves drawn into religious rituals which they could not fathom, and whose theological and sociological import are still disputed today. Cook found himself conducted to a temple, pushed and prodded to assume certain postures, wrapped in special garments, chanted at and sung over, fed with food previously chewed for him; all without a clue as to whether in their eyes he was a man, a mighty chief, indeed a god, or just the next sacrificial victim – or whether their theology might be so unlike his, that it was possible that in the Hawaiians' eyes, he be all of these at once.

Little attempt was made at inter-faith dialogue; the Britons did not understand or respect the Hawaiians' kapus, but insisted on imposing their own, punishing what they considered to be crimes. The Hawaiians were more inclined to obey their own taboos than the sailors'. So in a bid to impose British justice, Cook, full of resolution, decided to take the king himself hostage. Kalaniopu'u, in initial trust, went with Cook willingly to discover his desire. But the incident ended with the killing of Cook in Kealakekua Bay by the king's followers; and a much greater number of Hawaiians were slain.

Maita'i!

A debate has erupted in anthropology around the events of Cook's stay in the Hawaiian Islands. Marshall Sahlins at the University of Chicago has devoted intense study over the years to Cook's reception by the Hawaiians, investigating a tradition that Cook was taken by the Hawaiians to be their god Lono and fleshing out this thesis in great detail.[95] A Sri Lankan anthropologist, Gananath Obeyesekere, was provoked by this and led a counter-offensive.[96] Is it really the Hawaiians who took the European for a god? he wonders. This is hardly possible; they, like any other people of the world, possess practical rationality and would not have done so. It is really the Europeans *who take themselves for gods* in relation to the 'natives'. It is not the Hawaiians who suffer from a mythical view of the world. 'To put it bluntly, I doubt that the natives created their European god; the Europeans created him for them.'[97]

Sahlins defends himself against Obeyesekere's criticisms with two interesting counter-charges. First, he observes, Obeyesekere claims a greater understanding than Sahlins of what the ancient Hawaiians would have thought because

Obeyesekere too is a 'native'. He claims both moral superiority and better theoretical praxis on that basis, explicating Hawaiian concepts on the basis of his
memories of Sri Lanka. Sahlins points out the tacit imperialism and colonialism
towards the Hawaiians that grounds Obeyesekere's claim that, as Sri Lankan, he
knows how Hawaiians must think. No Hindu would make that mistake; therefore Hawaiians couldn't make that 'mistake'.

The second charge is even more interesting for our purposes, for Sahlins
targets Obeyesekere's own presuppositions about rationality in attributing 'practical rationality' of a specific kind to the Hawaiians and thereby deciding what
they must have thought. But Obeyesekere's 'practical rationality' is none other
than Western epistemology's picture of the mind as a mirror of nature, which he
attributes to the Hawaiians as superior to the 'mythical' way of thinking.
Obeyesekere, then, is actually submitting the Hawaiians to European philosophical prejudices about rationality.[98]

> A certain pseudo-politics of anthropological interpretation manages to
> express its solidarity with indigenous peoples by endowing them with the
> highest Western bourgeois values .... Not many have dared to ascribe to
> Polynesians such a bourgeois relation to reality – in the guise of a universal
> human disposition to rational cum practical action. Yet Obeyesekere then
> doubles the compliment by reversing the usual prejudices: the 'natives' are
> practical and the Westerners mythological. Moreover, he knows this to be
> true of Hawaiians because he is a Sri Lankan himself.[99]

This spat among anthropologists is fruitful for the questions it raises when one,
so to speak, tries to understand how another culture's shipping is built. Do all
peoples possess this rationality that is demanded of religious believers by Anglo-
American philosophers of religion?

One of the many things for which Obeyesekere takes Sahlins to task – one of
the more trivial points, perhaps – is his apparent acceptance of the accounts of
King on the *Resolution* and Samwell on the *Discovery*, about an incident on 17
February shortly after Cook's death. Despite the state of enmity at this point
between the British and some of the Hawaiians, Hawaiian women are still
aboard the British ships, although those Hawaiian men still sympathetic to the
British are afraid to be there. Some buildings in the town are on fire; the royal
heiau or temple had burnt a few days before. It was possibly some of the resi-
dences of priests that were burning in the village when the women observed this
from the decks of the British ships.

On both ships, the sailors report with astonishment that 'so entirely uncon-
cerned did [the women] appear', that 'some seemed to admire the sight, and
frequently cried out that it was *maitai*, or very fine'.[100]

Obeyesekere rejects this anecdote as prejudiced and refuses to allow it any
authenticity.[101] Such childlike delight in the pretty flames burning down one's
own town would clearly be irrational. As the Hawaiian women possess practical

rationality, it is impossible that they could have said this. One cannot divorce utterances like this from their context, Obeyesekere insists.

Quite so. But if we want to inquire into the context for this alleged exclamation, Obeyesekere is no help. Here are the women, persistently breaking kapu, eating prohibited foods in a prohibited setting, swimming out to the ships, especially at night, to socialise liberally with the British, virtually living on board, staying out all night, indeed for days, and refusing to come back when those few men brave enough to risk the kapu against it paddle out to plead with them to return. *What are these women getting up to*? Standing on *Resolution* and *Discovery* from the perspective of the sea, they look back at the village and watch the conflagration of the homes of the religiously and politically powerful – perhaps the priests of Ku, the god of war, who perform human sacrifice, currently consolidating their power-base with the king – and *cheer*. '*Maita'i!*'

Is it impossible that they cried 'Excellent! Well done!' as the priests' building went up in flames? Only if the women could not possibly have had a theological, religious, political, social agenda of their own. Only if it is not possible for them to have had interests and aims that differed from the particular male religious elite who imposed the practice of human sacrifice upon a not altogether willing community. In short: only if the Hawaiian women could not – for all their 'practical rationality' – have *thought for themselves* on religious and ethical issues.

Perhaps something revolutionary was happening, which neither the Hawaiian men nor the British men perceived at the time, nor anthropologists later. Perhaps this was ecclesiastical guerrilla warfare,[102] or an activism at once social, political, and religious. The first public repudiation of the social, gender-related kapu happened a few decades later, at the instigation of queens (although before then the powerful and esteemed Hawaiian queen Ka'ahumanu admitted to the British that she broke certain kapu in private, but asked them not to tell on her). The final religious taboo was performed defiantly by a queen at Halemaumau crater.

However, Obeyesekere insists on the Hawaiian women's behalf that they too have 'practical rationality' as he defines it – and thereby he has silenced them utterly. They were *rational*, and they did *not* say '*Well done!*' We could not now hear what they might have been saying in this outrageous and impossible cheer. By knowing in advance what 'rationality' means in all cultures, and insisting that all cultures have it, he has disallowed the women their cognitive autonomy and their historical agency. He has also failed to see the potential rhyme and reason in seeming 'irrationality'.

It can be rational not to be rational to the utmost extent .... On the other hand, rationality is all too ready to engage in destruction when it fails to recognize the rationality of things for which no rational foundation is given, and believes it can get carried away by the process of establishing rational foundations. Descartes thought that the best way to build cities

rationally was to begin by razing the old cities. Not even World War II
yielded proof of this prospect for rationality.[103]

On the rocks

Our resolute voyage, then, brings us particular dangers. Our shipping may be
wrecked on the rocks of our own discovery.

'The only time I was lucky at sea was the time I was shipwrecked.'[104] Zeno,
founder of Greek Stoicism, was driven to a life of philosophy after being
wrecked off Piraeus. It is not only a stoic calm in the face of adversity that we
could learn from his example, however, but perhaps more importantly: the
heuristic importance of failure. Without this failure, Zeno would have been less
wise. If you are in an unseaworthy ship, or sailing in the wrong direction, or
navigating with the wrong instruments and methods, then perhaps being shipwrecked is your only salvation, paradoxical though it may seem. Perhaps
inadequacies, imperfections and gaps in the planking and are actually a good
thing, if they can signal to you the need for self-examination and transformation.

It is Cook's own discovery, his own agency, that has brought his downfall. It
is not an accident external to his own undertaking, that has befallen him in an
chance blow of fate. His failure is the result of his own methodology, his own
aims.

Surely this fate, finding one's ships driven on the rocks by one's own navigation, can never befall a philosopher, so long as he is sufficiently rational.
Being rational entails the prediction and prevention of such failures. Yet it was
precisely this sort of eventuality that had Kant, as a supremely intelligent man,
pacing nervously on the shore, seeking assurances of safety and success before
starting, hoping for maps.

Wittgenstein, in the penultimate sentences of his first philosophical work,
seems to have realised that his own pronouncements on what it is proper and
possible to say, necessary though they were for the salvation of philosophy,
didn't meet his own conditions for what can be said:

> My propositions serve as elucidations in the following way: anyone who
> understands me eventually recognizes them as nonsensical, when he has
> used them – as steps – to climb up beyond them. (He must, so to speak,
> throw away the ladder after he has climbed up it.)[105]

He didn't explain how he could get away with this blatant self-contradiction; nor
why, if all of his work was true, a faultline of self-opposition should run through
it. For the absence of contradiction is the most sure and reliable guide to philosophical navigation. The foundation stone of rationality is the Principle of
Contradiction.

In an essay dedicated to Kant, Hamann introduced a marine image rather different to the one evoked by its dedicatee several decades later.[106] In it, Hamann describes not a single island of truth, but an archipelago of writing. This image contrasts with Kant's (and Mau'i's) vision of an island of truth and rationality. Where Mau'i wanted to impose unity, and Kant never questioned it, Hamann delights in the multiplicity and difference of islands, and the fact that one must voyage between them.

Hamann's archipelago has no bridges or ferries. Hamann quotes Socrates speaking with approval of 'readers who can swim',[107] who can negotiate the submarine connection between one idea and its neighbour without being conveyed in a stately fashion from one landfall to the next with watertight inferential reasoning. Where Kant is concerned about the conveyance, and Clifford about its seaworthiness, in Hamann's picture there is no boat at all, of *any* degree of adequacy.

Hamann was something of a philosophical heretic, who had difficulty in accommodating himself to the demands of the all-important Principle of Contradiction in the first place. Wittgenstein's paradox, that what we need to do seems to go beyond what we are allowed to say, would have neither surprised nor hindered him. And in fact, some of the most keenly intelligent philosophers have sat lightly to the prospect of self-contradiction. Maimonides in his *The Guide of the Perplexed* (what a misnomer) provides a list of the ways contradictions may arise. 'Sloppy thinking' does not exhaust the possibilities. Sometimes it is necessary for teaching purposes, sometimes the truth cannot be articulated in any other way. And in fact a fundamental contradiction runs through Maimonides' work, as with Wittgenstein; and again it centres precisely on what can or cannot be said. In the *Guide*, it is precisely whether anything at all can be said about a transcendent God: Maimonides tells us, most insistently, that nothing at all can be said about God's nature. On the other hand, his work runs to over seven hundred pages.

So perhaps philosophers make a mistake in their desperation to avoid contradiction in order show how their beliefs are possible and rational. First of all, self-contradiction may be methodologically necessary. Secondly, for the believer in a transcendent God, maybe it is an important affirmation about God's transcendence that we can't make these things all fit together in tidy human terms?

Hamann has other reasons for being sceptical about the authority of the Principle of Contradiction. In his view, reality and therefore knowledge are often contradictory:

Yes, daily at home I have the experience that one must always contradict oneself from two viewpoints, [which] never can agree, and that it is impossible to change these viewpoints into the other without doing the greatest violence to them. *Our knowledge is piecemeal ...*

There is the possibility, then, that reality itself contains contradictions and contrasts that cannot be reduced to one another in a tidy, self-consistent scheme.

From the nondualist Vedānta point of view, all opposition is phenomenal anyway: a matter of appearance, and a misleading one at that. The appearance of contradiction is superimposed by our own minds, and does not lie in the deepest reality of things. Zimmer's portrait of Vedic thought tells us that the pattern of life cannot be comprehended by logic:

> The rules of life are not those of logic but of dialectics; the reasonings of nature not like those of the mind, but rather like those of our illogical belly, our procreative faculty, the vegetable-animal aspect of our microcosm. In this sphere, the sphere of biological dialectics, the illogical sphere of nature and life's forces, 1 plus 1 is usually far from remaining merely 2 for very long.[108]

If this is so, then knowledge which is in communication with such a reality is itself piecemeal. Hamann continues:

> *Our knowledge is piecemeal* – no dogmatist is in a position to feel this great truth, if he is to play his role and play it well; and through a vicious circle of pure reason scepticism itself becomes dogma –[109]

Far from being a sign of rationality, the absence of contradiction is a sign of dogmatism; as in the political sphere, it is a symptom of absolutism. Knowledge arises dialogically, not united in a false synthesis. Hamann tells us: 'Every philosophy consists of certain and uncertain knowledge, of idealism and realism, of sensuousness and deductions. Why should only the uncertain knowledge be called belief? What then are – *rational grounds*?'[110]

Jain epistemology holds that in any given situation, structurally there are seven possible standpoints. No absolute affirmation or negation is possible; the nature of things is too complex to be exhausted in a single self-consistent predication. All predications are from a point-of-view. To criticise something as a 'contradiction' is felt to miss the point of the Jain doctrine of perspectivism: that contradictions can be 'avoided' only by understanding that statements as made from different points of view. 'The absolutists, the supremely unintelligent'(!), are afraid of contradiction because they have not realised that every assertion is made from a perspective. 'Afraid of contradiction, the dull-witted fall slain by the absolutist view.'[111]

On the rocks? Readers, I hope you can swim.

Seasick?

Why is it one gets seasick in a boat, but never swimming?

Like Zeno, Aristippus too was once shipwrecked. When he swam ashore, he realised there were other people on the land he had come to, because he saw their drawings in the sand. He was able to recognise other beings because they were like himself; he recognised himself in another. But of course, the other is not oneself; that is a mistake.

Psychoanalytic theory has confronted the question of the revelatory power of failure and mistake, as one can see in the importance of 'denial' in Freud's work, or 'méconnaissance' in Lacan's. In his early essay 'Negation', Freud articulates the concept of 'denial' as the mechanism that allows a truth to appear that is too painful to be permitted. By denying it, one can at least mention it, as opposed to blocking it out from consciousness altogether; at least it can get an initial hearing. Lacan's concept of 'mis-recognition' shows how the subject can 'misrecognise' what might be part of herself by displacing it, perhaps attributing it to someone else – in that everyday phenomenon, for example, of disliking in someone else a characteristic of one's own. At least this error is the first step in perceiving the truth – in making perception of the truth possible at all, even if its full import is not yet known.[112]

The question we have to pose, then, is what does philosophy of religion (or a philosopher of religion) misrecognise in another? What analogous 'denial' or 'misrecognition' takes place in discussions of rationality, wherein one denies possession of what properly belongs to oneself – and attributes it to someone else?

Certain styles of philosophy can only recognise subjectivity by its inversion in the other. This is called 'being objective'; being neutral, dispassionate, exhibiting a lack of bias and prejudice; whereas someone whose personality and viewpoint is less disguised is 'too subjective'. The danger in this is that one mistakes one's own subjectivity for objectivity – 'how I feel is simply how it is', 'this is how people are' – while being highly aware of the personal nature of the writing of the one who is different. The more 'abstract' and sterile one's writing style is, the easier this is to do. It does not entail that the philosopher whose writing seems the most abstract is the most 'objective', however. We just know what his subjectivity most values and desires for itself.

Anderson, developing the work of recent feminist epistemologies, suggests that the Enlightenment notion of objectivity is a 'weak' one, since it is blind to its own bias; 'both the method and the goal of objectivity are affected – to a greater or lesser degree – by biases of gender, including sex, race, and class biases.'[113] This renders it limited, with only a partial view of the world, and a distorted one at that. Feminist epistemologists call for a feminist, 'strong objectivity', with criteria which include 'empirical adequacy, novelty, ontological heterogeneity, complexity of relationship, applicability to current human needs, and diffusion of power'.[114]

What Harding, Anderson and other advocates of 'strong objectivity' suggest is that we try to 'think from the lives of others'[115] and to 'examine the basic background beliefs of the subject of knowledge'. 'The purpose of these moves toward objectivity is to gain less false and less partial knowledge, not absolute truth or impartial knowledge.'[116] Anderson and Harding suggest that adopting the standpoint of the marginalised other makes for greater objectivity because those on the margins actually have a wider knowledge of the social reality than those at the privileged centre. For the marginalised, in order to survive, have to know about what goes on at the centre, they have to know the reality of the dominant group; whereas the dominant group can remain completely ignorant of the lives and perspectives of the marginalised. 'And so the marginalised other will have a greater knowledge of social reality.'[117] Secondly, they have less of a vested interest in distorting the truth to maintain the status quo than those who profit from it.[118] So the critique of 'weak objectivity' from the standpoint of a desired 'strong objectivity' asserts the need for a recognition of 'the other'.

The critique of objectivity can be sharper still; it can consist in the rejection of so-called objectivity altogether. This can take the form of asserting that 'objectivity' is not possible; or one might assert that, even if it were possible, it would be undesirable.

Hamann wrote that 'the heroic spirit of a philosopher' consists in 'a thirsting ambition for truth and virtue, and a fury to conquer all lies and vice, which precisely are *not* recognised as such, nor wish to be'.[119] This does not suggest that one who quests after truth is a neutral, dispassionate scholar in a study, so much as a knight in a battle frenzy. To attain and to recognise the truth, according to Hamann, we do not require 'objectivity' or 'neutrality' but rather, passion, vision, even a little 'superstition'. (He writes this in deliberate provo-cation to the Enlightenment critics, such as his acquaintance Kant, who called Hamann's faith 'superstition'.) These are the 'leaven' needed 'to start off the soul's fermentation towards a philosophical heroism'.[120] Without a passionate commitment to something, one would never have the motivation and energy to embark on the quest, nor the audacity to unmask falsity even when it is attrac-tive and popular, let alone the courage to confront truths we find threatening.

For Hamann, personal commitment, passion, involvement are not a barrier to understanding and discovering the truth, but are in fact a helpful spur and guide to it. It is friendship and love, according to Hamann, that lead us to examine things most carefully and sympathetically, to have the patience to do so, and thus to understand them best. Where an uninvolved person sees only mould, and despises it, the lover sees a little microscopic forest.[121] Is the lover blind to mould's faults, or does he in fact have a clearer perception of what mould really is?

Thinkers working more within the Continental European tradition than the Anglo-American have not merely questioned whether neutrality and objectivity are *desirable*, but whether they are actually *possible*. The German philosopher Martin Heidegger observed that before we come to understand something, we already have some understanding 'in advance' of what we study. It may well be a misunderstanding; but on the other hand, it may be a useful guide to our inves-tigation – or at least a starting-point. We cannot get rid of our pre-understanding; it is a part of the way we are. However, it can be changed in interaction with what we study. This notion was explored in the context of interpreting the Bible by Rudolf Bultmann, and within interpretation theory or 'hermeneutics' by

Hans-Georg Gadamer.[122] Gadamer observed that in any act of interpretation there are two horizons: that of the interpreter and that of the creator. The goal is not for the interpreter to deny or suppress her own perspective, nor to impose it upon the writer from another age or culture; but to attempt to bring these two horizons together. For try as we might, we can never fully escape our own position and attain a completely neutral, god's-eye-view of things. This principle has been explored in the latter half of the twentieth century as it affects different aspects of our background, and hence our standpoint: in gender, race and ethnicity, and class.

Is this recognition of one's subjectivity a licence to prejudice? This is perhaps the most common objection to Gadamer's position; and it could be a damning one, for we see the dangers of religious prejudice not just throughout history, but also in many of the conflicts and atrocities of the last century. So it is worth asking whether the knowledge or understanding that results from this view is prejudiced; and for that we need to consider what the danger of prejudice is.

One danger is blindness; above all, self-blindness. One cannot see what is real, what is true, because one is dominated by one's own beliefs and assumptions. But neither Gadamer nor Hamann advocate simply imposing your own view, your own meaning, your own interpretation on things. Still less do they suggest that one's pre-judgements (prejudices) should remain, unchallenged, as one's final judgements. They suggest rather that one's own subjectivity is a *part* of the process of understanding. It is not to be suppressed or banished. Nevertheless, it is only a part. Philosophy, Hamann suggests, would be more successful if the philosopher was like a painter who steps back from her work.[123] In doing so, the painter does not become 'more objective' – as if she somehow cared less for her work; but she does become less myopic; and one not only sees one's work from a new angle, but the new standpoint also provides fresh views of the subject-matter. So what Hamann substitutes for objectivity as a 'control' or 'check' on self-deception and distortion is first of all, a wider, broader perspective; and secondly, a faithful relationship to what one studies and seeks to portray.

The other danger is deafness; that one cannot hear what is being said by the other person because one is certain that one already knows. But both Hamann and Gadamer propose a model for understanding that evokes the nature of an interpersonal relationship. They picture understanding like a dialogue, not a monologue. A genuine conversation has what Gadamer describes as a 'back and forth' – I may misunderstand you, but you have the opportunity for rejoinder and correction. There are two people involved here; both of them bring what they are to the encounter. Neither should dominate, though each seeks to correct misunderstandings that arise; neither should remain unchanged, though each seeks to maintain their own autonomy.

The viewpoint under discussion, then, does not amount to 'subjectivism'. It is not the domination of the subject and the subject's way of seeing that they advocate in their scepticism of 'objectivism'. It is inter-subjectivity that they are after; for like the feminist advocates of 'strong objectivity' the remedy is found in listening to the other person – as a fellow *subject*.

Richard Rorty has ascribed to the later Wittgenstein the view that philosophy is 'therapeutic'.[124] It does not consist in formulating truths, discovering knowledge; but in healing and improving our way of seeing and thinking about things.

We do need a remedy for seasickness as long as we are in a ship. But the therapy may consist in being shipwrecked on the rocks of an 'other' and having to swim for it.

Shipwrecked

Philosophy of religion can misrecognise its subjectivity, and perhaps more as well, by its inversion in the other. The Other may be the rocks on which our shipping could be wrecked. But perhaps we need to be shipwrecked, as Odysseus' sirens and the German Lorelei both threatened, when we are driven onto their rocks by our desire.

The project to which Anderson calls the philosopher of religion is to cease to contrast reason and desire, but to relate them. 'Philosophical analyses of and feminist concerns with a combination of reason and desire, as expressed in the yearning for truth, need to come to the top of the agenda in contemporary philosophy of religion.'[125] Actually, philosophy and rationality have always had desire. They just misrecognised it by an inversion into the other.

Blumenberg asked us the question: what else might we find adrift in the sea, when we are wrecked? Perhaps the remnants of previous shipwrecks? If so, we see the reason for Hamann's and Gadamer's insistence on our need for a tradition; for someone like Pōhaku to send us plank to cling to, to make it to the other shore. No others, no tradition – no planks.

But the other is also the lure, which calls us onto the rocks. Odysseus was desirous of hearing the sirens' song, which none could hear without driving themselves onto the rocks and wrecking the ship. He plugged the ears of his oarsmen with wax, so that they could row on for Scylla and Charybdis undistracted. But he would have himself bound to the mast of the ship, so that he could hear and experience without perdition.

Odysseus wants to experience the sirens without experiencing them; to encounter them and be changed forever without being destroyed by them. He wants to surmount the contradiction by having unblocked ears but bound limbs, the reverse of the blocked and unbound sailors; and his repudiation of the Either/Or, his embrace of a contradictory position is epistemologically successful.

This story of Odysseus and the sirens is, after all, an epistemic one. Odysseus is questing for knowledge – the vibrant experiential knowledge of immediate perception. But what prompts his epistemic act is desire: a desire that threatens to wreck his ship, destroy him and all his crew; but does deliver knowledge.

It does not deliver the knowledge he could have had: the sirens sing to him that they know all of what comes to pass on the fruitful earth, and that every man goes away from them a wiser man if only he will stay. But all this Odysseus does not learn from them. What he wants to experience is the desire itself: what it is like to experience desire to that self-destructive intensity. And this is the knowledge that he gains: knowledge about *desire*.

This is what philosophy of religion can misrecognise by inversion into the other, in its Odyssean lust for knowledge. Longing, desire, passion, commitment to a direction: these are inverted in Anglo-American philosophy into the other, 'theology' as philosophy's other perhaps, or just 'religion'; recognised there, disavowed here. Here is neutrality, but there engagement; here is knowledge, there only belief; here is understanding, there blind faith; here is reason, there irrational desire …. Here there is wax in the ears.

The Chāndogya Upaniṣad tells us: 'Verily, when one thinks, then he understands, one who does not think does not understand. Only he who thinks understands. But one must *desire* to understand faith.'[126]

Landfall

Others are the lure, the rocks, the plank – and are also what await us when we stagger onto dry land like Aristippus.

Nietzsche speaks of the astonishment of the survivor of a shipwreck, as he clambers on shore 'and stands with both feet on solid earth – astonished that it is not swaying'.[127] The sea voyage and shipwreck are not the end of the story. There is also the question of what happens when you make a landfall.[128]

The story is told in a Hawaiian legend of the goddess Pele (older sister of Hi'iaka) leaving her original home to find a new one. In their canoe she and her relations set forth and reach the archipelago of Hawaii. They test the suitability of each landing with a magical staff or divining rod called Paoa. On reaching one rock, one of her little brothers is marooned as a punishment for loading the canoe incompetently and causing it to nose down in the waves. But Pele is moved by compassion for her little brother and they return to collect him. Visiting each of the islands in turn, they explore it and its charms, but their divining rod discerns that each is not to be their home. Only when they reach the island of Hawai'i does Paoa confirm that this is to be Pele's new home. The people unload useful plants to support them in their new habitat: breadfruit, banana, pala'a (an edible fern) and 'awa (kava kava).

Here we see a voyage made not by a solitary philosopher-sailor but by a loving community. Tensions and disagreements arise but they are resolved, the desire for resolution being motivated by compassion. Their goal is not truth, rationality, or being right, but finding a 'home' – a place where one can actually *stay*. Although many places are not destined to be their home, each place is explored and enjoyed in its own right, and when departed, affectionate farewells are sung to it. There is nothing intrinsically wrong with these places; they are homes for someone else, but not for this family. Finally, when they arrive, steps are taken to ensure a good life. After all, a home has to be made, and maintained by somebody. Whereas we imagine Kant arriving on his island of truth, sitting plunged in solitary reflection on a beach and eventually wondering why no one has brought him his dinner; in this tale, responsibility is taken by these sailors for looking after themselves. There is no need for an unmentioned wife, mother or servant to care for their bodily needs and thus render them invisible and beyond the scope of philosophical consideration. The new arrivals do take care to provide for their physical needs, by bringing breadfruit, banana and pala'a plants. But they also have provided for other needs, for they also bring with them, plant and nurture, the 'awa plant, source of an intoxicating drink for plea-sure, religious trances, ecstasies.

And who is in the boat?

Have you ever heard of the madman who on a bright morning lighted a lantern and ran to the market-place calling out unceasingly: 'I seek God! I seek God!' As there were many people standing about who did not believe in God, he caused a great deal of amusement. Why? is he lost? said one. Has he strayed away like a child? said another. Or does he keep himself hidden? Is he afraid of us? Has he taken a sea voyage?[129]

2. The Tincture of Speech

Religious language

The teacher

St Augustine had a semiotic dialogue with his teenage son Adeodatus (as one does). This supposedly real conversation on the subject of signs and language was recorded in Augustine's early work, *De Magistro* (On the Teacher).[1] (Which one was the teacher, I wonder?) Augustine took a verse from Virgil's *Aeneid* – '*Si nihil ex tanta superis placet urbe relinqui*', 'if nothing of such a great city shall remain'[2] – and talked Adeodatus through it, asking for the meaning of each word. Adeodatus agrees that 'if' must mean something, and likewise 'nothing', but cannot point to some *thing* that these words signify. Maybe 'if' means a feeling of doubt? – 'Nothing' clearly means something that doesn't exist. But Augustine perplexes him with the challenge that what doesn't exist cannot 'be something'. By the time they reach only the third word, Adeodatus is floundering, and is reduced to trying to explain the meaning of a word or sign not with a thing, but with another sign, trying to explain 'of' with 'from' ('ex' with 'de').

The concern with the meaning of signs is not a new one, then. Yet it is chiefly epistemological questions which have dominated religious-philosophical debates for centuries. Then at the beginning of the twentieth century, the primary question shifted from 'What can we *know*?' to 'What can be *said*?' Wittgenstein's aim in his first work was 'to draw a limit to thought' (also Kant's aim in *The Critique of Pure Reason*). But then Wittgenstein corrects himself: 'or rather – not to thought, but to the expression of thoughts', for it is 'only in language that the limit can be drawn, and what lies on the other side of the limit will simply be nonsense'.[3] Thus Kant's Enlightenment project, to question whether we can think about and know things, like God, which are held to be beyond our sensory experience, has been transformed into a parallel linguistic question about what can be talked about meaningfully.

Simon Blackburn suggests that philosophy of language is an attempt to achieve some understanding of a triangle of elements: speakers, language and the world.[4] (Where do listeners come in the triangle, I wonder?) The task of the philosopher is to obtain some stable conception of these three and their relationships.[5]

Blackburn alludes to '… a certain tension, which arises because we can easily come to feel both that our understanding of referential expressions must be intimately connected with the object referred to, and also that it cannot be.'[6] This is the 'problem of reference'. How do words attach onto things in the world, so that we can talk about them? This is what Adeodatus was forced to think through. The theory of the Indian logicians of the Nyāya and Vaiśeṣika schools – that the meanings of words, the connection between words and their referents, is willed and established by God – would not satisfy many today.

If this is true of everyday language, might it not be even more true of language about the transcendent? This is not only a decadent Western worry. Ancient Indian philosophers raised the same problem. The Advaita Vedāntin Sureśvara maintains that words cannot directly denote Brahman, the ultimate reality.[7] His predecessor Śankara even went so far as to say that language is the instrument of ignorance. Both agree that it is impossible to use language directly to designate reality; ultimate reality still more so.[8] (This is not their last word on the subject, however.)

John Macquarrie stated: 'Before one can discuss whether a statement is true or false, one must have at least some idea of what the statement means.'[9] But, he asks, 'What does the theologian mean when he talks ... about God, angels, immortality, sin, grace, salvation and all the rest? Can we find an intelligible sense for these utterances?' No, say many philosophers. Anything supposedly 'transcendent' cannot be talked about. If words mean something by virtue of the objects to which we point, then words about 'God' and similar religious insights or entities cannot mean anything; for we cannot point to a God in our world. So religious utterances cannot make sense.

Thus 'the problem of reference' has provoked the greatest anxiety and energy in twentieth-century philosophy of religion. What do religious words refer to, if anything? What gives meaning to these words that name what you cannot display?

There is another challenge to religious language, however, which has been widely recognised for several millennia by religious believers themselves, before it was resurrected by sceptics. I shall call it 'the problem of effability'. Religious thinkers have struggled with the question of whether transcendent reality can be adequately expressed in human language. Mystics of every faith have repeatedly stressed that what they experienced was beyond words; but they have nothing but words with which to communicate their ultimate truths. Śankara and Sureśvara both maintain that the highest knowledge is a direct intuition without words; this finds its ultimate expression in the famous Upaniṣadic saying that Brahman is not this, not this (*neti neti*).

There is a problem then of relating the known and the spoken. We can consider this question under the concept of language as a form of 'representation'. The whole notion of a 'Problem of Reference' – Blackburn's triangle – presupposes that language *is* all about referring; that is, that language is 'representational'. It assumes an idea of language that says its job is all about making a picture of the world with words, hopefully an accurate picture. Language has to match the world, perhaps in a one-for-one way, in which each word represents a thing, and each thing has a word. That is why representation is an issue at all.

There is a two-fold problem, then: about whether and how language can reflect reality, and secondly how adequately it can do so. Both questions are made more difficult if one wants to say 'God is love' rather than 'The cat sat on the mat'. It is certainly more challenging to describe the Divine Essence accurately than to describe a feline one. The reasons why this is so reflect the epistemological difficulties already examined; the questions of language ride on the back of the challenges to religious knowledge: how can you *know*? Can you know the Ultimate as it really is? And never mind the *philosophical possibility* – what about the *theological propriety* of speaking about the Absolute in finite human terms?

Pointing out the variety of factors which influence the way we see things, Sallie McFague worries about the Scylla and Charybdis of idolatry and irrelevance that confronts language about God: either we take it literally or find it meaningless. Can we refer to God without identifying our language exhaustively with the divine? Does religious language refer to anything? If it does – how?[10]

Augustine's conclusion in *De Magistro* is that all words do 'refer' – but what they refer to is other words.[11]

The little asparagus tip

In the *Tractatus Logico-Philosophicus*, Wittgenstein sums up his attempt to draw a limit to the expression of thoughts: 'what can be said at all can be said clearly, and what we cannot talk about we must pass over in silence.' Language has a logical structure, and if we understand it we see the limits of what can be said meaningfully. Beyond this, both language and thought become nonsense.

In this account the structure of language mirrors the structure of the world. Language consists of propositions which are made up of 'elementary' propositions, which in turn are made up of names. Names are the ultimate constituents of language. Correspondingly, the world consists in the totality of facts; this is comprised by states of affairs, which is made up of objects. Each level of structure of language matches a level of structure in the world. The arrangement of the names logically mirrors or pictures the arrangement of the objects in the states of affairs. A proposition, Wittgenstein tells us, is a picture of reality, a model of reality as we imagine it.[12] It is because of this picturing relation that the propositions have sense. The meaning of a proposition is found in the situation it depicts; whether it is true or false depends on whether the situation it depicts exists or not.

Tying together these theses about the structure of language, the structure of the world, and the 'picture theory' of meaning results in a set of assertions about the limits of language, and therefore of thought. The only significant propositions (and hence thoughts) are those which are pictures of reality. This means that the only significant discourse is *factual* discourse – discourse about things that can be pointed to. That which does not fall within the realm of facts is nonsense: such signs or strings of signs fail to express a proposition, they say nothing at all because they fail to picture anything in the world and hence have no connection with the world. ('Most of the propositions in philosophy', Wittgenstein tells us, are in this class.[13]) Only when there is that picturing connection to things in the world do our signs have sense. Thus, because many things that we do talk about – ethics, religion and 'the problems of life' – lie 'outside the world' (that is, outside the realm of facts and their constituent states of affairs) nothing can be said about them. They 'show' themselves, Wittgenstein asserts, but they cannot be stated. 'There are, indeed, things that cannot be put into words. They *make themselves manifest*. They are what is mystical.'[14]

Wittgenstein was never a member of the 'club' called the Vienna Circle which shared many of his attitudes, and which began to meet in 1925. Its principal members had largely come from disciplines other than philosophy, chiefly science and mathematics.[15] A.J. Ayer spent some time with them as a young man, and returned to splash Logical Positivism across British philosophy in *Language, Truth and Logic* in 1936, when he was only 25.[16] Its approach and attitudes have remained dominant for decades, even though specific tenets have been set aside.

The fundamental aim was, once and for all, to destroy 'metaphysics' – any attempt to speculate or discuss anything beyond the material world. This rules out talk of God or an afterlife, as well as discussion of 'souls'. Unfortunately, it also threatens talk of things that the Logical Positivists wanted to talk about, like ethics and aesthetics, for these are difficult to articulate in purely material terms.[17]

The Logical Positivists' tools were logic and science. All sensible utterances are either what Hume called 'relations of ideas', connections between abstract concepts as in logic or mathematics, or else they are 'matters of fact', the domain of science. In later life, Ayer commented that it was not so much that they used science in their philosophy, as that they thought all knowledge *was* science.[18] Science is the correct way to describe and understand the world, and there isn't anything but the world to be known. All philosophy has to do, as Wittgenstein suggested, is criticise and refine the statements of science.

With the picture theory of meaning at its base, Logical Positivism put forward its principle doctrine: the Verification Principle, which determines which sorts of statements have meaning. Any statement that isn't either empirically verifiable or else a formal statement (in logic or mathematics), is nonsense. Anything that cannot be confirmed by observation is nonsense, unless it is a tautological proposition as (they asserted) the statements of mathematics and logic essentially are. This clearly excludes any talk of God or religion, for how can these assertions be verified in material terms?

As formulated by Schlick, the Verification Principle runs: 'The meaning of a proposition is the method of its verification.' This has the further corollary that what a proposition means can be described by saying what would verify it, which amounts to a reduction of all statements to statements of immediate observation. They originally thought that you could 'translate out' all statements into statements about sense data, but it proved impossible to put this into practice in a thorough-going way. General statements, like 'All ravens are black', are ultimately impossible to 'translate out' into sense perceptions because the subject extends to infinity. Who wants to undertake the arduous and tedious task of observing '*all* ravens', even if possible?

Moreover, this tends to reduce any statement about other people to observations about their behaviour, which is contentious. But even in dealing with its own ideal subject-matter, scientific inquiry, it is difficult to translate out very high-level items like electrons into visual sensations observed by the scientist. So the principle was weakened; instead of being able to translate the principle into sensations, it was simply required that the proposition, to be significant, should be confirmable by sense observation. Ayer later admitted that this led to some unconvincing views, particularly about the past. One had to assert that a statement about a past event actually means 'If you look it up in a history book you will see it written that ...' – a view Ayer asserted in *Language, Truth and Logic*, but later found desperately implausible.

Ayer's later verdict on the Verification Principle is that it was never well formulated. Ayer said himself that in his various attempts, he 'always let in either too little or too much' (which leaves one wondering what his real motivation was: to draw the line where the line *should* be drawn, or just to exclude what he disliked and include what he fancied?) The Verification Principle faces another embarrassing hurdle in trying to pass its own test. It is not a mathematical statement, nor a tautology of logic. How could you possibly verify the Verification Principle in the material world? It trespasses on a realm of non-empirical reality which it refuses to recognise as significant. The Verification Principle itself must be meaningless.[19]

Leaving aside these intriguing questions, what is the understanding of language and meaning that operates here? Language is seen as a system of signs; words are signs referring to objects, language involves propositions and assertions of fact pertaining to these objects. Meaning is found in the object to which the word refers.

Cognate issues are raised by two theories of meaning from ancient Indian philosophy.[20] Some took the view that the meaning of a sentence comes from its parts, like the Logical Positivists; this view is known as the *khaṇḍārtha* theory. The Bhāṭṭa Mīmāṃsakas and the Nyāya-Vaiśeṣikas held that the meaning of a sentence comes from the individual words in it, and one understands the meaning of a sentence by understanding the words first. The Prābhākara Mīmāṃsakas believed that although the meaning of a sentence is composed of the individual word meanings, nevertheless one understands the meanings of the sentence immediately on hearing the words. One doesn't have to understand the meanings of the individual words first and then synthesise them.

But this theory was countered by a more holistic approach to meaning and the relation of a sentence to its constituent words, the 'partlessness' thesis (*akhaṇḍārtha*), of the 'Synthetic' or 'Holistic' approach. The syllables of a word do not 'add up' to make its meaning; analogously, Bhartṛhari believed that the meaning of a sentence was manifested in its constituent words, but not made out of them. Maṇḍana Miśra followed this holistic approach to meaning.

Maṇḍana's discussion of what words 'aim at' is of interest here, for 'meaning' in Sanskrit, *artha*, literally means target or aim. So, Maṇḍana asks, do words only 'aim at', 'mean' the objects to which they refer? Or do they aim at a union with the thing to be done that is urged in speech? Or a union with the meanings of the other words in the sentence? It cannot be only the first, that words mean their objects. Otherwise there could be no understanding of the purpose of a sentence, especially such injunctions as make up much of the sacred scriptures of almost any religion, perhaps. And then words would be pointless. On the other hand, they must nevertheless aim at their objects in order to be explicable and so that cognition of the object can arise. Otherwise, meaning becomes solely dependent on a speaker's intention. That is counter-intuitive; one could mean whatever one liked by a word, simply by intending it, whereas words carry with them a limitation of possible meaning. Also, in situations where there is no speaker (as in scriptures) there could be no meaning. Words cannot aim simply at the action which they enjoin, without the mutual word-to-word connections; otherwise meaning would hang solely on the verb, and no qualification of action is possible. Consequently, words must 'aim at' a number of levels: things to which they refer, actions or purposes which they convey, and connections of meaning that arise from their relationship with other words.[21]

It seems that Maṇḍana Miśra would cope much better than Ayer with Augustine's challenge to Adeodatus to account for the meaning of words. To which objects do 'If' 'nothing' 'of' refer? And how do you verify 'pass the salt'? Theories of meaning which ignore the importance of action and motivation, not least the function of relations between words, cannot take us very far in understanding our everyday language.

The Logical Positivist has a fall-back position, such as the one taken by Antony Flew in the 'University Debate': if one cannot demand the possibility of verification, one can at least require that sensible statements can be susceptible of *falsification*. He tells the story of two people in a clearing the forest. One asserts that this wild place is actually tended by a gardener. The second insists that he has never seen such a person. 'Ah,' says his friend. 'He is invisible.' So traps and wires are set, but no gardener is caught. – As each successive test is set, and failed, the one who believes in the Invisible Gardener has an excuse ready to hand.[22]

Flew maintains that it is the unwillingness of believers to let anything count as evidence against their belief which gives rise to the suspicion that in the end this is empty and meaningless. If religious believers would at least be willing to allow that in principle, under some condition or circumstance, their beliefs could be falsified, we would have more confidence; but as it is, their assertions 'die the death of a thousand qualifications'.

Flew's objection that believers refuse to allow anything to falsify their belief cannot be allowed to slide past too quickly. The same complaint could be made of analytic statements, such as 'a bachelor is an unmarried man'. These too are unfalsifiable by empirical considerations. If someone claims to know a married bachelor, I would say 'Then he isn't a bachelor', or 'That isn't what I mean by a bachelor' or 'You don't understand what the term "bachelor" means or how it is used.' If someone who is a bachelor marries, we do not say 'Now he is a married bachelor', but rather, 'He was a bachelor, but now he's married.' Flew might retort that statements about God's existence are empirical statements, statements about what exists; not analytic statements. But certainly some religious discourse (such as the ontological argument) seems to function as if it thinks of itself as expressing necessarily true propositions.

Stephen Davis counters Flew's claim that believers will not allow anything to count against religious faith, by claiming that many believers do have a psychological limit to their acceptance of religious claims. Secondly, he maintains that religious statements can conceivably be verified in the future; if for example, someone invents a new, successful proof. It may still remain the case that the statement may not be *falsifiable*, but there are other statements recognised as possessing cognitive meaning, which can be verified if true but not falsified if false. He gives 'There are three successive sevens in the decimal determination of pi' as an example.[23]

Despite his own criticisms of Logical Positivism in later life, Ayer still maintained there was something right in the approach. One still needs to be able to say how you would go about testing what people say to see if it is true. There has to be some backing to the 'currency' of our language. The early Logical Positivists erred in thinking we could maintain the gold standard – that we could present our words like bank-notes and cash them in for the gold of objects and methods of verification. This is not possible. But one can still have legitimate concerns about counterfeit notes and counterfeit speech.

Unlike Ayer, Wittgenstein later turned against his own early theory. In *Philosophical Investigations* he deconstructs it patiently, using as a crowbar the idea of 'ostension' – of pointing to something to indicate the meaning of a word. The later Wittgenstein observes that, far from being the clear and obvious gesture he once thought, *every* ostensive definition can be interpreted in a variety of ways. Ostension can only make the meaning of a word clear 'when the overall role of the word in language is clear'[24] – when you already have a good idea of what the person is talking about. 'Point to a piece of paper. – And now point to its shape – now to its colour – now to its number (that sounds queer). – How did you do it?'[25] In any act of pointing, how do we know which feature is being indicated for our understanding?

Augustine – whose theory of language Wittgenstein thinks he is refuting – got there before him.[26] He and Adeodatus wondered about how to define 'walking' ostensively when one is already 'walking'. 'Walk faster,' Adeodatus suggests. But maybe that would be taken as defining 'speed', or 'acceleration' or 'hurrying'. Augustine suggested that maybe *nothing* can be known by words, except what is already known.[27] Words refer to other words;[28] this applies even to 'things' and 'activities', the easiest words point to or demonstrate. Augustine and Adeodatus consider the example of a fowler teaching the art of bird-catching,[29] and conclude that every form of demonstration requires a prior, shared context of understanding. Maṇḍana similarly disputes that all language learning can arise from such situations.[30] – What 'ostension' in fact would require is for us to be able to step *outside* language, outside a shared world, in order to teach the meaning of a word. But this Archimedean desire is quite impossible, according to Maṇḍana Miśra, Augustine, Wittgenstein, or Lacan, who writes: 'Either we already know the truth in question, and it is not, then, the signs which teach it to us, or we do not know it, and we cannot locate the signs which relate to it.'[31]

The value of such discussion, suggests Lacan, is that it shows 'that it is impossible to deal with language by referring the sign to the thing term by term'.[32] The Logical Positivists' picture of language and meaning is one that Lacan, like Augustine and the later Wittgenstein, finds inadequate. 'Language cannot be conceived of as the result of a series of shoots, of buds, coming out of each thing. The name is not like the little asparagus tip emerging from the thing.'[33]

According to these thinkers, we must look elsewhere for an understanding of language, meaning and reference.

The metaphysicians' coins

... the metaphysicians, when they make up a new language, are like knife-grinders who grind coins and medals against their stone instead of knives and scissors. They rub out the relief, the inscriptions, the portraits and when one can no longer see on the coins Victoria or Wilhelm or the French Republic, they explain: these coins now have nothing specifically English or German or French about them, for we have taken them out of time and space; they now are no longer worth, say, five francs, but rather have an inestimable value, and the area in which they are a medium of exchange has been infinitely extended.[34]

Anatole France's simile plays on an ancient tension between the 'universal', the abstract, the general; and the particular, individual, concrete. Our language is a language of the particular. The way we speak is heavily conditioned by contingent factors, our race, class, gender, tastes in music perhaps; and this is what we speak about. This restricts the scope and relevance of our talk, which is unfortunate for the metaphysician who thinks his science has universal applicability. The metaphysician's solution is to strip language of all particularity: of all the features that locate it in a history, a culture, a context. Then it does not refer specifically to a place, a date, a value. What Anatole France recognises is that this supposed neutrality does not make a coin (or a word) universal. A defaced coin does not have an infinite worth all over the world in every century; on the contrary, by losing all its particularity, it loses all its value.[35]

Is this what happens with religious language when it struggles against its problem of reference? The believer wants to refer to something that is not an object; using everyday language nevertheless but tugging at it to make it fit. The Christian says 'God is a father'; but has to circumscribe this with so many qualifications, restrictions, and alterations like 'not exactly like a human father' ... that the neutralised word has neither meaning nor use left to it. The dilemma is: either human language is allowed to retain its meaning, drawn from human experience of the finite, in which case it can't be about a transcendent God; or, language is 'purified' of its anthropomorphic roots – in which case, is it as meaningless as the metaphysicians' defaced coin?

Religious philosophy has a tradition of different solutions to this problem. Aristotle distinguished 'univocal' and 'equivocal' uses of words. A word is used univocally when it is used in exactly the same way in two cases: as when one says the ace of clubs and the ace of spades are both cards. It is used equivocally if it is used in two completely different ways, as when one says that a flying mammal and a wooden implement for ball games are both 'bats'.

There are some who believe that univocal assertions are possible in religious language. The evangelical theologian Carl Henry claims that only univocal knowledge is real knowledge, so language must be used univocally about us and God if we claim to have knowledge about God. 'The logical difficulty with the theory of analogical [word use] lies in its futile attempt to explore a middle road between univocity and equivocacy. Only univocal assertions protect us from equivocacy; only univocal knowledge is, therefore, genuine and authentic knowledge.' There must be some literal truth about God, there must be some similarity between man and God; otherwise we cannot have genuine knowledge of God.[36]

Another tradition, however, asserts that language about the divine must be equivocal. This is not only a philosopher's position, but also a mystic's, and it is found in many different religions. 'Negative theology' in a strict form maintains that nothing or next-to-nothing can be said about God. Plotinus insists repeatedly that The One is beyond all knowing and saying. The *Tao te Ching* informs us that the Tao that can be spoken about is not the real Tao.

The milder version says that while we cannot necessarily make positive assertions about what God is, we can at least make confident assertions about what God is not. Maimonides warns us of the great danger in applying positive attributes to God. Every perfection we can imagine – even if God possesses it – would not in reality be in God the way we conceive it. It might be called by the same name, but it would in fact amount to a negation. Truth becomes manifest, Maimonides tells us, when we realise that language can only be used equivocally of God.[37]

The role of negation is prominent in Upaniṣadic thought; most of the attempts to speak about Brahman do so by means of negations: sometimes pithy: 'This Self is not this, not this';[38] sometimes in lengthy chains of negations:

> It is neither gross nor fine, neither short nor long, neither glowing red (like fire) nor adhesive (like water). (It is) neither shadow nor darkness, neither air nor space, unattached, without taste, without smell, without eyes, without ears, without voice, without mind, without radiance, without breath, without a mouth, without measure, having no within and no without.[39]

Maṇḍana combined a kind of optimism, compared with the austerity of Śankara and Sureśvara, about the possibility of speaking about the ultimate, with an espousal of what Christian tradition was to call the 'via negativa'. An entity which is unknown by any form of knowledge (*pramāṇa*) can nevertheless be described by the negation of all particulars. Although one does not know Brahman or how Brahman connects with the word 'Brahman', nevertheless one knows the words of particulars – and the word 'not'. Thus the scriptures can teach us about Brahman.[40]

Striking is the way that negation can be taken as the basis for a theory of meaning. This was the point reached by some Buddhists: universals do not exist. On the other hand, particulars are transitory, fleeting, and have no stable existence. How and to what can words refer? In the understanding known as *apohavāda*, words function by exclusion: by cutting out everything to which the word does not apply.

If one is not satisfied with univocity or equivocity, however, there is a third possibility, famously associated with Thomas Aquinas.[41] He agrees with his more mystical colleagues that a word, such as 'good', cannot be used univocally of us and of God because God is so utterly different to us that his goodness cannot be the same as ours, differing only in degree. My 'goodness' may consist in paying my taxes and not beating my husband. God's doesn't. On the other hand, when speaking of God our use of language cannot be purely equivocal, he argues. If God's goodness is completely unlike mine in every respect, as unlike each other as a fruit bat and a cricket bat, how can we know what we mean by saying God is good? Isn't there anything in common between God's goodness and mine – like being loving, for example? The middle route lying between these two extremes is 'analogy'. Words are neither used with completely the same sense nor with a completely different one; the analogical use of words is sort of the same and sort of different. If we say God is good and my husband is good, we can see differences. My husband bears no moral obligations for maintaining the world in existence, and God does not have to be home in time to collect the children from school like he promised. However, perhaps we can see similarities. Both may be 'loving Fathers', who care for their 'children' and strive to bring about the best for them. They are not good in *exactly* the same way, but there is a kind of common ground.[42]

Analogy has been taken up in a novel direction by Barry Miller almost as a side-effect of his discussion of God's existence and simplicity.[43] Miller distinguishes a 'limit case' from a 'limit simpliciter'. A limit simpliciter differs only in degree from the things of which it is a limit, but it is still one of those things, a member of the set or series. The upper limit of speed, the speed of light, is itself a speed. So it is a limit *simpliciter*. A limit *case*, on the other hand, draws a limit without being a member of that group. So the bottom limit of speed, 0 kilometres or miles per hour, is not actually a speed, it is the absence of any speed. So it is a limit *case* of speed. A series of lines getting shorter and shorter might be 'stopped' with a point; but a point is not a line, not even a tiny one, so it is a limit *case* of the set of lines. A series of polygons, with progressively greater numbers of sides, becomes 'rounder and rounder' and closer and closer to a circle. A circle, then, is that to which such a progressive series points, or 'implies', as it were -- but a circle is not a polygon and does not actually belong to the series, and so a circle is the limit case, not the limit simpliciter, of a series of polygons. (A triangle would be the *lower* limit *simpliciter*.) The limit case, then, 'is that in which a defining characteristic of the members has been varied to the point of extinction', in other words, it does not belong to the series at all.[44]

Miller uses this to understand God's attributes, and so it functions as a kind of theory of analogy. God's attributes are not limits *simpliciter*, e.g. maximal goodness, which is how they are often dealt with by philosophers of religion whom Miller describes as 'Anselmian' or 'perfect being theologians'. God's is not the greatest possible goodness, on a scale that embraces the moral goodness of horses, dogs, humans, angels, and God. Perfect-being theologians have 'ensured the falsity of their claims about the nature of God ... by ignoring the possibility of there being anything similar to, but *beyond*, the maximum of a series'.[45] God's attributes are *outside the series*, as a limit case is. And yet the series clearly points to its limit case, and gives an indication of what it is like, though an imperfect or inexact one. So practitioners of negative theology, he suggests, also err in the opposite direction, in 'not recognizing the possibility of some *likeness* between that entity and the members of the series beyond which it lay'.[46]

So God's existence and attributes are limit cases and not 'instances' of their creaturely counterparts; hence they are neither univocal nor equivocal. There must be some similarity between the limit case and the series for it to be a limit case of that series and not some other. There is some community of meaning between them, so they are not equivocal. On the other hand 'It is not that one has the option of using univocal terms but is either too ignorant, perverse, or slovenly to do so. Rather, there are simply no terms that could be used univocally in such cases: the only possible alternative to using them analogically would be to use them equivocally.'[47] Miller concludes 'neither the divine transcendence nor the divine simplicity preclude all likeness between God's attributes and those of creatures. On the contrary, the limit case account of divine transcendence and simplicity has proved to be quite integral to the case not only for the possibility of such likeness but for one that is entirely devoid of anthropomorphism.'[48]

When Hamann was challenged with 'anthropomorphism', he retorted provocatively that he embraced a '*privileged* anthropomorphism'. This he suggests is actually legitimised by God's own opting for 'anthropomorphism' in the Incarnation. It is grounded in a theology of divine condescension: that God accommodates Herself to our epistemological and linguistic limitations, just as parents do not scorn their toddler's baby talk but rather respond in the same vein. Current research has shown that 'baby talk' or 'motherese', even when ungrammatical, actually facilitates language learning. Those parents who refuse to 'talk down' to their babies can actually make it more difficult for their child to learn to speak. But by accommodating their speech style to the level of the child, 'The adult shows an awareness of the child's level and seems to unconsciously promote the linguistic development by using structures slightly more advanced than those used by the child.'[49]

Hamann crafts a creation myth, his own reworking of the tale of the Garden of Eden, that takes the biblical anthropomorphism of Genesis even further: God plays with his children in the garden. For Hamann, the more concrete or scandalous the anthropomorphism, the more we are reminded of our linguistic horizons – and God's gracious accommodation. Hamann even confides to his friend Herder in letters that he finds it difficult to imagine a Creative Spirit without genitalia; and if the Bible can speak of God's mouth, hands, feet, why not his 'euphemismo'?[50]

What this approach tacitly requires, however, is an appreciation of paradox (indeed, irony, at which Hamann excelled), to avoid wilful distortion. Paradoxical language is found more in theology, particularly in the Christian Protestant traditions, than in analytical philosophy. This kind of approach can be articulated in a more philosophical framework, as Ian Ramsey did with his notion of 'models and qualifiers'.[51] One constructs a model of what God is like, and hedges it with qualifiers. Our partial and inadequate understanding is unfolded in terms of models; but in religious language these models are always qualified – qualification is built into the model; and they cannot be taken for a description of God.

However, it is theologians such as Luther or Karl Barth, and religious philosophers like Kierkegaard, who are masters in its deployment. For such thinkers, the Being of God is and remains a mystery; our affirmations then must have the paradoxical character of statements in which contraries are declared to be inseparable and equally necessary. Such paradoxes are not logically self-contradictory statements, like statements about 'square circles', but rather are evocative images: such as 'finding life and losing it', 'God everywhere present and nowhere included'. The negating aspect functions as an indication that the speaker is aware of the impropriety involved in making affirmations about God. The justification for being able to make either an affirmation or a negation is strictly dependent on a religious attitude: a strongly 'existential' one, resting on a perceived relationship with God in which God communicates with the individual; put alternatively, one that believes in the possibility of God's self-revelation as the source and ground of the claim made.

Although Hamann did not develop this systematically, one can see his insistence on daringly concrete language as a counter-reaction to the syndrome of the metaphysicians' coins. Hamann opened his 'Metacritique' of Kant with concerns about the empirical backing to Kant's linguistic currency. He maintains that the use of abstract terms can mislead us. Our language is grounded in particular terms, in ordinary language; every word has an empirical root.[52] Then we strip the 'particularity' from the word's field, generalising it to enable it to fit all cases. But the danger in this is that we begin to believe that the existence of the abstract word demonstrates the real existence of abstract objects to which these words refer. Hamann has in mind, above all, the word 'Reason'. In his view, there are a variety of ways we reason, varieties of activities we perform; but there is no such 'thing' as 'Reason'. Creating this word, we can debate whether 'it' is universal, pure, what 'it' can do, whether savages or other races or women have 'it'. The way we use language, then, conditions our thinking. This is why Hamann suggested that language is the crux of 'reason's misunderstanding with itself'.[53]

If we resist the lure of thinking that this abstract noun denotes the real existence of a thing, however, and remember that *reasoning* is something we *do*, we are more likely to realise that we do it differently after a heavy meal than on an empty stomach; we might reason differently when we are in a rage than when we are in love; we might be able to observe people of other cultures actually doing it, and so on. In Hamann's 'Metacritique', the remedy urged for this scissors-grinding temptation is to pay attention to ordinary language – as Wittgenstein was to urge two centuries later.

Meanwhile, the metaphysicians' demand that language about God must be decently abstract in order to avoid gross theological misunderstanding plays upon our shame about the earthy vigour, the life, the 'pudenda' of our language. But it strikes a death blow at language. 'The purity of a language deprives it of its richness; a correctness that is too rigid, of its strength and virility.'[54]

The way to revive language is not to aim at philosophical purity, abstraction and obsessive correctness and precision. The way to bring language back from the dead is through 'hyperbole', poetic exaggeration, creative provocation; to court the humble language of the people who experience and believe. This crude language is sanctioned by God:

By what means however shall we raise the extinct language of nature from the dead? – With pilgrimages to Arabia Felix, with crusades to the East, and with the reconstruction of their magic, which we must take for our booty with ancient women's cunning, for it is the best .... Because silken feet in dancing-shoes will not bear you on such a burdensome journey; then let the right way be shown to you through hyperbole ....[55]

The point of such critiques as Hamann's is that language must be brought into connection with the real. The creation of words that do not refer to real entities does not confer real existence on those concepts; sterile abstraction only tempts us to make an idol of our concepts, rather than an icon of our poetry.[56] However, this insistence on a kind of linguistic empiricism does not imply that *only the material is real*. For Hamann and Berkeley do not deploy their empiricist instincts to rope off the realm of the divine and its impact on humanity, as Logical Positivism sought to. Human experience of God is perfectly empirical. It is our experience. It is part of the real. Hamann struggles to break down the divide of the empirical and the conceptual that he finds dualistic in Kant's work, and the healing sacrament which performs this mediating function is language. It is embodied and material – Hamann emphasises the physicality of sounds and letters, even of breath; but language also contains a reference beyond that to the signified, which escapes the capture of matter.

Teaching an old word new tricks or teaching a new world old tricks?

Aristotle told us that the ability to create a good metaphor is a sign of genius; it implies that someone can grasp the similarity that exists in dissimilarity. Nelson Goodman just says it is a matter of teaching an old word new tricks.[57]

Although most are acquainted with metaphors as ornaments in language, 'near relations' of other figures of speech, such as simile,[58] metaphor is linguistically and epistemologically a much more complex and rich phenomenon than childhood lessons in grammar and literature ever suggested.

Among the various theories of metaphor, the simplest view is that it is another way of saying what can be said literally. A metaphor is a *substitution* for a more straightforward expression. I *could* say 'Her son is badly behaved' but I say instead 'Her son is a monster'. It is not difficult to translate my metaphor into more direct speech. This is the view of metaphor usually attributed to the ancients.

Janet Martin Soskice objects that this makes the value of metaphor negligible; not only does it reduce metaphor to the level of a riddle, it also reduces the intelligibility of language.[59] You could misunderstand my unkind reference to a friend's son as meaning 'Her son eats large quantities', perhaps. This explains Hobbes' negative evaluation of metaphor; it is an abuse of speech 'when they use words metaphorically; that is, in other senses than that they are ordained for; and thereby deceive others'.[60]

Soskice argues that in fact this view is untenable. A metaphor extends the meaning beyond what is contained in a single literal translation. Her strongest objection is that it suggests that those who use metaphors as part of their art, like the poet, the theologian or the scientist, are 'doing no more than translating from a prior and literal understanding into an evocative formulation'; whereas the thinking itself is undertaken as metaphor.[61] 'What interests us in metaphor is precisely that we find in it an increment to understanding.'[62]

This, then, is the direction that reflection on metaphor has taken: metaphor is not something you can easily replace; often it cannot be reduced to literal speech for it has its own cognitive content.[63] Richards observes that a metaphor is two thoughts or things held together, 'whose meaning is a resultant of their interaction'. This permanent tension or interaction is crucial in understanding what a metaphor does. It is not a question of substituting one word for another, but bringing into connection two different regions or contexts. The corollary of this is that metaphors are not merely rhetorical devices, but are new and unconventional ways of interpreting reality. Black claims that metaphors do not just help us discern reality, but sometimes create reality.

In the hands of such thinkers, metaphor becomes a model for how we understand, as well as how we embody our understanding in speech. When we encounter something new, we begin by partly assimilating it to what is known, as well as pointing up the differences with what is already familiar. This plays on the tension of similarity/dissimilarity that exists in metaphor, and extends it to a view of the method of understanding, or a way of seeing the world, or indeed the way in which the human mind itself works. 'Metaphor is as ultimate as speech itself, and speech as ultimate as thought .... Metaphor appears as the instinctive and necessary act of the mind exploring reality and ordering experience.'[64]

If this viewpoint is accepted, then religious language is not at all unique if it claims that language about God is fundamentally metaphorical. The same has even been said of scientific language.[65] This could possibly ease problems of language referring to the Transcendent, and show that religious language is not different in principle to other forms of discourse.

One corollary of this is that the assumption that univocal language comes first, and that metaphor is a later supplementation or ornamentation has virtually been reversed. We perceive or understand first metaphorically, and univocal propositions are later developments, refinements, clarifications of the initial 'metaphorical' perception. Nietzsche and Derrida both suggest that *all* language is metaphorical. Lacan takes this understanding of metaphor as fundamental to epistemology further, and uses metaphor and metonymy not just to indicate how conscious thinking and language operate, but primarily and fundamentally how the unconscious operates as well, as we shall see later. 'What need is there to talk of a reality which would sustain the so-called metaphorical usages? Every kind of usage, in a certain sense, is always metaphorical.'[66]

In contrast, it is striking that Blumenberg's 'metaphorology' is thoroughly *historical*, not simply theoretical. He examines particular, concrete metaphors (such as metaphors of truth) throughout the history of ideas with an impressive range, as well as engaging in theoretical reflection on metaphorology – such as, can metaphors be true? They cannot be verified. The issue cannot be decided theoretically, at least according to dominant contemporary understandings of truth and meaning. What Blumenberg is after, then, is the *historical* truth of metaphors, which is *pragmatic*. They answer to the question: what genuine guidance does it give? They give the world structure; they allow us to do what is impossible, that is, gain an overview over the totality of reality: 'the funda-mental, enduring certainties, conjectures, valuations, from which the attitudes, expectations, activities and idleness, longings and disappointments, interests and indifference of an epoch are regulated.'[67]

I agree with the view of metaphor as cognitive, as a model for how we learn, understand, and think. But the story of metaphor as languishing under the ancients, under-appreciated, as a mere figure of speech, until its rightful episte-mological status was recognised in modern times has a clear set of presuppositions and prejudices, although these have gone unchallenged in the discussions of metaphor. Metaphor as a 'mere' figure of speech in ancient Greece has its roots in rhetoric. While 'rhetoric' is not a term of approbation for most modern philosophers, it was held in considerable esteem in Greek philo-sophy – indeed, as Blumenberg points out, it was so important that Plato named the decisive phase of mythical cosmogony in *Timaeus* as the rhetorical act of persuasion. The power of persuasion was a quality of reality itself, extended into the arts and methods of rhetoric.[68]

It could be argued, then, that claiming it is a greater dignity for metaphor to be a way of perceiving and representing the world, actually rests on modern Western assumptions that the primary task of philosophy is description of mate-rial reality, and the primary task of language is to service thought by representing its cognitions accurately. In short, careless talk about 'mere figures of speech' and the 'greater importance' of metaphor as cognitive *privileges epistemology* over communication, interpersonal interaction, social change and transforma-tion.

Perhaps the point of metaphor is not to teach an old word new tricks, but to teach a new world old tricks. We might then see that metaphor as a device of rhetoric is more powerful than if is viewed as a mode of private cognition. But that would require a recognition of the priority of language as *communication* over language as representation; and who has expressed any interest in that?

The death of idols?

'Man's ultimate concern must be expressed symbolically, because symbolic language alone is able to express the ultimate.'[69] Paul Tillich characterises the symbol partly in distinction to the 'sign'. Both point beyond themselves to something else. They are given a special meaning by convention. The decisive difference is that signs do not 'participate in the reality of that to which they point', while symbols do; they 'participate in [the] meaning and power' of what they symbolise. Therefore, signs can be replaced for reasons of expediency or convention, while symbols cannot; their relationship to what they symbolise is more than arbitrary or conventional. Although changing stop-signs might cause some initial confusion, it would not have the impact of changing a country's flag, which is not a 'sign' of the country but a 'symbol'.

According to Tillich, symbols, as for example in art, give us access to levels of reality which we cannot reach scientifically. At the same time, they unlock hidden depths of our own being. Symbols cannot be produced intentionally, however. 'They grow out of the individual or collective unconscious and cannot function without being accepted by the unconscious dimension of our being. Symbols which have an especially social function, as political and religious symbols, are created or at least accepted by the collective unconscious of the group in which they appear.' These means that they grow, live, and die. They die when they no longer produce a response in the group in which they originally came to be.

Tillich applies his account of symbols to religious faith by naming God as the fundamental symbol of our ultimate concern. 'God is a symbol for God.' We need therefore to distinguish the ultimacy, which is not symbolic itself, from the concreteness of the symbol, which is taken from ordinary experience and applied to God. Faith, then, does not require belief in these concrete images from earthly life, 'but it is the acceptance of symbols that express our ultimate concern in terms of divine actions'. These are not susceptible to empirical criticism; their truth lies in the adequacy or lack of it to the situation for which they are created.

Randall has used an account of symbol and myth to highlight the non-representational function of religious language in particular.[70] Religion, he argues, is an activity which makes its own special contribution to society. It works with a body of symbols and myths that are non-representative and non-cognitive, that is, they do not symbolise some external thing that can be indicated apart from their operation, but rather it is a question of what these symbols and myths actually do. Religious symbols, according to Randall, have a fourfold function: they arouse emotions and stir us to action, and thereby may strengthen our practical commitment; they stimulate co-operative action and thus bind a community together through a common response to its symbols; they are able to communicate qualities of experience that cannot be expressed by the ordinary literal use of language; they evoke, and also clarify our experience of an aspect of the world that can be called the Divine. As artists can teach us to use our senses in a new way, so can prophets and saints open our hearts to new qualities in the world, the religious dimension of the world. Randall, however, does not believe that God or the Divine exists as a reality independent of the human mind. God is rather an 'intellectual symbol' for the religious aspects of the world, our ideals, our values, what Tillich calls our 'ultimate concern'.

Paul Ricoeur observes that the symbol gives rise to thought. It is prior to philosophy, theology, even myth. It has a 'double intentionality', that is, points in two directions: the first, the literal intention, is the only way into the more cryptic meaning. There is always more to symbols (and myths) than in the whole of philosophy.[71] But Ricoeur also calls our attention to a danger. We continually seek to make the Wholly Other into an object; 'metaphysics makes God into a supreme being; and religion treats the sacred as a new sphere of objects'[72] – with the result that sacred *signs* become sacred *things*. This is how 'idols' arise. The sacred can be a meaningful bearer of the Wholly Other, or can be a set of idols as one group of things in our culture alongside others. 'The ambiguity is inevitable: for if the Wholly Other draws near, it does so in the signs of the sacred; but symbols soon turn into idols.' For the symbols to live, the idols must die.[73]

Such accounts of symbol may seem to take us further than one expects to go when dealing purely with language.[74] Or do they? The symbol, apparently, makes something present. The symbol gives access to what we otherwise could not reach. The symbol gives rise to thought. It points in two directions at once. What does language do?

It may be, instead, that the difficulty lies in saying what of language is *not* a symbol.

The striptease that wasn't

Rudolf Bultmann claimed that much of the Bible is 'mythological'; by which he did not mean 'untrue', but rather that it belonged to the genre of myth. The New Testament cosmology of the world, for example, three-tiered as it is with heaven, God and his angels above, hell with Satan and his devils below, and the earth in the middle, is clearly, according to Bultmann, mythological.[75]

When the preacher confronts his listener with the Gospel message of redemption, this is the mythical view of the world which the New Testament presupposes. But this makes the Gospel message unbelievable to modern people, who (Bultmann says) cannot believe in this cosmos of demons and angels. Do we expect our converts not only to accept the essential message of salvation, but also the mythical view of the world in which it is set? And if we do not, does the New Testament embody a truth which is independent of its mythical framework? If it does, theology must undertake the task of stripping the message from its mythical setting, of 'demythologising' it.

We cannot, Bultmann tells us, simply subtract the bits of the Bible we find mythological and believe what is left over: the sophisticated wisdom, the inspiring ethical exhortations, or whatever takes our fancy. We must re-interpret the myth. That is because the real purpose of myth is not to present an objective picture of the world as it is, but to express our understanding of ourselves in the world in which we live. Myth speaks of the power or the powers which we suppose we experience as the ground and limit of our world and our activity and suffering. We describe these powers in terms derived from the visible world and from human life. We speak of the other world in terms of this world, and of the gods in terms derived from human life. Myth is an expression of the human conviction that the origin and purpose of the world in which we live are to be sought not within it but beyond it. It is also an expression of our awareness that we are not the lord [*sic*] of our own being. Hence the importance of the New Testament mythology lies not in its imagery but in the understanding of existence which it enshrines. This means that mythology needs to be reinterpreted existentially. We have to discover whether the New Testament offers us an understanding of ourselves which will challenge us to a genuine existential decision.[76]

What are the presuppositions of language and meaning underlying this account? It is clear that it presumes that meaning can be separated from the language in which it is nesting. One can extract the meaning like a kernel from the coarse husk which contains but also conceals it.[77] It is this notion of the relation of meaning to the language which gives it expression that has aroused some of the most energetic criticism of Bultmann's programme.[78]

However, Bultmann's programme, although it is a central focus for twentieth-century theology and religious thought, is only part of a larger tradition that has developed in Europe over the last several centuries. Odo Marquard characterises the fundamental attitude to myth of modern Europe as 'demythologising', whether one is referring to Bultmann or not. Myth is what we have 'behind us'; we are in the course of progress from 'mythos to logos', that is, from myth to rationality. Opinions divide principally as to whether this is a bad or good thing. But this history of the processes of demythologising is itself a myth, Marquard argues; the fact that 'the death of myth' has itself become a myth shows the relative immortality of myth. For Marquard, myth is what we cannot do without. We cannot take it off like clothing, an image which Marquard develops with pleasing frivolity. Mythic nakedness – and Marquard reminds us of Blumenberg's investigation into the metaphor of the 'naked truth'[79] – is a nakedness that humanly doesn't exist. Marquard is sceptical about the striptease of demythologising; the more that myth takes off, the more that it seems to keep on. A little child in the crowd might cry out: 'Look, the Emperor of the later Vienna Circle still has myths on!' Mythonudism is simply impossible.[80]

Blumenberg, in his monumental *Work on Myth*,[81] suggests that myth is needed not just by so-called 'primitive' peoples but by all of us; we need it to prevent the 'absolutism of reality'. Our knowledge is always only partial, but the absolutism of reality is total. Knowledge of the 'scientific' kind is not enough; we need something more than knowledge to cope. He disputes the myth of the progress from 'mythos' to 'logos'; scientific rationality is not the end-state. Rationality and myth are both indispensable to us, from the start and forever afterwards.

What comes to light in Blumenberg's examination is that people oppose rationality to myth in a relatively hostile (he might have added: 'indiscriminate') manner: whatever contrasts with rationality is 'myth'. So, for example, discussions of Nazi propaganda often speak of it as 'myth' with an air of acceptance that 'myth' is what their stories truly were[82] – although by the same token Nazi ideas of race and health are not considered 'philosophy' and 'science'. Setting myth and rationality against one another in this way makes myth subject, at best, to carrying the blame for the failures of rationality, or at worst, a kind of demonisation: which is ironically 'the mythicization of the difference between myth and rationality'![83]

Blumenberg chronicles modern attempts to bring myth to an end, in literary treatments of the Faust legend and in German philosophy, principally the German idealists. He suggests that both of them are trying to bring myth to an end *by means of itself.* If the work of myth is to counter the absolutism of reality, then myth comes to an end when we have solved that problem – when our knowledge is complete; when the absolutism of reality is replaced by the absolutism of the human subject. The German Idealists and those who succeed them (e.g. Nietzsche, Heidegger) compete to create the final myth, the story which is so complete that there is room for no other. 'To bring myth to an end was once supposed to have been the work of logos. This consciousness of itself on the part of philosophy – or better, the historians of philosophy – is contradicted by the fact that work aimed at putting an end to myth is again and again accomplished in the form of a metaphor of myth.'[84]

Anderson cites Irigaray on the need for transformation of the social structures which the myths in part support and justify. The work on myth that Anderson imagines (she is not invoking Blumenberg here) is mimesis, which means imitation. But Anderson has in mind a 'disruptive miming', which transforms patriarchal myths and theistic beliefs. Mythical configurations can be refigured. In particular, she performs her own refiguration of the Indian myth of Mirabai and the Greek myth of Antigone.[85]

Anderson cautions that there are dangers in separating myth too sharply from reason. We need a distinctive form of rational scrutiny, she maintains, to assess a myth's truth and justice.[86] I would suggest that rationality is even more in need of scrutiny, a distinctive form of *mythic* scrutiny, to assess *its* truth and justice.

Marquard warns us against the dangers of 'monomythia', the domination of a single myth. What we need is the plurality of myths, polymythia, for our own protection; for like mushrooms, some myths are poisonous. With the Enlightenment (perhaps poisonous?) myth of reason and rationality in mind, Hamann wrote: 'If one single truth rules like the sun, that is day. If you see in place of this single truth as many as the sands on the shores of the sea', what you have instead is night. Rationality prefers the clear light of day. But Hamann observes that it is night that poets love.[87]

Elephants in the room

In his first year of seminars, Lacan observed, by way of example, that the word 'elephant' allows us to take decisions about elephants in their absence, 'even before touching them', that have much greater impact on them than our immediate presence can. Once he had alluded to elephants, he observed: 'it is clear, all I need do is talk about it, there is no need for them to be here, for them really to be here, thanks to the word *elephant,* and to be more real than the contingent elephant-individuals.'[88] Later he referred to himself as having brought an elephant 'into the room the other day by means of the word elephant'.[89]

What happened when Lacan talked about elephants? He was not describing some unusually large and noticeably grey members of the student body in the room, either in literal assertions of existence or in metaphors. He was *doing something* – making elephants present – by means of language. There are, then, accounts of language which eschew the emphasis on the 'representing' function of language, description, report, assertion. There are accounts that prioritise instead the non-representational aspects of language; that it does not merely *say* things, it *does* things.

John Searle tells us that there are five things we can do with language. 'You can tell people how things are (assertives); tell them to do things (directives); commit yourself to doing things (commissives); express your feelings and attitudes (expressives); and bring about changes in the world through your utterances (declarations).'[90] Searle's approach has come to be known 'Speech-Act Theory'. Terrence Tilley claims that this schema can be used to throw light on much of religious language. He suggests as examples that petitionary prayer is a 'directive', that preaching is an 'assertive', that pledging is 'commissive', that swearing is 'expressive', and confession a 'declarative'.[91] Doubtless readers can reflect on the praxis of religious individuals to flesh out Searle's taxonomy still further.

What Speech-Act Theory does, first of all, is to underline that language is *act*, as well as 'speech'. Further, it asserts the right of language to be diverse. One needs to recognise the plurality of functions it possesses. However, one can question whether a tidy list of five is the best way to encourage a recognition of diversity. The enumeration of a list always begs questions – and where it does not irritate listeners, it sometimes silences them. I remember sitting in a lecture in which a distinguished Catholic psychotherapist and marriage counsellor said solemnly: 'There are five reasons why married people have sex.' I suppose, like Searle, he was trying to encourage recognition of more than one proper function. However, it made me wonder if one was repressed if one could only think of four reasons; or if, on the other hand, six things came to mind, might one be polymorphous? But I didn't like to ask.

Austin claimed that whenever we say something, we perform a number of acts. (So that's all right, then.) Contrary to representationalist views, much of what we say does not match the world; we say it in order to *do* something: to swear an oath or to make a vow does not *describe* the world, and yet such utterances are not meaningless. He called our attention to 'performative utterances' – times when speech is effective, when it brings something about. Much religious language does not describe;[92] there are times of worship, of making commitments, in which the action rather than the assertion is the important thing.[93]

It is the later Wittgenstein's account of language that has had the most impact, however, on non-representational understandings of language. Having repented and done penance for his earlier positivist leanings, he was born again into the new life of ordinary language. Like Hamann, like Lorenzen,[94] Wittgenstein had decided that the search for the ideal logical scientific language was misguided; that ordinary language would do very nicely. In fact, many philosophical problems can be untangled by paying attention to it, as was observed earlier by the Nyāya theoreticians.[95] Many traditional philosophical problems arise because we don't see the real nature of language; these problems arise when language is being used 'out of gear'.

What we see when we examine ordinary language is that it is much more complex than Logical Positivism allows. It is not just a tool for making assertions – 'As if there were only one thing called "talking about a thing". Whereas in fact we do the most various things with our sentences.'[96]

With an expansion of his view of what language *does*, Wittgenstein has to revise his earlier theory of meaning – his own picture theory. The word is not a unit of meaning, he now sees, nor is the sentence composed of word-units. 'If', 'there', 'now', only have their meaning in their use in language. So as compared to the *Tractatus*, where the meaning of the word was the thing to which it referred, in *Philosophical Investigations* the meaning of language is to be found in the many uses to which it is put. (Maṇḍana also asserted that children learn the meaning of words from their use in 'language-games', although he did not describe them as such; however, he disagreed with a hypothetical objector that the sole use from which they learned was in the form of injunctions.[97])

But how many kinds of sentence are there? Say assertion, question, and command? – There are countless kinds: countless different kinds of use of what we call 'symbols', 'words', 'sentences'. And this multiplicity is not something fixed, given once for all; but new types of language, new language-games, as we may say, come into existence, and others become obsolete and get forgotten. ... Here the term 'language-game' is meant to bring into prominence the fact that the speaking of language is part of an activity, or a form of life. Review the multiplicity of language-games in the following examples, and in others: giving orders, and obeying them – Describing the appearance of an object, or giving its measurements – Reporting an event – Speculating about an event – Play-acting – Guessing riddles – Asking, thanking, cursing, greeting, praying. – It is interesting to compare the multiplicity of the tools in language and of the ways they are used, the multiplicity of kinds of word and sentence, with what logicians have said about the structure of language. (Including the author of the *Tractatus Logico-Philosophicus*.)[98]

While in the *Tractatus* using language correctly consisted in following certain rules, an idea taken up by Logical Positivists, in *Philosophical Investigations* this is replaced by the idea of 'language games'. This contains the recognition that there are a variety of different systems of rules governing how we speak, and that these do not have a universal, objective, eternal validity, but are agreed, and apply to the matter at hand, without external justification. 'If you do not keep the multiplicity of language-games in view you will perhaps be inclined to ask questions like: "What is a question?" – Is it the statement that I do not know such-and-such, or the statement that I wish the other person would tell me ...? Or is it the description of my mental state of uncertainty?'[99] – in a perhaps unconscious echo of Augustine's son Adeodatus.

The corollary of this for religious language is that, if language functions in all kinds of different ways, and not just in the single assertive function that the Logical Positivists claim, then one can claim that religious language performs its *own* function. Thus, one can claim that religious language is its own language game, or set of language games, and each has its own purpose, meaning, and internal justification. This has, initially, the comforting consequence that religious believers can no longer be derided for not being able to display an object, 'God', that corresponds to the word.[100] Moreover, language cannot be considered apart from other aspects of life and behaviour; language is always embedded in a 'form of life'. The corollary is that one cannot make the rash assumption that religious statements function in the same way as mathematical propositions and scientific assertions of fact. To understand a religious statement as a philosopher, one must take into account the whole context in which the statement occurs. We have already seen how these notions have been appropriated epistemologically.

To see how some have essayed to flesh out these insights, let us look at an early attempt by R. Braithwaite. He adopted Wittgenstein's principle that meaning is found in use, and tried to consider the meaning of religious language from this starting-point. He argued that the primary element in the use of religious statements is the making of moral assertions; they serve a primarily ethical function. He further presupposes that moral statements are not verifiable propositions but express the attitude of the person making the statement, express the speaker's adherence to a certain policy of action. To say one 'ought' to do something is to say that one intends to do this. Religious statements, then, express the intention to live life in a particular way. So, for example, a Christian's assertion that 'God is love' means 'I intend to follow an agapeistic way of life.'[101] Differences in ritual between religions are essentially unimportant; as is the fact that they tell different stories, which need not be true in order to inspire. To assert the doctrines of a religion is both to tell its doctrinal story and to confess allegiance to its way of life.

For an account that bases itself on Wittgenstein, this is strikingly un-Wittgensteinian. Braithwaite reduces the complex phenomenon of ethics to a single function, and the even more elaborate and multivalent phenomenon of religion to a single purpose. The particular force of Wittgenstein's later position, especially his rejection of his own earlier theory, is precisely to eschew such single-mindedness and assert the primacy of diversity and plurality. If language does not have a single function, or a single nature, how can ethical *or* religious language be so ruthlessly singular?

More consistent is Gareth Moore's attempt to think through belief in God from the standpoint of how the language of religious believers functions.

> Christian belief in and language about God is logically linked to the way Christians live and see their lives. It is through the attitudes and dispositions and activities of Christians that their language gets its meaning. It is not that belief in God … is somehow given an independent, theoretical meaning, and that we are then exhorted to develop the attitudes appropriate to such a being. … The attitudes, dispositions and activities are not just appropriate in the light of the beliefs we hold about some being called God, they are what gives *sense* to our belief in God and what we believe about him. Our religious beliefs and language have their place within the context of a particular kind of human life, a life in which gratitude, generosity, lack of self-seeking, a sense of dependence and mystery, among other things, play an important, even a defining part.[102]

Moore takes seriously the context of belief and real life against which religious utterances have meaning. He is like a metalworker trying to restore the place, date and value to neutralised coins to reinstate their worth.

Moore's account could be subtitled 'God as Nothing'. Again and again he drives home the point that to say God did something is to say that no one did it. Paradoxically, however, the absence to which Moore continuously refers is overlaid with the presence of a name, which makes sense in the absence of its bearer, which introduces its bearer into the room by means of the word.

The cat's not on the mat

A philosopher and a theologian were at a party engaging in the usual jousting. 'You philosophers,' complained the theologian, 'are like blind men in a darkened room, looking for a cat that isn't there.' 'That may be so,' retorted the philosopher; 'but you theologians *find* the cat.'

For robust accounts of language, it is clear what language does when it announces: 'The cat sat on the mat'. What can it do about a cat that isn't there?

Freud described a baby playing his own little game of throwing a cotton reel away, saying 'Here!' while it is gone, then pulling it back to himself, saying 'Gone!' once it is present again. Lacan takes this game as the phenomenon of symbolisation taking shape: making something present in its absence, by means of the word. 'When the object is there he chases it away, when it isn't there he calls it. Through these first games, the object passes … on to the plane of language. The symbol comes into being and becomes more important than the object.'[103]

The word makes the absent present, like cats and elephants. Less commonly observed is that it can also make the present absent, as those from despised social or ethnic groups can feel when language used by others doesn't include them. This notion of the word as making-present is arguably a more adequate basis for understanding how language refers to the world than accounts of language as representational and picture theories of meaning. The word is *not* the label of what it names; the relation of word to object is the symbolic function of making something present in its absence. Lacan actually says that the word is the thing itself.[104] The object is almost the incarnation of the word.

In Lacan's conception, words are joined into a 'signifying chain', which links one signifier or word to another. With this image, the focus shifts off the connection of each word to its little *thing*; now the attention is on the connection between one word and the next. A graphic example may illustrate the impact that such a paradigm shift may have on something's meaning.

A friend who is a Roman Catholic priest (let's call him 'Johannes') was at my house for dinner. Johannes found himself in the company of psychotherapists and made the mistake of relating a dream that he had had several times lately, and canvassing opinion. He dreamed that he desperately wanted a pet cat. He reflected that he could go out in the street and pick one up, a stray, and pet it. But what he really wanted was one of his own to cuddle and take home and keep by him all the time for company. On the mat, perhaps.

The Jungian psychotherapist present observed that around the world, cats are symbols or archetypes for the underworld. The underworld is the image of the unconscious. Johannes was now at the time of life where it was time to make that descent of self-examination into the unconscious. This is not to be done casually ('pick up one in the street'); one needs to make a commitment to do this ('take the cat home with you and keep it'). What the dream was trying to tell Johannes was that he should now embark on a Jungian psychoanalysis.

The Lacanian was not interested in connecting the word 'cat' to an object, to then interpret the symbolism of the *object* – what that *animal* symbolises, as the Jungian had. Her focus was on a word-to-word connection: not *what* the word 'cat' brings to mind, but what *word* the word 'cat' brings to mind. One word came immediately to her mind: 'Pussy.'

With this an entirely new direction of interpretation opened up.

The Lacanian account of meaning does not grapple with the question of how the word attaches to the thing. It examines the way that words connect to other words. In this way, it is 'Augustinian' – it echoes the insight of Augustine and Adeodatus, with which I opened this chapter: words *do* refer, despite our sceptical doubts; but what they refer to is *other words*. This also recalls Maṇḍana's suggestions. Every signifier only leads to another signifier; 'no signification can be sustained other than by reference to another signification'.[105] Language is not supported by the existence of things outside it. 'So, you will get caught up in paths which are always dead ends … if you fail to take account of the fact that signification only ever refers back to itself, that is to say to another signification.'[106] Language is not justified by its connection with the 'real world'.

Language consists of signifying chains, which are made up by two structures: 'metaphor' and 'metonymy'.[107] Metonymy is the device in which one word stands in for, or replaces, another; almost like a euphemism. (Indeed, Hamann's 'euphemismo' is an example.) One says 'Downing Street announced ...' and means not a talking road, but the British Government's spokesperson. So metonymy is a word-to-word connection. Metaphor Lacan conceives as a substitution of one signifier for another; 'the occulted signifier remaining present through its (metonymic) connection with the rest of the chain.'[108] In the signifying chain of Johannes' dream,[109] 'cat' was a metaphor in this sense, blocking out 'pussy' (the occulted signifier). But because 'pussy' is metonymy for something else, what is blocked out is nevertheless still present in the signifying chain through this metonymic connection. (Johannes, in an act of anti-Freudian subversion but Lacanian one-up-manship, insisted that if 'cat' was metonymy for 'female genital', then the female genital was in fact a metonymy for a well-rounded relationship with a whole woman, as evidenced by his desire to keep the cat for company and not just have a quick patting session with a 'street'-'cat'.)

Metonymy, in those languages and cultures which encourage it, allows an extraordinary depth and richness to one's speech. The Hawaiian language enjoys a phenomenal degree of polysemy (multiple meanings to a single 'word'); and Hawaiian poetry makes extensive use of the possibilities inherent in polysemy and metonymy. Most songs and poems contain more than one meaning: not only the most obvious, but also a 'kaona' or hidden meaning. Once Hawaii was invaded by a different culture which was somewhat hostile and critical of its mores, yet desirous of enjoying it aesthetically, a kind of inter-lingual metonymy took place and still does. The original multiple meanings of poems and songs can be occulted behind a single translation – or lack of one. When certain things are forbidden and cannot be said, they can still find expression. The biblical genre of 'apocalyptic' functions in a similar way, to allow one to speak to those who will understand, when under conditions of repression or censorship.

For example, a Hawaiian prince, Lele-iō-Hoku, had written a love song in the Hawaiian language which unreservedly describes making love in the sea ('we two in the spray, oh joy two together, embracing tightly in the coolness' it begins). In my childhood it was sung at tourist shows, but in the original Hawaiian, never translated or sung in English. It was described to the tourists as 'The Hawaiian War Chant'. As a small child, I was even taught the hula to it. It is difficult to know which is more curious: the thought of little children dancing out this throbbing eroticism ('oh, *such spray*!', cries the refrain);[110] or the American cultural values that pronounce it more seemly for small children to celebrate making war than making love.

Wittgenstein's problem at the end of the *Tractatus* – 'I need to say something that my rules won't permit me to say' – is the problem faced by religious believers, even if they reject Logical Positivism; so long as they hold fast to the affirmation of divine transcendence. How then can we say the unsayable? How can we do this impossible thing? Simple: by metonymy and *kaona*.

The Hawaiians were wiser than Europeans and Americans to the possibilities that metonymy holds for religious language. Lacan was possibly aware of the use that religious language might have for his notion of signifying chains, but chose not to advert to it. Let us take forward these ideas for an understanding of religious language: of metonymy, as the possibility for saying the unsayable; of the word as making present what is seemingly absent or occulted; and of the signifying chain, which does not look to the world of things for its meaning – or its justification.

> We will fail to pursue the question further as long as we cling to the illusion that the signifier answers to the function of representing the signified, or better, that the signifier has to answer for its existence in the name of any signification whatever. For even reduced to this latter formulation, the heresy is the same – the heresy that leads to logical positivism in search of the 'meaning of meaning', as its objective is called in the language of its devotees.[111]

Lacan is adamant that it is not 'picturing' which justifies language. The later Wittgenstein similarly asserted, 'When we say: "Every word in language signifies something", we have so far said *nothing* whatever'.[112] Neither thinks that language can be explained by reference to the things or situations in the world that it is supposed to *mean*, or represent.

So, if we are to reject the picture theory, and maybe even a sense of language as representational, what are we left with? Words lead only to still more words, never things; language is a blind alley from which there is no exit into the real world. Language is a bubble in which we live, as the theologian Don Cupitt put it, with nothing outside it.[113] We are on the road to relativism and non-realism.

That is not, however, where Lacan ends up. He recognises the 'lure' of the picture theory and commonsensical notions of language as depicting reality: 'this lure is structural to human language and, in a sense, the verification of every truth is founded on it.'[114] In Lacan's view, words just point you to other words, not things; and yet if this order of language is a blind alley with no exit, it would be an order without meaning. Truth requires something 'beyond' signification. 'But it is in relation to truth that the signification of everything which is expressed is to be located.'[115] Like Wittgenstein, he needs a ladder to climb out of the threatened confines of his own theory.

His 'ladder' is the insistence that language ('the Symbolic' in his vocabulary) does have a strong relation to what he calls 'the Real'; language does not lack a relation to the things in our life. 'We are talking about things, and not about some eternally unidentifiable I know not what.'[116] For although one word may always send us off after another, 'all our experience runs counter to this linearity'. There are 'anchoring points' for language. 'There is no signifying chain that does not have, as if attached to the punctuation of each of its units, a whole articulation of relevant contexts suspended "vertically", as it were, from that point.'[117]

Although each signifier is linked to the next signifier in the chain, each signifier is also grounded, anchored – but not in a simplistic word-to-thing, one-to-one correspondence. The anchors are *contexts*, and what anchors the signifiers are *associations*. We cannot say, ' "cat" symbolises x' – but even if 'cat' connects to another word like 'pussy', a context and associations still exist to anchor these words in our world and our desires.

Language, says Lacan, 'introduces the dimension of truth into the real'.[118] It throws a net over things, and thus brings them to us for speech; in this way the world of things is brought into the human world of speaking. So although it does not 'picture' or simply 'mirror' reality, what language does to 'things' is to bring them into being for us, reveal them and their significance for us. Aristotle says that 'voice', as the expression of pleasure and pain and emotion, is something we share with animals. But 'language' makes clear what is expedient, what is harmful, what is good or evil, what is just and unjust, and so on.[119] Thus according to Aristotle, language does not passively describe the world, it *interprets* it according to human interests, needs, and desires.

'All speech always possesses a beyond.'[120] The beyond of signification is of course beyond language; but it is not a-linguistic and utterly ineffable. 'When you understand what is expressed in the signs of the language, it is always, in the end, on account of light coming to you from *outside* of the signs .... The truth is *outside* of the signs, elsewhere.'[121]

The beyond of 'language'

I have a few suggestions to make for thinking about language, religious language in particular. I should warn readers who are new to the discipline that these are somewhat unconventional; they might bring some philosophers out in hives, while others may not like the uses to which I have put their own accounts.

I suggest first that we restore the primacy of 'communication' to our reflection on language. During the writing of this chapter, I was involved in training for language therapy for small children with language disorders. The seminars on language focused entirely on the question of communication as what language is all about. ('Reference' didn't get a look in.) What does communication presuppose, what does it consist in, what facilitates it? It was striking that I could not think of philosophers of language who put this issue at the top of their agenda, or saw the challenges that exist in *communicating with someone else* as 'the problem of religious language'.

It is interesting that it is the atheist Lacan who suggests:

A creature needs some reference to the beyond of language, to a pact, to a commitment which constitutes him, strictly speaking, as an Other, a reference included in the general, or, to be more exact, universal system of interhuman symbols. No love can be functionally realisable in the human community, save by means of a specific pact, which ... [is] at one and the same time within language and outside of it. That is what we call the function of the sacred ....[122]

Language presupposes a pact; with a family, with a community. Children cannot learn language without it. In this community we are initiated into a shared symbolic system that unites us in solidarity with other human beings, both in language and beyond it. It is this pact that, first, converts 'The Other' into 'another human being', as Blumenberg comments; but further, allows us to undergo the sometimes humbling experience of becoming an Other to someone else.

This pact connects us with a tradition; a relation to our forbears, as Hamann and Lorenzen showed us, is presupposed in the very existence of this ship in which we sail. The Rgveda speaks of language 'as grain is shifted through the sieve and becomes clear of cockle' over time. This is accomplished through the tradition, 'after many labours and efforts', 'for the benefit of all the initiated – so that they could communicate by this language, so enriched and ennobled, in their gatherings'.[123] Above all, without this pact, this community, tradition, and language – love is not possible.

This is why I suggested earlier that rhetoric was important in considering metaphor; perhaps more important than epistemology. This pact commits us to engagement with our community – to conflict; to the need for change, for persuasion in the resolution of conflict and the maintenance of solidarity. Metaphor, myth and symbol are only important as ways of representing the world if we are trying to convince, persuade, inspire. Why else should we spend our time 'representing the world' – what *for*?

The Indian philosophers are indispensable to those in the West in reminding us of a central purpose for religious language: enlightenment and liberation. For although both Śankara and Sureśvara are pessimistic about the ability of language to create knowledge and describe ultimate reality, both are adamant that it is indispensable in attaining enlightenment. Although Śankara even goes so far as to say that the Upaniṣads are ultimately false because language is an instrument of ignorance, we can still be liberated by something that is false. Sureśvara asserts that although words cannot directly denote Brahman, they can help to dispel ignorance, just as someone can be woken from sleep by words even if she doesn't understand their meaning.[124]

Something of this spirit may lie behind Hamann's willingness to consort with anthropomorphism, at the risk of courting idolatry and blasphemy, and to urge us to the hyperbole that he himself practiced. Careful accuracy has its dangers; but error can be liberating. The crudities of anthropomorphism, if crude they are, continually remind us that the target of our speech lies beyond our verbal achievements. The worst temptations to idolatry may be words such as 'Perfect Being', 'Being Itself' or 'Ultimate Concern' rather than carved statues.[125]

What possibilities exist then for reference, for effability? Maṇḍana maintained that all the universe is accompanied by speech, because everything is known by cognition, and cognition always has the 'tincture of speech'. Here Maṇḍana weaves together two relationships: the relationship of speech to cognition, and of language to the universe.

On the first point, Maṇḍana tells us that cognition or thinking cannot appear 'without a support'. (Hamann similarly reminded us that the ability to think, along with other things such as emotional development and social interaction, all rest on language.[126]) Even babies' activities, in reaching for their mothers' breast, for example, show the 'tincture of speech': 'this!' is the baby's target. Even if you maintain that some cognition is possible in advance of speech, it becomes more vivid and distinct after language has been learned: the examples he gives are notes of the scale and herdsmen naming their animals. And when language has been lost, things are as good as unknown.[127] Some Indian philosophers spoke of ultimate knowledge, *śāstra*, as *śabda*, the spoken (or spoken word), others as *vāc*, speech; thus solidly identifying language and knowledge.[128]

In the Jewish and Christian creation account, the world is created by language; by the word. Hamann, in his re-working of the biblical creation myth, suggests an identification between the world and speech which smoothes away the difficulties in their relationship:

> Every phenomenon of nature was a word, – the sign, symbol and pledge of a new, mysterious, inexpressible but all the more intimate union, participation and community of divine energies and ideas. Everything the human being heard from the beginning, saw with its eyes, looked upon and touched with its hands was a living word; for God was the word. With this word in mouth and heart the origin of language was as natural, as near and as easy as child's play.[129]

Indian traditions join the cosmos and language or speech in their own way.

> The meaning of *śabda* (lit. 'what-is-spoken') is able both to create everything, and to make everything known. It follows therefore, that the closest correlation between *śabda* and *artha*, the spoken matter and its referent … must pertain to the original condition of the world. Identity is certainly the strongest form of this pertinence. And indeed, it was proclaimed that Transcendent Speech *is* the Universe; both of them shape knowledge of Reality as itself, i.e. as it is. At the same time, to have a structured cosmic shape means to be *vānmaya*, 'made of words' or 'manifested in words'.[130]

Speech was identified with the world in a succession of levels.[131] But even when knowledge and speech descend through the various levels to the level of ordinary human speech, it is still 'universal', in the sense of being a manifestation of the universe.

This account would of course be rejected by analytic philosophers who deem that as a starting-point for an account of the question of meaning and reference, such myths are wholly inadequate. They prefer their own.

Metonymy, however, has good prospects for reference to the transcendent. Metonymy removes the imperialist remnants of positivism, the insistence that language can only be justified by the existence of something solidly material. Metonymy makes it possible to refer to the immaterial; it can cope with the absence of what it names because its function is to replace, or even displace. It stands in for what is missing; it is the locum for the absent target. Moreover, its fluidity means that it resists idolatry; as significance shifts easily on to it, so too it can easily shift off and onto another signifier.

The Hawaiian device of the 'kaona', familiar of course to other cultures and traditions, also allows the speaker to say the unsayable, to refer to what one is not allowed to name. It allows discourse on at least two levels, which are not unrelated to one another, but do not reduce one to the other. Its closest European relative is perhaps the way that Lacan speaks of the way one discourse takes hold of another and uses it as a support, when describing the activities of the unconscious, in dreaming, for example.

It is worth considering the adoption of the idea of meaning as *artha* – as a target. Language 'aims at' something; words don't sit permanently attached to their objects. Language does not *possess* meaning, but *aspires* to it. It is not a given, something we can thoughtlessly assume, but is rather an achievement when it strikes its target. This humbler, less certain stance sits well with the focus on language as communication, not representation; for representation takes its relation to the world for granted, though not the truth of its constructions. But to speak of meaning as a target brings out the *venture* of language as communication, the risk. One can never be certain in advance of success; neither of its 'reference' nor its reception.

If meaning is a target, it also keeps in view the idea of the 'beyond' of signification and language. Miller's notion of God as a limit case brings out the fact that linguistic reference to the divine is a pointing to, a pointing-beyond-itself-to, which never really arrives at its destination. Like Zeno's stadium runner or arrows, language of the divine then can be seen as flying accurately towards its target, thus indicating clearly where it lies – but never reaching it. Both its power to reveal, and its inability to master, are clearly expressed in this image.

One of the more suggestive ideas from Indian semantics is the theory of meaning held by the grammarians and by Maṇḍana Miśra. For them, meaning is not found in any of the ways we have examined throughout this chapter. Meaning is 'sphoṭa'. – that which bursts forth when it is revealed by speech. Kunjunni Raja calls it 'the partless, integral linguistic symbol'.[132]

Maṇḍana Miśra, in contrast to Śaṅkara and Sureśvara, tells us in fact that Brahman *is* language. Brahman is consciousness, consciousness is the power of speech, so Brahman is of the nature of speech, whose universe is a manifestation of speech. Brahman is the word. The word *is Brahman itself*, and not just a symbol of Brahman.[133] Lacan tells us: 'For the human being the word or the concept is nothing other than the word in its materiality. It is the thing itself. It is not just a shadow, a breath, a virtual illusion of the thing, it is the thing itself.'[134]

> The fundamental phenomenon revealed by analysis is this relation of one discourse to another, using it as a support. What we discover manifested in it is this fundamental principle of semantics, that every semanteme refers to the whole of the semantic system, to the polyvalence of its usages. Moreover, for everything which properly speaking pertains to language, in as much as it is human, that is to say utilisable in speech, the symbol is never univocal. Every semanteme always has several meanings.[135]

In the semantics of belief, in which 'every phenomenon of nature is a word', perhaps every discourse in fact relates to one discourse; one register of speech supports all the others. Every semanteme recalls it to us, multiple though its meaning be.

PART II

Religious Experience

3. Going Mad?

An introduction to religious experience

The woman who knew about pantyhose

A woman temporarily admitted to a psychiatric hospital told us that God had just spoken to her that day, through an advertisement for tights on the television she had seen in the patients' day-room. Apparently, these tights 'stay with you' throughout the day; no matter where you go, how you twist and turn, they stay close to you and don't bag and come away from you at the knees and ankles. She added that, as a modern urban woman, parables about fishermen and sheep didn't communicate anything to her about God, but 'she really knew about pantyhose'. She asserted that God was speaking to her through this advertisement, in order to reassure her and console her in her present period of distress. The psychiatrists felt confirmed in their diagnosis of paranoid schizophrenia, for it is a classic symptom of a such a condition that one feels that God or some other 'voice' is speaking to one personally through the television, radio, electric sockets, wires allegedly planted in the brain, etc. I felt uncomfortably aware that, had the woman been speaking to a different audience in a different room, the reaction could have been very different. Had she spoken in a prayer meeting she would probably have received a positive reaction; her words would have been accepted as mediating a religious insight, perhaps indeed as a 'word from the Lord'.

Ironically, some months later the woman did turn up at a pentecostalist prayer meeting. Unfortunately, she did not repeat her soothing message of divine presence. Apparently she stood up in the group to say harsh and condemning words that God had revealed to her about the presence of evil in the group and its members. The words had an eerie and disquieting effect upon the listeners. The experienced members of the group diagnosed them as the voice of Satan, and it was felt that the woman required an exorcism to drive out her demon. I don't know the end of her story.

The prevalence of religious experiences is impressive. The British psychologists David Hay and Ann Morisy in their first enquiry into the distribution and frequency of religious experience found that slightly more than a third of a balanced sample of the population of the United Kingdom reported having had an experience of a 'presence or power, whether referred to as God or not, which was different from their everyday selves'.[1] This proportion of a positive response was broadly similar to the results found by North American researchers at roughly the same time: positive responses at rates of 20-50%, perhaps depending in part on the exact question asked.[2] More recent research in the UK, USA and Australia has found positive response rates of 33-48%, when the investigation was conducted in the form of a poll.[3] When, however, the research is done in a more intimate and confidential setting, such as an interview, the positive response rate rises dramatically to 62-67%.[4] So a significant proportion of the population has these experiences. Are they all mad?

All it takes is some basic familiarity with psychology or sociology, and a little ingenuity, and one can generate a host of natural factors to offer as explanations for an alleged 'experience of God'. One can replace notions of divine presence and activity with intense social pressure, like brainwashing, mass hysteria, or parental pressure; one can think of repressed sexuality, a projected parent complex, the psyche's process of individuation; one can consider the effects of emotional stress or a personal crisis, an overwhelming sense of guilt or perhaps hypersuggestibility, hypnotic suggestion and indeed auto-suggestion; the effects of culture or social structures, education and upbringing, and expectation; psychological disease or disorder, and psychological well-being; or physiological factors such as disease, or the ingestion of hallucinogenic substances. All of these, in fact, have been suggested as explanations for (by which is often meant, the real causes of) religious experience. If any of the above factors are present, does this mean that the experience was not religious? (Can you think of many experiences or moments in your life in which at least one of these factors was not present?)

To maintain that a religious experience must be religious because it could not be explained in any other way, then, is to make the religious significance of an event dependent on one's imagination and ingenuity. Some thinker will be able to come up with an alternative, even if it seems implausible to the believer. These accounts may be revealing; they may be true. As long as there is disagreement about not just the validity but the sanity of such experiences, accounts from psychology need to be considered seriously. They raise specifically philosophical problems as well.

One can helpfully distinguish between 'naturalistic' and 'reductionist' explanations. Naturalistic explanations are ones that operate purely in terms of the natural world. They seek to explain spiritual experiences or behaviour in terms of psychology, sociology, anthropology, or even physiology; but not in theological terms. They may leave the religious or theological import unaffected. 'Reductionism', on the other hand, seeks to 'reduce' a phenomenon and the account given of it (its origin or cause, explanation, 'meaning') to a single explanatory context and specifically rejects any possible religious significance.

Proudfoot differentiates 'descriptive reductionism' from 'explanatory reductionism'. Descriptive reductionism describes a phenomenon under the wrong category: 'To describe an experience in nonreligious terms when the subject himself describes it in religious terms is to misidentify the experience', which Proudfoot believes is wrong. Explanatory reduction, however, is to explain an experience in a way that the subject himself might not like or agree with; but that Proudfoot argues is justifiable. What is to be explained is set in a new context;

it stands or falls on how well it can account for the evidence.[5] What Proudfoot calls 'explanatory reductionism' is not always 'reductionist' in our sense. His 'explanatory reduction' may 'relocate' an experience into a new framework without 'reducing' it. While one needs to take care in laying violent interpretative hands on someone else's experience, it is unnecessary to limit ourselves just to spelling out what people say about their own experiences. But Proudfoot's distinction between a wrongly reductive 'description' and a rightly reductive 'explanation' is not so easy to identify in practice. Where does describing stop and explaining begin? Let us imagine that we respectfully *describe* an experience as religious but maintain that one cannot *explain* it in those terms. What have we just said?

How do you know what it means?

Does the network of scientific accounts exclude the possibility of any religious truth or meaning? As we shall see, one probably could give a thorough causal explanation of any religious experience in psychological terms. Two questions still hang in the air: does that say anything about whether the experience really happened or not, and does it say anything about the meaning of the experience?

The meaning a subject gives to her experience, then, while not unaffected by natural factors, may not be something that is identical to the event's 'cause', 'explanation' or 'origin'. It is something that requires its *own* interpretative framework in order to cope with it. Karl Jaspers introduced a distinction between 'understanding', which is proper to the humanities, and 'explaining', which belongs to the natural sciences.[6] But in recent years that sort of tidy distinction has become eroded.[7] This recent critique from the philosophy of science rejects the simple ascription of 'facts' to science and 'values' to the humanities; and of factual explanation to scientific method and a different sort of 'understanding' to the arts. It indicates that scientific inquiry is also value-laden, and can contribute to reflection on values. What it does not do, however, is to indicate that scientific methods are well-equipped to deal with the existential questions of meaning that other hermeneutical (interpretative) disciplines are designed to do.

Further, even when an experience is provided with such a hermeneutic for its psychological aspects – if, for example, a religious experience is considered for its psychoanalytic import – the question of its specifically *theological* meaning remains. Each interpretative discipline is designed for its own clients; and not necessarily well-equipped to deal with styles of inquiry for which it has not evolved.

Optimally, every aspect of a phenomenon should be examined and accounted for within an appropriate interpretative framework. The fundamental difficulty with the attempt to explain religious experience in a reductive way is that the experience and the human being having it are both complex, while most explanatory frameworks are highly specialised. They are not competent to interpret every aspect of human existence; they are designed for a very specific job.

They, and their advocates, lose credibility when they are overextended, much as in a job interview we become increasingly suspicious of the candidate who claims to be able to do every conceivable task with equal expertise.

How do you know it was true?

Returning to the woman who knew about pantyhose, one reason the doctors treated her religious experience as a symptom was that they assumed that what she claimed about God wasn't true. Whatever the sincerity or conviction that lay behind it, it did not occur to them even to consider that God might really have communicated to her as she claimed.

So what is it that makes a statement true, or that makes knowledge genuine? Philosophers have offered different accounts of truth and of the relationship which knowledge and the statements purporting to express it has to reality.

The commonsensical view, perhaps, is 'realism'. There is a world out there that is independent of my mind and my way of seeing things, says the realist. The goal of knowledge is to reflect the world 'out there' accurately. A notion of truth that cohabits happily with realism is the 'correspondence theory'. If a statement corresponds with the facts, the world 'out there', it is true. Applied to religious statements, the realist-correspondence theory sort of person wants *claims* about God to accurately reflect the *facts* about God. In deciding whether the woman's religious experience was true, they want to know if the experience in some way really 'came from' God. Did She intend to reach out to the woman in her distress, and therefore lead her to interpret the television advertisement in a way that gave her consolation? Did God feel concerned about the workings of the prayer group and in some way communicate this to the woman, to have her address the prayer group on Her behalf?

Realist-correspondence theory people tend not to be satisfied with phrases or suggestions that something can be 'true for you', if this implies that truth is relative to individuals and that truth somehow changes from one person to another. But that is how many people do see things. Consequently, there are a variety of opposed stances to realism. 'Idealists' maintain that ideas are what really exists; what we experience as reality, as the world out there, is really mind-dependent in some way. Idealists are difficult to find in practice, nowadays at least. What one finds more commonly are different varieties of anti-realism or non-realism. In current religious thinking, one approach maintains that God is a construct of our own minds, an internal ideal which is valuable and important, but not an 'objective', independently-existing being 'out there'.

Versions of anti- or non-realism often require a different notion of truth to fit their metaphysics. If you are sceptical about the existence of a world 'out there' or the possibility of knowing it as it really is in itself, then perhaps it is unwise to make your criterion of truth consist in something which you think impossible to attain. An alternative notion of truth, then, is the 'coherence' theory. The coherence theorist maintains that knowing whether my statement accurately reflects 'how the world is' demands more than I can ever know or perceive. All I can know is *how things seem to me*; to assert that that is how they *really* are is to make a claim that I can never support. All that is required for truth, therefore, is that that statement coheres with other things I claim to be true; and if a claim blatantly contradicts other claims I feel are true, this new contradictory claim is suspect.

The coherence theorist, then, is concerned with the integrity and harmony of a person's system of beliefs. If a person claims to believe in a loving, forgiving, compassionate God, but also claims to have revelations from God that someone is irredeemably damned for a small offence, the coherence theorist may find these revelations do not meet his criteria for truth. So the coherence theorist wants to see how the religious experiences fit in the context of the Pantyhose Woman's life and how well it accorded with her other beliefs. He might observe that the first experience was valid and insightful and revealed religious truth, because it cohered with her general picture of God as loving, compassionate, and always available in times of need. The second experience, perhaps, contradicted that picture of God and its validity should be questioned.

The 'pragmatist', finally, suggests that what is true depends on what leads to the best results. A false claim just doesn't pan out in practice. True theories, on the other hand, have a way of working when tested and applied in the world; that is what indicates their truth. So the pragmatist observes that the first experience gave the woman a sense of support, a sense of not being alone in her depression, that clearly helped her through a difficult period. The second experience, however, led to negative results and a destructive social situation and was not therefore an authentic or genuinely religious insight. The claims about the authenticity or veridicality of her experience thus have to be tested for their 'fruits' in the rest of her life.

There are shortcomings and disadvantages to each of these positions; that is why there are three of them. Of the realist-correspondence theorist, we might ask: how do you propose to ascertain whether God 'spoke' to this woman or not? Since most people hold that God is not available for examination, it will have to be some feature of the experience itself that reveals its divine origin or lack of it. There are in fact many systems, rules of discernment, criteria and so on that have been developed within particular religious traditions precisely to do this. Some of them involve conformity with what is already believed or known of God by the tradition in question – rather like coherence criteria, as it happens. But inevitably many of the criteria in fact concern the 'fruits' of the experience – which, disconcertingly, looks like pragmatism.

The coherence theorist might reasonably be asked, why must it be the case that a religious experience is only 'true', or 'genuine', or 'valid' if it conforms with a certain system that he already holds? Perhaps his system is bizarre, or even harmful, and if the religious experience in question conforms to it – well, that is a bad thing. As the Pantyhose Woman was (allegedly) paranoid, a perception of others as demonic and hostile certainly conformed to her beliefs. On the other hand, if an overpowering experience contradicts a distorted world-view, perhaps *that is precisely why it is genuine*. Maybe some religious ideas and beliefs should be challenged and revised in the light of experience; why should the prior beliefs be given priority over the most recent experience?[8]

The pragmatist has to confront the fact that what seems to be the case does not always seem to be the same as what is beneficial. We can in some situations distinguish between 'the truth' and 'what is helpful'. This is precisely what creates certain ethical dilemmas, such as whether to give a terminally ill patient the 'full facts' of his condition. Perhaps in some situations it is not helpful to know the 'truth'. Further, the pragmatist has to meet the challenge of declaring on what basis we decide what is beneficial to a person's life or *what* 'works in practice'. Was it helpful for the woman to believe that God was looking after her – or did it infantilise her and encourage escapism and lack of responsibility? The decision on this question surely rests on some prior notion of what is good for people. How do you justify this in a non-circular way, without recourse to 'correspondence' or 'coherence'?

One might argue that religious experience is 'self-authenticating': it doesn't need external confirmation or falsification to say it is true. This claim is usually scornfully rejected; as Alston observes, it is in fact hard to find someone that actually asserts it in the form that its critics give it. Yandell argues that any proposition that is put forward as self-authenticating must be radically restricted in the scope of what it claims, so that 'one could not base a religion or a philosophy or even plans for a picnic on what it epistemically contains'.[9] One might say a claim 'to have felt something' is self-authenticating; but one cannot base a religion on that minimal claim. The more you increase the scope of the claim, however, the less plausible it becomes to assert that it is really self-authenticating. Self-authentication for 'propositions of the wealth of ramifications possessed by basic religious claims' 'is just out of the question'.

I suspect the claims and counter-claims about self-authentication rest on a misunderstanding about the nature and scope of the claim. Few mystics themselves really make a claim for self-authentication; and if they do, it is for the validity of *their experience*; not the entire edifice of Christianity or Islam or Advaita Vedānta, on the grounds of a single experience in meditation. Yandell is attacking a straw man.

However, I suspect what many do feel is that it is not appropriate to put the meaning or significance that someone's experience has for her out for tender, to be dismissed by a sceptic for lack of objectivity or scientific proof. That is a different claim; and does not entail that everything one says on the basis of a religious experience has universal validity and needs no support from anyone else. We ought to observe a distinction between the subject's right to take her experience seriously, and the experience's value as evidence for general knowledge and truth-claims that are held to be valid for everyone.

In the discussion that follows, I will write without prejudice on this issue for now, referring in most cases to the 'veridicality' of the experience. By 'veridicality' I mean truth value, authenticity or integrity, in a way that is to apply to each theory of truth we have examined. As appropriate, it refers to the properly religious origin of the experience, and/or the reliability of the believer in her understanding and report of the experience, and/or the religious value ('growth', 'utility', 'fruitfulness') of the experience, and/or the epistemic value of the experience: that it conveyed authentic religious insight, or knowledge, enlightenment or consolation.

This broad term and its use arise from my own conviction that all three concepts of truth have something to offer, and it is not epistemically promiscuous to seek to unite all three in an interactive model of what makes for 'truth' in a phenomenon as complex as religion. Perhaps we would do best to regard correspondence, coherence and practical benefit as mutually supportive 'criteria', rather than mutually exclusive 'concepts'.

How do you know it was God?

Pantyhose Woman claimed to have an experience 'of God'. How do you tell that an experience is 'of God'? Interestingly, many people who claim to have religious experiences are reluctant to claim that it was specifically *God* whom they experienced.[10] Is experiencing God one mode of consciousness or kind of experience alongside others – so that we can talk about 'religious experience', as opposed to 'aesthetic experience', 'sensory experience', and so on? Or is it a dimension of the whole of experience; so that, for the believer, whether you are talking about a Beethoven symphony, a prayer meeting, or watching the sunrise, all of these experiences disclose the being of God? A religious believer might not like the implications of the first position; it might seem to compartmentalise his faith too much, making God one object or aspect of life alongside others like symphonies and sunrises. But if we opt for the latter understanding, how do we distinguish between moving experiences of beauty and religious revelations, between sunrises and divine self-disclosures?

Nevertheless, some people make a very explicit claim to have *experienced God*, like the woman who knew about pantyhose. How do you adjudicate their claims? Did she know about God too, or just pantyhose?

Potentially there is a problem of circularity here. To identify God as the 'object' of an experience, we need to be able to recognise God; to recognise God, we need to know God. This would seem to indicate that one needs to know God already in order to experience Her, otherwise you would never know that you *were* experiencing Her. But how can you know God even before you have experienced Her? Experience is a ground of knowledge even for those who are not empiricists or positivists; and in a time when the possibility of offering strictly logical proofs for the existence of God is unfashionable, some regard it as the only possible source of knowledge of God.

This vicious circle might exist, in theory, with any new experience. Jerome Gellman suggests that there are two general routes for identifying the object of an experience. There can be 'auto-identification', where the object of one's perception identifies itself: 'This is God speaking to you.' There is also 'recognition-identification', which is analogous to the way we identify physical objects in our perception. 'Oh – there's Susan.' The factors that affect our recognition of mundane objects, Gellman claims, are also at work in our recognition of God: we cannot always explain the process, or the reasons we have for making the identification. Often it is immediate, habitual, or unconscious. It may be based on past experiences, or on descriptions others have given us. All of these, Gellman maintains, can apply to God, just as to women or birds. According to Gellman, identification of God as the one who is experienced is not uniquely problematic.[11]

It *is* uniquely problematic, however, if the very existence of the being in question is disputed; or if there is dispute about the nature of the being even between those who agree such a being exists. Because God is not just a being alongside other beings, and the experience of God is different from the experience of Susan, problems do exist concerning the possibility of *experiencing* God and *knowing* God.

A positivist might observe that an allegedly incorporeal, transcendent God cannot be perceived with the senses and therefore cannot be the object of experience. A philosophical 'rationalist' like Kant, whether a believer or not, might argue that the very notion of 'knowing' something which transcends our human faculties of knowledge is contradictory, unintelligible, impossible. 'Experience' in Kant's terms does not include experience of what is transcendent; 'the object of pure thought'. God cannot be 'experienced'; therefore experience cannot yield knowledge of God. Any claims to knowledge about God cannot be justified in this manner.[12]

Meanwhile, a religious person, whatever their philosophical stance, might also deny that God can be the 'object' of religious experience, precisely for reasons of piety. 'God does not offer himself for observation,' maintained Hegel.[13] Such a person might say, 'God cannot be the object of experience because God is not an object. God is not something that can be experienced the way of work of art can, or even another human being can. Therefore, whatever religious experiences are, they cannot simply be experiences *of* God in the way that we can have an experience *of* a sunset.' The Jewish theologian Martin Buber, as well as the Catholic Gabriel Marcel and the Protestant Paul Tillich, were unhappy with the notion of God as an 'object' of human experience for these reasons. For these thinkers, God cannot be approached as object of knowledge; but can only be known as a person. 'If to believe in God means being able to talk about him in the third person, then I do not believe in God,' wrote Buber.[14]

Of course, religious experiences are not only 'of God' in the monotheists' sense. People also claim to experience an impersonal ultimate reality, or a non-Being beyond all being; so if there is a Being, She is given different names, qualities, and opinions. The experience can be 'of' something worldly while having a religious dimension, or it can be an experience of nothingness.

Different writers on the subject tend to present their own typology or taxonomy of religious experience, accordingly. Glock and Stark, for example, distinguish confirming experience, responsive experience, ecstatic experience, and revelational experience (in ascending order of rarity and intensity).[15] Caroline Franks Davis categorises religious experiences according to their nature or content, with the following result: religious experiences can be 'interpretive', in which a believer interprets experience in a certain religious way (like seeing an event as an answer to prayer); 'quasi-sensory', in which the experience is primarily of a sensory nature, something is 'seen' or 'heard' (visions, dreams, etc.); 'revelatory', which includes sudden convictions, revelations, enlightenment, flashes of insight; 'regenerative', these renew the subject's faith and improve his well-being; 'numinous', in which the divine is revealed in its awesome, even terrifying majesty; and 'mystical' experiences.[16] Yet another scheme is provided by Keith Yandell who divides experiences by their 'object' rather than by their distinctive style, and distinguishes between experiences that are monotheistic, nirvāṇic (Buddhist), kevalic (Jain, seeing oneself as the indestructible subject of experience), mokṣa (Hinduism, of Brahman, as Yandell describes it, although this is not what mokṣa means) and nature mysticism.[17]

One question then which has occupied those who reflect on these matters is whether each experience or type of experience is utterly different and incommensurable with another, or whether there is a common core to religious experiences. Almond has outlined five different attitudes on the question: from asserting that all mystical experience is the same to claiming that there are as many different types of mystical experience as there are interpretations of them.[18] In between these extremes are claims that all mystical experience is the same, but the interpretations differ according to the mystic's religious framework, or that there are a few different types of experience which cross religious or cultural divides; or maintain that there is only one form of interior mystical experience, even if one can subdivide it into types.[19] Stace suggests that there is a basic unity involved in religious experience: what we have is a case of a fundamentally identical experience being interpreted in different ways by different mystics. 'The language of the Hindus on the one hand and the Christians on the other is so astonishingly similar that they give every appearance of describing exactly the same experience.'[20] Steven Katz, on the other hand, allows for no such common core, and maintains instead a radical particularity of religious experiences.[21]

What is the point of this debate? The impatient could complain that it is clear, on the one hand, that religious experiences are each unique in some respects, and on the other hand, that there are many features which they share. Are there not some questionable philosophical assumptions behind this insistence on nailing down their identity or difference? Must they all *really* be the same or else all totally different; and what does it mean to say there are five types, and most definitely not four or six?

One can slice up the cake any number of ways, and the number of slices, their size and shape, say more about the intentions of the slicer and the needs of the eaters than they do about the cake itself. Why not borrow a notion from Wittgenstein? While it is pointless to find a single unifying characteristic in religious experiences, we can detect 'family resemblances' among the different accounts. There may not be a single feature which they all share; but it is not impossible to relate one to another.

There is however one central issue at stake in this dispute about the diversity of religious experiences: the value that religious experiences have as truthful or false witnesses. The descriptions they give of the God that they claim to experience can differ so radically, that one can legitimately ask whether they can all be telling the truth. 'How can "ultimate reality" be both a personal being and an impersonal principle, identical to our inmost self and forever "other", loving and utterly indifferent, good and amoral, knowable and unknowable, a plenitude and "emptiness"?'[22] If one can argue that, despite apparent conflicts, all religious experiences witness to one religious truth it undercuts one argument made by the sceptic.[23]

We should not, then, assume that a religious experience is an experience *of* *God*, for even amongst religious philosophers it is disputed whether or not God can be the object of experience. For that matter, it is also disputed whether one ought to suppose that all other experiences are *not* of Ultimate Reality.[24]

'Lightning is Brahman, they say. It is called lightning because it scatters darkness. He who knows it as such that lightning is Brahman scatters evils, for lightning is, indeed, Brahman.'[25]

Godfather man

Another patient was brought in and was diagnosed as a paranoid schizophrenic. Walking down the corridor of his block of flats, he had looked in the open front door of one of the flats as he passed by. Inside he saw a man sitting at a table, one hand in his lap, one hand on the table. In the film *The Godfather* the eponymous character sat in the same way. Our friend inferred from this man's posture that he must be a Mafia 'godfather', and moreover, that as a Mafia godfather he would expect regular payments of protection money. In fear that he might otherwise be harmed or even killed, the unfortunate man regularly slipped envelopes of cash under his bemused neighbour's door.

How you interpret something is a vital question that lies behind many of the issues provoked by people's religious experiences. A few moments' reflection on an experience reveals that one can distinguish different 'moments' within the whole 'phenomenon'. There was the perception of the man, there was what the patient made of it and how he spoke about it. What relationship do these different 'moments' have to one another?

One view is that experience and the interpretation of it are something like a *kernel in a husk*, or a nut in its shell. There is a fundamental, uninterpreted experience, which is then interpreted, clothed, fleshed out in the concepts, images, terminology and world-view belonging to the individual. The interpretation, however, is in some sense separable from the experience. The man saw the same thing that any of us would have seen: someone sitting at a table. But his *interpretation* of it was different.

This brings out two fundamental stances towards experience and interpretation. Experience and interpretation can be seen as separate, either conceptually or in practice. One might see experience as something that happens, which is then interpreted. Concepts, beliefs, language and other forms of organising one's thought and one's experience can be applied or withheld. Or one can see experience as *inseparable* from interpretation.

Let us look first at the impact of the first issue on questions of religious experience. Is experience separable from interpretation? If it is, even if one can distinguish reality from what we make of it only in theory and not in practice, it makes it much easier to cope with the fact that people's religious experiences are so diverse. If you experience Kuan-Yin and I experience Laka and someone else experiences Mary and a Hindu experiences Lakhmi, it might seem like a conflict in testimony and thus call the veridicality of all our experiences into question. However, if we each experience a female figure which we each then *interpret* as a figure from our own religious tradition, using the language and beliefs of our own religion, it might not be that we are all deluded. All witness to the same truth in their very different ways, it can then be argued.

'Experiencing-as'

Alternatively, one can argue as John Hick has that all experience is an 'experiencing-as'. The paradigm for this view is those ambiguous pictures which can be seen, with equal plausibility, as one thing or another; the two wavy lines that can be seen as a goblet or as two faces in profile; the female figure that can either be a roman-nosed crone or a young woman with a necklace; or Jastrow's figure that can either be seen as a duck or as a rabbit looking upwards (the duck's beak forming the rabbit's ears). Like such figures, this view claims, experience is inherently ambiguous; it needs to be 'experienced-as' something, in a kind of interpretative act, for it to have any meaning. The original event or phenomenon is constituted as an experience by the interpretation which is embedded in the very act of perception. Thus a religious believer might validly experience the sunrise as having a religious power and significance, while his atheist companion (perhaps equally validly) does not. The woman in the story, then, immediately experienced the voice *as God's voice* as it was happening; she did not first hear 'a voice' then later interpret it as 'Oh, that must have been God back then.'

Hick's *experiencing-as* is an attempt to deal with the questions raised by religious pluralism. Hick tries to explain how diverse religious traditions can all bear witness legitimately to religious truth. As we have seen, Hick's pluralism suggests that we cannot know 'The Real' as it is in-itself; it has masks or faces which differ, depending on what a particular culture or religion brings to or imposes on its experience of the Real-in-itself. 'The great world faiths embody different perceptions and conceptions of, and correspondingly different responses to, the Real from within the major variant ways of being human'.[26] There is a fundamental divine reality, which our religion, culture, upbringing lead us to see and name a certain way. Christians have experiences of 'Jesus', Muslims of 'Allah'; Jains and Theravāda Buddhists do not experience a personal being but strive for mokṣa and nirvana. How it is in itself is beyond our knowledge.

This is useful if one's concern is not just with other faiths than one's own, but also with atheists. Both the atheist and the religious believer can agree that, on one level, the experience was 'of' nature or art or another person, and the believer need not be driven to say anything peculiar about the object of the experience. Moreover, the fact that the believer 'experiences-as' in this case is not peculiar either, if *all* experience is 'experiencing-as'. The atheist is 'experiencing-as' as well. This can create parity between claims about religious experience and other kinds of experience in a way that some think desirable. It can also be used to indicate the broad area of agreement that exists or can exist between the atheist and the believer, suggesting that they are really in agreement about 'the facts' and only differ in their interpretation of them.

To this Caroline Franks Davis objects that one has to leave out a lot if one really wants to claim that the atheist and the believer agree on the facts. She thinks that the atheist and the believer *don't* have the same experience.[27] (I would qualify this point somewhat: they can agree on 'the fact' that S had a religious experience in which he felt something and differ on their opinion of the veridicality of the experience.) It is an open question whether the theist and atheist friends admiring a sunset together are experiencing the 'same thing with a different interpretation' when one experiences it as a revelation of God's majesty as creator, and the other does not. Davis and Donovan both make the point that the paradigm cases of 'experiencing-as', such as the duck-rabbit, are both cases of genuine ambiguity, in which there *isn't* a 'right' perception. Is that what most religious believers mean to assert about their experience? Further, when asserting (as Hick has) that 'all experience is an experience-as', it is perhaps misleading to offer the duck-rabbit or one of his colleagues as a paradigm case. Not all visual perception has *that* nature, it is not all genuinely ambiguous. That is precisely why such optical illusions contain a moment of surprise for us. In other cases, there is instead an accurate perception-as (of a branch sticking out of a loch) which is mistakenly experienced-as something else (a monster). Donovan suggests that we should keep the category of 'experiencing-as' for the unusual ambiguous cases like the duck-rabbit. It makes it harder to preserve the difference between 'taking something to be the case that really isn't the case, and taking something to be the case and being right in doing so.'[28] Moreover, not all religious experience happily fits this model; arguably, there are religious experiences which arise precisely as a result of holding the religious world-view, and which are not just ordinary experiences interpreted in a religious way. 'For only under the religious interpretations do they have the profound personal significance and the subtle interconnections with an overall world-view and understanding of life which they have when experienced by the believer.'[29]

The place of interpretation

Both these approaches, the kernel-and-husk and experiencing-as, can be inclined to stress the *disjunctive* relation that can exist between experience and interpretation, perhaps emphasising the role that concepts or conceptualisation play in shaping our experience. These concepts might well come from us, it is thought, and not the divine reality itself.

In this division between the divine or ultimate reality *as it is in itself* on the one hand, and on the other hand *as it appears to us*, all the phenomenal features of the experience (that is, the qualities we experience) are thought to lie on the human side. Not merely my feelings, but my sense that this was this or that God or Goddess, are interpretations which I made of the original pure experience.

Of course, this can leave the testimonial value of the experience in jeopardy. Might it be the case, then, that religious experience is 'nothing but' interpretation; an ordinary experience cloaked in religious language? If this were the case, spiritual experiences would provide no independent evidence for religious truths.[30] One might further object that religious experience cannot, even in principle, justify religious belief, because religious experience is already shaped, interpreted or even created by someone's religious beliefs. On this view, to attempt to justify religious belief on the grounds of some (supposedly prior) religious experience is actually circular.[31] Only what is directly given in experience, without subjective interpretation, can be reliable evidence, because the interpretation could be infected by a person's bias or prejudice. The interpretations themselves must be justified by some form of evidence which is actually independent of the experience itself. Flew, for example, demands prior evidence that religious doctrines are probably true before a person is warranted in placing a 'religious interpretation' on an 'experience'.[32]

So we have two more questions to consider. Can you divide experience and interpretation – is there such a thing as pure, unmediated experience? And if so, does the interpretation risk distorting the 'original, pure' experience?

Take an experience, let us say, of an oak tree. Remove the phenomenal features: how it looked, sounded, tasted, felt, smelled – green, brown, rough bark, leafy odour; what is left? Remove now your understanding of what you were experiencing, how you identified it, what you thought it was or recognised it as: no category of 'deciduous', no identification as *Quercus*, or even as 'tree' as opposed to 'shrub'. Consider now the thing itself, without your overlay of sensory and emotional features, your interpretation of its identity, nature, being. What precisely is left?

According to Yandell, nothing is left. 'In the case of tasting a lemon drop, remove the sense of smooth round hard object on my tongue and a lemon taste, and nothing whatever is left. In the case of sensing the presence of a holy God while partaking of the Eucharist ..., remove the sense of a holy presence, and your religious experience is gone.'[33] How does an experience with no content differ from 'no experience'? One cannot remove all concepts from experience to leave the pure experience: the idea of a 'pure experience' is itself a concept.[34]

As Donovan points out, it is in the nature of such experiences to be *someone's* experience, hence it is artificial to speak of neutral, uninterpreted experience. Experiences can't be compared at an 'uninterpreted' level. The fact that we can be undecided or change our interpretation doesn't demonstrate that experience is just there prior to interpretation; experiences are interpreted from the beginning.[35] Katz asserts that the experience of the mystic is shaped by the beliefs and concepts of the mystic's own religion. These shape the experience that the mystic seeks to have, as it were, shaping the experience even before the believer has it. There is no 'core' experience that is religiously neutral, which is thereafter interpreted.[36]

Proudfoot stresses that experience is constituted by beliefs and concepts, in a way that shapes the experience even as we are having it:

> there is no uninterpreted experience. Our experience is already informed and constituted by our conceptions and tacit theories about ourselves and our world. All observation is theory-laden. We can design procedures in which certain hypotheses can be tested, but any perception or experience is already shaped by the concepts and implicit judgments we bring to it. In this sense, we are constantly engaged in interpretation and reinterpretation.[37]

For Proudfoot, this position allows for 'optimism' in understanding people from very different cultures: if we study their concepts and beliefs and the rules that govern them, we can in principle have 'access to the variety of experiences available to persons in that culture.'[38]

However, one can observe, firstly, that this view is in danger of being self-defeating. If all observation is theory-laden, so too is this very observation. If being theory-laden makes something suspect, then this claim itself must be suspect along with all others. If this view escapes the conditions under which all others suffer, the objector must provide reasons why *his* belief is not thus compromised, but the religious believer's is.

One can take a sceptical attitude towards the claim that all experience is shaped by interpretation or by the subject's concepts; as Alston and Yandell do. Alston sees perceptual experience as 'essentially independent' of interpretation, conceptualisation or the application of concepts, beliefs, or judgement. The contrary idea, that no experience comes to us unmediated by general concepts and judgements, he calls a 'baseless prejudice.'[39]

One can aim, still more tellingly, at the assumption that our concepts or interpretations mitigate against the truth-value or reliability of a belief. Perhaps interpretation is harmless, and does not distort experience, or even is positively helpful by organising otherwise meaningless sense data into actual knowledge? Donovan has questioned the assumption that the less interpretation, the nearer one gets to the genuine experience and its meaning. 'It is, after all, just as possible to miss the genuine significance of an experience through under-interpretation as it is through over-interpretation.'[40] An 'uninterpreted, neutral' experience is not a source of information in science or any other form of knowledge; experience only becomes 'knowledge' or 'understanding' when our basic experiences of the world are transformed by 'quite elaborate theoretical interpretations'. This may be true of mystical experiences as well; they can only be understood by interpreting them within the belief-system of the person who has them. 'If so, then trying to strip off interpretations in search of a neutral, core experience could be quite the wrong approach to take.'[41]

One can indeed draw comparisons with other kinds of experiences, which must therefore also be shaped by beliefs, concepts, expectations or interpretations.

> Here too people articulate their experience as they have been culturally taught to do. The commonsense *physical objects dispersed in space* conceptual scheme is inculcated in a thousand subtle and not so subtle ways in the course of socialization. Does this imply that we are not proceeding rationally in forming perceptual beliefs in the standard way? If not, how can we condemn [religious experience] for this reason?[42]

Davis urges that even unconscious interpretations can be innocent until proven guilty; 'if they were not generally reliable, the human race would not have survived so long'. She concludes that 'it is reasonable to believe that in ordinary, real-life situations these rules of inference generally lead to veridical perceptions.'[43]

Clearly there is a tension here. If all the phenomenal features and qualities of the experience, including those attributed to the divine Object, really belong to the human side only and are said to be inapplicable to the divinity, it becomes difficult to know what is left of the divine in one's experience. Even 'divinity' and 'ultimate reality' are human concepts. If the suggestion is that we ought to strip our experience of its conceptual disguise – well, it is difficult to know where to stop. At the personal name given to the Divinity? But why stop there: 'personal' versus 'impersonal' is a conceptual distinction. Hick, for example, maintains that the Real is neither personal nor impersonal in itself. 'I experienced a divine presence, which I interpreted as personal'? But not only is 'divine' a concept, so too is 'presence'. One might think the distinction between presence and absence is a fundamental distinction that lies in the nature of things, not merely in how we perceive them. But certain sophisticated mystical experiences make even the distinction between 'presence' and 'absence' of the divine look questionable, having more to do with human interpretation and expectation than the divine existence.

For that matter, so too is 'experience' a concept, in the way it is being handled throughout this discussion – as is 'religious'. I doubt an ancient Hawaiian would think of such a thing as a 'religious experience' in this way at all.

In any case, if we strip all features and qualities from the Real, in order to harmonise our differing accounts – precisely by doing that, we make it impossible to claim that the Real I experience is one and the same as the Real which you experience. We have no features to compare in order to proclaim an identity between my 'The Real' and your 'The Real'; we can only assert *a priori* that there can only be one 'The Real'. It becomes impossible to ground the claim that the Contentless One whom I worship is the same as the Qualityless One that you adore. 'What has always seemed objectionable to me in the Hickean universe is the way the self must strip off all that is closest and dearest to it in order to reach the supposedly truly religious point of view; what sort of person can jettison their values and judgements and ascend to the Hickean pluralist mountain top? Moreover, once you reach this position, values and judgements and attachments having been ditched, on what basis can you make a choice? The very ascent destroys the self's relationship with its own values etc. but also makes it impossible to choose (i.e. rationally decide on as opposed to plump for) any others.'[44]

On the other hand, it is difficult to deny that many features of our experience *are* 'contributed' in some way by us. If I feel a sense of a powerful presence when there is no one visible in the room, if I am a Christian I am inclined to assume without argument that it is the God of the Bible. And in many cases (unless I am Samuel or Isaiah) I do *assume* it, rather than deduce it from a self-evident principle, or demand identification from the Presence in order to settle the question, or compare its qualities with qualities ascribed to various deities to see which God the Presence most resembles. If I am an Advaita Vedāntin, or a Buddhist, *all* the features of the experience are said to be purely my superimposition upon it anyway – not least the having of the experience itself, including my 'self', the one having it.

A suggested approach

On the principle that, whenever possible, it is always preferable to have one's cake and eat it too, let us see whether we can arrive at a comprehensive model of interpretation that allows us all the benefits of these different points of view.

Ideally, our understanding of experience and interpretation ought to allow for this double truth: on the one hand, we must take responsibility for many of the ways in which we see things, recognising that 'it seems that way to me, and I could be wrong'. On the other hand, many of the ways we perceive things *are* genuinely perceptive (in the colloquial sense); and perhaps this possibility of genuine discovery exists not only in 'passive' experience but also in the more 'active' moment of bringing it into language, and interpretation. That is: interpretation can be accurate, and might reveal deeper insights than a mere 'recording' of an experience can.

It does seem an error of judgement to seek to rope off a 'pure experience' from what one makes of it. It is part of the meaning of the word 'experience' that *I* experience it. Perhaps all perception, even a simple one like seeing a tree, is 'interpreted' to some degree. It would be misleading, then, to isolate kinds of experiences or perceptions as 'subjective' or as ones based on interpretation, and to suppose from this that other kinds of perception or experience are not. This is perhaps the most helpful use to which 'experiencing-as' images can be put: to show that even sensory perception involves a considerable degree of interpretation of the sensory data.

This is because many of the ways in which interpretation operates are unconscious: as Davis observes, there are unconscious rules of inference, interpretation, selection procedures at work that are analogous to conscious inference. Because they are unconscious, however, they seem to us to be part of what is 'given', that is, simply there rather than part of a mental act of construction. As she goes on to observe, the rules that govern interpretation come in large measure from our culture, language, training, beliefs, experiences, upbringing, personality, and so on. So an experience could have a different *significance* for a believer and non-believer, even if they seem to have similar *perceptions and emotions*. Even emotions use these unconscious rules of inference; studies show that people decide what it is they feel in part on the basis of how they interpret their situation.[45]

One can distinguish, then, between situations where I know I am having to do a lot of work to make sense of what I experience, and experiences where identifying or understanding what I experience is straightforward. Whatever the difference between such experiences may be, however, it is not the case that I am a judge in the first instance and a video camera in the second. The difference between them is not an imagined difference between 'subjective' and 'objective', still less between 'biased' and 'accurate'.

Rather than conceiving of experience and interpretation according to a single model, like a kernel and a husk, our notion of interpretation then ought to be as broad and as varied as possible. In some uses of the term, interpretation is a matter of *bringing something to expression*. Perhaps it is an original, inexpressible, or at least wordless, phenomenon which is then brought into speech as an act of interpretation. The paradigm for this view might be the act of playing a piece of music on an instrument; one speaks of the performer's 'interpretation', but the latter is not merely something added on to the piece. The piece only exists in its being performed and thus inevitably 'interpreted'. 'Interpretation', while not creating the thing, nevertheless is the only manner in which it can exist. The language used to describe experience then – even if it is 'added on later' – does not so much conceal as reveal. This would mirror the experience we often have of not really understanding something until we have talked about it, explained it to someone else.

Another meaning of the word 'interpret' is 'to translate' – as in 'an interpreter'. Translation is performed precisely in order to make something more intelligible than it was before. Thus 'interpretation' does not damage truth so much as facilitate understanding. This model also contains useful possibilities for understanding accuracy, truth or falsity in a situation of diversity. Many translations of a poem can exist, all of them correct, although they are different. One might be more literal, thus preferred for study; one might rhyme and scan like the original, thus is to be preferred for performance. To insist that, because they are different, one must be right and the other wrong is to fail to understand the complexity of languages and the business of translation. However, this does not mean that *every* translation is correct. While there may be no single *right* translation, there nevertheless is such a thing as a *wrong* one, and a competent person can easily identify it. There is variety in language, but there are also rules.

Interpretation can also name what happens when one person seeks to understand another in conversation. 'You misinterpreted what I said,' is a sentence which makes sense and is often said.

All of these paradigms bring out one particular insight: what is going on is a linguistic event; acts of language. They also suggest a further point: that interpretation is *relational*, that is, if interpretation is a question of language, it is most like that language that takes place between two people: dialogue, that moves back and forth between one and another.[46]

If this account of experience is justified in portraying it as a relational phenomenon, then a relational account of interpretation is all the more apt. This relational view of interpretation can also incorporate the single views of interpretation we have just considered: there can be cases of coded speech whose real meaning or intention has to be extracted from the actual words uttered, like a kernel from a husk; there can be cases of ambiguity, in which one can 'experience-someone-as' threatening, or hostile; there is often the experience that one is actually bringing into speech something which is not yet formulated in words, and thus not only making sense of it but in some sense bringing it into a real existence, as in performance; and as in translation, a sense that something difficult to understand is rendered comprehensible. It also contains the notion that an experience and the interpretation of it are not identical, without being overly precise in how they differ. It further allows for an active, shaping role in understanding and perception, but also for the possibility of correction. For example, there can be aspect of 'experiencing-as' as its initial moment; what it has in addition, however, by using the model of dialogue, is the possibility of a corrective response: we can 'experience-as' falsely, and if so, we can be corrected. 'I thought you were angry.' 'No, you misinterpreted me.'

Thus this broad relational model of interpretation matches the broad notion of truth that was suggested earlier. Rival models can be incorporated into a multi-aspect model; the way to have one's cake and eat it too is to reject the assumption that there must be only one piece of cake.

4. Seeing God or Seeing Snakes?

Naturalistic explanations of religious experience

> From a scientific point of view, we can make no distinction between the man who eats little and sees heaven and the man who drinks much and sees snakes. Each is in an abnormal physical condition, and therefore has abnormal perceptions. Normal perceptions, since they have to be useful in the struggle for life, must have some correspondence with fact; but in abnormal perceptions there is no reason to expect such correspondence, and their testimony, therefore, cannot outweigh that of normal perception.[1]

In this passage, Bertrand Russell equates religious experience with abnormal non-religious experiences. Since, Russell maintains, perceptions received in an abnormal physical condition cannot be trusted as true, as 'correspondence with fact',[2] religious experiences have no truth-value, and cannot be genuine sources of knowledge. Although the argument is a little scanty, Russell is articulating some popular ideas and assumptions: religious experiences are only true if they cannot be explained by any non-religious or natural factors. – There are perfectly good scientific explanations for spiritual experiences, therefore no religious explanation is necessary; the psychological explanation has 'explained them away'. – Religious experiences arise from natural causes and therefore have no value as sources of knowledge or insight.

The possibility of providing a scientific account with full explanatory power affects the truth-value of religious experiences, and with it the rationality of belief based on religious experience and the possibility of religious knowledge. So it is crucial to explore first what explanations psychological accounts can offer.

Psychological accounts of religious experience

Broadly speaking, psychological accounts of religious experience attempt to explain it in three ways: by the physiological generation of experiences, the artificial induction of experiences, or the motivation of experiences by desire or need. Naturalistic explanations need not conflict with religious interpretations, however. It depends on the ambitions of each. Scientific accounts might 'reduce' the supernatural to purely natural factors, but if a religious point of view insists that God alone is responsible and no consideration of human involvement is

valid, we might consider this a form of 'religious reductionism'. Religious sensitivity does not commit someone to this. A theological account can be given
which does not see God as an *alternative explanation to natural phenomena*, but
rather as *present in natural phenomena* or working through them. So a believer
might see God as working through the phenomena of the natural world to reveal
Herself in human experience. As Alston observes, many religious traditions see
God as causally related to everything that happens. So even if every religious
experience has sufficient causes in the natural world to explain it, that by no
means rules out a causal connection with God; God can't fail to be causally
connected to anything.[3] Further, religious believers themselves might want to
make use of naturalist explanations on occasion to account for experiences
which they find suspect, as well as to deepen their understanding of experiences
they think genuine. So the religious believer need not fear naturalist explanations, indeed, one might even find them useful as an aid to discernment. An array
of naturalist accounts, then, might even be of service to the religious believer;
just as the scientist need not ignore the personalistic aspects of an experience.[4]

Physiological generation of experiences

Some people think they can see an immediate similarity between religious experiences and experiences that are psycho-pathological. Prince defines religious
experience as 'states of mind which their subjects invest with supernatural or
preternatural meaning (interpreting the experiences as related to such agencies
as spirits, gods, devils or magical influences)'. He goes on to remark: 'Defined
in this way, we can immediately see a significant kinship between psychiatric
disorders and religious experiences.'[5]

Because people who are thought to be disturbed in some way have experiences that they describe in a similar fashion to the way other people, usually
considered sane, describe their religious experiences, it could be tempting to see
all religious experience as essentially pathological. Religion is abnormal behaviour requiring psychiatric analysis, 'absolute insanity';[6] religion is 'mental
sickness ... that *must* make you self-depreciating and dehumanized'.[7] Perhaps
all religious ideas originate in psychosis.[8] On the other hand, 'the communication of personal psychopathology ... might be the occasion for [religious]
innovation',[9] which is an unusually upbeat suggestion.

Is there no intrinsic difference then between 'pathological experiences' and
'spiritual experiences'? Is it impossible to distinguish them, as Russell and
Mackie[10] both suggest? To carry through this assertion properly requires greater
precision than either philosopher gives it; for if religious experience is difficult
enough to define, understanding mental illness or psychopathology is even more
problematic and controversial. After all, before one can equate two phenomena,
one needs to be clear about what each phenomenon is. Perhaps it is no coincidence that Russell and Mackie are both philosophers, and not psychiatrists, for
in current psychiatric research there is no consensus on whether, for example,

mental health and mental illness are discrete variables (two completely different things), or whether there is rather an overall continuity between mental illness and the normal personality.[11] Some telling research showed that whether one found a positive, negative, or no relation between mental health and religion depended on the criteria for mental health used (they compared seven different conceptions of the latter).[12]

Leslie Francis failed to find a relationship between neuroticism and religion, and in fact found a significant *negative* relationship between psychoticism and religiosity. 'According to these criteria, there is no evidence to suggest that religious people experience lower levels of mental health, and some clear evidence to suggest that they enjoy higher levels of mental health.'[13] Peter Fenwick, having suggested that the right hemisphere of the brain 'contributes' to mystical experiences, goes on to conclude: 'A parsimonious view would be that mystical experiences are normal and that temporal lobe structures are involved with their synthesis but that their expression in fragmented form is frequently associated with pathology.'

As a philosopher, rather than a psychiatrist, Davis describes a number of features which demonstrate a clear difference between psychotic experiences and religious ones from her review of the literature.[14] The value of the insights obtained, the religious components of the experience, the emotions felt, the welcome given to such experiences (or not) all differ. Non-religious features of schizophrenic experiences such as thought disorders, delusions of grandeur, hallucinations of fantastic objects, fears of extra-terrestrial forces are all absent from religious experiences. Superficial similarities, such as the sense of a loss of control, or a dissolution of the ego, are not alike on examination, and are welcomed by the mystic while feared by the psychotic. Religious experiences are 'life-enhancing' while psychotic experiences are not. Finally, the mystic's freedom from the material world and the psychotic anxiety to escape the real world are, she says, radically different.

Recent research by Jackson suggests that while there are apparent similarities between religious experience and schizophrenic experience, their pragmatic effects are opposite. He hypothesises that both are a function of a personality trait that allows one to enter altered states of consciousness more easily than usual: a 'schizotypal personality trait'. His theory is that the onset of such experiences typically occurs in time of crisis. Benign experiences involve effective solutions to the problem; they are part of a ' "homeostatic" problem-solving process'. This process is triggered by high levels of cognitive tension, and is normally adaptive because it reduces the tension through 'cognitive restructuring'. But when this process is triggered, yet fails, psychosis results and begins a self-perpetuating cycle of psychotic experiences.

Interestingly, this suggests not only a positive view of religious experience but also of schizophrenia. Jackson in fact suggests that the ability to have such experiences is normally adaptive, linked not only with problem-solving but also with creativity.[15] Rather than seeing religious experience as a sub-category of pathological experience, perhaps it is more apt to consider pathological experiences a sub-category of spiritual experience.

Some accounts attempt to explain the processes involved in religious experience in the context of some natural mechanism or facility that we have, that is not necessarily pathological. Fenwick observes that the features of mystical experience are part of everyday experience, as well as of pathological experiences such as psychoses. In this case, 'it is logical to assume that there must be a brain mechanism which allows the expression of the experience.'[16] Deikman suggests that what takes place in mystical experience is 'deautomatization'. 'Deautomatization' undoes the automatic, unconscious operating we use for much of our activity and perception; we concentrate, unusually, on things that we have normally ceased to notice. Deikman argues that in mystical experience, the psychological structures that organise, limit, select and interpret perceptual stimuli become 'deautomatized'. Pragmatic modes of selection break down, 'in favor of alternate modes of consciousness whose stimulus processing may be less efficient from a biological point of view but whose very inefficiency may permit the experience of aspects of the real world formerly excluded or ignored'.[17] He is careful to note that such an explanation does not say anything about the 'source' of transcendent stimuli; 'God or the Unconscious share equal possibilities here and one's interpretation will reflect one's presuppositions and beliefs.'[18]

Altered states of consciousness could be important in everyday functioning. Ludwig suggests that altered states of consciousness 'might be regarded ... as "final common pathways" for many different forms of human expression and experience, both adaptive and maladaptive'.[19] Valla and Prince interpret religious experiences as self-healing mechanisms; endogenous psychological healing mechanisms analogous to other mechanisms which exist in the human organism and function to right or stabilise body temperature, blood sugar, blood pressure, and other systems.[20] Hay reminds us of Hardy's Hypothesis: 'that religious experience involves a kind of awareness that has evolved through natural selection because of its survival value to the individual.'[21]

Artificial induction

There are also other conditions under which people have highly unusual experiences, without suffering from a psychiatric disorder. People have odd experiences when they have taken drugs, or are suffering from sensory deprivation, or when subjected to excessive psychological stress or pressure. So on the one hand, we have examples of the generation of unusual experiences under unusual physiological conditions (sensory deprivation, intoxication etc.) but with no religious content or spiritual import. On the other hand, we have unusual experiences with religious content and import, that are achieved without the aid of unusual physiological conditions. Can these two be connected to explain the generation of religious experience?

Pahnke's 'Good Friday' study involved the administration of a hallucinogenic drug to experimental subjects (all of them theology students), followed by placing them in a religious service.[22] Most of them obliged by having a religious experience. Perhaps it is interesting that religious experiences can be produced by the combined effects of drugs and liturgy, and it may be useful to know that if one is going to take a drug, the setting can influence the experience. But as an attempt to explain the occurrence of religious experiences across the board, it is difficult to see how this experiment can explain the generation of religious experiences which take place without pharmaceutical (or even liturgical) intervention. So such studies cannot take us very far in explaining the majority of religious experiences, which mostly occur chemically unaided.

The connection between odd spiritual experiences and other kinds of odd experience therefore must be made in a different way; for example, by claiming that all religious experiences *do* take place under unusual physiological conditions, identical or equivalent to the conditions that produce other kinds of hallucinations or hysteria.

Can religious experiences be produced by coercive techniques of psychological manipulation? This was a suggestion made by William Sargant in *Battle for the Mind*.[23] He argued that much of what goes on in religious settings operates like brainwashing. Comparing religious experiences with the phenomenon of combat stress and hysteria, he asserts that the level of stress on a person at a revivalist prayer meeting could easily equal the stress experienced by soldiers in the trenches in a war, so that it is difficult if not impossible to withstand it by failing to have a conversion experience.[24] Not having been to war, I may not be qualified to comment; but I would be amazed, even relieved, if it were true that the horrors of war were no greater than the pressures exerted on the recalcitrant unbeliever at a prayer meeting.

However, it is certainly plausible that suggestion can produce experiences in people who would not otherwise have had them. It can be suggested to people that they *will* be healed, or experience *satori*, and maybe if they are 'suggestible' enough they will comply. 'Suggestible' people unconsciously oblige more readily than most people will, even without the aid of explicit hypnotic techniques; it is often argued that those who have spiritual experiences, or indeed religious people generally, are more 'suggestible' than most people, and that this explains their religious experiences.

Several studies have attempted to test the hypothesis that religious people or those who report religious experience are hypersuggestible.[25] Douglas-Smith's study of 249 subjects of mystical experience found only 38 who could be suspected of hypersuggestibility.[26] Gibbons' and De Jarnette's study compared two groups of religious believers, those who were 'highly suggestible' and those whose suggestibility was low.[27] Their conclusion was that the 'existential phenomena' which make up conversion experiences, and perhaps 'transcendental experiences' generally, are hypnotic phenomena.[28] But it is interesting to compare the two groups to see what the differences are. Actually, the most striking difference between the highly suggestible group and the less suggestible group was whether or not they thought their mother was 'moderately to deeply religious', a finding which Gibbons and De Jarnette do not explore. But as far as religious experiences are concerned, the chief difference between those who were highly suggestible and those who were not is the way they described their religious experiences.

The suggestible types, without exception, described their conversions as 'primarily an experiential phenomenon' – as emotional and perceptual.[29] (The quotations from the subjects describe feeling a warm tingling glow, feeling scared to death, feeling something like a bolt of lightning, feeling Christ's presence, feeling great happiness.) The low-susceptible group report their experience in a way Gibbons and De Jarnette describe as emphasising 'cognitive and situational determinants', 'which appear to be caused by a desire to conform to socially sanctioned standards of morality or to gain group acceptance'.[30] 'No, I never felt too much emotion about it, but one day I just went forward and accepted the Lord' is a typical utterance of this group. So the differences between those who are very suggestible and those who are not were not in the number of religious experiences they had, but in their nature – or in the language they chose to describe these experiences to a stranger. Gibbons and De Jarnette's research does not support the idea that converting, being saved, or being religious is connected with suggestibility (in their study, they find there is no correlation between suggestibility and church attendance, for example). Rather, it demonstrates that the conversion experiences of highly suggestible people are more dramatic and emotional in a dramatic and emotional setting than the conversions of those who are not.

A connection has been made, then, between someone who can be easily induced to feel something, and an experience which is highly emotional. A certain kind of person is more likely to have a corresponding kind of religious experience; but this tells us nothing about other kinds of people and less dramatic and emotional experiences. Thus there are problems with accepting suggestibility as a global explanation of religious experience. Both religious experience and suggestibility itself are complex phenomena, which makes the examination of their relationship more difficult. Each has many aspects. People can be 'suggestible' in some respects but not in others, just as some people who have spiritual experiences never go to church, and some people who go to church are not especially 'spiritual' or 'religious' when measured against other criteria. The relationship between these many different factors is not clear.[31]

Even if one were to accept a link, there is nothing in the studies to advise the philosopher on the question of veridicality. There is nothing to help us decide between the implication that religious experiences are 'nothing but' misplaced emotion, and Ralph Hood's suggestion, on the other hand, that the correlation is 'indicative of an ability to become aware of "wider" or "deeper" aspects of reality of which hypnosis is only another indicator'.

One can also enquire into the role of education, or even conditioning, where religious experience is concerned: do people have these experiences because they are brought up to have them, or pressurised into having them? Associationist, operant conditioning, and social learning theory accounts have all been given of religious behaviour and experience.[32] Religious behaviour might be explained in terms of coincidental connections between stimuli and responses, so that one has a religious experience in a learned, automatic way just as Pavlov's dogs salivated at the sound of a bell (Guthrie and Vetter). Religious behaviour or experiences might be reinforced by what happens subsequently and thereby strengthened (Bufford). Social learning theory stresses the importance of human beings in the reinforcement and learning process, and also places a greater emphasis on cognition or thought. This is said to explain the adherence of devotees to their respective religions, and when people deviate from their education or upbringing, this can be explained by factors which made the imitation difficult.

It is clear that education and imitation can influence or even create specific behaviours, beliefs and practices. However, some further argument or account must be given to justify a claim that actual *experiences* undergone, events that happen to someone, can be inculcated by conditioning. One might also note that 45% of the positive responders in Hay and Morisy's study (see Chapter 3 above) were not church attenders, and this is not an uncommon finding. Where the dominant social forces and culture are secular, as in most Western industrialised nations where such research is carried out, educational or behaviourist theories cannot account for a significant proportion of religious experiences.

However, the role of a community and a tradition in supporting religious practice and experience need not be seen as inevitably deleterious. Religion can also be investigated in detail for the psychological value of its particular practices. Such an inquiry is offered by Stuart Linke, who examines the psychological impact and value of specific religious practices and experiences in Judaism.[33] Basing his work on an understanding of the twofold psychological function of religious ceremony and ritual, as expressing and moderating emotion and as transmitting cultural traditions – he also attends to the complexity of different cultural traditions, the different places people occupy on the spectrum of faith, tradition and observance. For example, after a bereavement the mourner is prohibited from greeting friends. Linke observes, 'the Jewish tradition has astutely anticipated the psychological needs of the bereaved individual. At the point where shock is normal and withdrawal natural, the tradition allows for this to happen and, in fact, encourages it. We do not carry on as before but give ourselves, wholeheartedly, to the business of grieving.'[34] So religious structures can also offer psychological support.

Finally, can odd, spiritual things be made to happen by engaging in certain practices? Isn't it likely that breathing in an unusual way, or even just concentrating and excluding sensory stimuli, can produce curious results? After all, sensory deprivation does produce a number of unusual phenomena and sensations, as does simply hyperventilating.

There are similarities between practices in disciplined meditation and other mind-altering physiological circumstances. However, these suggestions may apply to some religious experiences, but not all. Highly disciplined meditation accounts for only a small proportion of the religious experiences that are reported. Many others come out of the blue, with the subject of the experience unprepared. Secondly, while many meditation techniques are austere, none that I know of is so total as to constitute true sensory deprivation, nor are most mortals capable of sustaining them for the number of hours or days required to produce hallucinations and other symptoms of sensory deprivation. Thirdly, as Davis observes, the negative things that happen to those subjected to sensory deprivation (hallucinations, unpleasant experiences) do not happen when meditators focus their attention in an allegedly analogous way.[35] Such explanations may give an account of what is going on physiologically in the subject. However, curiously, many practitioners take measurable physiological changes as confirmation that the experience is genuine and that something really is happening.

In traditional Hawaiian religion, 'awa or kava kava is taken to facilitate spiritual experiences, awareness, revelation. Peyote is used in a similar way among American peoples, and iboga has a similar sacred function in certain African religions. Here we see the deliberate generation of experiences that are nevertheless understood as spiritual, indeed as gifts of the divine. The people concerned are not in ignorance of the effects of the ingested substance, yet the botanical origin of the visions is not felt to be inimical to the sacred power of the experience, nor does it invalidate the insights reached in it. It is simply the necessary herbal accompaniment to divine revelation. This ability to distinguish between different layers of significance and give each its due weight shows a theoretical sophistication that some researchers seem to lack.

Needs and wishes

Some accounts suggest that various forms of need underlie human religiosity, and therefore religious experiences. Those who are deprived in socio-economic terms, or who are neurotic, dysfunctional or maladjusted are more likely to have these experiences than those who are not, it is claimed.

The evidence to support this thesis is equivocal. Clearly it will not be without a bias of its own, for certain assumptions, explicit or not, need to be made about who is 'healthy' and who isn't. Similarly, US studies often conclude that the 'deprived' are more religious; this is supported by pointing to higher rates of religiosity in the elderly, women, the uneducated, the poor, rural dwellers, black people. Surely these social assumptions are not invulnerable to critique?

Meanwhile UK studies, while agreeing that in general women and the elderly are 'more religious', find that religious experience is more common among those of a higher socio-economic status; moreover, when enquiring specifically into the propensity to have religious *experiences*, spiritual *experience* (as opposed to 'being religious') is *positively* correlated with higher social class and education in both the US and the UK. National surveys from 1978 to 1987 in the UK, USA and Australia find that reports of religious experience increase as one goes up the social scale. For example, in Britain, 47% of the upper middle class as opposed to 32% of those identified as 'unskilled/subsistence' report such experience.

One might observe that, while Marx suggested that religion was the 'opium of the people', Lenin described the way it was used as a 'ticket to heaven' by those who owned the means of production; in short, Marx's suggestion was not that the poor are more likely to be religious than the rich by virtue of their oppression; he and Lenin were simply describing how religion was used by both rich and poor in different ways in the unjust socio-economic structures of the time. This is perhaps a more valid vector of critique.

Various attempts have been made to find the origin of religious experiences in sexual frustration or sexual sublimation; in regression, lack of ego strength, and other forms of dysfunction or maladjustment.[36] Psychoanalytic theory is pre-eminent in this field, stemming from Freud, who addressed the question of religion in many contexts and offered a variety of explanations for religious belief. Freud's accounts generally focus on the broader phenomenon of religion, rather than merely the question of striking religious experiences themselves, and the explanations he gives of religion vary and develop over time. A principal theme, however, is the association he makes between 'God the Father' and a person's own father. The belief in God is thus connected with Freud's theory of the Oedipal conflict. In Freud's exegesis of the letter from the American physician, he interprets a man's auditory religious experience as an outbreak then a resolution of his Oedipal conflict, which took the form of a rebellion against God the Father followed by a return to filial submission.[37] In contrast, in *Civilisation and its Discontents*, he is sent back to the question of religious experience by the complaint that his focus on relations with the father and on certain kinds of religious experience failed to explain the 'oceanic' experience of unity that characterises so many religious experiences. This Freud then interprets as a regression to the infant's state of bliss when united with his mother while breast-feeding.[38] Psychoanalytic theorist Julia Kristeva connects religious experience with the primary experience of infants in this fashion:

> In reading about famous mystical experiences, I felt that faith could be described, perhaps rather simplistically, as what can only be called a primary identification with a loving and protective agency. Overcoming the notion of irremediable separation, Western man ... re-establishes a continuity or fusion with an Other that is no longer substantial and maternal but symbolic and paternal. Saint Augustine goes so far as to compare the Christian's faith in God with the infant's relation to its mother's breast. 'What am I even at the best but an infant sucking the milk Thou givest, and feeding upon Thee, the food that perisheth not?'[39] What

we have here is fusion with a breast that is, to be sure, succouring, nourishing, loving, and protective, but transposed from the mother's body to an
invisible agency located in another world.[40]

Jung began with a standard Freudian view of religion as a symbolic illusion, a
protection against anxiety, a sublimation of infantile sexuality, a projected father
complex;[41] but his estimation of religion changed with the passing years. First
he decided that the view of religion purely as sexual sublimation does not in the
end do justice to the empirical reality of religion. Religions had helped to create
culture, a higher civilisation and morality; it violates the whole principle of
scientific method to just reject all this as the results of auto-suggestion. But
although he asserts that religion has the greatest significance culturally, and the
greatest appeal aesthetically, it is time for humanity to move beyond this delusory set of beliefs, which only serve to guide us to an imaginary reality. Belief
should be replaced by understanding, so we can keep the beauty of the symbol
without submitting to belief.

However, in his psychoanalytic practice, Jung began to see how religious
symbols aided psychic healing and growth, and what he called 'individuation'.
He still resisted an emphasis on any objective content to religion, but subjectively it had a powerful role to play as the mediation of the contents of the
unconscious through symbols and rituals. Our psychic and spiritual health
depend upon it. 'What are religions? Religions are psychotherapeutic systems.
… It is the most elaborate system, and there is great practical truth behind it.'[42]
His attitude towards religion grew ever more positive; if such experiences make
your life healthier and happier, you may describe them as 'the grace of God'.[43]
Shortly before death, in an interview with the *Listener*,[44] when asked if he
believed in God, Jung answered: 'I don't believe – I *know*.' This provoked such
a response that he sent a letter to the *Listener* in an attempt to explain himself.[45]
What he 'knows', is not the existence of an objective God, but 'that I am obviously confronted with a factor unknown in itself, which I call "God" ';
somebody or something stronger than himself, the power of fate, which is
personal inasmuch as one's fate is personal; the overpowering emotions and a
superior will in his own psychical system. He does not assert the reality of a
universal, metaphysical Being, the traditional God.

Object-relations theory shares Freud's interest in early love relationships and
their effects on later life. It interprets 'the experience of communion, merger, or
"encounter", reported in many religious traditions … as either a return to what
once was infantile reality, or, more likely, an attempt to recreate imagined infantile bliss that never was'.[46] There are many variations on the theme of the
infant's feeling of symbiosis with the mother in breastfeeding and similar
moments.[47] Sometimes early loss or trauma are found behind powerful conversion experiences and mysticism. Masson, for example, found that three forms of
trauma in childhood (loss of a parent, sexual or physical abuse) were often found
in the lives of Indian ascetics. It is suggested that these experiences made them

extremely aggressive to others, an aggression which they turn on themselves in self-punishing asceticism.[48] Another theory, arising from the suggestion that many mystics have suffered childhood loss, is that mysticism is an effective outlet for the emotions of grief.[49] Why not argue that early loss encourages a few to turn their needs, desire and dependency to a more dependable Object? Why not argue that, as in the example of the Buddha, suffering encourages reflection on what is ultimately important, or most truly real; and that a few (those who become mystics) decide to place their trust and direct their energies beyond the transitory material world of suffering?

Attachment theory compares our relations with God to our relations with the figures in our early life to whom we were attached, and finds similarities in the way we relate to God and the way we relate to other human beings: how 'one's relationship with God is constructed from the building blocks of one's own actual experiences in close relationships'.[50] Thus, as it is commonly accepted that our adult love relationships are affected by our relations in childhood, attachment theory suggests that our relationship with God will follow a similar model. However, Kirkpatrick suggests this important difference between the effect of our behaviour on relationships with humans and with God: humans can be driven away by our inappropriate behaviour – thus our negative expectations can be self-fulfilling – while God cannot be driven away.[51] This, she suggests, is important because some might find the kind of secure attachment relationship they never had in human interpersonal relationships in a relationship with God.

So are neurotic people are more likely to have religious experiences? Or are people who claim to have religious experiences more likely to be neurotic? As we have already seen, this is a question that comes loaded with presuppositions about normality and health, as well as methodological difficulties in determining well-being. Some studies that have investigated the prevalence of religious experience have also included questions about the psychological well-being of those who report having had religious experiences. Hay summarises the results as either showing no association between religious experience and mental health, or a positive relation.[52]

This suggests a preliminary disconfirmation of the suggestion that all religious experience can plausibly be ascribed to psychological instability. There is insufficient support, then, for the suggestion that having religious experiences is by itself a sign of neurosis. On the other hand, it can easily be argued that spirituality meets various psychological needs.

There are psychologists and psychotherapists who have investigated the correlations between religious experience and psychological well-being. William James was one of the first and most famous.[53] Humanistic thinkers, such as Abraham Maslow, focus on the happy and healthy individual rather than the unhappy and unwell, on the theory that the end product of growth is perhaps the best way to learn about the growth process.[54] Maslow maintains that everyone shares a basic set of needs, but the satisfaction of needs and the removal of tension are not the only motivations for behaviour. Instead, Maslow distinguishes two categories of motivation: 'deficiency motivation' (response to a need, both physical or psychological) and 'growth motivation'. These push the person out of her security and put her in situations of tension and challenge. Growth then is not just gratifying basic needs so that they go away, but also involves motivations 'over and above these basic needs, e.g. talents, capacities, creative tendencies'. So 'basic needs and self-actualisation do not contradict each other any more than do childhood and maturity'.[55] This growth and self-actualisation is punctuated by 'peak experiences', a moment when 'the powers of a person come together in a particularly efficient and intensely enjoyable way, and in which he is more integrated ... more open for experience ... fully-functioning ... more truly himself'.[56] These experiences he often describes as 'transcendent' but is adamant that they are natural phenomena. They are our moments of greatest maturity, of individuation, they are both the means and results of true growth. Peak experiences constituted the private revelation or ecstasy of the founders of the great religions, and hence are the essence of every religion. This transcendent, ecstatic core of religion is later objectified in ritual, regulated and institutionalised by 'ecclesiastical non-peakers', and the original revelation or peak experience was made into sacred objects and activities.[57] Since Maslow, 'transpersonal psychology' and psychosynthesis have grown like a tropical climber reaching for the sun.[58]

Even the people who are eager to defend the value of religion (precisely these people, in fact) admit that spirituality can meet our psychological needs. What does this mean?

It would be odd to suggest that, because something met a need, it was therefore unveridical. It is more often the case that the satisfaction of a need constitutes a kind of justification of something, rather than its disqualification. But maybe one can produce a theory that says that people can meet their needs in an inauthentic way by experiencing something that doesn't exist. Psychoanalysis provides such a theory, and in many cases it carries considerable force. People can meet their emotional and psychological needs with fantasies, illusions, and delusions.

In *The Future of an Illusion*, Freud makes the distinction between an 'illusion' and a 'delusion'. An illusion is a belief you have because you want to believe it, not because it is true. It may be true or false. A delusion, on the other hand, is a belief you have that is false. Freud maintains that religion is an 'illusion'; but although he clearly believes it is a 'delusion' (i.e. false) he is careful not to assert that it is, on the grounds that he cannot know that religious claims are untrue. Freud, then, accepts that a distinction must be made between seeing the origin of a belief in wish-fulfilment, and the truth or falsity of a belief. Freud also accepts that psychoanalysis is not competent to decide on the truth-value of religious beliefs; what makes the difference between an illusory and a delusory religious belief does not come under the scope of psychoanalysis.

In psychoanalytic culture, one has grounds for calling a religious belief an 'illusion' if one finds a need that is met by the religious experience, and can do this by observing a similarity between one's image of God or relationship to God and that of one's parent. However, even if one accepts that there can be a similarity between our human and divine relationships, that fact alone is ambiguous. What does it mean that one conceives of a certain relationship in a way that one habitually conceives of relationships? Or if one construes a relationship in a way that meets one's psychological needs? It could mean that the relationship is a total fantasy, that one has imagined a relationship that does not exist, because the love-object does not exist, as with a fantasy lover. Or it could simply be that the relationship is like many of our relationships – indeed, according to some theories, like *all* of our relationships: that is, a relationship with a real other, which is refracted through the expectations and assumptions arising from our early love relations.

So there are two possibilities here. Does a similarity between the way I see my father and the way I see God undermine the likelihood of God's existence: *God the Father is fantasised*? Or does it mean that early relations shaped my perceptions of God, leaving the question of God's existence unaffected: *God is fantasised as Father*? This may be an illusion, in Freud's sense; but it does not entail the non-existence of God. If my relations with my children mirror my mother's relations with me, does that entail that my children don't exist?

Psychoanalytic or psychodynamic theories can in fact say a great deal about why a putative relationship with God has the character it does; without being categorical on the issue of whether God exists or not. The creative ingenuity of some religious believers can be seen in the paradox that naturalist explanations can be very fruitful avenues to explore for religious believers wanting to deepen their understanding of their own experience. Thus, instead of damaging the credibility of such testimony of experience, naturalistic explanations actually are used by many people to refine their spiritual lives. Psychoanalytist and semiotician Julia Kristeva writes:

> To the analyst ... the representations on which the Credo is based are fantasies, which reveal fundamental desires or traumas but not dogmas. Analysis subjects these fantasies to X-ray examination. It begins by individualizing: What about *your* father? Was he 'almighty' or not? What kind of son were *you*? What about *your* desire for virginity or resurrection? By shifting attention from the 'macrofantasy' to the 'microfantasy' analysis reveals the underlying sexuality, which prayer circumvents but does not really proscribe; for though the object of desire be transformed, desire itself remains a feature of Christian discourse.[59]

So theories whose intention may be atheistic or reductive can actually be deployed by believers to refine their spirituality. Anthony de Luca's examination of Freud and religion argues that Freud calls us to a 'purification' of our religiosity. Freudian psychoanalysis purifies our personal concept of God from any elements that may come from our own unresolved conflicts:

Human and Divine

Freud more than any other contemporary thinker leads us through an excruciating purification. No idea is left secret; it must be exposed to brilliant flame. This is not God; that is not God; this is you, that is you. Now we are enlightened: we know all that He is not. Thus man is caught in a dilemma in his search for God. He has had to sacrifice all his idols.[60]

The deconstructive scalpel of psychoanalysis, or the 'X-ray examination' is deployed on the image of God. As a Kantian, Freud himself could not assert an identity between the analysand's image of God and the actual existence of God. This gap allows the believer to use the same critical tools to purify and refine God's image – precisely for the sake of fidelity to God, or at least, for the sake of psycho-spiritual development. In fact, de Luca suggests that the atheist may be not less in the grip of unresolved Oedipal conflicts than the believer.

The person who is fully mature is no longer a victim of unconscious infantile longings which seek satisfaction in their beliefs about God; nor is the mature person one who has unconscious hostility toward the father which finds expression in doing away with him, i.e., atheism. The important factor is to examine the *character* of the belief or disbelief. Belief or disbelief, to be considered mature, must be the distillation of a mind which has gone through the infantile stages of development successfully. As the child has had to resolve the relations with the parents, so the mature person has resolved these attitudes toward God.[61]

Lacan had the courage and self-criticism to consider this point. Although he felt obliged to maintain, along with many other intellectuals after Nietzsche, that 'God is dead', he did wonder whether in fact this might not be a shelter against castration. One kills off God the Father before that Almighty Father can castrate little atheistic Oedipus.

Are psychological explanations exhaustive?

Entertain a new thought for a moment: it is not parsimony and simplicity that are desirable in explanations, as scientists and philosophers often suppose, but richness and diversity. In this case, the reductionist urge is moving in the wrong direction.

Why might this be so? Because religious experience itself is diverse. Most accounts tend to focus on a single style of religious experience. Researchers who equate religious experience with psychotic or pathological experience stress dramatic, quasi-sensory religious experiences such as visions and voices, experiences of demons or other entities – the kinds of religious experience that most resemble psychotic experiences, in fact, but the majority of reported experiences are not like that. Meanwhile, investigators who attribute religious experiences to suggestion or hysteria tend to focus on spectacular emotional experiences such as those that happen at revivalist meetings, prayer meetings with a strong emphasis on conversion and being saved, or on public instantaneous healings. These also are numerically in the minority. Ascetics who renounce things are associated with traumatic loss, and people who pray the rosary are deemed to be anal characters.[62]

One thing that is clear from this unconscious display of preference on the part of the researchers is that a single psychological explanation cannot fit every believer's psyche. Nor, perhaps, can a single cause cover all the aspects even of one particular case.[63] Do scientists investigating the causes of such afflictions insist that *only* genetic factors must be responsible for lung cancer, or *only* family relations responsible for schizophrenia? As genetic predisposition and environment are both considered, so too a complex interrelation even of purely natural factors provides a more plausible account of religious experience than a single natural explanation.[64] A Zen master may trigger a religious experience in his novice by suggestion, but he does not spell out what the content of the experience is, what thoughts or insights will be experienced. Even if 'suggestion' adequately explains *that* the experience happened, it does not account for *what* happened. A number of different naturalistic accounts may be needed even to give a full *psychological* picture of the event.

No single psychological theory then, is exhaustive. It seems that one needs a variety of reductionist explanations to supplement the limitations and deficiencies of each. But many of these competing theories are 'natural enemies': Freudianism and behaviourism, for example, are inimical to one another. They 'reduce' in different directions. Even apart from their mutual hostility, if a single reductionistic account *isn't* adequate for all cases, it subverts any reductionist claim to be the sole explanation for the phenomenon.

What is often misguided about 'reductionist' explanations is the reduction to a *narrower* frame of reference than can provide an adequate and profound understanding of the phenomenon. Often, it is a more limited scope than the subject himself currently possesses. But what is most often needed when a subject 'misunderstands' his experience is a *wider* frame of reference, something that comprehends what he leaves out of account.

What seems disordered in Godfather Man's reasoning was that only one possible explanation was considered. It was not merely the logic of deducing a man's identity from his posture that seemed odd; it was the assumption that this was the only possible inference to draw. When we feel someone is misguided in their understanding of their own experience, we often feel that way because their range of possible explanations is too narrow: they only consider one possible meaning or interpretation. An earnest Catholic teenager feels called to give herself completely to God and assumes that the only way to do so is to become a nun in an enclosed order, which she wants to do forthwith. Someone who is depressed and lonely has a dramatic emotional experience with a friendly group, and thinks this must mean that all their religious claims are true and he must join this new religious movement and break off contact with his family and former friends. If we feel that they have misjudged their experience and drawn a false inference, we would do better to *widen* their interpretative horizons, not reduce them to a different explanatory context which is even narrower.

No single theory is adequate for the whole of religious experience, nor can a single theory give a total explanation for an individual experience. Naturalist explanations, therefore, are helpful in deepening or expanding one's understanding of religious experience. It is simplistic, however, to take them as 'explaining it away', for a single style of explanation leaves too much unaccounted for.

Naturalist explanations and truth-value

Is the truth-value of a phenomenon determined by its origin or cause? As we have seen, Freud's own view in the case of religious belief was that it is not. He reached this conclusion because he thought that Kant had successfully demonstrated that such transcendent things cannot be known, but only believed; neither proved nor disproved empirically.

Reductionist explanations need to be carefully put if they are not to saw off the branch that they are sitting on. Can all mental experience, all beliefs be explained in purely naturalistic terms? Does one prove the falsity of a belief with an explanation in purely naturalistic terms of why it is believed? If one answers 'yes' to both these questions, reductionism itself is false: as a belief, it too can be accounted for in purely naturalistic terms, no less than religion can. So if the reductive explainer does not wish to have his own science explained away, he must allow that his explanatory framework does not preclude the truth of a belief – in which case a religious belief about experience might be true, even if his scientific explanation is also true. Alternatively, he faces the arduous task of persuading the rest of us why *his* views uniquely escape falsification despite behavioural conditioning, social pressure, brain function or unconscious desire.

It would be unwise, however, to decide that psychological issues have no bearing at all on issues of veridicality. Even mystics, gurus and spiritual directors of different religious traditions have considered the origin of an experience to have something important to say about its truth or status. For the practitioners, it is an important matter to discover whether an experience is from God, from the devil, from misplaced excessive desire or an overactive imagination or an excitable nature. Precisely in mystical traditions, a sceptical attitude is often taken to florid experiences:

A monk in Thailand sat down to meditate as he usually did for an hour or so in the afternoon. This time though it seemed that he travelled down a long dark tunnel and found at the end someone who took him on a tour, guiding him with his hand. The monk never saw the rest of this person, only the hand on his arm, and heard a voice explain the various bloody and horrific tortures which he saw. This was a vision of a hell-realm. The voice explained what different kammas [karmas] had brought on the various forms of intense suffering. The tour was long, the place immense and the monk emerged from his experience only when the dark night sky was full of stars ....[65]

When he told his Teacher about it his comment was, 'Why didn't you find out *who* took you on the tour before you followed?' Had he done so, instead of permitting the mind to ramble on and be fascinated, he might have investigated *who* was producing it all. The upshot of this discussion is that a psychological explanation can affect our estimation of the veridicality of an experience, and the veridicality of an experience can be compromised at a number of different stages in the process: one can hallucinate something that isn't there, or one can perceive something accurately but wildly misinterpret it. However, the sheer fact of providing an psychological explanation that satisfies our curiosity on a certain point and thus seems adequate for a certain purpose, does not exclude the possibility that an experience or some moment in it is nevertheless veridical.

So where people have religious experiences when they are distressed, this suggests a reason why people may *want* to have such experiences. If one believes that one can make things happen by wanting things to happen, it suggests why people have these experiences when they do, or even why some people have these experiences more often than others. What it does not decide, however, is the question of the veridicality of the experiences or what is experienced. Someone who suffers from low self-esteem and desperately needs to be loved may 'fall in love' more often than someone who does not. Psychological factors may thus 'explain' her propensity to get involved in such relationships. They may also 'explain' much about how she views the men she becomes involved with, why she chooses certain men, and why her relationships often fail. What such an explanation does not do is to demonstrate that she does not really have those feelings, still less that the men she seeks out do not really exist. Some further argument would be needed to justify reaching a similar conclusion about spiritual experiences and the divine.

A student of mine once responded to psychoanalytic accounts of religiosity with this insight: 'A courageous enemy is better than a cowardly friend.' Insights from the social sciences are, I believe, essential not only for a wider and deeper understanding of the phenomenon; not only indispensable to the atheist; they are also helpful to help the mystic become a wiser mystic.

A courageous enemy is more to be treasured than a cowardly ally. Let us play with a Lacanian idea to see if his apparently atheistic account can be used by the religious believer for a paradoxical purpose.

Lacan's account of the formation of the subject, the development of individual identity, is given in terms of the infant's relation to the other. The baby sees herself reflected in the gaze of the mother, or sees her image in the mirror – an image that is at once herself, of course, but also not herself. In jubilation, seeing this glorious image, she adopts this form or image as 'me'; but this is untrue as well as true. This cycle of seeing an image, identifying with it, taking it into oneself, then projecting it (oneself) outward again, continues in our perceptions of others.[66] In this way our identity is made up in layers of partly mistaken identifications with the Other, for what is inside us we can only recognise by inverting it into another. But that is a *misrecognition*, for it is really ourselves that we are beholding. 'The relation to the Other always contains negation, takes the form of inversion.' Desire for the Other and identification with what one desires swings like a see-saw between oneself and the Other.

What is inescapable, however, is the necessity of another in the formation of one's own self. One's idea of oneself and one's ideas of other people develop together. And one needs the Other to make *oneself* into an other, with a 'pact', a commitment, as we have seen.

Can this not serve as a model in which to interpret the psychological dynamics of religious encounter? The spiritual 'infant' joyously beholds a glorious other outside herself. Only after identifying with it does she realise how true, and how false, that identification is: she realises how much her perception of the Other owes to her own narcissism, her inversion of herself into the other. Yet the need remains for an other who always accepts, yet always transcends, this projection. Without this 'pact' with someone who can never be reduced to oneself, there can never be love.

Modern Man, then, will not, without more ado, call God back, when the time for it has arrived. Jupiter and Thor, after their fall, have never been restored to their altars, and rightly so. So also will the man of the future not call back a 'God' who has to make up as a sort of physical energy, for the loss of energy in the macrocosm, who has to make the poor accept their wretched lot on earth, who must keep the oppressed in their social and political state of degradation. He will not be a God who acts like a French king or a German emperor, who can be inspected as a factor in an Oedipus-complex, who is a kind of 'unstared stare' and pursues man with his threats, who produces man as a kind of utensil, who makes man's cultural activity superfluous. He will not be a God who lets theologians have a look at the maps of His Providence, who lets Himself be invoked as a meteorological and agricultural factor. He will not be a super-economist, a super-physician, a super-psychiatrist who puts all economists, physicians, and psychiatrists in the shade, who so greatly prompts man to forget his fellow-man that charity becomes unimportant. The man of the future will call God back, but this call will be only for the true God. With the heaven above his head empty of pseudo-gods, he will walk through the world and history, calling for a Transcendent God.[67]

5. Being Eminently Rational

Arguments for the existence of God based on religious experience

In recent years, there has been an increase in the attention given to the question of whether religious experience can provide the key premise in an argument for the existence of God. Let us imagine that someone claims to have received a message from God. No obvious psychological or social reasons exist for thinking his experience delusional or hallucinatory. It coheres with other purported religious truths of his belief system, and seems to have a positive effect on his life. What can be claimed on the basis of his experience? Can it be counted as evidence, maybe even as part of an argument, for the existence of God?

The argument

Analogy with sense perception: Wainwright and Alston

I have an experience of a tree, I believe that the tree exists. I have an experience of God, and I believe that God exists. Admittedly there are some differences between these two experiences, but any similarities might justify truth claims based on religious experience, just as we are justified in our beliefs based on sense perception.

This argument was put forward by William Wainwright.[1] Based on an analogy with sense perception, which he takes as a paradigm of cognitive types of experience, he claimed that mystical experience is probably cognitive as well – that is, it gives us information. Both are noetic; they have an intentional object (an object of the experience), both give rise to states of affairs that can be checked independently, and checking procedures for both kind of experience exist. Wainwright admits that there are dissimilarities as well, which mostly focus on the procedures for checking whether the experience was veridical or not.

This argument has been developed over a number of years in greater depth and detail by William Alston, in a series of articles and finally in a book-length treatment. He deploys the notion of a 'doxastic practice', a practice of forming beliefs based on experience.[2] Sense perception is a doxastic practice: we perceive something and form beliefs on the basis of this perception. 'I see a tree' becomes the belief that 'There is a tree here'. Religious experience also has its own doxastic practice: we form a belief in God based on an experience of God's presence.

Alston's main strategy is to examine arguments for the reliability and rationality of sense perception as a doxastic practice, and to argue that Christian mystical practice has the same epistemic status because it enjoys essentially the same conditions as sense perception. He is chiefly concerned to rebut the idea that we have sufficient reason to trust sensory doxastic practice but not mystical doxastic practice.[3] He argues that there are no arguments for the reliability of sense perception that are not circular, and claims that *any* doxastic practice exhibits this kind of non-vicious circularity: one cannot test or prove the reliability of that way of forming beliefs without using (and trusting) the very things in question. How can we test our memories without using memory somehow? How can we test sense perception without double-checking by using our, or someone else's, sensory input? So rationality does not come from being able to prove the reliability of the ways we have of forming beliefs; we are acting rationally when we form and evaluate beliefs in the ways that are accepted and established in our society. If there are no 'overriders' to the belief, one's rationality cannot be faulted for reaching it, and one can take this doxastic practice and its results to be reliable.[4] Christian mystical practice satisfies all the conditions for rational acceptance, and therefore 'can be rationally engaged in, and rationally taken to be reliable and a source of justification, provided it is not disqualified by reasons to the contrary'.

If the theist can successfully maintain that religious doxastic practice is on a par with other ways we have of forming beliefs, such as sense perception or memory, a significant battle has been won in the quest to justify religious experience as a source of knowledge. Opposition to Alston's account, however, comes from defenders of the epistemic value of religious experience as well as those who oppose it. Most objections surround the question of the parity of religious doxastic practice and sensory doxastic practice.

Yandell argues that with sensory doxastic practice, experience may provide evidence *against* something without calling into question the substantial support sensory experience provides in general. Thus we can doubt that we are *really* seeing a pink elephant late on New Year's Eve, without undermining the credibility of all of our senses, all of the time. But for religious doxastic practices, no religious experience can count as evidence against the existence of God without calling into question the presupposition of its own doxastic practice. Sensory practice does not need to make a prior presupposition of the existence of material objects; it can remain neutral on the question until they appear. Religious doxastic practice, however, must first assume God's existence, Yandell maintains. But it is difficult to see why this must be so. Quite apart from the fact that non-theistic religions exist in which people have religious experiences, unbelievers can have a powerful religious experience which contradicts their previous atheistic world-view.

Yandell also objects – as many sceptics do: 'If no experience could count as evidence against belief, then none can count for it either.'[5] To be trustworthy, the doxastic practice must allow us to discover that God does not exist, if God doesn't – just as sensory doxastic practice allows us to discover that unicorns don't exist. But Yandell holds that 'within pietistic practice, no experience can count as evidence against God's existence. So, within pietistic practice, no experience can provide evidence in favor of God's existence.'

There are other disanalogies between the two ways of forming beliefs. It is easy to test one's sense perceptions against another person's, or the evidence of one sense (sight) against another one (touch). These allow for a degree of 'checking' and confirmation that are difficult, if not impossible, to obtain in spiritual experiences.[6]

Yandell's conclusion is that sensory doxastic practice is rational but the religious version is not, because the analogy between them is insufficiently close. Alston expressly denies, however, that he intends to assert a 'parity' between the doxastic practices based on sense experience and religious experience respectively, or that the two are 'analogous'.[7] If this disclaimer is allowed, then it does not demolish his argument to find important ways in which the two differ; any more than finding crucial differences between swimming and rugby undermines the claim of either to be considered a 'sport'. At the same time, one can make the rejoinder that there must be sufficient common ground to support the claim. Finding crucial differences between swimming and warfare *does* undermine any claim of warfare to be a sport. Before arguments that at least *flirt* with the idea of 'parity' or 'analogy' (whether they consummate the union or not) can succeed, we need an agreement on *precisely* how much similarity is required, and how much dissimilarity tolerated, for something to be considered an analogy (or accepted as parity). But this we can never have. Analogical language is not capable of such stringent control, just as 'parity' cannot be supported with a list of exhaustive criteria. Both rely on their power to *convince* – thus properly belong to rhetoric, as I suggested earlier for metaphor. This means that where a sceptic has a powerful disinclination to be convinced, an argument that suggests an analogy or parity will always fail, whatever its merits or insights.

In that case, however, the sceptic's rejection of analogy and parity is not then based on *rational grounds* and *alleged failures of logic* ...

A 'cumulative case' from religious experience

Basil Mitchell, followed in different ways by Swinburne, Donovan and Davis, suggests that religious experience can be evidence for the existence of God as part of a 'cumulative case'. It is reasonable to believe that religious experiences are genuine only if the religious system within which they are understood is itself found to be plausible. 'The correctness of any particular interpretation cannot be guaranteed simply by the experience itself, but relies on a conceptual framework which draws support from other, independent evidence.'[8] Mitchell argues that, although religious experience itself is not a theoretical matter, showing that the beliefs based on it are able to be rationally justified *is*. One needs to employ experience and reasoning. Knowledge only comes through the systematic relation of experiences to what we already know and the integration of them into the belief-system as a whole.

Swinburne's causal theory of perception applied to religious experience means that one can only have an experience of God 'if and only if its seeming to him that God is present is in fact caused by God being present'.[9] One could immediately complain that this latter point – 'if in fact ... God is present' – is precisely what is so difficult to establish. However, this difficulty is treated with Swinburne's now famous Principle of Credulity [PC]: 'It is a principle of rationality that (in the absence of special considerations) if it seems (epistemically) to a subject that x is present, then probably x is present; what one seems to perceive is probably so.'[10] This he takes as a fundamental 'principle of rationality', which means that anyone who is rational has to accept it; but it also means that it stands on its own terms, in other words, it does not need other justifications for its acceptance. The alternative to accepting the PC in general is a 'sceptical bog', he says, in which one must doubt everything that is not capable of deductive proof.[11]

What the PC does is to shift the burden of proof onto the sceptic. Instead of providing cogent arguments why someone should be believed if he claims to have had an experience of God, it is up to the sceptic to provide arguments why he should *not* be believed. 'In the absence of special considerations, all religious experiences are to be taken by their subjects as genuine, and hence as substantial grounds for belief in the existence of their apparent object.'[12]

The subjects of religious experiences might take their experiences as genuine, but need the rest of us do so too? To deal with this issue the Principle of Testimony [PT] joins the fray. It legitimises 'the assumption that other people normally tell the truth'; in which case 'the experiences of others are (probably) as they report them'.[13] By combining both principles, we find that it is rational that 'other things being equal, we think that what others tell us that they perceived, probably happened'.[14]

Rowe rejects Swinburne's PC altogether. It is a serious problem that God does not let Herself be experienced predictably, he thinks, and in such a case the PC is not a rational foundation for belief. Gutting thinks that while Swinburne is right that the PC is *prima facie* evidence for existential claims, he misrepresents the strength of that *prima facie* case. Gutting understands Swinburne to think that the evidence of the experience is decisive unless something overrides it. He claims that experiences and the PC only allow some, but not sufficient, support; and only as part of a cumulative case, for existential claims.[15] But Swinburne himself insists on the need for a cumulative case.

Davis, however, argues that something like the PC must underpin any successful argument from religious experience.[16] Like Swinburne, she also argues that these principles must be considered fundamental principles of rationality. Philosophers cannot give inductive justification for trusting our reasoning, memories, or other people's reports, but these are things that we could not cope without trusting. It is not irrational to trust them without inductive proof that they are reliable.[17] Admittedly there are 'defeaters', reasons for rejecting some claims based on experience, and it does not absolve believers from any need for further justification for what they believe. But the main point of the PC is that most experiences are innocent until proven guilty; and by shifting the burden of proof onto the sceptic, the PC avoids many of the problems and paradoxes which arise when one tries to draw up criteria and conditions for the justification of belief and for the veridicality of experiences.

Subsequent arguments

Subsequent treatments of the issue have often taken up Swinburne's PC, improved or modified as they see fit. Yandell's formulation of his foundational principle is a little more elaborate than Swinburne's:

> For any subject S and experience E, if S's having E is a matter of its (phenomenologically) seeming to S that S experiences a numinous being N, then if S nonculpably has no reason to think that:
> (i) S would seem to experience N whether or not there is an N that S experiences, or
> (ii) if E is nonveridical, S could not discover that it was, or
> (iii) if E is of a type T of experience such that every member of T is nonveridical, S could not discover this fact, then E provides S evidence that there is an N, provided that
> (iv) *O exists* falls within the scope of both collegial and lateral disconfirmation.[18]

So Yandell gives epistemic credibility to religious experience provided that it clears a number of hurdles: there must be no good reason for doubting that the person is capable of distinguishing a veridical experience from a non-veridical one, and there must be some possibility of ruling out the existence of the apparent object of experience, should it *not* exist. If people have numinous experiences under conditions that satisfy all of Yandell's conditions, then there is experiential evidence that God exists. Persons do have numinous experiences under conditions that satisfy all of the conditions. Hence there is experiential evidence that God exists.

Gellman has constructed an argument which he dubs BEE (Best Explanation of Experience) which carries with it a STING (Strength in Number Greatness) to constitute an argument for the evidential value of religious experiences.[19] 'If a person, S, has an experience, E, which seems (phenomenally) to be of a particular object, O (or of an object of kind, K), then everything *else being* equal the best explanation of S's having E is that S has experienced O (or object of kind, K), rather than something else or nothing at all.' Its dependence on Swinburne's

Principle of Credulity is clear (although he has introduced some modifications).[20]

Like Swinburne and Davis, Gellman also claims that BEE is a principle of rationality which people use continually and cannot do without, and as such does not require proof. When we dispute someone else's experience, we feel the burden of proof is on *us* to say why we do not believe it; this common-sense fact indicates to Gellman that in general we give experiential reports the benefit of the doubt.

Gellman's 'STING', 'Strength in Number Greatness', argues that the more people have such experience, the stronger the case for its veridicality.[21] This allows the numerous experiences of God that have been reported to carry some weight in an argument. Together BEE and STING can ground specific claims about God, he claims: if many people experience God as loving, it is rational to believe Her to be so.[22]

Objections to the arguments

Is parity even possible?

These arguments are clever and well-thought-out. They are convincing accounts of how we must and do operate in everyday affairs, when watertight proof of a matter is lacking or impossible. The PC in Swinburne's, Davis's or Gellman's versions, or Yandell's PN*, are persuasive when viewed in action in our experience of mundane affairs.

However, they stand or fall on the question of whether something which is applicable to mundane affairs and entities can be applied in even a broadly similar way to a transcendent entity. For the sceptic – even for some religious believers – the gulf between God and other entities cannot be breached so easily. The problem is that for the atheist, the religious account will *never* be the Best Explanation of an Experience – *any* explanation, even an improbable one or indeed implausible one, would be better. A religious account is not so much a BEE as a WASP (What Astonishingly Silly Propositions).[23] Even if Yandell's argument were accepted by a sceptic, he would assert that *all* experiences of purported numinous beings are either a type of experience that is always nonveridical (iii), an experience such that if it were nonveridical, one could not know it (ii), and indeed that the person would have that experience whether or not the being existed (i) – since the being doesn't.

Yandell could retort that the critic must provide *evidence* for his assertion that all religious experience comes under (i), (ii) or (iii); we would then discover that the sceptic and the theist both have difficulty in supporting their assertions in ways that are not circular, or do not simply arise from their respective basic beliefs. We reach an impasse – the very impasse the argument from religious experience has been trying to escape, that is, having nothing to ground one's argument on but one's own belief. Proponents of the evidential value of religious experiences may be rationally justified on the basis of their own presuppositions, but are not on the basis of the sceptic's, and vice versa. They may shift the burden of proof onto the sceptic, but the latter is likely to drop it as swiftly as they have.

In doing this, they have not created an indubitable foundation for believing the claims of religious experience. What they have done is to suggest that other kinds of experience which are generally considered reliable (sense experience, memory and the like) also rely on their own selves to provide grounds and justification for their claims. This is a very valuable critique. But there are nevertheless good reasons for saying that this does not confer parity on religious belief and other kinds of belief; chiefly, the alleged transcendence of God. So while the challenge to the foundation of *all* belief may go some way to placing the burden of proof on the sceptic to show what is deficient about religious doxastic practice as opposed to other practices which are usually taken to be uncontroversial, there is a wealth of reasons why religious experience is more problematic and controversial than sight, smell, or memory.

Problems in reporting

Unreliable witnesses

We have already examined the question of naturalistic explanations for religious experience, which clearly could be a major reason for rejecting the claims made on the basis of it. Here I shall just add to defences against this challenge.

One challenge arises from an alleged inability to distinguish psychotic from religious experiences. Davis observes, however, that religious communities themselves usually contain a distinction between healthy and unhealthy mystical or other religious experiences. She acknowledges that there may be no 'intrinsic' differences between experiences which theists reject as pathological and many that they accept, if what is meant by that is that subjects are able to consult background knowledge and the way things are before they can be sure that the way things seem to them is not the way things really are. But she observes that the same is true for vivid sensory hallucinations. If I see snakes coming out of the wall, I cannot 'double-check' and look at how things really are outside my hallucination, in order to verify or falsify my perception. No one suggests that because of this, all sense experiences ought to be understood as hallucinatory. 'To insist that the experiences themselves must carry some mark of their veridicality would be to impose far harsher conditions on religious experience than on non-religious perceptual experiences.'[24]

Secondly, it seems that many people who have religious experiences cannot be considered pathological. What of those who are? Surely we can discount their experiences. Gellman in fact disagrees, suggesting that there is no reason to believe that in the pathological cases the subject is *not* really experiencing God. Moreover, although the evidential value of the pathological experiences is weak, it nevertheless still might provide some evidence for the existence of God. Indeed, he argues, it may not be that being pathological makes it more likely just to *think* you are experiencing God, it may also make it more likely for you actually to experience God. Such people may actually have a heightened sensitivity, an increased openness to extraordinary experiences, or a greater need to experience God.[25]

Reports of absence

Not all people report religious experience; some report a definite absence of any religious feeling or experience. Indeed, some have actively tried yet failed to have any experience of God. Should this not therefore be allowed as evidence *against* the existence of a God? Why should the experience of religious people be given priority as 'evidence' over against the experience of the atheist or sceptic? Michael Martin has argued, for example, that the absence of a chair is good evidence for there being no chair in the room.[26] Bertrand Russell adds the further objection that not only do some fail to experience God, even when they try; but even to do so makes questionable demands to change the observer himself:

> The man of science, when he wishes others to see what he has seen, arranges his microscope or telescope; that is to say, he makes changes in the external world, but demands of the observer only normal eyesight. The mystic, on the other hand, demands changes in the observer, by fasting, by breathing exercises, and by a careful abstention from external observation.[27]

Several arguments have been put forward for why there should be a lack of parity between reports of presence and reports of absence. One might account for the differences by suggesting analogies with aesthetic experiences. I may experience rapture while listening to the quintet in Wagner's *Die Meistersinger*, because of the stunning counterpoint and the extra-musical significance of the *Leitmotiv* and the way they are transformed. But if you are tone-deaf and musically ill-educated to boot, you will not. Does that mean I am hallucinating the aural perceptions, or my delight is deluded? Should the judgment of my sister-in-law and her colour-blind husband be given equal weight when choosing new curtains? Should we expect a professional wine-taster and a teetotaller to report identical reactions when tasting Lalou Bize-Leroy's latest Burgundy?

   The point of this analogy is that even sense-experiences which are in principle public and available to all may not be reported, or reported identically, by everyone. The differences could be down to different abilities, capacities, or education in the subject of the experience. Not all the features of the experience (or lack of experience) can be ascribed *tout court* to the 'object'. The nature of an experience, or having the experience at all, may also be down to the subject. In this case, the variation is no more problematic than the variability of human beings generally.

It can also be plausibly argued that reports of *presence* and reports of *absence* cannot be given the same weight, nor do they have the same implications for the existence of the thing. Let us imagine that Kimo fails to see a dolphin on Tuesday afternoon when he is surfing at the North Shore of O'ahu, even though Hoku claimed to see dolphins there the day before. Do we know for certain that there were no dolphins in the ocean off Waimea at that time? They can be difficult for a surfing human to spot. Moreover, are we justified in claiming that, because Kimo failed to see one at the Banzai Pipeline on Tuesday afternoon, dolphins must be as mythical as dragons or unicorns?

The first point is that there might be a disparity between claims of presence and of absence if the thing in question is shy or hard for us to perceive. Gellman articulates it as the difference between observing the absence of something and trying but failing to observe the presence of something; sometimes these two are effectively the same, but not always.[28] To know for certain that something is absent, we need enough information and experience of it, and of what constitutes 'thoroughly searching' for that kind of entity. In Gellman's view, we do not have enough knowledge to say when or whether S has *failed to experience God*, or S has *experienced God's absence*.[29]

We cannot always extend the claim of absence of X to a claim of the non-existence of X, moreover, we cannot always extend the claim of the non-existence of X here and now to the claim that no X's exist anywhere. Presumably Martin does not really mean to claim that evidence for there being no chair in a given room at a given time is reason to believe that no chairs exist anywhere, at any time. The appropriate analogy to Martin's example, then, would be this: one could say that there was evidence for the absence of God to a certain person at a certain time. But just as one cannot claim, based on specific claims of absence, that there must be no chairs or no dolphins at all, one is not entitled to generalise that there must be no divine being because some people, unlike others, fail to experience one on named occasions.[30]

The sceptic could reject this claim, as Martin does, by saying that because God is allegedly 'omnipresent', according to the believer, She must always be 'there', wherever and whenever 'there' is, to be experienced. But few believers feel themselves committed to this point of view. Most are comfortable with the suggestion that there may be reasons why someone does not have an experience of God: God's freedom or sovereignty, problems to do with the individual in question, his willingness or openness to the experience, and so on. The question of whether or not God can or will be perceived by a certain individual may not be a simple question of God's 'actual' 'presence' or 'absence', but may depend on other factors. It is interesting, moreover, that the experience of the absence of God is a salient theme in Christian mystical literature, often understood as a crucial phase in the mystical journey.[31]

Conflicting reports

Flew, among others, has challenged the notion that religious experience can provide any support or evidence for religious belief on the grounds that what or who is allegedly experienced is so various that the testimony is in conflict.[32] The challenge to the believer who wants to maintain that religious experience can provide such support or evidence is this: he must rule out all experiences which don't agree with his own theology, on the basis that they are misguided or fallacious. Once he does this, he ought to say how fallacious experiences arise. In which case, then, the same argumentation can be applied to experiences in his own tradition, which Flew presumes the believer would wish to avoid. Or, if he wants to maintain the possibility of different religions having valid experiences which can provide evidence for the existence of God, then he needs to provide some way of reconciling the diverse religious experiences without weakening their evidential value.

A variety of arguments have been deployed against this sceptical challenge. Difference in testimony does not necessitate, first, for example, that some might be right and others wrong. There can be conflicts in scientific testimony: as when there is agreement about the existence of something but not its nature (as in early research into AIDS: did it come from a virus, or combined assaults on the immune system?) Alston makes light of the difficulties of conflicting claims, in part by drawing on this kind of analogy with scientific discovery. It is not clear that the different revelations are incompatible, he suggests, partly because it is not clear what diversity can be embraced by the divine nature. Moreover, the fact of conflicts in beliefs does not mean that both believers cannot be rational – even if one is wrong. It can be rational to believe something incorrect, if the limited evidence one has points in that direction. Finally, sceptics often point to an unfavourable contrast between the diversity of religious opinions and scientific unanimity. However, Alston observes, there was no such unanimity in science 300 years ago. Perhaps religion is in a position comparable to that of science several centuries ago; perhaps now with the increased communication, awareness of and dialogue between religions, we are working towards a common understanding in religion too.[33] These reflections, though perhaps helpful, seem insufficient to deal with the intractable issues involved. Few believers who are not Anglo-Saxon analytic philosophers would be consoled by the suggestion that, although wrong, they are rational. I think most would prefer to be right, whether 'rationally justified' or not.

Swinburne advocates an 'ascent to generality'. Specific conflicts between religious claims are just that: conflicts between *specific* descriptions of the religious object. They do not support scepticism about all religious claims based on experience.[34] The conflicts can be avoided by avoiding detail, reducing the claim, and rising to a sufficiently general level of discussion so that conflicts do not appear. This may be useful advice for avoiding disputes in inter-faith dialogue, but it does nothing to resolve the philosophical problem of whether the contrasting claims from different religious traditions can all be accepted as true.

Davis claims that, while different types of numinous and mystical experience cannot all be reduced to 'the same type of experience with differing interpretations', nevertheless a complex reconciliation of mystical and numinous experiences is possible. She argues that most alleged conflict among mystical experience is superficial, and a less superficial reading indicates that mystics essentially have the sort of experience: 'freedom from all sense of time, space, personal identity, and multiplicity, which leaves them with a blissful, "naked awareness" of perfect unity and a sense that "this is it", the ultimate level of reality.'[35] Differences in description can arise from a number of factors; she points out that religious traditions themselves allow for diversity of experience, and that the major religions have thus developed theories to reconcile the apparently incompatible experiences and integrate them in one system. So she maintains that it is possible to distil a 'common core' to these experiences.[36]

Gellman provides several arguments to defeat the sceptic's challenge from diversity. He denies that most experiences amount to propositions about God which conflict with other peoples' propositions; most experiences of God pertain to that person alone, and are not in logical contradiction with God's communication to another. Even where the content of the experience was propositional and it conflicted with another proposition, it is not necessarily delusory that it was *God* who was experienced. Both people could have experienced God, and the incompatibility could be put down to 'local differences' in their two perceptions of Her.[37] One person may have misunderstood, or truly experienced God but only *imagined* what the revelation was; both of which can happen often enough between human beings without reducing our sense that such encounters are generally reliable.[38] Or the incompatibility could indeed originate from God, who may wish one person to believe one thing and another person something else. Further, it is not so much the case that all conflicts fall between religions; the differences in experience and testimony arise principally within the religious traditions themselves. It is harder to make the incompatibility argument work here than one might think, he alleges. Experiencing God as 'loving' and as 'just' might *feel* very different, but they are not logically incompatible such as to preclude both being true. Experiences are only incompatible if one claim is that God's nature is exclusively one kind, and another claim is that God's character is of a different kind that is logically incompatible with the first.[39]

Gellman's answer to the dilemma posed by 'multiple theisms' is to speak of 'networks' of experiential knowledge about God, which build up over time and inevitably diverge.[40] This breadth of knowledge which encompasses resemblance and divergence in a single 'network' can also be ascribed to different religious traditions. There will of course be differences between one network or set and another, but these differences exist in a larger context of similar experiences of God. 'The situation here no more bars the identification of God from one member of a network set to another than it does with respect to varied richly endowed ways of identifying a single human person.'[41]

There is one great stumbling-block, however, to unifying religions by claiming that they all ultimately worship the same God, though they perceive God differently. That is the fact that some religions do not believe in a God, or they do not conceive of Ultimate Reality as being personal. Gellman however asserts that God exists in inexhaustible fullness, in plenitude, which can never be encompassed in a single experience or aspect. Even being 'personal' is too limited. Borrowing Buber's idea that God is personal and enters into a personal relationship with us, but the concept of personhood is utterly incapable of describing the nature of God, Gellman suggests that God could be experienced either as personal or impersonal without a real contradiction.[42]

Confirmation and falsification

One difficulty many have with taking religious experiences at face value (or allowing them to have *any* value) is the difficulties that are said to exist in confirming or falsifying them and their claims. First of all, it is said, simply seeming to have an experience which has the nature of 'being *of* something' does not entail that that thing exists. Allegedly having an experience *of* God does not entail that God exists. Flew, for example, objects to making inferences from religious experience, 'considered as a purely psychological phenomenon, to conclusions about the supposed objective religious truths'.[43] It is not difficult to make short work of this objection. How can I argue from my necessarily subjective experience of seeing my word processor (considered as a purely psychological phenomenon) to my objective claim that it exists? And yet I make this sort of assumption continually, and could hardly cope in the world without doing so.

But the disquiet of the sceptic cannot be dispatched so easily. Should there be any doubt about my sense perceptions, I can call in another witness. 'Do *you* see aliens in my garden, or am I going mad?' Or if the evidence of my eyes is in question, I can test other modes of sense-perception: try to grab an alien and feel it, smell it, hear it squeaking when I squeeze it. Neither of these options is generally thought to be possible with God. Russell complains:

> When a man of science tells us the result of an experiment, he also tells us how the experiment was performed; others can repeat it, and if the result is not confirmed it is not accepted as true; but many men might put themselves into the situation in which the mystic's vision occurred without obtaining the same revelation .... Science depends upon perception and inference; its credibility is due to the fact that the perceptions are such as any observer can test. The mystic himself may be certain that he knows, and has no need of scientific tests; but those who are asked to accept his testimony will subject it to the same kind of scientific tests as those applied to men who say they have been to the North Pole.[44]

Perhaps this shows a touching faith in the repeatability of experiments; or the narrow view that all empirical data that is reliable results from experiments under the control of scientists. Vulcanologists have difficulty in repeating experiences exactly to double-check results, as do those who study other aspects of the climate and the natural world.

Still, sensory perceptions are more easily confirmed or falsified in a second manner: if no one is available to corroborate my perception, I can check again on a later occasion to see if the experience recurs. When I become familiar with the situation, I can even make predictions: 'The aliens never turn up on weekends, but they always arrive on a weekday if I've baked my famous lemon cake. So if I bake my lemon cake on Monday, they should appear by the time it's cooled enough to eat.' But many religious believers are reluctant to make predictions about how and why God will or must appear. (A few do, but are usually embarrassed by predictive failure.)

Thirdly, if my husband does not, in fact, see aliens in my garden after I serve up my lemon cake or at any other time, it is usually considered to be disconfirmation or falsification of my claims to have seen aliens and to bake the universe's best lemon cake. Religious believers are often charged with refusing to let anything falsify or count against their religious beliefs. They have shown themselves capable of producing plausible arguments for the non-appearance of God to many: those not favoured with an experience of God have blinded their eyes, they are not among the chosen.

So, the sceptic complains, nothing is allowed to falsify an experience or count against it; if someone predicts that God will appear on a certain date, and God does not, most would-be prophets and their followers claim that they had just miscalculated the date, rather than concluding that God doesn't exist after all. This refusal to allow testimony *against* ever to count as valid, according to the critic, vitiates its claim to count as respectable evidence, for there can then be no basis for adjudicating experiences in the case of God, since we don't know what makes for delusory religious experiences. Therefore no experiences can count as evidence, Rowe argues.[45]

So the two most common tests of someone's sensory experience – corroboration and prediction – are not generally admitted as fair tests of God's existence by religious believers. On the one hand, it is difficult to obtain any kind of independent confirmation of someone's religious experience; and on the other hand, one cannot predict the mysterious ways of God. In the face of these sceptical difficulties, is Swinburne's Principle of Credulity really enough to defend the credibility of religious experience? Might not something more be required by way of confirmation of the veridicality of the experiences?

Attempts at saying that falsification is possible

Supporters of the evidential value of religious experience have with great energy attempted to meet the challenge of falsification by providing lists of criteria or conditions which could challenge the veridicality of a given religious experience. One needs to be clear here that what is on offer is not, so to speak, the global falsification of the validity or veridicality of *all* religious experience; but rather the means to identify spurious or deluded experiences. This is done precisely to safeguard the evidential value of *some* experiences.

Davis, rather encyclopaedically developing Swinburne's 'special considerations', lists numerous 'challenges' that can be made with respect to the description, the subject or the object of the experience.[46] 'Description-related challenges' include obvious logical inconsistencies or incoherence, conflicts with background knowledge, or faults in beliefs taken to be background knowledge, such as claims to see an animal now extinct, or conflicts between the subject's actual and expected behaviour if he had had the experience, evidence that the subject is a habitual liar or prone to exaggeration, or has a poor memory, or is not competent in terminology used,[47] or is retrospectively interpreting the experience in an inappropriate way. Subject-related challenges include a past unreliability of the subject, or that the subject was in a certain state such that experiences under those conditions usually are unveridical, or that the subject would likely have had that experience whether the percept was there or not, or the subject hasn't had the training necessary for that type of experience, etc. Object-related challenges include conflicts with the background evidence: that against the background evidence, it is probable that the alleged object of the experience was not present, or if present was not the cause of the experience, or that it is highly unlikely the percept was there as described.

Yandell distinguishes between 'polar', 'collegial' and 'lateral' forms of confirmation or falsification. 'Polar' disconfirmation is a situation in which not experiencing God could be counted as evidence against God's existence.[48] Yandell argues that this kind of disconfirmation is nonsensical in relation to an omnipotent, omniscient God, who presumably has the power to prevent Herself being experienced.[49] 'Lateral' disconfirmation occurs if something very like the Object has a quality which contradicts qualities the Object ought to have. Thus, if one had an experience of an omniscient, omnipotent, awesome being who was horrid and evil, this could count as experiential evidence against the proposition that an omniscient, omnipotent, awesome and all-good and holy being exists.[50] 'Collegial' disconfirmation occurs if it is logically possible for an experience to take place which would provide evidence of O lacks A, e.g. God exists but is not holy. Where it is logically necessary that O has A, and an experience takes place that contradicts that notion, one has collegial disconfirmation. (Where, for example, one experiences something very like O but lacking A, like an evil omnipotent being that one cannot call God.)

Yandell claims that, while the theist must surrender polar disconfirmation in the case of God, one can conjoin the other two. One could then construct possible disconfirming experiences, such as: 'What I thought was God turned out not to be holy. This putative-God is omnipotent, and if so then there cannot be a real omnipotent God that is holy. (This assumes, as monotheists mostly assert, that there cannot be two omnipotent beings). Putative-God has some of the properties of God, but lacks a property God must have, and it is not likely that there be two beings with the properties that God has.'[51] If Yandell is right, then the believer in religious experience could allow for the possibility of disconfirmation in a manner that is not self-contradictory or absurd.

Yandell also allows that there are situations which could disqualify a given religious experience as worthy of being taken as evidence; but he disputes that this fact disqualifies religious experience as a whole. First, if there are conditions that make it possible to have delusory experiences of a numinous being, if one were in such a condition, one could know it, then one could know that it would call into question the veridicality of that experience.[52] One *can* know that an experience is nonveridical, he maintains against the sceptic's complaint, if an anti-theistic argument succeeds, or if the 'putative information content' of an experience conflicted 'with the information content of most others in a context in which there was no good reason to overturn the majority testimony'.[53] Specifically, numinous monotheistic religious experience could be shown to be nonveridical if any of the following were true: if an appeal to evil disproves theism; if there is a contradiction in the concept of a numinous being; if some other contradicting variety of religious experience shows that numinous monotheistic experience is non-veridical; or if some purely secular explanation is shown to be sufficient in a way that rules out causation by anything numinous.[54]

Confirmation?

Attempts have also been made to supply criteria for confirming the validity or veridicality of religious experiences, though this is more challenging. Gutting argues that we would expect, if there was 'a very good and very powerful being concerned about us', that those who have had those experiences would have them again; that others would have similar experiences; and that those who have them would be empowered to lead better lives. All three of these conditions he sees fulfilled; so religious experiences of God's presence can be taken to establish Her existence. 'The experiences themselves give *prima facie* warrant to the claim that he exists, and the fulfilment of the expectations induced by the assumption that the experiences are veridical provides the further support needed for ultimate warrant.'[55]

Davis provides four criteria for genuine versus delusive mystical experiences that exist in several different religious traditions: internal and external consistency; the moral and spiritual 'fruits' or consequences of the experience; consistency with orthodox doctrine of the religious tradition in question; and the evaluation of the subject's general psychological and mental condition. There are many kinds of criteria other than sense perception which we use to assess things of undisputed reality and importance: 'other people's emotions and character, causality, the passage of time, and the meaning of words and signs.'[56]

Foreshadowing Alston's later work, Davis calls for an argument which does not treat religious experience as analogous to some other kind of experience less controversial; but rather treats it 'as one type of perceptual experience among others'.[57]

Yandell observes that a degree of corroboration is possible with religious experience; we can compare descriptions of experiences in different times and places, cultures and religious traditions, in a way similar to the useful comparisons made with sensory descriptions, for example when testing an astronomical theory against past records of astronomical events made from with different cultures.[58] Allowing for different metaphors and symbols, Yandell finds 'considerable agreement' between the accounts. One can thus draw useful corroborating evidence from different cultures, places and times. This diversity of confirming evidence, in his view, supports the claims of religious experience against the charges that it cannot be corroborated by other persons or the other senses of the subject in the way that seeing a visible object can.[59]

*

So a number of arguments for the existence of a Deity based on religious experience have been devised, but they are not a very diverse group of arguments. Meanwhile there remains a body of objections to taking religious experience seriously as a source of knowledge. Although the cases put forward by Swinburne, Davis, Yandell, Gellman and their colleagues address these challenges, perhaps one could step outside the accepted circle of argument, evidence and proof to look at the question afresh.

6. Or Maybe Not?

Another way of looking at it

A rather surprising analogy

There is nothing like a telling analogy, so let us explore a new one. I apologise if some readers are offended by it. (They could perhaps substitute 'falling in love' for the offending analogue, though it won't fit perfectly.) I can only say that I tried, but failed, to find a more prosaic one that has all the features and characteristics that I want to explore.

Let us imagine someone who is a sceptic about orgasms. Prudence has never had one, nor seen anyone else have one, although she has many friends who claim to have had one.

Her orgasmic friends, who tell her of the bliss that these experiences bring and the positive benefits such experiences have in their lives (relaxation and stress reduction, improved health and happiness, better marriages, etc.) try their best to convert her. They tell her what she must to do have one, go into great detail about techniques, and so on. But their advice is conflicting, and moreover, like Russell, Prudence is sceptical of the requirement that changes are demanded in the observer in order to observe the phenomenon. Nevertheless, curiosity and fair-mindedness prevail and she follows the quite different, indeed conflicting, instructions given by two friends on different occasions, but without the desired result. Like Russell, she expects that as a person of science she ought to be able to repeat the experiment and get the same result; so when she is not successful in achieving the same result using the specified methodology, her suspicions are deepened.

Her scepticism is further increased by the conflicting testimony contained in others' reports of their experiences. Classical French sources describe it as '*le petit* mort'; but her cousin, a recent convert, paints a vivid picture of herself at the relevant moment which sounds anything but dead. How are these to be reconciled, without either doubting the veracity of one source, or concluding that they must be referring to different things altogether? Prudence decides to make allowances for poetic language and personal differences. However, her older brother speaks of 'an internal explosion' (which sounds neither pleasurable nor beneficial, thus conflicting with other claims made on the behalf of such experiences), and which is very specific to one area, very localised; while her best friend says it's like wave upon wave of ecstasy, rolling over her whole body (which sounds nothing like an explosion, and precisely contradicts her brother's report of anatomic localisation). These two reports cannot be harmonised, or reduced one to the other. And this troubles her, for she normally thinks of both these trusted intimates as truthful. Comparing their descriptions point by point, it is difficult to believe that they are really having the same experience. But a more direct contradiction between her two closest sources is that her brother says such a thing can happen only once at a time, while her best friend says it can happen again and again in one session. Returning to her brother to put this question to him again, he flatly contradicts this, and declares it impossible for the experience to come again right after the first one.

Still more contradictions attend on the question of whether such experiences are 'of someone else' or not. Most of Prudence's friends say that the experience is an experience of someone else, someone else indeed who 'gives' it to you, and that this is the whole point; that it would be 'meaningless' otherwise. Others, including her teenage younger brother, have only had experiences of this kind that involve no other being whatsoever, and when the allegation of the 'mean-inglessness' of such an experience is put to him, he can make no sense of it. The situation is further confounded by this younger brother, who seems to imply that this experience can take you unawares, when you aren't even expecting it, nor doing anything that should lead to it, like when you're asleep. Meanwhile, an energetic friend reports such experiences not only of *one* entity but of *multiple* entities.

This is an even more irreconcilable contradiction than the conflict concerning repetition of the event, for that one could have been explained away by some incapacity of her brother, or some extraordinary talent on the part of her best friend. But this one appears to be a logical contradiction. Either someone else has to be there, and give it to you, or there is no one there and no one required. And either the one who is experienced at that moment is single, or multiple. She appeals to her older brother for an explanation, who unhelpfully indicates that all are true. So everyone who has one, has them all these ways? No, some may only have it in one of these ways. Then how do you know that it is the same experience they are having? Prudence wants to know, reasonably enough. How can you claim they are the same experience? Do they all feel the same, have the same phenomenal features? No. Are they of the same intentional object? No. Her brother finally becomes somewhat inarticulate on this point, and mutters that all these are possible, just, well, different, and finally ends by echoing her best friend, who maintained: 'You can't really describe it. Words don't get it across. You just have to experience it for yourself.' This is precisely what our heroine cannot do, so this is rather unhelpful as well as unconvincing. In the face of all these contradictions, Prudence is now a confirmed unbeliever.[1]

Although friends have been willing to boast about their experiences, they are strangely coy about actually letting her observe them having one. Why should that be the case if they are telling the truth? So Prudence secretes herself in the closet of her younger brother, who allegedly has these experiences regularly. What she observes, while perhaps novel, is singularly unedifying; and it does nothing to convince her that actually experiencing one of these for oneself can possibly be as her friends describe.

Her intense curiosity and puzzlement persist, and when Prudence becomes a medical student she decides to conduct some proper scientific research into the matter. She wires up several volunteers with many electrodes, placed in the most relevant areas, and with a few extra impartial witnesses, stands in intense scrutiny of the experimental subjects – who fail to achieve their aim under these laboratory conditions. They maintain that it is the conditions, not their ability, still less the experience they describe, that is at fault. She is about to abandon her researches with the conclusion that it is either a hoax or else all these people are highly suggestible, when her indefatigable younger brother comes through with the sought-after result in the laboratory, despite the unfavourable ambience. Prudence is at last able to measure a variety of things about the event.

At last she knows the truth. Something does happen, but it is purely physiological. It can be adequately explained in purely materialist terms, its cause (just a very simple stimulus), its mechanism (very like an involuntary reflex, of which there are other uncontested examples), and its effects, for which she can easily conjecture an evolutionary explanation, in terms of selfish genes and their mode of transport.

Her friends, while perhaps not exactly lying, were at least grossly exaggerating or merely deluded when they spoke of ecstasy, being out of their heads or beside themselves, feelings of union with another, and the like. This at most may, as Russell puts it, express an emotion, not a fact; and it is due to their inability to separate emotional importance from scientific validity. Further, when her best friend went on to draw conclusions from her experience and make claims about her partner – his love for her, his concern about how she felt, his desire to please her, his acceptance of her for who she was, his fidelity, and so on – it is clear that these beliefs were motivated by emotional needs and wish-fulfilment, and in no way justified as deductions from the experiences.

If the objections considered in the previous chapters mean that personal experience cannot serve as evidence for religious truth, then we have every reason to doubt the veridicality of orgasms: the credibility of claims of an orgasmic experience will suffer under all of the objections raised. Not everyone has one, including those who try religiously, and we can investigate a number of different frames of reference to understand this: psychological, physiological, interpersonal. Those who do have them give reports and descriptions which frequently conflict; yet not only are these not allowed to vitiate the claims to such experience, the very different experiences are still somehow recognised as 'the same thing'. Perfectly good naturalistic explanations exist that exclude all reference to the emotional or ecstatic phenomena that are often claimed for such experiences, and which say nothing about any purported 'meaningfulness' to the subject. It is also either extremely difficult or impossible to confirm or falsify certain aspects of the experience. We may measure the brain waves of someone meditating and see something physiologically measurable, such as an alteration in their brain waves, but this tells us nothing about any religious import or the content of their experience, still less establish the truth of any religious claims. Similarly, physiological evidence may establish one aspect of someone's orgasmic claim, without saying anything about the phenomenology or the experiential aspects of the event: how it felt. Yet those who are experienced can ask questions to verify whether someone experienced the phenomenon in question, but the questions and the answers all presuppose a prior commitment to and experience of the thing in question.

Getting personal

Why *this* analogy?

Perhaps the category of 'perception' is not the best category for understanding and interpreting spiritual experiences. If the analogy fits, and convinces, might this be because such experiences more resemble interpersonal exchanges than moments of sensory perception?

One alternative to the classification of religious experience as a 'mode of perception' is to see it as a mode of personal encounter. As we have seen, not everyone is satisfied with the notion that God can be the 'object' of experience; and therefore, not every religious believer would be happy with the suggestion that religious experience is appropriately compared to the sensory experience of a tree or a chair. The analogy with sense perception distorts the personal, even intimate nature of religious experience. For such people, a more appropriate analogy is the experience of other persons.

Alston very briefly alludes to the possibility of such an analogy, but does not explore it. Davis lists a number of similarities between religious experiences and interpersonal encounters.[2] But Davis disputes that this personal encounter analogy can extend sufficiently far to be an adequate conceptualisation of the divine-human relationship. She notes that there are also serious disanalogies between experiences of the divine and personal relationships. We can feel certain about something and not be right; so too with an I-Thou encounter. We can be mistaken in thinking we have knowledge of someone on the basis of a personal relationship, she observes. This indeed is true, but is it really a disanalogy? Is it not rather an unfortunate truth about both, and therefore strengthens the analogy? I can be wrongly, but implacably, convinced that I perceive your 'real' motives, thoughts, desires. People can also have unshakeable convictions that God has told them something or other, and perhaps they can also be quite wrong about it. Not only is this not a disanalogy, it isn't even a ground against using personal knowledge as a model for religious knowledge. We can be mistaken in *any* knowledge claim (with the exception of kinds of knowledge that are said to be incorrigible, if any there be).

The most crucial disanalogy in her view, however, is that the things we do to test the veridicality of our experience of one another can only show whether an *individual* experience is veridical or not; they cannot show that such experiences *in general* are veridical. Some general principle of rationality is needed for that. However, while conclusions based on personal encounters in general are uncontroversially held to be veridical, despite the occasional misunderstanding, conclusions based on religious experiences *in general* are not. That is the very point in question. She concludes that this analogy (like that with sense perception) only succeeds if it is part of a more general framework based on more basic premises.[3]

Only succeeds in what? In providing a fruitful model for understanding religious experience, or in providing a knock-down argument for the existence of God? Only in the most abnormal situation would we be inclined to argue for the existence of someone based on the claim to know them well. The personalist would say that this in fact represents one of the *strongest* points of analogy between human and divine relationships: that one does not speak about the one in question as an 'object of knowledge' so much as relate to Her personally. Only a philosopher who had lost his grip on everyday interpersonal dealings would think it necessary or even appropriate to infer the existence of the person to whom he had just spoken from the fact of their conversation.

Davis' distinction between individual encounters and encounters 'in general' is also misplaced. It may be true that our personal encounters 'in general' are veridical with only an occasional mistake, though one could not establish this in any non-circular way, that is, without using precisely the interpersonal knowledge that is in question. It is certainly true that the veridicality of religious experience in general is controversial. But shouldn't it be? Few religious believers, if they were to survey the religious experiences and claims – not just of saintly mystics but also of men of war – would want to assert so loosely that religious experiences are veridical 'in general'. What one asserts on the basis of a personal relationship with the divine is *only* a specific, personal claim. Moreover, Davis is clearly still working within a tacit model of perception here. What does it mean to say that our personal encounters are veridical 'in general'? That we almost always understand each other accurately, and rarely misinterpret others' intentions, and only infrequently misrepresent what others have said? Hardly. All it can mean is: that we rarely hallucinate seeing another human being. But that demonstrates that she is still thinking about interpersonal knowledge fundamentally *as perception*: all that is 'personal' in her shift of viewpoint is the shift from seeing an object like a chair to seeing a person.

Davis' misunderstanding of the personalist position is to assume that it, in common with most of the current discussion in analytical philosophy of religion, sees religious experience as a kind of perception, and secondly to see it as directed towards the assertion of the existence of the object in question. The real utility of the model of personal encounter is, however, found in the question of understanding and interpretation, not the existence of something; its concerns are hermeneutical, not ontological or metaphysical. One appeals to personal knowledge to justify one's claims about another person in issues of understanding and misunderstanding, of slander and misrepresentation; not in issues of existence or non-existence.

The personalists

There is a philosophical stance called 'Personalism' which is quite different to the style of philosophy in which these debates have been undertaken. Sometimes called 'Dialogism', its chief exponents, who were influenced by Hamann, wrote mostly in the first half of the twentieth century.[4]

For the Personalists, the relationship is the fundamental principle of thinking and being. A human being cannot be viewed in isolation, but is constituted by his or her relationships. 'In the beginning is relation.'[5]

This conviction also extends to epistemology. The personalists are sceptical about objectivity. This is partly because of its implicit denial of one's own standpoint: 'I really believe that a philosophy, to be adequate, must rise out of thinking that is done from the personal standpoint of the thinker. To achieve being objective, the thinker must proceed boldly from his own subjective situation.'[6] But it is also because of the detachment from others that it is felt to entail. 'No one can have an "objective", standpointless, and perspectiveless relation to the spiritual in others. The I has no absolute existence, for it exists only in relationship to the Thou.'[7]

This dialogical, intersubjective, relational stance in turn becomes the ground for articulating the relationship between human beings and God. For the personalists, the relationship between humanity and God is no more philosophically difficult than relationships between human beings; for the relational principle of dialogue exists in both, and the basic understanding of 'Person' applies to God (however differently) as well as to human beings: 'The I and Thou of human discourse is without more ado also the I and Thou between God and [humanity]. The distinction between immanence and transcendence disappears in speech.'[8] In fact, our human relationships also point us to God: 'Every particular *Thou* is a glimpse through to the eternal *Thou*; by means of every particular *Thou* the primary word addresses the eternal *Thou* .... The inborn *Thou* is realised in each relation and consummated in none. It is consummated only in the direct relation with the *Thou* that by its nature cannot become *It*.'[9]

'The relation with man is the real simile of the relation with God; in it true address receives true response; except that in God's response everything, the universe, is made manifest as language.'[10] What this relational approach suggests is the central role that language plays in intersubjectivity, a point stressed by Ebner. How else is a relationship between 'I and Thou' shown, except in dialogue? It is through and in language that human beings are human, are persons. The human person is characterised by the fact that everything that it is can speak and be expressed in language. But language also reveals to us our neediness, our lack of self-sufficiency. In conversation, I come in contact with another, over whom I do not have disposal. And that turns us to other human beings; if I only exist in language, the relationality of dialogue means I need the other in order to exist. Every sentence means the relationship of the I and the you, Ebner tells us; the use of words is always fundamentally the relationship of I to the You.[11]

Neither of us is the origin of the other, nor of language, Ebner reflects. Nor is language the origin of us, nor our ground. The origin in itself remains dark and cannot be expressed in a word; but the word God refers to it. Language names its own origin 'God'.[12]

The relationship we have with the origin of our being is revealed in the fact that my fundamental experience is not of being in the first person but in the second person: not 'I' but 'you' – one who is addressed, who is always called by the origin into dialogue. The beginning of my own speaking is grounded in the fact that God as origin calls to me in the granting of language. I find myself and my self-expression in being addressed by the origin of the relationship of speech.

This also means, conversely, I can never have a relationship with this origin that consists in 'talking about' the origin of my being in the third person rather than the second. The origin can never become an object, something about which I speak; I cannot talk of or about God, only *to* God.[13] This relationship of address is the only original relationship I can have to the origin. It is the basis of every portrayal of God and every name for God.[14]

In the moment in which one steps from the sense of 'Thou art' into a sentence in the third person – as it were to grasp God in a predication of existence in the 'objective' sphere of the third person, outside the human-personal relationship of 'Thou art' – one loses God in his reality.[15]

Conclusion

Our surprising analogue, coupled with a relational or 'personalist' framework, proves quite fruitful in exploring other thorny questions that arise in considering religious experience. What sort of intentional structure does it exhibit? Is an orgasm an experience 'of' someone or not? Well, yes and no. If you have this experience with the participation of someone else, does that person 'give' you the experience or cause it? Again, yes or no, depending on what exactly is meant. It could be said, quite correctly, that 'an orgasm' (rather than some specific sensation in a causal relation to the orgasm) is an experience 'of your-self'. It's different from the feeling of someone else stroking your arm; for it is 'internal to yourself' in a sense. But does the fact that you experience it 'in your-self' mean that you are deluded to think another was involved in the experience? Clearly not. Thus we have a model for how something could be experienced 'in oneself', 'of oneself', while it still makes sense to speak of the intrinsic partici-pation of another. When a friend tells us of a rapturous love experience with her new beau, we don't dismiss it like this: 'It was *your body* having the orgasm, so no one else was there' – as we might dismiss a religious experience as 'it was just your subconscious'. It was indeed her body, but not in opposition to the involvement of another. That was the joy of it. Something similar might be the case with religious experiences. Something can be experienced 'within' oneself, mediated through one's own being, without entailing that one's own being was the sole cause of the experience, excluding the participation of another. At the same time, it seems inadequate to define an orgasm just as 'an experience of one's lover'; so too with the definition of a religious experience as 'an experi-ence of God'. That would seem to be a presupposition of such an experience, rather than its definition.

This peculiar intentional structure – that this particular experience 'of another' can only be experienced through oneself – can also clarify the confu-sions that surround psychological questions about spirituality. If God is immanent within an experience, facilitating the deeper experience of oneself the way a lover does, it can be quite germane to employ the critiques of psychology and physiology in trying to understand the experience. Much enlightenment could be had by embracing such forms of examination. Most people in psycho-analysis analyse their sexual experiences for what they reveal about themselves, without thinking that such analysis explains away the existence of their partners. Their analysts, I presume, do not then inform them that the experience wasn't really sexual, because it was shown to be 'just psychological'. After such an analysis of a religious experience, there is no need to discard the theological aspects either. What such analysis can do, however, is to explore and clarify which aspects of the experience – spiritual *or* sexual – may be due to the subject's own distorting interpretation.

Still considering psychology or psychopathology, in our analogue we can also see a way that someone can have both religious and sexual experiences that are odd, 'perverted' or 'psychotic' – and while it can be undeniable that the experi-ence happened as described, that does not oblige us to share their views, join in their practices, or in any way endorse what has occurred, even if we believe in what you might call the 'veridicality' of it.

The question of meaning arises here too. In our analogue, we can also see distinguishable levels of physiology and a super-physiological import that is given to the experience. 'Meaningless sex' is a phrase that is often heard, which only makes sense if sometimes sex does have a 'meaning' over and above all the other ingredients which qualify an event to be 'sex'. That the physiological events can be induced without love or desire in no way entails that one is deluded to say that *other* experiences of the same kind *do* have a meaning that is absent in those rudimentary cases.

The question of interpretation in connection with the event also arises press-ingly in love acts. How should one interpret such an event, what difference should it make to one's future decisions, plans, and commitments? The kind of interpretative framework we are considering here is one that is relational; to adopt this framework and to use it *puts you in a relationship*. Whether we are thinking of the love of a man or the love of God, all one's experience, one's whole life could be interpreted and related to this relationship; within this frame-work. In the case of religious experience, it becomes clear then how experiences that are otherwise 'aesthetic' might also be 'religious', in the same way that for a couple hearing 'their song' is a 'love' experience as well as a musical one. In this way, all experience could be 'religious', just as every part of life can be related to one's love of a spouse. At the same time, it is possible to distinguish orgasms from fond thoughts, and likewise one can distinguish spiritually uplifting experiences of nature from the more overwhelming experiences of encounter that some report.

Moreover, the circularity or spiral character of experience and interpretation is evident here also. How one interprets the experience strongly affects its nature or how it is experienced; and the experience likewise affects the kind of inter-pretation one comes up with, and it is difficult to say which comes first. If the interpretation is a happy one, the experience might be more pleasurable, and vice versa. But if the interpretation can affect the quality or the perceived meaning of the experience, does that compromise the subject's report? One might say, 'You wouldn't have enjoyed it if you hadn't believed that he loved you'; but does one conclude from this that her enjoyment was not legitimately part of the experi-ence, since it came from her interpretation? In fact, our analogue suggests that a rigid distinction between experience and interpretation is misguided; not least because the interpretation is *part of* the experience. Does one tell the rape victim that, while the physical pain was part of the 'core' of the experience, the humil-iation was only her 'interpretation'?

And again, the larger interpretative context plays a role in how one experi-ences the event. Wider cultural and social factors, as well as personal, religious or familial ones, can shape the experience as 'fulfilling' or 'dirty', as 'shameful' or as something to boast about. And yet, while powerful, it is still possible for an event to transcend the shaping tendencies of a certain framework. One could be raised in a context in which such experiences are seen as shameful, shocking, and dirty, and then have an overpowering experience with a loved one which caused one to rethink the values of one's family, religion or culture – thus begin-ning to transcend it.

The importance of language in what goes forward and how it is understood is seen in both cases. There is always the temptation to say that an experience could not be adequately captured in words. But, true though this may be, it is also true that the experience cannot be adequately captured *without* words. What are acts of love without love-talk? And how best do you know how your partner has felt, what your partner has experienced, what the significance of the event was for him? Do such words – even if felt to be a pale version of the feelings and sensations – obscure the truth of the event, or in fact help to constitute it?

Russell's objection to changes to the observer being required seems foolish in the case of our analogue; it is not at all unreasonable to say an orgasm just cannot be had by simply sitting in one's study and introspecting. It does not call into question the reality of the experience at all; it simply indicates the special kind of experience that it is. Something similar might hold for spiritual experience as well. There are many examples of uncontroversial experiences that can only be had if one moderates oneself in some way, or even undergoes some specific training: winning a dressage competition, being able to hear the inner parts in four-part harmony or being able to discern whether a wine is oxidised or not. The special demands placed on the observer, the modifications made, do not make the experiences unveridical.

Likewise, the fact that no one else can scrutinise the experience need not be a sign of suspicion, but simply a sign of the kind of experience it is. Many experiences are 'non-transferable'; in the sense that although they can be described, although people can have them together, although people can understand one another's experience – nevertheless one cannot have this experience 'on behalf of' another, or feel someone else's feeling. But the same can be said of pain, and no one really doubts the veridicality of that.

The genuineness of an experience becomes a non-question. Can an orgasm *not* be genuine somehow? I am not suggesting that either orgasms or religious experiences are simply self-authenticating; I suggest that 'self-authenticating' is the wrong way to understand it. Yandell and Alston have a point in their carefully constructed arguments against the idea that an experience is not obliged to provide any other justification for its propositional claims than its own occurrence. Nevertheless, I believe we have to allow an element of incorrigibility here, such as we do allow for other sorts of experiences and sensations, such as emotions and pains. The disputes can arise at the level of interpretation, or proposition. Using the traditional hermeneutical distinction of 'explication' and 'application', when we start to explain and expand upon an experience, or apply the conclusions we have reached on it to our lives, we can make mistakes. Considering explication, I don't dispute that my friend had a fabulous experience with her new man, but I can dispute her enthusiastic inference that he must therefore be all that she fantasises he is. Likewise, one cannot dispute the phenomenological details of the religious enthusiast's experience, but could dispute the theological or pastoral conclusions that they reach from that starting-point. Further, accepting that someone must be allowed to be right about what he felt does not mean that one need accept the 'application' of his experience to the rest of his life – or to one's own. Incorrigibility on the one side must be met with autonomy on the other; your experience does not 'authenticate' the repression or persecution of another. But as with religious experiences, the task of interpreting and assessing the event and one's understanding of it is a relational one, and must be dealt with case by case.

The analogy with love experiences also suggests that absence of religious experience may not be a question of the existence or not of some entity, or a problem with someone's religious (or other) 'apparatus'. The failure to experience ecstasy in a situation where another claims to may be down to the quality of the relationship or experience, in both cases.

What I suggest, by employing this unconventional analogy, is that there are other undisputed areas of human existence which share most of the epistemological 'problems' of religious experience. Given that, as far as I know, even people who have never had one do not seriously doubt the reality of orgasms, the question must be asked whether the criteria set for accepting the validity of spiritual experience are too stringent for many less controversial areas of human experience.

Sense perception is a relatively simple affair; religious experience is terribly complex. Perhaps then our interpretative model for religious experience should not be sense experience or other kinds of 'perception'. Experiencing God may not be at all like perceiving a chair. This I suggest is not merely because of the phenomenal or emotional content (few report feelings of ecstasy and union when looking at a chair). Nor is it simply that God is not an object to experience like a chair. Alston denies that he means that God is an 'object' in the wrong sense, but only in the 'proper sense'; I am not convinced that *any* sense is proper, not even the sense in which another human being can be the object of my perception.

My ultimate reason, however, for rejecting perception as a model for spiritual experience is that it is much more complex than *any* form of perception. There may be something perceptual about the experience, as there may be with falling in love or making love; and yet 'perception' as a classification or category doesn't do justice to such experiences. There is much more to them than that: reflection, interpretation, creation, communication, transformation .... Perception may be a sub-category of such experiences, rather than the other way around; it may occur in acts of love, but perception is not what an act of love is.

Instead, we should consider relationships themselves as a model for understanding spiritual experience, not least because both are complex. Relationships are multi-faceted; ambiguous, contestable. Human relations also share with religious experience the fact that their import cannot be summed up in propositions. The knowledge and understanding we arrive at through relationships can never be purely propositional, nor veridical 'in general'. Nor is it an ingredient in an argument for someone's existence. To construct an argument on the basis of a relationship can only be appropriate in a situation where the trust proper to such relationships has degenerated; or, if used to justify oneself to a third party, risks the affront of exploiting a friendship to confirm one's own rightness. Finally, to treat such personal knowledge as 'evidence' can only be appropriate where matters have so deteriorated that the partners have ended up in a court of law.

There is one all-important point at which this analogy breaks down – as all analogies must, for they are not identities. I do not want to dismiss it as a trivial difference; indeed, if I intended my analogy to be an argument for the existence of God, this difference would undermine my whole case. The crucial difference between certain kinds of spiritual experience and human love experiences is this: if there is a God, She is transcendent. Lovers are earthly. Lovers can be seen, smelled, squeezed. God cannot. The analogy of human love, like the argument based on perception which it challenges, cannot encompass the uniqueness of the divine 'Lover'. Depending on your theological tastes, this is either an irremediable defect in *any* attempt to justify religious experience as we do other things – or else it is a point of faith on which there can be absolutely no compromise.

PART III

Evil and Suffering

Not, I'll not, carrion comfort, Despair, not feast on thee:
Not untwist – slack they may be – these last strands of man
In me or, most weary, cry *I can no more*. I can;
Can something, hope, wish day come, not choose not to be.

But ah, but O thou terrible, why wouldst thou rude on me
Thy wring-world right foot rock? Lay a lionlimb against me? scan
With darksome devouring eyes my bruised bones? and fan,
O in turns of tempest, me heaped there; me frantic to avoid thee and flee?

Why? That my chaff might fly; my grain lie, sheer and clear.
Nay in all that toil, that coil, since (seems) I kissed the rod,
Hand rather, my heart lo! lapped strength, stole joy, would laugh, cheer.
Cheer whom though? The hero whose heaven-handling flung me, foot trod
Me? or me that fought him? O which one? is it each one? That night, that year
Of now done darkness I wretch lay wrestling with (my God!) my God.

Gerard Manley Hopkins, 'Carrion Comfort'

7. Problems of Evil

An introduction to the variety of problems of evil and suffering

Who knows the will of the gods in heaven?
Who understands the plan of the underworld gods?
Where have mortals learnt the way of a god?
He who was alive yesterday is dead today.
For a minute he was dejected, suddenly he is exuberant.
One moment people are singing in exaltation,
Another they groan like professional mourners ...
I am appalled at these things; I do not understand their significance.[1]

This text was written more than three thousand years ago. Philosophical reflection on suffering is not a recent development in the history of ideas. Nor is it the product of modern scepticism to suggest that evil and pain raise religious and theological problems in particular.

If anything is universal in philosophical reflection, across ages and cultures, it is systematic inquiry into the problems of evil. What is not universal, however, are the actual problems that arise within particular religious frameworks, nor the underlying attitude towards suffering. Ramakant Sinari contrasts the basic world-view of the 'Vedic Indian' with the Western, Greek-based mindset (admittedly with some generalisation on both sides). The Greek-influenced European mind displays a zeal for explanation and epistemological mastery: 'epidemics, depressions, revolutions, wars, or concentration camps have been looked upon as objective phenomena, scientifically explainable and avoidable rather than as human misfortunes that must leave everybody crestfallen.'[2] The Vedic tendency to 'transcendentalism', on the other hand, inspires a different attitude and approach to the existential problems of suffering and evil; 'one of melancholy and distress at the very emergence of man in the world.' Despite the world-affirming aspects of Indian philosophy, Sinari suggests that in the Upaniṣadic world-view, existence is a menace.[3] 'Human existence is too formidable a disaster to be only intellectually explained, or to be looked at objectively.'[4]

It would be misleading, however, to characterise the 'Western view' as 'positive' or 'optimistic' or 'world-affirming', and denigrate the Indian world-view as 'negative', 'pessimistic' or 'world-denying'. They manifest a network of rela-

147

tions and stances too complex to be described so simply. The 'Western view' may inspire change – but it also inspires complaint and indignation. The philosophical discussions betray an unconscious air of entitlement: that we are entitled to a better world and a better nature, and the fact that we don't have one is a fundamental metaphysical problem – for God even more than for us. On the other hand, while the 'Upaniṣadic world-view' may lead to a resigned futility, it can also lead to a more profound acceptance of the conditions of human existence and a willingness to embrace whatever it offers.

> The mortal individual identifies his mind with the principle that brought him into existence, that hurls him along and is to wipe him out, feeling himself to be a part of that supreme force as its manifestation, a part of its veil and play. One submits to the totality. One attunes one's ears to the dissonant as well as to the consonant strains of the cosmic symphony, regarding oneself as a brief passage, a momentary melody, now raised but soon to fade and be heard no more. Thus comprehending his part and function in the everlasting, joyful-woeful song of life, the individual is not melancholy at the prospect of the pains of death and birth, or because of the frustrations of his personal expectations. Life is no longer evaluated by him in terms of sorrow. Both the sorrows and the joys of the round are transcended in ecstasy.[5]

Until one reaches this stage of enlightenment, however, there remains a philosophical problem: not a 'problem of evil', but multiple problems of evil.

The problems

The multiplicity of problems do not simply arise from the number of different religions; suffering and evil raise a number of different questions for *each* religious tradition. Why is there pain, but why is there also *wickedness*? What can we do to make it better? Where does it come from? What function does it have, or purpose does it serve? How can massive, horrific evil or pain ever serve a good purpose? Why does God allow it? Why do we do it?

'Existential' and 'philosophical' problems

In Anglo-Saxon philosophy of religion, the 'Problem of Evil' refers narrowly to a problem concerning God's existence and attributes. Surveying the mass of literature, one finds authors who argue coolly about 'possible worlds' and 'middle knowledge', and others who quote *The Brothers Karamazov* and Elie Wiesel with passion. A commensurate distinction is often made between the 'logical' or philosophical problem and the 'existential' or pastoral problem. Alvin Plantinga explains that the philosophical problem 'has do with fulfilling epistemic obligations, or maintaining a rational system of beliefs, or following proper intellectual procedure, or perhaps with practising proper mental hygiene'.[6] The existential problem is how this impacts on one's life:

> faced with the shocking concreteness of a particularly appalling example of evil in his own life or the life of someone close to him, a believer may find himself tempted to take toward God an attitude he himself deplores; such evil can incline him to mistrust God, or to be angry with him, to adopt toward him an attitude of suspicion and distrust or bitterness and rebellion.[7]

The most intractable problem is how one copes with it.

In making this distinction, philosophers tacitly concede that solving one problem does not automatically solve the other – the philosopher of religion is concerned to defend the utility of his arguments against the complaint that they are pastorally useless and give no comfort to those who suffer. One who is intellectually satisfied that the existence of God is not ruled out by the philosophical problem may find this to be of no comfort when her child is suffering from leukaemia. Likewise, one may lead a relatively untroubled and contented life, and still find the philosophical question an insurmountable obstacle to faith in a Deity.

I am not sure that this is the best place to draw a distinction. It seems to divide human beings too sharply into 'thinking and reasoning' parts as opposed to 'feeling, suffering, experiencing' ones. Even to excuse one's arguments from giving comfort is questionable. Comfort is a relative phenomenon. Sometimes what is precisely most distressing about the so-called 'existential' problem is the 'intellectual' or cognitive conflict between our beliefs and their immediate experience. At such times, philosophical questions and defences are a *practical* answer; sometimes the *pastoral* challenge faced by those who talk with people in distress is precisely to address these philosophical issues. The example of Indian religions – Hinduism, Jainism, Buddhism – demonstrates that suffering as an existential problem is a profoundly philosophical question; not least an *ethical* question, one in which human action, not divine inaction, is the point at issue.

Problems of origin for the atheist

Everyone who thinks about it has a philosophical problem with the origin of evil: monists and monotheists, believers and unbelievers. Even those who reject belief in a God have serious anthropological problems to face, if not in explaining 'natural evil', then at least in accounting for 'moral evil'.[8] (Moral evil is what most people mean when they say 'evil': the whole panoply of human awfulness from mere rudeness to mass murder. 'Natural evil' signifies the ills of existence that are not attributed to human moral choices, such as the illness and death of human and non-human animals, or natural disasters.)

'How did it happen, that the human being from the situation of Nature passed over into the present evils? if in his nature lay the enclosed treasure of capabilities, of inclinations etc., which for his happiness must remain enclosed, why … this kernel of wrongness? how did it germinate?'[9] Herder and Hamann discussed the problem that Rousseau had not solved: if 'man was born free', as Rousseau maintained, why was he 'everywhere in chains'? In leaving behind belief in a Creator God, one may substitute Nature as the mother of humanity, and speak of what is 'natural' in place of what is 'good'. But if one loses the specific question: why do we behave *badly* – we have the even more contradictory problem: why do we sometimes act 'unnaturally'? How is *that* possible – to be something other than what we in fact are? If 'evil' is what is unnatural, as in an optimistic form of humanism, and everything comes from nature as there is no supernatural, it remains a philosophical challenge to explain where evil as 'the unnatural' comes from.

The most consistent approach would be something like the ancient materialist and atheist Indian school, Cārvāka[10] – or the Enlightenment thought of the Marquis de Sade.[11] To detach goodness from God and try to retain a sense of morals grounded in 'nature' is only an inadequate half-step in the right direction, in their view. The materialist and atheist critique must be completed in a total evacuation of Nature itself of any kind of norm or value: nature is neither good nor bad, in any sense at all.[12] The very notions of 'goodness' and 'evil' then become empty; 'good' action is devoid of any intrinsic value. There is only pleasure and pain; and these thinkers advocate seeking out the former (at least for oneself).

Yet not even in his most extreme writings did Sade attain the desired consistency of thinking. In his novel *Juliette*, the Pope tells the eponymous heroine: 'Man thus has no relationship to Nature, nor Nature to man; Nature cannot bind man by any law, man is in no way dependent upon Nature, neither is answerable to the other, they cannot either harm or help each other.' Nothing is forbidden by nature; consequently 'what we improperly call evil is really not evil at all'. On the other hand, the Pope also tells her he must commit murder daily, for 'whenever Nature feels the need for murder she inspires in us a longing to commit it, and willy-nilly we obey her'. He complains that all human laws contradict the laws of Nature, and this is the justification for overthrowing human moral regulations. Indeed, 'atrocity in crime pleases Nature, since 'tis according to this factor alone she regulates the delight to provide us when we commit a crime. The more frightful it is, the more we enjoy it; the blacker, the fouler it is, the more we are thrilled by it.' So Nature does have laws after all; moreover, we are to obey them.

These contradictions show that Sade has not really freed himself from a normative view of Nature. This is because he is caught up in a fundamental antinomy. He wants to dispense with all notions of value, but as long as one prefers pleasure to pain, one is still employing the idea of a value: pleasure itself *is* the value. He is trapped in a further contradiction that arises for the perverted:

if you eradicate good, you rob yourself of the pleasure of transgression.[13] His third dilemma arises from his slant on hedonism. Even to torture another while experiencing orgasm, in the most emphatic attempt to accentuate pleasure and appropriate it for oneself, cannot extricate pleasure from pain. Pleasure and pain are sometimes inseparable. Sade himself unconsciously betrays this while trying to refute it, by depicting female characters achieving an unwilling climax as a result of unspeakable torments and degradations.[14]

Worst of all, in the end, Sade still faces an existential problem, the hedonists' existential Problem of Evil: how to have more pleasure and less pain. The extremes to which this quest takes him, at least in fiction, are no less laboured than the theodicial efforts of the most pedantic Christian philosopher.

So while non-believers can avoid the theological conflicts, they still have to account for humanity's destructive behaviour; and of course they still face the existential problem of encountering evil and coping with suffering (or a deficit of pleasure).

Problems of origin for the believer

The problem of the origin of evil confronts believers in a benevolent Deity differently. They must explain why a well-meaning and competent God has bungled so badly in creation. Couldn't God do better?[15] Didn't God mind?

Monotheists have to deal with the embarrassing implication that God created evil when creating the world. This issue arises in a different way for monists, who believe that all reality is ultimately one, identical with the Supreme Self, Brahman. In the Advaita Vedāntin tradition, the fact that immediate experience contradicts this alleged unity of all is put down to ignorance (avidyā). It is an illusory projection of our own subjectivity (māyā). Where does this ignorance come from, that generates the entire world of everyday experience? Brahman is the ultimate, the source of all; and yet Brahman is in no way reprehensible, defective, or defiled. So how does this ignorance originate?

Meanwhile, any monotheist who asserts the existence of an omnipotent God of perfect goodness has to puzzle over the conflict of God's attributes with the reality of evil. I once intended to set this classic question for a Philosophy of Religion exam paper: 'How can the omnipotence of God be defended in the face of evil?' I was horrified, when I saw the proofs of the paper, to read: 'How can the *impotence* of God be defended in the face of evil?' (None of the students attempted it, on the day.)

Like most 'Freudian slips', this one seemed to betray something significant. Why doesn't God intervene to ameliorate suffering and prevent evil when we, less powerful and less good creatures, would surely wish to do so? Isn't God good enough? Powerful enough? Or is there just no God?

Alvin Plantinga has argued that, despite this traditional challenge put by Epicurus, Augustine, and David Hume, there is no *contradiction* as such or *logical incompatibility* between the affirmations that the theist wants to make about God's omnipotence and omnibenevolence, and the proposition that evil exists.[16] Yandell has argued similarly.[17] 'God is good.' 'God is omnipotent.' 'Evil exists.' – None of these propositions are formally opposite to or the contradiction of any of the others, so the theist's set of propositions are not self-contradictory in a strict or formal sense. 'Atheologians', Plantinga remarks, have not been able to formulate a necessarily true proposition which renders the set of theistic propositions contradictory.[18]

Plantinga thinks that the theist can even forestall the looser claim that evil is a *contra-indication* for the existence of God. What is required to show that these propositions are consistent with one another is to formulate a third proposition that harmonises them. This proposition must be consistent with one of the propositions (e.g. 'Evil exists') and entailed by the other (e.g. 'God is good').[19] It would look something like this: 'Because of God's goodness and omnipotence, God must necessarily x; and x is fully consistent with the existence of evil.'

Plantinga offers here a 'defence', which has recently been distinguished from a 'theodicy'. A defence of belief in God is considered more modest in scope and ambition; it merely tries to show (variously) that belief in God is not irrational, or is more probably true than false, or that the existence of evil is not incompatible with the existence of an omnipotent and omnibenevolent God. A 'theodicy' is a more ambitious attempt to 'justify God'; it goes beyond the task of minimal defence, and attempts to give some account of why God might allow suffering and evil events to happen. Plantinga's 'defence' is the idea that human beings have free will; we shall examine this idea in a later chapter.

The atheist challenge

> If there exists some Lord all powerful to fulfil
> In every creature bliss or woe, and action good or ill,
> That Lord is stained with sin. Man does but work his will.[20]

So maintained the Theravāda Buddhist. Faced with the horrors of the world and human history, it seems reasonable enough to doubt that God exists. For if religious experience, as we have seen, can be taken by the believer as some kind of evidence for the existence of God, the reality of evil can be taken as evidence *against*.

Non-theistic traditions in Buddhism made this point repeatedly against the Hindus. If all good and evil is the creation of a supreme god, then it is the achievement of that god that people become liars, thieves, unchaste, heretical, murderers.

> He who has eyes can see the sickening sight;
> Why does not Brahma set his creatures right?
>
> If his wide power no limit can restrain,
> Why is his hand so rarely spread to bless?

Why are all his creatures condemned to pain?
Why does he not to all give happiness?

Why do fraud, lies, and ignorance prevail?
Why triumphs falsehood – truth and justice fail?

I count your Brahma one th' injust among,
Who made a world in which to shelter wrong.[21]

This rejection of belief in a God based on the reality of evil has been relentless. Antony Flew mounted this challenge to the rationality of religious belief:

> Now it often seems to people who are not religious as if there was no conceivable event or series of events the occurrence of which would be admitted by sophisticated religious people to be a sufficient reason for conceding 'There wasn't a God after all' or 'God does not really love us then'. ... Just what would have to happen not merely (morally and wrongly) to tempt but also (logically and rightly) to entitle us to say 'God does not love us' or even 'God does not exist'? I therefore put the ... simple central questions, 'What would have to occur or to have occurred to constitute for you a disproof of the love of, or of the existence of, God?'[22]

Is it reasonable and right, then, to believe in a God *despite* the evidence? Does the speech of one who believes in God suffer the 'endemic evil' that any assertion of God's providence or care – or even existence – must be qualified so often that it 'may thus be killed by inches, the death by a thousand qualifications'?[23]

Plantinga's and Yandell's claim that the theist's propositions are not contradictory is somewhat supported by the fact that most atheologians have shifted their attention from the claim that there is an actual *contradiction*, to the claim that God's existence is rendered less *probable* by the extent of evil,[24] or alternatively that the existence of evil is at least evidence against the existence of God.[25]

The main difficulty philosophers of religion have with the notion of probability is that, in most cases, it is calculated on the basis of numerous examples; how many races the horse has won so far, for example. Such numerical evidence is rather difficult to acquire in the case of God's existence. The other way probabilities are normally determined is by propensity: we do not need to roll a die a number of times, experimentally, to determine the probability of rolling a 6. The characteristics of a thing can allow one to work out a priori what the probability of a given result should be. This is also difficult, if not impossible, in our case: we do not know and could not plausibly calculate the intrinsic propensities of universes containing evil to have a God or not to have a God in order to come to a reasoned decision in the matter. Nonetheless, some philosophers of religion have gone to work undeterred, using Bayes' Theorem.[26] J.L. Mackie uses the theorem to establish an atheistic argument, while R. Swinburne uses it to demonstrate a theistic argument – a fact which already might lead to cynicism about how impartial or conclusive the results of this approach might be.[27]

Michael Martin has argued that the existence of evil is at least evidence against the existence of God. He claims that there is no uncontroversial evidence that God exists. The existence of evil in great abundance would falsify the claim that God exists unless one assumes either that God has sufficient motive for allowing the existence of evil in great abundance or that it is logically necessary. Despite repeated attempts to do so, no one has provided a good reason to believe that God has sufficient motive to allow evil to exist in great abundance or that it is logically necessary. Therefore on rational grounds one should not believe that God exists.[28] Many of these assertions will be examined in the next chapters.

The anthropological question

Not only is the problem of evil not just a theist's problem, it may not principally be a *theological* problem, but an anthropological one. The really disturbing question is not 'Why does God *let* it happen?' but 'Why do human beings *make* it happen?' One might reflect on the fact that, after the senseless slaughter of the First World War, the atheist Freud found it necessary to reconsider his understanding of human nature, and thereafter placed greater emphasis on aggression, hostility, and the death drive. Even a non-theistic view of humanity and the world has to take the problem of evil into account, and provide an account (as has been said about theologies) that is credible 'in the presence of burning children'.[29] The atrocities witnessed by the last century alone challenge *any* claims about moral goodness, human as well as divine.

The problem of evil, then, has provoked not just attacks and defences of God's character. It has also called forth assertions and counter-assertions about what it is to be human. The theological and the anthropological issues are perhaps more inseparable here than in any other area of the philosophy of religion.

Making the problems disappear

There are two ways to make the problems swiftly disappear. One is to deny the reality of evil, and the other is to deny that God is in any way accountable to us for it.

How evil is evil?

There are religious traditions that hold that evil is really an illusion, and that the aim of the spiritual person should be to rise above the level of superficialities to see reality as it truly is – which means seeing suffering and evil for the illusion that they are. Hinduism and Buddhism are particularly associated with this meta-physic.

The Upaniṣadic view, developed particularly in the non-dualist or monist schools such as Advaita Vedānta, is that the variety of beings we perceive and the experiences we undergo are not ultimately real. Consequently, evil and suffering are not ultimately real. Paradoxically, they can further spiritual growth and enlightenment, if they serve to detach us from worldly things and experiences. 'The tangible realm of māyā, which is the veil that occludes Truth, is at the same time the self-revelation of truth. Everything is a mask, a gesture of self-revelation. The dark aspects of life ... counterbalance the bright.'[30]

The idea that evil does not have positive existence in itself is also present in the Christian tradition. Augustine and Aquinas, in part following Aristotle, maintained that evil is fundamentally the lack of a good quality that an entity ought to have. All created being, since it was created by God, is good; evil implies an element or a tendency towards non-being:[31] evil is 'the privation of good'. This includes corruption, and something that is defective or wrong, full stop.[32] Moral evil, according to Augustine, is a human choice not to fulfil the true nature and being that God intended for us. This evil originates from basically good, rational creatures (angels, human beings) whose will falls short of the 'unchangeable good'.

The designation of something as 'evil' can also be a question of our point of view. (Augustine describes evil in this way as well.) Some things are called evil from one perspective but may not be from another. My cold may be a natural evil to me; but may be the cause of great joy and prosperity for the virus responsible. Earthquakes resolve the pressure building up on tectonic plates. Much suffering arises from such conflicts of interests. Where species are in conflict or in competition, situations may arise which cause humans suffering but are in the interests of other species, such as in areas of India today where human beings are encroaching on the tiger's habitat, resulting in an increase in the killing of human beings by tigers. From the human perspective, such things cause suffering; but they are part of natural processes, and human pleasures and desires are not necessarily coextensive with 'the good' that God maximises. Perhaps God does not play favourites among species. Viewed as a whole, it is claimed, creation is good, even if aspects of it or events in it are not desirable from the point of view of a particular individual or a particular species.

Spinoza argued that in nature there is no good and no evil; things exist the way they are necessarily. To call existing things good and evil is an act of the imagination, and it reflects our own concerns and interests, not their own intrinsic natures. Therefore, there is no philosophical problem of why there is evil in the world. Buber, like Spinoza, relativises the evilness of evil, suggesting that we reject the notion of evil and goodness as opposites. 'Good', claims Buber, is the orientation and motivation towards God (or 'home', as he puts it) while ' "evil" is the aimless whirl of human potentialities without which nothing can be achieved and by which, if they take no direction but remain trapped in themselves, everything goes awry.'[33] This implies that evil is just a misdirection of good, or of a good impulse, drive, or motivation. This implication is clearer in Buber's *Images of Good and Evil*:[34] the evil urge, which is more important than the good one because of its creative potential, is identified with passion, and is only evil if it is misused. In a similar vein Mordecai Kaplan suggests that evil is chaos and good is the purposive force that produces the cosmos out of chaos.[35] But Eliezer Berkovits argues that this account does not chime with most people's experience, which indicates that 'evil and wickedness, sorrow and suffering, failure and sin'[36] are much more than mere unformed nature or chaos.

There is an element of interpretation, as well as point-of-view, in naming good and evil. Can I really be certain that what is painful or seems evil to me is intrinsically, necessarily so? And if I suffer from a state of affairs that benefits another, for example, does that really represent serious grounds against the existence of a loving God? Nevertheless, unless one subscribes to a religious or metaphysical traditions which denies *all* evil as a reality, these reflections do not eliminate the problem of evil; they just reduce the tally of evils to be contended with.

The unaccountable God

'This is the hidden problem of theodicy: to affirm the necessary rightness of things without simultaneously subjecting God to necessity. ... The problem is to assert the necessary rightness of things as they are, but to do so in a way that they are seen as proceeding from God's will, wisdom, and power, and not from a necessity of His nature.'[37] This is the tactical problem for one who believes in a kindly God: to avoid accusations that God is cruel in allowing suffering, one portrays evil as somehow inevitable or necessary. But then the Lord of All becomes entrammelled in the requirements of logical necessity as well as moral obligations, which is unseemly in one so transcendent.

Nevertheless, certain philosophical and theological schools have held their noses and jumped into the water: God is subject to necessity in some respects. Islamic Mu'tazilites, Christian scholastics, Jewish rationalists have all accepted the notion that God is at least bound by logic. The Indian analogue is to wonder whether the gods are subject to karma.

A contrasting approach is to question what right we have to call God to account. In the Book of Job, God's own self-theodicy is this one: why should God have to justify Himself to His own creatures? If God is omnipotent, the ultimate in justice, and our Creator, shouldn't God be unaccountable to us, his inferiors? Is not God the standard for justice – rather than being held accountable to some prior, more ultimate, standard?

Perhaps the most uncompromising statements of this nature come from the Islamic Ash'arite school, in opposition to the more 'rationalist' Mu'tazilite school. In a form of reasoning familiar to many as the 'Euthyphro' dilemma, from Plato's dialogue of that name, the Ash'arites argued that God does not 'do what is just because it is just'; rather, what God does is just because 'just' is defined as 'what God does'. Justice takes its definition from God, rather than God being obliged to conform to a prior standard of justice. Indeed, we cannot judge God for we have no independent ability to discern 'good' and 'evil' – for these are not objective realities. Instead,

> In this version of theodicy, divine wisdom is the ultimate justification for things as they are. Whatever happens for good and evil in the world results from the eternal decree of God, but this decree itself has been issued in accord with what 'wisdom demands'. In the Islamic theodicy, divine wisdom is the final refuge of necessity.[38]

Maimonides asserts that God's providence does not consist in arranging things for our convenience and comfort, or even our physical well-being. In Maimonides' opinion, the idea that God's providence means that He guarantees health, wealth, and happiness for us is explicitly repudiated in the Book of Job; Job had previously held this opinion, and that precisely is what he learns to reject. The lesson that God teaches in his speech in Job is that

> the notion of His providence is not the same as the notion of our providence; nor is the notion of His governance of the things created by Him the same as the notion of our governance of that which we govern. The two notions are not comprised in one definition, contrary to what is thought by all those who are confused, and there is nothing in common between the two except the name alone.[39]

Maimonides concludes, 'If a man knows this, every misfortune will be borne lightly by him. And misfortunes will not add to his doubts regarding the deity and whether He does or does not know and whether he exercises providence or manifests neglect, but will, on the contrary, add to his love.'[40]

Aquinas' way of removing blame from God was to deny that God is a moral agent. If you are a moral agent, that is, one who can be said to have moral obligations and duties, then being good consists in meeting your obligations and fulfilling your duties. But the theist is not obliged to suppose that God is bound by any kind of duty or obligation – least of all the obligation to justify Himself to His creatures. Brian Davies observes that discussions of the problem of evil frequently presuppose that God's goodness consists in God meeting His moral obligations.[41] But God is not a moral agent.[42]

One can sympathise with the motivation behind Davies' argument: that God is not to be thought of as an agent subject to moral duties and obligations as people are; his goodness, if you like, ought not to be conceived in such creaturely terms. He concludes: 'We are in no position to say that God ought or ought not to have done something and that he is morally at fault or morally excusable for not doing it. In this sense, so one might argue, there is no problem of evil.'[43]

Childhood readers of the Narnia books by C.S. Lewis might recall that, when the christological lion Aslan was absent in times of trouble, the children would reason (theodicially), 'He's not a *tame* lion.' Nevertheless, Aslan always did redeem the problematic state of affairs in the end. He simply decided on the methods and timing himself. In that way, although not predictable, he still came through with all the compassion and redemption that the children required. Does there not come a point at which one must say: 'If to be "good" doesn't entail x, then what on earth can goodness mean?' One can give God a lot of slack on the question of whether moral goodness entails doing or refraining from this or that, but is there a bottom line – a point at which one says, 'If God's goodness does not involve doing even *this*, in the end, there can be no more reason to call God good'? How far can we let go of our anthropomorphic conceptions of God's nature, and go into theological free-fall?

Some might find this 'bottom line' in the notion of ultimate redemption. Davies' position, however, is different. It is not a question of allowing God some moral slack and having a bottom line. Following his interpretation of Aquinas' position, he understands God's 'goodness' as consisting in perfection, which does not imply moral excellence.[44] 'Perfection' means perfectly actualising all that something can or should be. He quotes Aquinas: 'For things are called perfect when they have achieved actuality, the perfect thing being that in which nothing required by the thing's particular mode of perfection fails to exist.'[45] At the same time, Davies claims not to know what such perfection amounts to.

The second meaning he gives to God's goodness is that it means that God is 'the maker of all creaturely goodness, which must therefore reflect him somehow'.[46] This creaturely goodness does include moral goodness. Another, more Aristotelian way to put it is: 'God can be called "good" as the source of all that is attractive.'[47]

I have considerable sympathy for the argument that God is not bound by human moral standards and opinions, but I wonder how far this account simply sidesteps some of the valid problems that exist and receive discussion in the philosophy of religion. It is true that many philosophers do fall into a way of speaking that implies that God is slipping up on his moral obligations. However, most people who are sincerely troubled by the existence of evil, given their belief in the existence of God, see the problem differently, in a way that Davies' Thomist account perhaps cannot escape.

What part of perfection, including the divine perfection, is it to allow unjust and unavoidable suffering? If God is failing to actualise his potential for omnibenevolence, this is an imperfection in a divine being, perhaps. So one needs to explain why unjust and unavoidable suffering, despite appearances, does not constitute a wobble in divine omnibenevolence.

If God is good because He is attractive, what is attractive about maintaining pain and viciousness in being?

If God is the source of all human moral goodness, why is the supply from this perfect source so erratic? If God fails to actualise moral goodness in humanity consistently, there is a potential problem here. This is not because God is disobeying the Ten Commandments and failing as a moral agent. Even under the job description for divine goodness that Davies provides, in which 'behaving well' plays no part, the appearance of things is that God is not altogether successful.

Davies might claim that I am failing to see the point, and still wrongly holding God accountable to some prior standard of perfection. I am only doing so insofar as it is necessary to in order to claim – as Davies and Aquinas do – that God 'is as divine as it takes divinity to be. It is for God to be fully God and, therefore, perfectly God'.[48] Although Davies claims not to know what this amounts to, I think he is being too modest.

Thomist accounts do, after all, consider a number of attributes that God fully is or actualises, and omnipotent and omnibenevolent are two of them. It is difficult to know on what grounds we can assert that God is good, and is achieving all that He can and should as God, and still maintain a modest negative theology which knows nothing at all of what it is to be God and whether God is succeeding at it.

No, I think the choice is more stark in this instance. Either one really holds to the Unaccountable God, consistently follows the *via negativa*, and does not even make the bare claim to know how God truly is good – or one takes a Thomist stance which positively predicates goodness of God, albeit the goodness of a Creator and not a model citizen. This case, however, is still open to challenge from the imperfections of the creation. If one wants to be believed, agreed with, or considered 'rational', one needs, for example, to give some account of why the goodness of creation and humanity 'reflect' or 'show forth' the goodness of God – but the imperfections and evils in the world do not likewise reveal evil and imperfection in God's nature. There are many possible arguments and accounts which could achieve this, so it is far from a hopeless task. But these are the theodicies and discussions of philosophy of religion which Davies accuses of futility because they view God as a moral agent.[49] Nevertheless, we will examine them in the next four chapters.

These problems and issues now require further investigation – although even to say that is to take a philosophical stance:

The cosmic dynamism of which we ourselves are minute manifestations cannot be fitted to the dimensions of our brain, any more than to the brains of ants; for the universe is the holy revelation of an absolutely transcendent essence. We can be glad to understand it even a little, in terms appropriate to the range of our egocentric sensual and mental faculties. Though characterized every moment by perishableness, the universal whirling process in itself is everlasting, even as is the hidden power from which it derives. It is everlasting, indeed, through the very transiency [*sic*] of its continually appearing and vanishing phenomena – all these evanescent forms. And precisely because these break, it is everlasting. The cloud-shadows of death and bereavement darken the face of the world every second; these race across the moonlit, sunlit scene – but they do not outbalance the light, the fulfilment of life's joy in the perpetual begetting of new forms. The world, in spite of its pain, is as it were enraptured by itself, and does not count the hurts that go with the procedure: as though lovers in their rapture should mind whether the kisses hurt, or a child eagerly swallowing ice cream whether the chill was a little painful. Everything depends on where one puts the emphasis …. A continuous blending and transformation of opposites through a relentless vital dynamism – even asking for pains, to balance and enhance the intensity of delight – goes spontaneously, power- fully, and joyously with this terrific Oriental acceptance of the whole dimension of the universe.[50]

8. Origins of Evil

The problem of the origin of evil and different attempts to answer it

One way of trying to 'account for' something is to say where it came from. Much reflection on evil and suffering tries to explain why there is pain and wrongdoing, in an attempt to give us an enlightened perspective on it.

Although the notions are commonly distinguished, there is at least an inter-penetration of moral and natural evil. Accounts of the origin of evil and of suffering may need to comprehend both. First of all, much so-called 'natural evil' is caused by humans, whether through malice or ignorance. Many of the so-called natural disasters that occur in our world occur directly or indirectly because of human action: severe flooding, for example, is often caused or at least exacerbated by wanton deforestation. How much suffering and loss of human life is caused by an earthquake largely depends on how much and what quality of housing has been constructed on the fault line. Many sicknesses or illnesses are either directly caused, or are worsened or further spread by human behaviour, even if unintentionally. The results of human actions are manifested in the natural sphere as well as the interpersonal one. Secondly, humans *are* part of the natural world – part of 'creation' – and if one deals with the imperfections in the natural world, one touches on imperfections in the human species.

The source of all

Some thinkers boldly assert that God is the source of evil as well as good. Passages in the Hebrew Scriptures stress that God is the source of all: weal and woe. Islamic thinkers who insist on the absolute supremacy and omnipotence of God would rather cope with the tensions raised for God's goodness than compromise God's transcendence and power. Ash'arī wrote: 'Good and evil (occur) through the decree and power of God. We believe in God's decree and power – the good as well as the evil, the sweet as well as the bitter.'[1] The Ash'arite position was that God is the only agent, God alone 'creates acts', even human action; thus God is the source even of evil. And although Christians often shy away from any association between God and evil, some theologians, such as Oswald Bayer, do not hesitate to speak from experience of the incomprehensible, terrible hiddenness of God, in which he conceals himself in an omnipotence both dark and endlessly distant and at the same time infinitely close – consumingly, burningly, oppressively close, closer than I am to myself; in that omnipotence which creates life *and* death, light *and* darkness (Isaiah 45.7), love *and* hate (Ecclesiastes 9.1f.), conservation *and* destruction, weal *and* woe (Amos 3.6, Isaiah 45.7), evil *and* good (Lamentations 3.38), in short: that he works all in all – inextricably and impenetrably to us.[2]

For the German mystic Jakob Boehme, God is 'All' in this sense – as well as 'Nothing'. In his extraordinary cosmogony, God is not so much the 'highest' as the 'lowest': everything, including matter and natural forces, rises up from this primal foundation (*Urgrund* or *Ungrund*) and sinks back into it. This origination from the unmanifested Godhead is threefold, a triad of thesis, antithesis, and the synthesis that results from them. Thus the *inner* life of God is the original triad of 'Attraction', 'Diffusion', and what results from their interaction: 'Agony'! The life of God as *manifested* is the triad of Love, Expression, and their synthesis, Visible Variety. Human phenomena are explained with the same triadic structure: soul, body, spirit; and good, evil, and their resultant, free will.

Boehme's attempts to account for the origin of evil are the outcome of this unusual metaphysical structure, and they also demonstrate the evolution of his thinking as each attempt, presumably, was found wanting over time. In his earliest thought, he wants to maintain that nothing but good results from this *Urgrund*. Later he suggests that good and evil, as an opposition, arise from the same creative source of the divine; as part of life and movement. Finally, he reaches the conclusion that evil itself becomes a consequence of the first, ultimate divine principle: the wrathful side of God.

A world created

'When the rabbi reproached the tailor for taking six weeks to make a pair of trousers, while it took God no more than six days to create an entire world, the tailor parried. "Yes, Rabbi," he said, "but just see what a world created in a hurry looks like." '[3]

In the Judaic and the Christian traditions, when God created the universe He created His Other rather than His self. So in order to be differentiated from God, the universe cannot be perfect; there must be a metaphysical or ontological difference between God and the world. It is from this necessary inherent imperfection that evil arises.

Within the Jewish tradition, one way of conceiving divine creation evolves out of the notion of *tsimtsum*, or Divine contraction, found in Lurianic Kabbala.

[The] very essence of *Ein-Sof*[4] leaves no space whatsoever for creation, for it is impossible to imagine an area which is not already God, since this would constitute a limitation of His infinity. ... Consequently, an act of creation is possible only through 'the entry of God into Himself', that is, through an act of *zimzum* whereby He contracts Himself and so makes it possible for something which is not *Ein-Sof* to exist. Some part of the Godhead, therefore, retreats and leaves room, so to speak, for the creative processes to come into play.[5]

This absence-of-God's-presence is a necessary condition for the existence of other things, but also entails imperfection. It leads to the creation of 'vessels', one of which is 'primordial humanity', which then 'break' from the irresistible pressure of the divine light which they contain. This 'breaking of the vessels' leads to the roots of evil.

The point can be expressed in a rather Platonic way, in terms of the inescapable imperfections that exist specifically in matter. Maimonides sees matter as limited and a source of deficiency, and reasons that this makes imperfections in the material order unavoidable,[6] as if in Murphy's Law: 'If matter can go wrong – and it can – then it will.' It is just inevitable in a material world that things will not be perfect.

Both Augustine and Aquinas engage the ontological difference between God and the world to explain the existence of suffering and evil. They further develop the doctrine by suggesting that in order to have a full range of good things, a hierarchy of goods must exist. Not only does this entail some rather defective things at one end of the continuum, there are some things that arise from change, which itself brings imperfection. Vardy suggests that without this, 'there would be no fading rose, no spring and no autumn. No birth, no marriage and no death.'[7]

Kropf weaves this Thomist tradition across the woof of a modern conception of evolution:

Perhaps evil, or what we take to be evil, especially in the course of natural events, exists primarily because creation, understood as an evolutionary process, necessarily begins with forms of existence that are as totally unlike God as possible. This would not deny God's immanence or presence within the working of the process, but rather offer a new, dynamic understanding of what Thomas Aquinas said long ago: that the basic reason for God's immanence within creation (sustaining things' existence and providentially guiding them toward their fulfilment) is to be found precisely in his total 'otherness' from them as the transcendent cause of their existence. In terms of good and evil, this would mean that created things, at least in their primitive evolutionary beginnings, would be at the same time as totally unlike God and as imperfect as could be imagined![8]

Evolution and inevitably metaphysical imperfection can be used to reckon with the defects of the material world – but also with the defects of the moral world. Psychological and spiritual versions of 'evolution' appeal to the tastes of the times more than notions of original sin. Human mischief might result from psychological or biological dispositions that may be morally neutral in themselves, but can be turned in the direction of evil. This puts theodicy into the territory of the social sciences. One such account is given by Ervin Staub, who in a study of genocide and mass violence examines the complex biological, psychological and sociological factors that can give rise to horrific evil-doing by ordinary people.[9] Or the account can be of a theological or spiritual nature; such as the somewhat mystical evolutionary vision of Teilhard de Chardin, or the philosophical account given by John Hick.[10] Hick maintains that the tradition of the ideas of the early Christian, Irenaeus, in contrast to the 'Augustinian',[11] places less emphasis on a Fall and paints a picture instead of fallible human beings, created in the 'image' but not the 'likeness' of God. The 'image of God' is found in human nature as it is created, whereas the 'likeness of God' is our final perfecting by the Holy Spirit. This implies that, as with a likeness to one's mother, one has to grow into and mature into a 'likeness' to God for it to be visible. Thus while we are born with moral freedom and responsibility, we are only at the beginning of a process of growth and development which will eventually culminate in the finite 'likeness' of God. Sin, therefore, should not be seen as a wicked revolt against God calling for condemnation, but as a weakness calling for compassion; it is part of our growth and evolution.

These accounts bed the existence of evil into the very nature of a created, material universe, in a way that makes suffering and destruction seem inevitable. They suggest that evil is not something added on to the world which could just as easily have been forestalled, or could now be removed, by a decent Deity. Rather, the roots of evil are just part of the structure of the universe.

One can question several points in these arguments, however. Is it *necessary* that matter be limited and inherently imperfect, or is that just a Platonic prejudice? Do we have to have degrees of *defect* in order to have variety in creation? One does not need roses to fade in order to have contrast in the garden; one can have stately lilies and humble violets to contrast with the shape or form of tightly scrolled rosebuds or loosely blowing blossoms. Finally, even if one grants the basic features of the argument, the sceptic could still demand that God explain Himself on a crucial point: why do You not intervene to act and ameliorate, to mitigate the worst side-effects of materiality?

A stable world

Here the theodicist can appeal to natural laws and they role they play in our cognitive and moral development. In order for the natural order to remain stable and predictable, it is undesirable for frequent divine interventions to take place to subvert the course of nature. This would undermine our growth in causal and moral reasoning. Reichenbach and Swinburne argue along these lines.[12]

Swinburne insists that for us to learn and develop morally, we need to experience the consequences of good and bad actions: one cannot learn from one's actions if there are no consequences. If we are to make moral choices, we need to learn from past experiences, and 'if all knowledge of the future is obtained by normal induction, that is by induction from patterns of similar events in the past – then there must be serious natural evils occurring to man or animals'.[13] But for this knowledge to develop, 'laws of nature must operate regularly; and that means that there will be ... "victims of the system" '.[14] But could God not intervene to protect such victims? If He did, Swinburne replies, 'others will not take the trouble to help the helpless next time, and they will be rational not to take that trouble. For they will know that more powerful help is always available.'[15] This means that as an unfortunate but necessary consequence, serious evils will occur.

Basinger observes that given the great number of widespread causal factors in our world, God cannot significantly lessen the amount of evil and death without having to intervene directly and continuously in our world.[16] Each intervention that upsets the causal apple-cart requires further interventions to right things again; or as Birnbaum puts it, even an omnipotent Deity could not intervene to overthrow natural laws without unravelling the cosmos.[17] Moreover, Basinger argues that if God was continually circumventing natural and psychological laws, it would destroy our belief that anticipated consequences will normally follow certain actions; in which case, 'we must seriously question whether we can retain a meaningful concept of "free choice" '.[18] Basinger concludes that 'continuous widespread divine intervention into our present natural system would make meaningful human choice impossible (or at least greatly lessen its meaningfulness)'.[19] Could we function as rational people if natural laws were continually disrupted and our own decisions frequently undermined, with unpredictable results?[20]

Eleanor Stump disputes that we can only acquire knowledge through experience of cause and effect. Knowledge or indeed divine revelation could come through other means, such as through dreams, or scientific experimentation. 'If the emotional force of such a dream were not enough ..., the veracity of the dream's message could be tested – by animal experiments, for example.'[21] If such experimentation frequently proved such dreams to be true, we would come to trust them more and more.

I wonder how we would distinguish the informative dreams from the rest? If we could not, would we be obliged to test *all* the suggestions made by dreams, and test *all* substances to find out which were dangerous? That might lead to *increased* suffering, indeed needless suffering. For scientific investigation itself is neither morally neutral nor harmless. Experiments on animals are viewed by many as an increase of evil and suffering, not a reduction of it. The suffering of animals itself is already a theodicial problem, and not only for modern thinkers: al-Maʿarrī, who died in 1057, raised the problem of animal suffering as a serious challenge to God's compassion.[22] As long as we deliberately inflict or risk harm

to any beings whatever, it cannot be said that evil and suffering have been eliminated, or possibly even reduced. Experimentation may permit us a degree of
knowledge sufficient to avoid taking a harmful substance *in ignorance*, but the
substance could still be accidentally ingested or deliberately used to poison
someone. Stump's possible world may not be much of an improvement on the
present one.[23]

Human responsibility

'To be sure, it was often possible to put the blame on man himself. So tight was
the network of rules and prohibitions that surrounded him that to sin and offend
the gods was the easiest thing to do.'[24] Like the ancient Mesopotamians
described here, most religious traditions suggest that evil mainly exists insofar
as we create it ourselves or deserve it. This seems to be an idea that occurs easily
to human beings.

Karma

The simplest solution to the origin of evil within Indian religion begins with the
supposition that karma can be transferred from one individual to another. Then
one can suggest that evil results from the transfer of the Creator's bad karma
from to humanity: 'in particular, Indra and Śiva wipe off their moral dirt on us,'
as Wendy Doniger O'Flaherty relates.[25]

So what is this karma? Obeyesekere identifies the lineaments of the 'karmic
eschatology' shared by Hinduism, Jainism, and Buddhism:

- A theory of rebirth that postulates a cyclical theory of continuity, so
  that death is merely a temporary state in a continuing process of births
  and rebirths.
- A theory of karma that postulates that one's present existence is determined for the most part by the ethical nature of one's past actions.
- A theory of the nature of existence known as saṃsāra, which includes
  all living things in the cycle of endless continuity.
- A theory of salvation (nirvāṇa), the salient characteristic of which is
  the view that salvation must involve the cessation of rebirth, and must
  therefore occur outside of the whole cycle of continuity, or saṃsāra.[26]

Obeyesekere thinks this eschatology evolved out of a simpler belief in rebirth,
which was later 'ethicised' into the karmic eschatology.[27]

The foundation stone of Buddhism is the explanation of the origin of evil and
suffering, and the account given by the Tathāgata stands out against the backdrop of Indian philosophy and religion. The origin of the suffering of human
existence is set forth in the Buddha's doctrine of Dependent Origination,[28] the
lack of understanding of which gives rise to our misery. Each phenomenon of

human experience is dependent on, connected to, another; they arise inseparably in a chain, but can also cease as each link is broken.

> Karma depends on ignorance;
> Consciousness depends on karma;
> Name and form depend on consciousness;
> The six organs of sense depend on name and form;
> Contact depends on the six organs of sense;
> Sensation depends on contact;
> Desire depends on sensation;
> Attachment depends on desire;
> Existence depends on attachment;
> Birth depends on existence;
> On birth depend old age and death, sorrow, lamentation, misery, brief, and
>   despair. Thus does this entire aggregation of misery arise.[29]

On the other hand, with 'the complete fading out and cessation of ignorance' karma ceases; when karma ceases consciousness ceases, and so on; and thus the knitting of misery can unravel once that first stitch is severed. Ignorance, then, is the root cause of all suffering and evil in the Buddhist tradition.

In contrast, the Hindu scriptures all recognise a diversity of possible causes of trouble. It could arise from immediate or past human action, from divine action, from hereditary traits, from natural causes, from sorcery, or simply 'fate'.[30] The most salient network of ideas accounting for the existence of evil and suffering, however, is the combined doctrines of saṃsāra and karma. So crucial does the theory of karma become, that some effort went into ensuring that theories about causality in the natural world do not undermine the moral force of the karma doctrine. This rationale has been suggested for the origin of the concept of adṛṣṭa in the Vaiśeṣika philosophical tradition.[31] This 'unseen', the invisible controlling force, that moves things, thus accounting for various inexplicable phenomena in the natural world (such as magnetism), also moves minds and events. It is also used then as an overarching term for merit and blame, dharma/adharma, as that force which ensures the functioning of karma. In this way 'it functions as the key factor in reinterpreting the "natural" world as saṃsāra, that is, as a mechanism of reward and punishment, or karmic retribution'.[32] It not merely supplements but begins to replace conceptions of purely material causality, by offering a way in which natural events can be understood as punishment and reward in the karmic process.

Although karma is distinctively Indian in origin, the conviction that human responsibility is at the bottom of the matter appears in many different religions. The Jewish notion of *tochacha* (based on Lev. 26 and Deut. 28) tells us that trouble is primarily a divine punishment for sin, and should prompt us to examine our deeds. This punishment can extend to the children of sinful parents (cf. Ex. 34.7, 20.5) or to other members of the community. The agency of God in enacting this punishment is explicit in the concept of *tochacha*, whereas Indian traditions differ on the question of whether karma requires a God to oversee and administer it.

Whose ignorance?

As we have seen (in Chapter 7), the Vedāntin tradition faces a particular problem in accounting for the onset of evil and suffering. Suffering, evil, indeed the whole universe itself, good and bad, arises from ignorance. But Advaitins also maintain that we are not ultimately differentiated from one another but are all, at our most real, identical with Brahman. So how can Brahman give rise to what is delusory?[33]

Three styles of solution can be distinguished, although they are not opposed and indeed can be found in a single thinker. One form of justification is to emphasise human responsibility and dissociate Brahman from ignorance; another is to distinguish 'Brahman' from 'Īśvara' and hold the latter responsible; thirdly, one can boldly suppose Brahman itself to be the support of ignorance.

Śankara himself distinguished 'Brahman', from 'Īśvara', or 'nirguṇa Brahman' from 'saguṇa Brahman': the divine with and without attributes. The ultimate reality is Brahman without attributes: nirguṇa Brahman. It is unconditioned and indescribable, and cannot be separated into itself and its properties (for example, it doesn't 'have consciousness'). Beyond name or form, it nevertheless assumes different forms because it is its nature to express itself. Brahman as 'saguṇa', on the other hand, for whom Śankara uses the name Īśvara ('God', 'Lord'), possesses all qualities. Īśvara is a relational reality, a mode of Brahman's expression which makes the empirical world possible. This is what makes it possible to know Brahman by many names and forms; even though they themselves are ultimately unreal: they are mediated through Īśvara. Īśvara is phenomenal appearance, and unlike Brahman is conditioned by māyā. It is Īśvara who is the material and efficient cause of the world, is immanent in it, as its inner self, its 'inner controller', as the Upaniṣads so often put it. Īśvara is not, however, the highest, most ultimate reality. Thus Śankara can maintain the absolute purity and transcendence of the divine, while incidentally accounting for the origin of the world,[34] the misunderstood realm of appearance, and with it evil and suffering.

Nevertheless, Śankara will not be drawn on the question: whose ignorance is it that causes the sufferings of existence; ours or Brahman's? Where does it come from? These are philosophically irrelevant; to ask them betrays misunderstanding; he sets them aside with 'frivolity'.[35] Ignorance does not have a positive existence; insofar as it is not a thing you can have, no one has it. What is important, in Śankara's view, is to recognise the widespread misrecognition on which all our perception and action is based – better still, to get rid of it.

Followers of Śankara are less ascetic in their philosophical practice.[36] Maṇḍana attributes ignorance to individual souls,[37] to avoid making Brahman subject to saṃsāra, the cycle of births and deaths. Śankara's pupil Sureśvara, also arguing that ignorance is not a property, can thereby assert that it is therefore neither a property of Brahman, nor distinct from it. Instead, he associates it with individual souls, who in their ignorance generate the perceptions of the material world and its conditions. Under the sway of imagination, the souls thus constitute the māyā of the world. Both the souls and the ignorance he suggests are eternal, which answers the question of how they arise: they don't *arise*. They are themselves internally self-contradictory. This means that inconsistencies in the account can be placed at the door of māyā itself, not the philosopher. If one could give a rational and consistent account of it, it wouldn't be māyā; it would be a reality. – Nayak claims that this won't do; 'it is difficult to understand how a concept or a principle, which is inconsistent and is not itself explainable, can satisfactorily work as an explanatory theory of the origin of the world'.[38]

On the other hand, Sureśvara does grasp the nettle of the underlying identity of Brahman with individual beings, that gives rise to the very problem.[39] For he also asserts that ignorance, as the failure to perceive the ultimate oneness of the Self, *does* affect Brahman. Depending on how you construe Sureśvara, either this might be no serious matter, because ignorance is unreal and Brahman remains unaffected. Alternatively, he can be read as asserting that Brahman 'has transformed itself into the subject-object relation and has generated the entire domain of world distinctions. To account for ignorance, therefore, one must say that the pure Self is ignorant in regard to itself, and eventually produces the illusion of individual persons and empirical phenomena.'[40] This is, in comparison, an eyebrow-raising theology. Padmapāda and Prakāśātman develop this idea into the view that Brahman is both the object of ignorance, in that it is the absolute unity of Brahman that is misconceived, and also the support of ignorance. All the Vedāntin thinkers, however, are united in the belief that Brahman remains pure and undefiled by the superimposition of this ignorance; perhaps one should return to Śankara's own writing for the reminder that it is only important to know the source of suffering if one intends to remedy it.

The Fall

How did we come to be, from creations of God, what we now are, creations of *humanity*?[41]

The human origin of evil is sometimes depicted in narrative or mythological form. The story is told in Judaism, Christianity, and Islam, that an omnibenevolent God created a first human couple, to be his vice-regents on earth, as the Qur'an describes it, and created a paradise for them to inhabit. Other rational beings, angels, were also created. Both the humans and the angels were endowed with free will. One angel, Lucifer or Satan in the Christian tradition, Iblis in the Islamic, used his free will to rebel against God; to place himself first. He and those who followed his example fell from grace; their previously good natures became twisted and infected by evil. These angels became the Devil and the demons, who tempt others and create evils and suffering in the world.

Adam and Eve, the first human pair, were tempted by Satan into disobeying the rules God had laid down for the enjoyment of Eden. They changed thereby the course of human history: they were expelled from Paradise and condemned to live in conditions of greater physical hardship. In the Islamic tradition, they repented and their continued existence is portrayed as a form of second chance. In the Christian tradition, a continued faultline runs through humanity in the form of 'original sin': as Augustine interprets it, all human beings were present seminally in Adam, and thus all were corrupted. The notion of 'original sin' is traditionally interpreted as implying that no human being is born free of sin; none has the perfect will power to avoid sin. All evil is thus explained in terms of sin; not only moral evil, but also (potentially) natural evil, which could be attributed to demonic activity.

In the Mahābhārata, the sage Mārkaṇḍeya gives an account of karma and saṃsāra in a story of human origins that has interesting parallels with the Semitic 'Fall' mythology, albeit within a thoroughly Indian metaphysical framework.[42] In the primal age, human beings lived in 'pure' bodies, were free of physical and moral imperfections, were godlike, honest, and pious; were able to commute between heaven and earth and to see the gods directly, without any aid or special procedures. Their lifespan ran to thousands of years. But over time, they fell prey to wrath and lust, became subject to delusion, and then were reborn in unfortunate incarnations (demons, animals, mere human beings) and accumulated a store of evil and good deeds. Thus begins karma; our past actions 'follow us like a shadow'. But even in this fallen state, the wise may gain insight into this state of affairs and with lives of piety may gain control over their fates through good and wise action.

It may be observed that Fall accounts do not so much solve the problem of the origin of evil, as shunt it further back in human history. Why did the godlike creatures of Mārkaṇḍeya fall prey to vice; why did Lucifer sin? We need another answer to these questions, if evil is not to remain anthropologically inexplicable. The existence of a Devil is controversial (although both Plantinga and Vardy hold it out as a possibility).[43] Many also find the notion of an original human pair created at the beginning of the universe to be impossible to swallow in an age where most Westerners, at least, are convinced by Darwin. This picture of a Fall has also been attacked on ethical grounds, that is, that it has lead to some very undesirable results, for example in the view and treatment of women[44] (though the Islamic account of the Fall holds Adam and Eve equally responsible).

Subtle order

Reflect! The order of life
Is a subtle, marvellous, unique order,
For nothing but death endears life,
And only the fear of tombs adorns it;
Were it not for the misery of painful life,

People would not grasp the meaning of happiness.
Whomever the scowling of dark does not terrify,
Does not feel the bliss of the new morning.[45]

A final network of explanations for the reality of evil arises from logical considerations. Is evil the logically necessary counterpart to good? Can some good
results only arise by means of some bad things? Could we recognise and appre-
ciate good if there was no evil?

The appeal for a half-mercy

The Islamic theologian al-Naẓẓām argued that a just world required a mixture of
opposing components, including good and evil. These reflections were developed by his student, al-Jāḥiẓ. If creation were totally good, 'the requisite testing,
the trial-and-error conducive to thought, would also cease'.[46] 'It is the opposition of things within creation that provokes thought. Without thought, there
would be neither discrimination nor choice. Knowledge itself would no longer
be possible …. It is through the opposition of good and evil, perfect and imperfect, that we acquire knowledge.'[47] Where Swinburne, Basinger and others have
argued that one needs to experience consequences of action to develop moral
knowledge, here al-Jāḥiẓ extends the principle to all cognition.

Mackie has three responses to the claim that the universe is better with some
evil in it. None is devastating to the theodicist, and none addresses al-Jāḥiẓ's
epistemological point.[48] First, he notes that the goods which result from evil are
only derivative; why then does it make sense to promote misery in order to
maintain happiness? Secondly, this suggests 'that God is not in our sense benevolent or sympathetic: he is not concerned to minimise evil …, but only to
promote good …; and this might be a disturbing conclusion for some theists.'[49]
Then again, it might not. Believers in most religious traditions place a higher
value on 'virtues' than on 'pleasures', and are untroubled by the thought that
God allows some suffering because of its tendency to promote growth and maturity. We do the same for our children. Finally, Mackie states that 'first-order
evils' (suffering, discomforts) may be balanced by 'first-order good', i.e. pleasure. He claims that the theist invokes second-order good (virtues) that arises out
of first-order evil and makes it worthwhile. But this is cancelled out by second-
order evils (vices). So the theist has to posit 'third-order goods' to cope with
those, 'and we should be well on the way to an infinite regress, where the solution of a problem of evil, stated in terms of evil (n), indicated the existence of an
evil ($n + 1$), and a further problem to be solved'.[50] If this *structure* is absurd,
well, no one but Mackie has suggested that the joys and sufferings of life are
constructed like a multi-story car park. In real life, virtues or 'second-order
goods' respond both to pains and to vices and there is no 'further problem to be
solved' with a different level of goods.

If it were really *logically impossible* to have good without evil, God could not have arranged the world otherwise, (if you think God cannot do the logically impossible), and God's goodness is defended. But two objections can be made to this claim. The first is that evil and good are not really opposites, or not *logical* opposites. The second is that God could have created a universe in which natural and moral evils were not necessary for the good things to arise.

Mackie argues that good and evil are not logical opposites (unless evil is the privation of good, but not everyone accepts this Augustinian definition of evil). Moreover, not everything has to have an opposite in order to exist: 'it is not really impossible that everything should be, say, red, that the truth is merely that if everything were red we should not notice redness'.[51] In the same way, 'God might have made everything good, though *we* should not have noticed it if he had.'[52]

The other side of the coin is to say that there is no evil that does not contain some good in it; Muslim thinkers unpacked this idea frequently, often with examples such as the amputation of a gangrenous hand. 'God created nothing without there being wisdom in it, and He created nothing without there being blessing in it, either for all people or for some of them. Thus in God's creation of suffering, there is blessing, too, either for the sufferer or for someone else.'[53]

The second objection, that God could have created a world in which evil was *not* necessary for good, has some force. Generosity is still possible where there is no shortage. The world could be like Christmas for the middle classes: an opportunity to give freely to those who already have much. Empathy, if not sympathy or compassion, would still be possible: we could enjoy one another's pleasures and rejoice in their joys, and the consolation of sympathising with their suffering would be very easy to forgo.

But could we have forgiveness where there is no wrongdoing, or courage where there is no tribulation or danger? For *certain* goods, *certain* evils might be necessary. Without malicious injury, there could be no forgiveness; without danger, there could be no courage.

Mackie objects to this approach because it appears to set a limit to what a supposedly omnipotent God can do.[54] If God cannot create good without some evil, there is a limit to His power. 'It would be a *causal* law that you cannot have a certain end without a certain means, so that if God has to introduce evil as a means to good, he must be subject to at least some causal laws.'[55] This view, however, he thinks is unacceptable to theists, who believe that God created causal laws and is not limited by them. In fact, this is not so much a causal issue as a logical one, and the question of whether God is bound by logic is a disputed one.

Still, we could renounce such virtues as arise in response to vices, and we might be better off. Mesle argues that 'With regard to friends it is loyalty which we value, not the fear of betrayal.'[56] Quite so; who values the fear of betrayal? But why, precisely, *do* we value loyalty? It is because we know of, have experienced, the alternative. If there were no possibility of betrayal, loyalty would be unnoticed rather than celebrated, because the possibility of betrayal by a friend would be unknown.

This is why the logical point, rightly understood, is important to the theodicist. We do not require the full panoply of evils in order to have any good things whatever. We can imagine plenty, pleasure, and love in a paradise free from natural dangers and moral wrongs. But *some* evils are necessary for *some* goods, and this *is* a logical necessity because it is part of the definition of some goods that they are a response to certain evil or painful situations. It hardly seems like a weakness on God's part if we say that God could not have created a world without forgiveness without the existence of wrongdoing to forgive. For this inability is not the inability to do something very difficult or a bondage to a logical principle; it is just that the word 'forgiveness' would have no meaning, would not refer, in such a world.

Here is a Talmudic story: The Evil Tempter was captured. The captors started to kill him, but were warned that if they did, the entire universe would fall apart, so they contented themselves with imprisoning him instead. Three days later, they searched throughout the land trying to find a fresh egg, but could find none. When there is no sex drive, there can be no eggs. They were faced with a dilemma: if they did not release the Evil One, they could not continue with life as they knew it; if they did release him, evil would roam the land once more. They appealed to heaven for a 'half-mercy': the Tempter should live, but not tempt us with evil. A voice answered from above: 'They do not grant halves in heaven.'[57]

A zest, an edge, an ecstasy

… as though lovers in their rapture should mind whether the kisses hurt …[58]

Many phenomena are ambivalent when viewed from the perspective of human utility. Fire is both extremely beneficial and extremely dangerous. Many things can be the source of much pleasure, good, and benefit, but can be potentially dangerous. So to be rid of some evils we would have to do without some goods. I shall call this the Château Lafite Principle: no alcoholism means no fine claret.

Mackie might argue that an omnipotent God could have designed things otherwise. Red wine could have been divinely designed to reduce cholesterol without toxicity or intoxication, and an omnibenevolent God ought to have done that. Alternatively, as Mackie claims that God could have created human beings who always freely do good, God could have created human beings who always freely create fine wine but never *drink* it too freely.

The Château Lafite Principle however observes that sometimes the *same quality* can yield *both* pleasure/benefit *and* pain/harm. Recent research on diet and cancer has made the surprising discovery that a 'healthy' diet of fresh fruit and vegetables can *shorten* rather than prolong the life of cancer sufferers. The reason seems to be that fruits and vegetables and vitamins have anti-oxidants which do away with 'free radicals'. These free radicals kill cells and thereby cause damage and ageing and disease, so were thought to be unreservedly 'bad'. But the study has discovered that free radicals also kill cancer cells. So eating fruit and vegetables and taking vitamins helps to prevent cancer; but also helps cancer to spread once it is present by interfering with the now beneficially destructive free radicals. So the Château Lafite Principle states that to remove the harmful potential of some phenomena removes the beneficial potential as well.

The very name of the Château Lafite Principle indicates that pleasure is also at risk in a sanitised world. To remove the mind-altering or intoxicating properties of wine to render it harmless would remove much or perhaps most of the pleasures of drinking. We would only have *premier cru* grape juice. That would certainly be a less-than-best possible world. Danger and indeed naughtiness itself can also yield pleasures. God might have so created it that Belgian chocolates are as healthy to eat as broccoli. This is logically possible, but would it be as pleasurable? Would not the chocolates thereby lose some of their allure, their air of luxury and indulgence? God might have so created us as to always freely benefit from and take pleasure in what is wholly beneficial to us; drinking cod liver oil in a bubble-bath would be as luxurious and delicious as drinking champagne in the same location, and driving prudently would give adolescent males the same rush of adrenalin as driving too fast. But it could be argued that the delights of the freedom to enjoy things to excess so outweighs the tedium of a lifetime of forced moderation that it constitutes a greater good in itself; and the occasional pleasures to be had precisely in being naughty make free will and fallibility worth having.

It is rarely, if ever, observed in theodicies that there are even peculiar pleasures to be had in suffering and hardship themselves. An older woman, who had lived through the Second World War in Britain, once said to me, 'I feel sorry for your generation, that they never had a war.' My pacifist sensibilities were shocked at the time, but it was obtuse of me not to glimpse what it was she was trying to express. She was hinting not only at *virtue* but at *pleasure*: not only the courage and fortitude inculcated by the suffering and hardship, but also of some elusive *pleasurable* quality, the intensity of experience, some greater appreciation and enjoyment to be had from life in the face of death. I suspect it was vaguely akin to the extraordinary piece of advice which a friend's mother gave him: 'Arthur, when your back is to the wall, and you're fighting for your life, and even your friends seem to have turned against you – *enjoy it!*'

> Yes, to hunger and not have, yet hope on for,
> To storm, and strive, and be at every assault
> Fresh-foiled, worse flung, deeper disappointed,
> The turmoil and the torment, it has, I swear, a sweetness,
> Keeps a kind of joy in it: a zest, an edge, an ecstasy ...[59]

The perfect rightness of the actual

Overstretch one lute-string and the melody is lost.[60]

Ormsby describes al-Ghazālī's cardinal principle as 'the perfect rightness of the actual'.[61] His fundamental tenet is that the world as it is, is 'most wonderful', unsurpassable; as God has willed it and brings it into being moment by moment, it cannot be better. Even its defects contribute to its excellence; for it is what has been willed by God.

Maybe the world is so constructed, that 'good' truly is what pleases us and 'bad' what displeases us. Maybe these things are clear and unequivocal opposites. Perhaps it is easy for us to recognise and distinguish them. Perhaps in practice they could be separated neatly by a being with sufficient metaphysical clout, and when separated, the universe and we would be all the better for it. – But doesn't this picture seem simplistic and unreal when held up against the world as it is?

Of course, much of the discussion in contemporary Philosophy of Religion does not confine itself to the world as it is, the actual world. One common practice is to compare the actual world with evil in it to a 'possible world' – one different from this one in any respect: perhaps it has no evil, or human beings have no free will. Or one compares the world with a God, and a world without a God, to see which most resembles the actual world. Comparisons are then made between the actual world and the possible world. Somehow, the possible world usually seems to win at this game; at least when it is played by those sceptical of God's existence. But at any rate, if the possible world is better than the actual world, one has serious grounds for doubting God's goodness (or perhaps his judgement?) – above all, one has good grounds for doubting the existence of a God. The *actual* one is not the best possible world, and an omnipotent and omnibenevolent being would have created the *best* possible world. Meanwhile, the theists hasten to argue that the actual world *is* best possible world, or that the sceptic's possible world isn't as good as alleged, or perhaps simply allege that God is not obliged to create the best of all possible worlds after all.[62]

Aspects and moments of this procedure will become evident in subsequent chapters. Beforehand, however, it is worth voicing a few doubts about this particular theodicial game. I must confess that the confidence required to do this – to claim definitive knowledge of what the universe would be like under slightly different circumstances – simply eludes me. And there are more complex arguments against the notion of possible worlds and how it is used.[63] It does, however, have an historical precedent. David Hume seems to advocate such a procedure. His character Philo asks us to compare the way the world is with what someone would expect 'beforehand' from a Deity.[64] Hume's conclusion is clearly negative; there is too much evil in this world, and too much of it gratuitous and unjustified, to make it believable that it was created and is maintained by such a Deity.

The use of the word 'beforehand' is curious, however. For Hume generally asserts that knowledge can only come from experience. In fact, our inability to have a 'beforehand' kind of knowledge of practical questions concerning the existence of things is appealed to elsewhere in the same work, where Philo ridicules the possibility of knowing about the origin of the universe in the absence of actual experience.[65] So how can we form a reliable notion 'beforehand' of what the world ought to be like if created by a God?

The contemporary followers of Hume follow him also, perhaps, in this little inconsistency. Proper Humean scepticism, which rules out much metaphysical talk, ought to be applied to talk of possible worlds; or, even when such ontology is not explicitly evoked, needs to acknowledge the speculative and highly uncertain nature of its constructions. Such 'knowledge' about possible worlds is not merely held fast in the *absence* of experience; it is actually maintained in *defiance* of experience, of the actual. One should not lose sight, therefore, of the fact that such conjurings are imaginative constructions; like arguments for and against the parity of religious experience with other forms of experience, their true character is not one of ratiocination, so much as rhetoric; not inference, but attempts at persuasion. Its language is not logic, but analogy. Which depicted state of affairs is more *persuasive* in the end – how does it seem to you? That is the question to put to the arguments in the rest of this book, including my own.

Some defenders of God, however, take their stand on the actual world; and a world whose actuality is too complex to be reduced to a simple opposition of good (what we like) and evil (what we dislike). 'Through the combination (of disparate things) divine beneficence is perfected,' wrote al-Jāḥiẓ.[66] This suggests a different view of the world, one which recognises it as full of diversity, a coincidence of opposites which cannot simply be reduced to one another, and whose total appraisal requires a level of insight and discernment that we humans lack. 'In the negation of a single one is the negation of all,' al-Jāḥiẓ maintained.[67] 'The cosmos is like a living body; to remove or alter one part is to damage all.'[68] To eliminate a part of it which we designate evil or injurious is to amputate a limb. God has created a universe, full of defect and yet perfect in its actuality, for the divine purpose. 'Do you not see that the mountain is not more indicative of God than the pebble and that the praiseworthy peacock is not more indicative of Him than the disapproved pig?'[69]

This variety and plenitude of the world can be balanced and integrated into a dynamic and colourful conception of reality. Hawaiian religion does not spend much time musing on the metaphysical problems of evil. On the other hand, it espouses a principle called *lōkāhi*: unity, agreement, harmony. Lava is destructive of plant and animal life; but when its fire, its dryness, its barrenness is balanced with water, it makes a tremendously fertile soil, and the 'ōhi'a-lehua trees and the hāpu'u ferns move in and repopulate the renewed earth. For Hawaiians, the activity of the volcano was the act of the goddess Pele, in all her destructive power: a power for destruction, as so many stories tell, that often followed on human cruelty or hard-heartedness; but also the beginning of new creation and ever-increasing beauty. In Hawaiian thought, destruction is no less a witness to the divine than creation.

> 'ūhī 'ūhā mai ana 'eā
> ke nome a'ela iā Puna 'eā
> ka mea nani ka i Paliuli 'eā
> ke pulelo a'ela i nā pali 'eā

> the sound of the lava moving over the earth
> gnawing its way across the land of Puna
> making Paliuli beautiful
> the fine fire rising on the cliffs[70]

9. The Ends of Suffering

Different accounts of the purpose of suffering

If one way to account for something is to see where it has come from, another way is to see where it is going to. 'Why is there evil?' can be answered with respect to its origins or its purposes. This chapter moves into the terrain of 'theodicy' proper: patterns of explanation or even justification that defend God or the Gods for allowing evil, because of some purpose that is attained by it, or some greater good that comes from it.

Thus theodicies presuppose the principle held by Ibn Sīnā and al-Ghazālī: that God never wills evil for its own sake, but only wills it or allows it for the good that it contains or provokes. Stewart suggests that a number of these defences and theodicies are related and depend on a central pattern of justification which he calls the greater good defence:[1] that God permits evil for the sake of a greater good. There are different versions and variations, tailored for specific needs or to meet specific challenges.[2] Some argue that *every* evil is outweighed or counterbalanced by some good. The trouble with this is that it suggests that there is some specific causal or logical relationship between the evil and the good. This can be difficult to establish. So one might attempt to justify those evils not entailed by a specific outweighing good with the claim that they arise from or are made possible by other states of affairs which do lead to a greater good, such as free will, for example. A crime may not itself lead to a greater good, but it arises from a state of affairs – human free will – which opens the way for a greater good justification. Alternatively, rather than justify each individual evil as redeemed by a particular good, one might claim instead that the general aggregate of evil is outweighed or overbalanced by the aggregate of good in the universe, or evil is part of a world-history that, despite the evil it contains, will lead to a triumphantly good end.[3]

Mesle raises an objection to any form of greater-good reasoning with the claim that if it is argued that good comes from evil, that means that evil is really good. It is not then a 'real evil' but only an 'apparent' one.[4] Christian theology, by maintaining that all things work for the good or that all manner of thing shall be well as the mystic Julian of Norwich put it, 'implies that nothing is ultimately evil'.[5]

It seems that Mesle's claim relies on a confusion between derivation and identity. X may derive from Y without being *identical* to Y, and without possessing all of Y's qualities. My children derive from me, but are not me, nor does the fact that they came from me mean that they necessarily are everything I am. Hick, defending himself against Mesle, insists that in his theodicy evils 'remain unequivocably evil and such that it would have been much better if they had never occurred'.[6] Moreover, it is not the case that Christian theology 'implies that nothing is ultimately evil'. Rather, Christianity and other faiths inspire their believers to hope that no situation, no matter how evil, will go unredeemed. That is quite different from denying the reality of evil.

Yet there is another sense in which people of faith *do* maintain that evil is not ultimate – not only those who speak in terms of māyā, but Jews, Christians and Muslims as well. Christian Scriptures assert that while ultimate or absolute evil is separation from God, 'nothing can separate us from the love of God'; and that for those who love God, all things work out for the good. Al-Ghazālī and al-Jāḥiz also assert that even apparent evil is part of God's plan to work the good. But what they assert is not a perversion: that what is wicked, like torture, is in itself really a good thing. What they assert is the indefatigability of good.

Trau makes several distinctions which brings some clarity to these confused issues.[7] There is a distinction to be made between something being 'intrinsically' bad or good, and 'instrumentally' bad or good; something's instrumental value comes from what it contributes in the realisation of something else. The *overall* value of something comes from its intrinsic *and* instrumental value. If something's intrinsic goodness outweighs its instrumental badness (e.g. telling the truth even though it might hurt someone's feelings), or its instrumental goodness outweighs its intrinsic badness (telling a lie to save someone's life), then overall it has positive value. For the 'positive value' of something is not the same as its goodness; it is distinct from the 'good-making' or 'bad-making' characteristics of the thing. – The burden of Trau's argument, then, is to show how something which may be intrinsically bad may have overall positive value. It may be bad in itself to lie; but if by lying I can save a man's life by deceiving his murderous enemy, then my intrinsically bad act overall has positive value. Thus Trau's analysis is useful in providing a framework and vocabulary for articulating the complex interweaving of 'good' and 'bad' acts and consequences that we find in our lives.

Instrumental or consequential views

If one obvious way to account for the origin of evil is human responsibility, one common purpose ascribed to evil is human improvement. Such explanations of evil proliferate in the theodicial reflection of most religions.

Punishment and rectification

The Egyptian Jewish thinker Saadia ben Joseph Gaon named punishment as one of three purposes for evil. He balanced this with the idea that God awarded the suffering innocent a kind of compensation. The apparent iniquities in our destinities – that the good often suffer while the evil prosper – Saadia explains by distinguishing between the dominant tendency of one's action, which is rewarded or punished for in the hereafter, and the minority of one's acts. A good person might suffer because she is being punished now for her minor evil acts; but she will be rewarded later.[8] Saadia's Alexandrian predecessor Philo, however, disliked this form of reasoning and preferred the Stoic idea that virtue was its own reward; that God preferred us to choose virtue from desire rather than fear.[9] Much later, Moses Mendelssohn reacted against the idea of a punishing God as contrary to both reason and religion.[10]

This idea has even been used to address the problem of the Holocaust. By citing the notion of *tochacha*, it has been suggested that the Holocaust was a punishment on European Jews.[11] 'Lusting after Modernity was the sin, Holocaust was the punishment' is David Landau's paraphrase of the charge – a charge he rejects.[12] Needless to say, Landau is not alone in rejecting this suggestion as it is often seen as offensive to those who have suffered – many of whom seem unquestionably innocent.[13] The Book of Job can be seen as refuting this idea specifically.[14]

Ignaz Maybaum, however, has maintained that the suffering of the Jewish people in the Holocaust served a purpose. The role of the Jewish people is to bring the rest of the world to God:

> The suffering of the Jews in the Holocaust was the suffering of God's faithful servant for the sake of humanity. Auschwitz was like Golgotha in the Christian tradition, and the six million victims had purged western civilization so that it could again 'become a place where man can live peacefully, do justly, love mercy, and walk humbly with God'.[15]

For others, the creation of the state of Israel is the good that came about as a result of the sufferings of the Second World War.

The Christian and the Islamic traditions are more explicit in asserting that there will be a final reckoning to balance out any injustices that cannot or are not rectified on earth. The Last Judgement is necessary to convert an account of a Fall, as the origin of evil, into a theodicy, as the justifiable end; for most of us can see many instances of unresolved suffering or evil in our lives that call out to a just God for rectification.

However, the Last Judgement as a justification for evil is unpopular with many today. The picture of God involved is one that some find uncongenial; not merely does this God seem not-very-omnibenevolent; He does not seem even as benevolent as we like to think ourselves to be. Many believers would like to hold out the hope of all being redeemed, and thus the idea of a Last Judgement leading to everlasting punishment for some is less of a comfort to our sense of justice than an affront to our sense of mercy and compassion.

We have already seen the complex ways in which the doctrine of karma has been used to explain the origin of evil; but it has a kind of explanatory multivalence. It explains purely passive suffering: why things have happened to me through no apparent fault of my own. It 'justifies' God: as Śankara writes, the Lord cannot be reproached with injustice; for apparent inequities are due to the merit and demerit of creatures themselves. Ultimately, for all of the Indian religions that embrace the concept of karma, the essence of the doctrine is human responsibility and the inescapability of our own agency for good or ill. As that for which we alone are responsible, it sometimes contrasts with 'fate', to drive the message home. So it has another explanatory vector as well, most clearly seen in its Buddhist manifestation: it gives an account of *why* we are disposed to act wickedly.[16] Under karmic doctrine, however, while I am to blame for what happens to me, in a sense I am hapless: the activities of my past incarnation are beyond my awareness and control. In this way, the doctrine of karma can 'mediate between responsibility and non-responsibility'.[17] It does not simply engender passivity and fatalism. 'The acts done in former births never leave any creature. In determining the working out of karma the Lord of Creation saw them all. Man, since he is under the control of karma, must always have in mind how he can restore the balance and rescue himself from evil consequences.'[18] Jaina theory is explicit: all action, whether good or bad, causes karmic matter to attach to the soul, which weighs it down into rebirth. The only way to cease the cycle of death and rebirth is to avoid all action, in total ascetic renunciation.

How can this doctrine be used in a theodicy? Michael Stoeber suggests that reincarnation is a possible solution to 'dysteleological' (massive, pointless) suffering. It is 'a hypothesis of rebirth within which dysteleological evils might be understood as never utterly destructive .... This world, with all its terrible adversities, is justified as an appropriate realm of personal and spiritual progression to the divine life ....'[19]

I don't quite see how rebirth really solves the problem of unjustified, still less dysteleological, suffering – as long as it remains a reality or even a possibility in each existence. Life no. 75 may resolve any outstanding injustices either practised or suffered in Life no. 74, but insofar as it will contain new injustices committed or endured, another Life (no. 76) will be necessary to compensate for those. Clearly Life no. 76 will require no. 77 – and we are in an infinite progress, so to speak, of lives, each necessary to clean up the mess of the previous one. Readers of Dr Seuss's *The Cat in the Hat Comes Back* will be familiar with the structure of the problem.

I suspect the theory of karma is not best deployed as a theory of compensation, uprooted from the firmly ethical soil in which Jaina and Buddhist thinking above all have planted it. Karma is above all the result of one's own action, and does not serve to control the impact of others' action on oneself. (That is, it cannot *control* others' action, only account for it.) In the traditional Indian understanding, one can only bring an end to this otherwise endless cycle of rebirth by one's own ethical and spiritual endeavours in a life in which unjust *suffering* (as opposed to one's unjust *action*) is neither here nor there. If one suffers unjustly in a life which is blameless, that obtains the necessary release.

One does not have to be reborn *again* to be compensated. But where rebirth must do duty to make up for past suffering, God or apūrva must somehow guarantee that in the end there will be some life in which no unjust affliction takes place, so that one can progress to the divine life by one's own spiritual efforts, and not be bothered with the encumbrance of an offence against oneself which needs counterbalancing in a later life. And if God is prepared to control one's fate to that extent in one's last life, in order to prevent yet another rebirth, why does God not do it from the very first existence and spare us all the trouble of so much existing?

Testing

The book of Job in the Hebrew Bible examines the idea that suffering is a form of test; it is put on the lips of one of Job's friends as an explanation for Job's suffering. This idea figures prominently in Judaism, Christianity and Islam.

According to Saadia, testing was one of the three purposes of evil. 'An upright servant, whose Lord knows that he will bear sufferings loosed upon him and hold steadfast in his uprightness, is subjected to certain sufferings, so that when he steadfastly bears them, his Lord may reward him and bless him. This too is a kind of bounty and beneficence, for it brings the servant to everlasting blessedness.'[20]

This kind of account brings with it certain problems for the traditional conception of God. If God needs to test creatures to find out what they will do, then perhaps God is not omniscient. If God is omniscient and does not need to find out, what moral justification is there for subjecting people to hardship as a 'test'? Jewish exegetes wrestled with this particular question when interpreting the story of Abraham being commanded to sacrifice his son, Isaac (Genesis 22.1-12). Saadia interpreted verse 12, frequently understood as God saying, 'Now I know you are a God-fearing man', as 'Now I have made known [to all people] that you are a God-fearing man'; in other words, the 'test' was not imposed upon Abraham to inform God, but as a lesson and example for all people.[21] Hasdai Crescas made use of an Aristotelian idea, that virtuous action *makes one* virtuous; so the purpose of the test is to strengthen, exercise, perfect one's virtue which otherwise would simply have remained in potential. Isaac Arama set forth an account that strikingly foreshadows Søren Kierkegaard's notion that religion can place higher demands on one than rational morality (or 'the ethical', as Kierkegaard calls it).[22] 'God tested Abraham in order to teach him that rational, or philosophical, morality is not absolutely binding, that there are situations wherein this morality has to be "suspended" .... By commanding Abraham to sacrifice his son God taught him that there is a "higher morality", determined by God's will.'[23] Perhaps the advocate of this position could also claim that, while God might know that Abraham *would have* passed the test if he had been subjected to it, he could not justly be rewarded for it if he hadn't had to do it. So the purpose of the testing could be said not to inform God, but to give us the opportunity to earn honour and reward. There is also a kabbalistic theodicy of the 'bread of shame' which picks up this idea: 'If the good bestowed by God is not deserved (as in a world with no challenge), the recipient's pleasure will be lessened, or even negated, by the feelings of shame which always accompany undeserved favours.'[24]

Maimonides also finds fault with this notion of God's providence, and indeed argues that this concept is *not* found in the Bible, rightly understood. 'Know that the aim and meaning of all the *trials* mentioned in the *Torah* is to let people know what they ought to do or what they must believe ... the purpose being not the accomplishment of that particular act, but the latter's being a model to be imitated and followed.'[25]

The Islamic Ash'arite theologian al-Ghazālī also disliked this kind of account; he claimed that it likened God to a capricious tyrant who first slaps his servant and then makes it up to him with some financial compensation. He preferred the idea that suffering is medicinal; that, although human compassion may shrink from imposing a treatment that is painful, God who is all-wise does not.

The German Jewish Neo-Kantian philosopher Hermann Cohen (writing *before* the Holocaust) suggests that suffering, viewed as a form of punishment, is an important part of self-development and redemption.[26] This can be useful to oneself, for one is in a position to know what one has done; but is not to be used to blame others for their suffering. Nevertheless, suffering plays an indispensable role in salvation; it is a means to an end, an end which is understood in terms of better morality and ultimately redemption. Suffering marks the point at which religion emerges from ethics[27] and moves us to a deeper understanding of life and suffering, and a new relationship to my fellow creatures. 'In suffering, a dazzling light suddenly makes me see the dark spots in the sun of life.'[28]

Karma, as understood by Jains, Buddhists and Hindus, clearly points in the direction of self-improvement through suffering. The Sikh use of the concept brings a theodicial innovation. In a kind of theological pun, 'karamu' (Punjabi for karma) is juxtaposed to 'karma' – from Arabic karam, meaning the grace of God. While 'karma' does exist, it can be overcome by 'karma' in the theological sense; and it can bring us to union with God.

Suffering can be viewed as a punishment, then as a test, then as a way of purification, leading us to God. If one takes these instrumental or consequential views of evil as justifications for divine punishment, this view of God perhaps has more in common with capricious tyrants or harsh parents than with many people's notion of divine compassion, providence and wisdom. It can be criticised on grounds of anthropomorphism, of its notion of God's benevolence, omnipotence and omniscience. On the other hand, it can be viewed as an attempt to insist on *human* responsibility for human actions, and to exhort us to moral efforts rather than ethical passivity. It also serves as a way to speak of our inevitable sufferings within the framework of a relationship with God, an attempt which can be developed even further.

Redemption and union

Many religious traditions have a notion of redemption which may be brought into play in the attempt to justify or excuse God in the face of evil and suffering. Stewart, for one, has argued that all versions of the greater good defence are ultimately incomplete: what theodicy needs is to recover an appreciation of the idea of redemption. Against the backdrop of the question of whether evil is logically necessary for the existence of good, he writes: 'the good which logically requires the *existence* of evil is *redemption*.'[29]

The Orthodox Jewish theologian Michael Wyschogrod writes: 'The God of Israel is a redeeming God; that is the only message which we are justified in preaching, no matter how false it may seem in the eyes of unbelief .... If there is hope after the Holocaust, there is hope because for believers the voice of the prophets speaks louder than Hitler, and because the divine promise extends beyond the crematoria and reduces the voice of Auschwitz to silence.'[30]

That God will somehow redeem suffering in some fashion in the future is not demonstrable either empirically or logically to a sceptic, but what if such redemption is not 'pie in the sky' but a reality which can be experienced here and now? Stoeber claims that mystics in all faith traditions respond to the problem of evil in a uniquely 'mystical' way, and thus one can identify or create a 'mystical theodicy' across the differences in faiths.[31] This, he argues, solves problems that traditional theodicies cannot. Mystics claim a verification in their present experience of God's ultimate good purposes which redeem evil. Therefore, mystical experiences confirm theodicy's claim of God's goodness and look forward to the ultimate redemption of all suffering. 'Mystical theodicy does not merely point to a future spiritual eschaton that justifies teleology; but emphasises, on the authority of enlightened mystics, experiences of God's purposes in the context of the very transformative processes which are associated with the teleology.'[32]

Moreover, the consolation for suffering is also found here and now in the mystical experience of God, not in the hereafter. This is not purely a retreat from the real world, however; because mystics are also inspired to active love and compassion as practical responses to others' suffering. 'So in its treatment of the problem of evil, mystical theodicy offers a much more effective practical response than that which we find in non-mystical theodicy.'[33]

Yet problems attend on the notion of the 'confirmation' of God's good purposes in experience. How one understands and interprets an experience is not so straightforward. The idea that mystical experiences provide a 'verification' 'here and now' of God's ultimate ends, and that this is a new theodicy, needs to be addressed with more circumspection. To hear God telling you 'All shall be well, and all manner of thing shall be well' may be different from reading Romans 8.28, experientially, but it neither imparts any new information about God's purposes nor constitutes a 'verification' of them, so much as a reassuring repetition of what one has already repeatedly been told in the sources and scriptures of one's religious tradition. It is difficult to see how anyone can claim a *verification* of the end of history here and now. One can claim to have a vivid experience of what one thinks the end of history will be like, but the intensity of a personal experience is no indication of its truth or of its predictive power, nor does it constitute a new theodicy.

At the end of his lengthy *Guide of the Perplexed*, Maimonides suggests that the understanding of evil is inextricable from the spiritual journey. As long as we are united with God through our intellect, God's providence over us is complete and no evil can befall us. Such evils can overtake us only when we abandon God and are consequently separated from Him. The ability to achieve perfect and continual contemplation of God increases with age; in addition the great love for God increases 'until the soul is separated from the body at that moment in this state of pleasure'. This is how Maimonides understands the deaths of Moses, Aaron and Miriam: 'the three of them died in the pleasure of this due to the intensity of passionate love.'[34]

The Hebrew Scriptures speak of God as 'like a refiner's fire'. Hopkins, asking after the purpose of his suffering, answers his own question: 'Why? That my chaff might fly; my grain lie, sheer and clear.' Those who feel themselves in an intimate relation with God attempt to account for their pain as part of the spiritual path. Before we can be united with God, we must be purified; this is painful at times. Such lovers of the divine urge us to believe that suffering can transform us; therefore it is to be attributed to God's will, God's providence, even God's love: 'It is Love, manifesting itself in different forms, in one, it is a beseeching need, in another, a Perfect withhold. When manifest on the face of the lover, it is all suffering, when veiling the Beloved, it is all music.'[35] As we have seen, Sufi mystics like Junayd were explicit about the sufferings entailed in the mystic's development; a theme common in mysticism of most religious traditions.

'Whoever does not take pleasure in the trials of love is not a lover.'[36]

Developmental and evolutionary views

Soul-growth theodicies

In his teaching on Job, Saadia spoke of sufferings as 'instruction'; indeed as 'visitations of love' from God. In our own times, John Hick created a famous and influential theodicy which developed the idea that suffering is necessary for our personal growth and development.[37] As we have seen, he views humanity as in need of growth and development, rather than merely wicked by nature. So Hick tries to explain the mixture of good and evil in the world by characterising the world as a 'vale of soul-making', as Keats puts it. Hick observes that God's aim in creation must surely determine the nature of that creation; and that atheistic writers assume a purpose to creation which is at odds with Christian views. God does not want to create a hedonistic paradise, but an environment in which we can grow into 'children of God'. As parents want their children 'to become

the best human beings that they are capable of becoming', they do not treat pleasure 'as the sole and supreme value'.

> To most parents it seems more important to try to foster quality and
> strength of character in their children than to fill their lives at all times with
> the utmost possible degree of pleasure. If, then, there is any true analogy
> between God's purpose for his human creatures, and the purpose of loving
> and wise parents for their children, we have to recognize that the presence
> of pleasure and the absence of pain cannot be the supreme and overriding
> end for which the world exists. Rather, this world must be a place of soul-
> making. And its value is to be judged, not primarily by the quantity of
> pleasure and pain occurring in it at any particular moment, but by its
> fitness for its primary purpose, the purpose of soul-making.[38]

This theodicy has come under a attack chiefly for its optimism; it has been
charged with not taking evil sufficiently seriously, not giving sufficient weight to
'dysteleological' evil or the possibility of irredeemable evil. Critics wonder at the
sense of proportion that might allow the Holocaust to be considered an opportunity for moral development. Like many, perhaps all, theodicies, it must make an
appeal to 'mystery', or to put it more bluntly, to ignorance. To put it more bluntly
still, it must confess that it fails to spell out precisely why God permits massive
evils that seem to have no soul-growing purposes or results.

One has to ask whether this must be considered a fatal flaw in a theodicy,
however. The sceptic might treat the theist as falling short of her epistemic
obligations if she fails to give a precise, logical, and complete account of exactly
what God is up to in the universe. The believer might treat the theist as falling
short of her epistemic and religious obligation to humility if she thinks that she
has *succeeded* in doing so.

But let us unpack these theological suggestions as they appear in cognate
theodicies.

A Christian evolutionary theodicy

Richard W. Kropf has put forward a theodicy, largely inspired by Teilhard de
Chardin, in which he remains within the mainstream Christian tradition but
weaves the idea of evolution into the account.[39] Both the structure of the
problem and the solution remain largely 'traditional'; in that he insists on the
reality and goodness of God; the reality of evil; and the reality of human
freedom and responsibility.

In Kropf's view, God's activity is an evolutionary process; the claim that God
saw all that He created and said it was good refers more to his final end product
than to the present state of affairs. Kropf takes this to mean that moral evil and
natural imperfections are inevitable *en route*, and our image and likeness to God
is more God's intention than our present actuality.

The necessary unlikeness of the universe to God (especially in the beginning, before it has evolved) is part of the reason for its defects. Kropf also stresses the role that chance and indeterminacy play in evolution. Randomness lies behind both the 'progress' of evolution and the failures; which statistically outnumber the successes. 'Statistically, the failures far outnumber the successes when we judge them as individual ventures or experiments of nature. That we should call these failures evils is, of course, a human judgement, which must be balanced by the realization that evolution as a whole has been a success.'[40] The dimension of chance inherent in evolution, however, also entails great potential for things going wrong. 'Being ourselves the children of chance, it is not surprising that there also lurks, both within the void of the universe and within each one of us, a "dark storehouse" from which unknown potentialities may manifest themselves.'[41] There is always the potential for genetic mutation, for our own cells to go wild in cancers, and for the evolution of viruses and parasites.

So, on Kropf's view, there is no absolute distinction between moral and natural evil, because this world is one in which spirit and matter not merely coexist, but are indeed two aspects of a single reality. 'It is unreasonable' therefore 'to restrict what we call "suffering" to the purely human segment of creation.'[42] In the evolutionary context, suffering is a basic condition of the universe. All forms of evil await redemption, 'incompleteness and defect on all levels of created being share a common travail until all things are consummated in one great ecstasy of union with God'.[43]

Human suffering is the price of freedom. To accept the price of freedom indeed takes an act of faith.

> Yet the pattern is clear. Freedom has emerged, and with it, sin, while life has always meant death, and any degree of sensitivity has brought suffering with it. None of these has been possible without the other, nor have any of these fated pairs existed over the eons of time without a direct relationship to the rest. It is all of one vast piece. There is a solidarity in sin, as well as in retribution for it, and there is a solidarity in freedom as well. But there is also a solidarity in suffering, which makes it one with life and death, sin, and freedom.[44]

Ultimately Kropf's solution is to posit a God who suffers with us, indeed more than all of us; and 'God's response to the problem of evil is to be found in the mystery of his own suffering in Christ.'[45] The final answer for the Christian he sees in the Resurrection, the redemption of all suffering.

A Jewish theodicy of human potential

David Birnbaum has created a 'Quest for Potential' theodicy from traditions in Judaism coupled with conceptions of human potential. In Birnbaum's view, this theodicy both handles the classic problems of theodicy, and gives an answer to the painful question of how God could be understood as intervening in Pharaoh's Egypt but not in Hitler's Europe. Birnbaum expresses the core of his theodicy in the following five points:

1. The purpose of man [*sic*] is to quest for his potential – spiritual and other.
2. The greater man's freedom, the greater his ability to attain his potential.
3. Freedom requires privacy, responsibility, and selfhood.
4. In order to yield man greater freedom (along with greater privacy, responsibility, and selfhood), God has contracted His here-and-now consciousness, in correlation to mankind's ascent in knowledge.
5. With the Divine consciousness increasingly contracted from the here-and-now, and evil existent in the here-and-now, man is increasingly forced to confront evil on his own.[46]

At the heart of Birnbaum's theodicy is the notion of potential, both human and divine. 'Holy potential is at the epicenter of the Divine. Holy quest for potential is the underlying core dynamic of the cosmic order.'[48] The very first name for God revealed to Israel ('I-Will-Be-That-Which-I-Will-Be') is 'a declaration that the holiest state of the holy is God of Potential. God is the actualization of potential in its conscious holy form.'[48] This holy potential demanded more expression and so God brought the universe into being.

Birnbaum contrasts two dynamics: a 'Tree of Life' or 'Gilded Cage' existence, with a 'Tree of Knowledge' or 'Potential' existence, a life of challenge, possibility, responsibility. This latter is a state of higher dignity, greater knowledge and growth as opposed to stagnation, and greater potential for moral good; but it is also a state of greater potential for evil, and what Birnbaum describes as 'unleashed' natural evil. This is the path that humanity took.

We need freedom in order to develop our potential; the greater our freedom, the greater our potential. Birnbaum adds a new twist to his theodicy, however, with the claim that any expansion in our freedom and responsibility requires a contraction on God's part. This builds on the Lurianic idea that the creation of the universe could only come about by means of a Divine contraction, or *tsimtsum*. As part of a theodicy, Birnbaum postulates the possibility of *tsimtsum* as a contraction of God's 'here-and-now consciousness'. Birnbaum also uses the Hebrew concept of *Hester Panim*, or God hiding His face. This phrase occurs many times in the Hebrew Scriptures;[49] Soloveitchik calls it a 'temporary suspension of God's active surveillance'.[50] While the notion of God hiding His face was traditionally understood as a form of punishment or response to sin, Birnbaum considers it in a more positive light as necessary for the development of human potential. God's hiding His face leaves room for human freedom, privacy, and responsibility. Birnbaum sees a contradiction between Divine presence and human freedom,[51] and between

Divine omniscience and privacy. So this lack of God's conscious presence and intervention is not inexplicable, it is required by our need for growth. To give us the full freedom, privacy and responsibility we require, God chooses to withdraw, to contract his consciousness of what is happening. Birnbaum writes: 'As the contraction of real-time Divine consciousness continues, (as mankind ascends in knowledge and freedom) there is a commensurate lower incidence and level of direct particular Providence – for the sake of the general Providence of allowing mankind to reach its full potentialities.'[52] Just as the parent withdraws to let the child grow up, so does God deal with Israel.

This means, however, that not only are we given increasingly full rein; so too is evil unleashed as God withdraws his providential care and control. This could be viewed metaphysically, or, as Birnbaum does, as part of a kind of soul-growth dynamic; as we become increasingly mature and independent, so to speak, so we are challenged with greater evils. This applies at the level not so much of the individual, but of the history of Israel. So, Birnbaum's theodicy addresses one of the central challenges for traditional Judaism after the Holocaust, which is: why did God intervene to lead His people out of Egypt, and not intervene to lead His people out of Auschwitz – a much greater need?

It should be stressed that Birnbaum does not, in his use of *tsimtsum* and *Hester Panim*, intend to compromise God's goodness or loving kindness.

> If one wishes to challenge our thesis on the (incorrect) grounds that it denies Providence, one might be missing the larger meaning of Providence. For the ultimate Providence may be in securing mankind's freedom and potential for (primarily spiritual) growth and ultimate perfection, an attainment conceivably possible only in an environment of proportionate contracted real-time omniscience.[53]

This remains, firmly, a kind of greater good defence. 'To undermine "quest for potential" would undermine the very core of the Divine and of Divine Creation.'[54]

Ultimately Birnbaum's message is:

> Man is not alone in the cosmos, but in his own sphere man is indeed currently essentially on his own. Rather than being despondent that some cherished idols of dependency have proven fragile, man's spirit should be exhilarated. He should be uplifted by the awesome potential he has been given in trust; by the confidence placed in him by his Deity; by the magnitude of his personal freedom.
>
> When on his own, man is truly an extension of, and in the image of, the Divine. As the Divine is free, so is man.[55]

Clearly Birnbaum's theodicy contains an understanding of two traditional divine attributes – omnibenevolence and omniscience – that will disturb some.

The first is the somewhat wide notion of God's omnibenevolence, such that it encompasses (indeed, necessitates) God's partial negligence. (That is an unkind way to speak of Birnbaum's thoughtful and clearly devout theodicy.) The second, more radical and novel re-interpretation is the limit placed on God's omniscience. An allegedly necessary ignorance of future contingent propositions is one thing – intentionally hiding one's face is another. Birnbaum finds the thought that God is temporarily absent preferable to the notion that God, either through lack of concern or an extraordinary stoicism, is watching attentively but passively on the sidelines and does not intervene. But this is clearly a question of how one prefers one's compassion. Those who like to imagine God as being like a parent might object that children in hospital prefer their parents to be with them, even if the parents can do nothing to heal their children. For a parent to leave a child alone in pain, reasoning that he or she can do nothing to help anyway, is not usually felt as *less* painful for the child, but more. I suspect that most believers who hold to a meticulously provident and caring God would prefer a God of stoic restraint, who does not intervene for some mysterious but justifiable reason, to a God who finds our pain easier to bear if He does not notice it.

Admittedly Birnbaum's central thesis is that God does not want us to remain as dependent children. But most adults prefer not to be abandoned in their suffering either. A distinction needs to be made then between the desire for intervention and the desire for consolation; the former can imply dependence and lack of responsibility and maturity, but not the latter. Birnbaum's quest-for-potential defence would only absolve God of blame for not intervening, not for not noticing. Thus his solution to the problem does call God's omnibenevolence into question.

The implication I find chilling in this overall account of human history in relation to God is that the process of intensification of horror in history will continue – and the twenty-first century will contain even worse horrors than those seen in Verdun, Auschwitz, Bosnia, Rwanda and Kosovo. Birnbaum implicitly moves against this thought by suggesting that the process could conceivably be reversed. 'Should mankind become enslaved beyond an unknown threshold, or should the evil or its consequences penetrate the veil of cosmic consciousness, a decontraction is not entirely precluded regardless of the damage to human freedom. For freedom is of limited value if there are no living players left to practise.'[56] There is no point, perhaps, in asking Birnbaum at what point he thinks God *would* intervene; he could reasonably reply that that is God's concern.

On the other hand, the critic might also ask whether the twentieth century, horrible though it has undoubtedly been, has been more horrific and bloodthirsty than any other. Perhaps if one is working within the perspective of Jewish history exclusively, it is unquestionable that the Chosen People have suffered in the twentieth century more than in any other. However, if God's providence is conceived in a more universalist fashion, the argument for the escalation of violence in history is weaker and Birnbaum's schematisation of history limps a little.

Nevertheless, that does not particularly affect the central core of the argument. The crux of Birnbaum's theodicy is twofold: that human potential and the imperative of its development is the greater good that justifies God's stance towards us, and that God's relative abandonment of humanity is necessitated by the conflict between God's omniscience and our privacy, God's involvement and our freedom. To the former I have no particular objection. The second point, however, along with other aspects of Birnbaum's account, presupposes a view of the divine-human relationship that is open to challenge.

'Humanity should be, or become, independent of God; God's omniscience is an affront to our privacy; God's presence compromises our freedom.' – It is more conventional in Judaism, Christianity and Islam, to encourage dependence on God rather than to imagine independence of God even to be possible; but there is no obligation on Birnbaum to be conventional. More fundamentally, however, this account suggests a conception of God and humanity which is predicated on conflict and competition. Birnbaum's account of divine-human relations is perhaps one of those instances when an analogy breaks down and it is time to change horses. If a teenager's mother wants to know everything about her daughter's life and activities, it violates the girl's privacy; if a father is always hanging over his son, it restricts the lad's freedom; but do we need to extend these truths of human life and relationships to God? One can imagine that God wants to encourage human initiative and responsibility; but that does not entail that what is usually felt to be desirable in God (attentiveness) and these desirable human traits are diametrically opposed. Birnbaum's theodicy implies that it is impossible for both God and ourselves to be as good as our essences require. Without this kernel of opposition, the theodicy fails, because it is precisely this conflict that creates the *requirement* of God's absence and negligence that justifies His inaction in the face of evil. God's passivity in human history can only be justified by the greater good of allowing human potential to develop if divine and human responsibility are opposed.

Rethinking God

Of course, it is always possible not simply to juggle God's goodness and power and evil in order to keep them all going at once, but to rethink the concept of God so that His attributes don't conflict. This reconsideration of the divine has proceeded in three directions: in rejecting or redefining God's power, or God's goodness, or keeping both of these in play while loosening God's superintendence of the world.

Questioning God's power

Within Judaism and Christianity, there has been considerable discussion of late on the question of whether God still ought to be considered to be omnipotent.

Hans Küng, writing about the work of Hans Jonas, a Jewish philosopher of religion, articulates a new conception of God:

> Against God's omnipotence Jonas sets *God's impotence*, that of a God who in Auschwitz and elsewhere kept silence and did not intervene, 'not because he did not want to, but because he could not'. In other words, Jonas maintains God's goodness and his comprehensibility – even after Auschwitz. The omnipotence of God must be sacrificed.[57]

Process theology has taken the lead in re-thinking God's omnipotence. One of its chief attractions is precisely its treatment of the problem of evil. Indeed, Griffin[59] holds that the problem of evil is 'unique' to those who believe in absolute omnipotence and creation out of nothing. If, on the other hand, God, in creating, acted on some pre-existent actualities, they might have power of their own which they could use independently of God. Moreover, there might be some eternal and necessary principles that govern the possibilities of the situations these entities might be in. These entities, according to Griffin, have two-fold power: power at least partially to determine themselves, and power to influence others. God does not have a monopoly on power; these entities' power cannot be overridden by God. God's power, moreover, is understood as persuasive, not coercive. So to ask why God did not intervene to somehow *force* Himmler not to do what he did is to misunderstand God's power. God seeks to persuade, but cannot force, people to act morally. As Lewis Ford describes it,

> Divine persuasive power maximises creaturely freedom, respecting the integrity of each creature in the very act of guiding that creature's development toward greater freedom. The image of God as the craftsman, the cosmic watchmaker, must be abandoned. God is the husbandman in the vineyard of the world, fostering and nurturing its continuous evolutionary growth throughout all ages; he is the companion and friend who inspires us to achieve the very best that is within us. God creates by persuading the world to create itself.[59]

Why does God not intervene to minimise the effects of evil? Griffin responds: those things which cannot deviate much from the divine will also cannot be influenced by God very quickly. Those things which can be influenced by God quickly can deviate drastically from the divine will. Those things which can do nothing on their own cannot be directly influenced by God at all.[60] These propositions combined indicate that it is simply not possible for God to take the whip hand with troublesome entities in the world. He does what He can persuasively; but that mode of action, the only one open to Him, has so to speak a high probability of failure.

However, one corollary of the process view, which Ford concedes, is that believers have to give up the conviction that good will triumph.[61] There would be no grounds for claiming that it will, with any certainty; for God cannot step in to *make* it happen. Human beings – like God – can only hope for the best, and do their part to contribute.

Madden and Hare accept that God's power is persuasive in some respects, they do not accept that it must be persuasive in *all* respects.[62] Even so, process thought gives no theodicy that explains why so many people remain unpersuaded. Is God so ineffective in his persuasive efforts? Next, if a persuasive God only maximises creativity and freedom and not good acts and experiences, process theists have no more produced a theodicy that shows that the limitations of creativity and freedom in this world are compatible with the exercise of great persuasive power, than they have produced a theodicy showing that the extent and distribution of *evil* acts and experiences are compatible with great persuasive power. So we may just as reasonably believe that great persuasive power for *evil* is at work in the world, as great persuasive power for good.

Either you are attracted by the process view of God, or you are not. What is valuable, perhaps, even for those who are not, is the suggestion that God's omnipotence be re-considered. One need not reject the idea of maximal power or omnipotence in order to step back for a moment and reflect on what divine power might consist in, or how it might show itself (or not). God's power might not consist in massive displays of force and coercion; and just as human parents might refrain from corporal punishment on ethical grounds and pacifists from war, so might God not exercise coercive power; not from weakness, however, but precisely as a realisation of His omnibenevolence.

Questioning God's goodness

After the Holocaust, Elie Wiesel famously found God guilty, that is, responsible for the suffering of the Jews. But, nevertheless, Wiesel argued that Jews should not abandon traditional belief in God. Rubenstein disagrees on the latter point: how is it possible, he asks, to continue to believe in an omnipotent and beneficent God after Auschwitz?[63]

> If I believed in God as the omnipotent author of the historical drama and Israel as His Chosen People, I had to accept ... that it was God's will that Hitler committed six million Jews to slaughter. I could not possibly believe in such a God nor could I believe in Israel as the chosen people of God after Auschwitz.[64]

Despite this, Rubenstein feels Jewish identity and Jewish values should be maintained; he proposes a sort of Judaism without God.

Others have advocated, not atheism, but the rejection of the notion of an all-good God. From within the Christian tradition, John Roth has put forward 'a theodicy of protest'. On the basis of the 'slaughter-bench of history', Roth questions the assumption that God cares about history. 'This result testifies that such a wasteful God cannot be totally benevolent. History itself is God's indictment.'[65] The responsibility for all evil (including human moral evil) cannot be placed on humanity alone; God too is responsible – He is the one who started it. Moreover, human freedom, far from constituting a defence of God, is part of the offence. We have both too much and too little of it: we do not have enough freedom to overcome our limitations, but we abuse the freedom we have and thus have too much.

> Freedom's defense for God looks more and more like a ploy by the devil's advocate. That defense cannot avoid saying: only if freedom has the potential to be what it has become can there be a chance for the highest goods. But can the end justify the means? – that is the question. A protesting theodicy is skeptical because it will not forget futile cries. No good that it can envision, on earth or beyond, is worth the freedom – enfeebled and empowered – that wastes so much life.[66]

Roth believes in an omnipotent God who *could* intervene (because he thinks that a God who isn't omnipotent isn't worth bothering about), but chooses not to. Roth's God does not predetermine the future, and the past cannot be undone. Therefore, Roth's God is responsible for all evils: 'Thus, in spite and because of his sovereignty, this God is everlastingly guilty and the degrees run from gross negligence to murder.'[67]

Roth's call for action is complex. On the one hand, he advocates despair. Noting Rubenstein's observation that 'the Holocaust bears witness to *the advance of* civilization', Roth considers that there can only be worse to come. We can also only despair over the hope that there will be a future good that will justify what has happened so far. 'The irretrievable waste of the past robs God of a perfect alibi. Only if he obliterates truth by wiping out the memory of victims can a protesting "Why?" be stilled forever. So long as that question can sound, the whole human experience stands as less than acceptable.'[68]

Yet Roth also advocates trust and even hope – albeit the ambivalent hope of Wiesel: 'to have hope in God is to have hope against God.'[69] Rather than inaction, we should be fuelled by dissent against God to fight; for 'it is given to man to transform divine injustice into human justice and compassion'.[70]

> Such a God has no simple nature. He is tugged and pulled by multiple desires, but he is not at their mercy. They are controlled by his own acts of will. This God is no bumbler. He knows what he is doing, and that reality [*sic*] is the problem. Our protests do him no harm. Indeed, his license gives us a mandate to say what we feel, and we must … so long as we speak for the sake of human well-being. When dissent is raised in that spirit, its rebellious care may grip God's ear.[71]

Frederick Sontag advocates an even more robust indictment of God:

'Freedom' and 'will' as divine attributes become essential to any picture of a holocaust God. 'Contingency' and 'chance' are equally important. We must be dealing with a God who takes great risks and whose mode of control is at best quite loose. We face a God with a policy of non-interference, one who consciously created humans with a greater capacity for evil and destruction than any aim to enhance good can account for. And God did this by rejecting other options open to him, some of which are preferable from a human point of view. Such a God, certainly, is not easy or comfortable to believe in, but that is not so great a difficulty for organized religion as it might seem .... Only a God more difficult for us to deal with seems likely to account for a harsh world, once our romantic views of life have been exploded by passing through a holocaust.[72]

Is this a good answer to the problem? My inclination is to say, either we find an answer with an all-good God, or we adopt the perspective which says that we cannot justify God to ourselves, or we abandon religious faith altogether. There seems to be little sense in worshipping a God whose moral standards fall short of ours. Griffin's response to this account is to suggest that it will eventually undermine our own moral goodness.

The religious drive to be in harmony with Roth's God, rather than countering our own evil tendencies, will actually give support to them. This is the most unfortunate aspect of Roth's position: directly counter to his intentions, his position *does* legitimate evil, since it says that deity itself, the Holy One, the one with an all-inclusive perspective, fosters it unnecessarily.[73]

This is not to say that it is inappropriate to quarrel and rail against God. But the paradoxical statements of writers like Wiesel should be understood with the appropriate degree of irony, and the recognition of ambivalence that they represent – not as one-sided denunciations. 'The Jew has found it possible to simultaneously protest and praise.'[74] Wiesel himself expresses a complex and subtle ambivalence, as this quotation indicates:

I do not believe that we can speak *about* God; we can only – as Kafka put it – speak *to* God. It all depends on who is speaking. What I am attempting is to speak *to* God. Even if I speak *against* him, I am speaking *to* him. And even if I am angry with God, I am attempting to show him my anger. But that in itself contains a confession of God, not a negation of God.[75]

If one is to let go of the notion that God is straightforwardly good in the way that human beings are good, I think that rather than entertaining the idea that God might be at least partly bad, the theist would be better off following Aquinas, and claim that God's goodness is not identical but *analogous* to ours. God's goodness may not consist in arranging the world to our satisfaction, allowing us decent freedoms and rights but intervening when necessary; it may not consist in eliminating even horrendous sufferings. Thus the existence of evil is not necessarily incompatible with the existence of a God who is *transcendently* good. This in effect is the position of those who worship the Unaccountable God.

God's responsibility and providence

Should we, then, give up the notion of Meticulous Providence – that is, the notion that God is intimately involved in the world and takes infinite pains on its behalf, intervening continuously to work things out for the good?

Oliver Leaman summarises the Jewish philosopher Arthur Cohen's argument: 'To suggest that God could have prevented such events is to want him to intervene in the running of the world on our behalf, which would prevent us from exercising our freedom.'[76] In Cohen's view, God cannot be held responsible for the evil acts of humanity, because God no longer acts directly in the world. God has given us guidance on how to live; if we flout it, the results will be painful and disastrous – but not God's fault. God's goodness does not consist in His willingness to intervene, but in creating the world in the first place.

Although theodicies which deny or water down God's omnipotence or God's goodness may be unsatisfactory for many, they do inadvertently suggest one important insight: that in the usual case made against God in the problem of evil, there might be a problem with the concept of God in use. – Why did God allow that? Why didn't God intervene to stop it? – These questions suggest a Super-Social-Worker God, who ought to intervene with infallible judgement and timing to remove a person from a situation of danger and put her in a place of safety. It is clear however even from dealing with a toddler that people of any age and ability resent fiercely the restriction on their freedom that occurs when someone in a position of greater power thwarts their desires or disputes their judgement and prevents them from acting on it. They object even if the intervention is, or is alleged to be, 'better' or 'in their own interests' or 'towards a greater good'. It seems likely that were God to carry out this task continually, we should not be any more pleased with God than we are now; we would simply have a different set of objections against His omnibenevolence. And indeed, we would still see it as a problem of our suffering.

Against theodicy

Kenneth Surin quotes Greenberg's post-Auschwitz theological formulation: 'No statement, theological or otherwise, should be made that would not be credible in the presence of burning children'[77] and remarks: 'No attempted justification of God on the part of human beings can aspire to meet this test; indeed, the very thought that it is possible for someone to say, with the sufferings of these children in mind, that God is justified, is a blasphemy. This episode can only prompt penance and conversion; it cannot motivate a theodicy.'[78] Theodicy is a second-order discourse which 'has to confess its inability to address the "problem of evil" from a cosmic perspective which enables us to justify God'.[79] Our priority must be the first-order discourse of praxis.[80]

Tilley has extensively developed the notion that theodicy itself is an evil to be resisted:

> [T]he usual practice of academic theodicy has marginalized, homogenized, supplanted, 'purified,' and ultimately silenced those expressing grief, cursing God, consoling the sorrowful, and trying practically to understand and counteract evil events, evil actions, and evil practices. I have come to see theodicy as a discourse practice which disguises real evils while those evils continue to afflict people. In short, engaging in the discourse practice of theodicy *creates* evils, not the least of which is the radical disjunction of 'academic' philosophical theology from 'pastoral' counsel.[81]

His contention is that theodicy is purely theoretical, not practical. 'Theodicies do not respond to complaints or laments. They are not addressed to people who sin and suffer. They are addressed to abstract individual intellects which have purely theoretical problems of understanding evil.'[82] Both Tilley and Surin make explicit, and heated, criticisms of those who engage in theodicy:

> A theodicist who, intentionally or inadvertently, formulates doctrines which occlude the radical and ruthless particularity of human evil is, by implication, mediating a social and political practice which averts its gaze from the cruelties that exist in the world. The theodicist ... cannot propound views that promote serenity in a heartless world.[83]

> The practice of theodicy valorizes the spotless hands which write about evils without being sullied by them.[84]

James Wetzel joins in the criticism of what he calls 'speculative theodicy'; its vice is its inability to accept the possibility of irredeemable evil, since it appeals to an ultimate redemption of even the most horrific evils. The approach is 'one which may tend to deaden us to the harsher realities of our world'.[85]

Wetzel's assertion, however, is that 'practical theodicy' (such as Surin's; he is writing before Tilley's book) does not really constitute the elimination of traditional theodicy, but is more 'the tradition's loyal opposition' than 'the indignant rejection of theodicy's attempt to make sense of evil'.[86] It can suffer from similar defects. 'Questions of meaning and significance' can drop out of sight.

> But evil's challenge to faith's intelligibility fails to respect the contested border between the practical and the theoretical point of view, and expo-

nents of neither side can avoid coming to terms with the possibility of irre-deemable suffering. When presented with this kind of evil, practical theodicists are no less evasive than their theoretical counterparts.[87]

I have considerable sympathy for the passions and concerns of this style of critique (though I would dissociate myself from the tendency towards *ad personam* arguments against 'metaphysical theodicists'). I share their impa-tience with anyone who thinks that the life-and-death issues of injustice and suffering can be resolved with a correct application of Bayes' Theorem, or conjured away with logical quibbles and possible worlds. However, I think that the anger and the critique are somewhat misplaced.

This issue brings to the fore the question of the relation between practical and theoretical, or existential and philosophical ways of handling the problem of evil and suffering. To treat the distinction between 'practical' and 'theoretical' as a clear-cut and obvious disjunction is naïve. One gets the impression at times from passages in Tilley's and Surin's critique that the world is divided between acad-emics who never suffer, and victims of suffering and injustice who can never think.[88] It is not clear, in fact, what the alleged contrast between 'practical' and 'theoretical' responses is really meant to boil down to. Should we act without thinking, and are those who think necessarily inactive?[89]

Surin claims: 'There can be no possibility of rational speech in such condi-tions [Auschwitz]. This is virtually a truism (except, of course, for the metaphysical theodicist).'[90] But is that a description of how actual individuals felt and behaved? Or is it, as it appears, a prescription of how Surin assumes they must be? For some people do reflect on their horrific experiences, even while they are happening. Some people do remain capable of rational speech, indeed, theological reflection. Are they *wrong* to do so, are they thereby 'justifying' their own maltreatment? Or are they mistaken in believing that they are 'thinking', because Surin has declared *de jure* that one cannot? Is it not patron-ising, in fact, to declare that those who suffer, be they shanty-town dwellers or concentration camp inmates or rape victims, are incapable of rational speech? And if they are, does that mean that, despite the credibility as 'practical theodi-cists' they might have gained through their suffering, they too are really merely 'metaphysical theodicists'?

For all the good intentions of such a protest, it is surely unacceptable to decide that those who suffer intensely are somehow debarred from rational reflection on their suffering, just as it is unfair to assume that academics do not suffer, and do not 'sully' their 'spotless hands' with real, practical evils. Surin's claim, like much of Tilley's argument, in my opinion, creates a radical but in fact false opposition between 'practical' and 'theoretical', between experiencing something and reflecting on it. Of course peoples' minds can be numbed with horror and shock; but that does not mean that reflection cannot be done by anyone, at any time. Wiesel, so often called to support such protests, describes a concentration camp scene in which the prisoners see a boy hung on the gallows.

In response to one man's agonised question: 'Where is God?', another responds: 'God is there, on the gallows'. Is that not only 'rational speech' but more, in fact a theological critique of a highly profound sort? Is it a credible theological claim to be made 'in the presence of burning children'?

To demand that those who write on the problem of evil display a practical approach instead of dealing in abstractions actually makes a self-contradictory demand: that the theodicist make *practical* evils *abstract*, to speak of evil and treat of peoples' sufferings in a 'theoretical' way, which Tilley and Surin rightly deplore. What in fact Tilley demands is an 'abstract practical answer': for in a book, one cannot give a practical 'answer' to the problem of evil because *there is no practical 'problem of evil'* – there are a myriad of different problems. One can be raped, one's child can die of incurable cancer, one can live in extreme poverty, one can be imprisoned and tortured. In practical terms, these are not the same problem 'of evil'; the causes and the effects of the pain are not the same, the issues and questions raised are not all identical. One can hardly assume then that all of these problems require the same practical response, not even the same pastoral and religious response. Although Surin complains that theodicists write about evil as an *abstraction*,[91] there is a form of *generalisation* that is ethically acceptable, however. It wants to address the common questions and issues that arise for people who have suffered from numerous *different* evils; and arises from a solidarity that is trying to find a way to speak that respects peoples' differences, without reducing them all to an identical kind of person, belief or experience – or 'problem'.

What does the 'theoretical' theodicist not do in her text that she should do? Express moral outrage? Propose solutions to practical problems? Offer more personalised, or maybe less 'intellectual', comfort to the suffering? We have just seen that this is not appropriate or even possible except at a very narrow and specific level of experience. Or, alternatively, what does the theodicist do that is unacceptable? The aim of the theodicist is to resolve or at least reduce the painful philosophical tension that believers experience between the misery of their existence and the optimism of their faith. As a specific discourse of its own, it addresses the cognitive dissonance that one experiences. Sorting out what one thinks and believes is not somehow in opposition to feeling, experiencing, being angered by evil, or being moved to compassion or action. On the contrary, such reflection is a necessary accompaniment to action that is effective and compassion that is wise. The implicit anti-intellectual, anti-academic prejudice is ultimately founded on a faulty anthropology, that opposes thinking to feeling, experiencing to reflecting, suffering to pondering.

This does not legitimise evil acts. It offers the suffering reasons for having hope that good is the overarching context for evil, rather than seeing good events as sporadic and inadequate in an overarching context of pain and sin. It supports them in 'not choosing not to be'.

Finally, Tilley complains that theodicy wrongly tries to get God off the hook with regard to evils in the world. But – sharing, as I think I do, Tilley's and

Surin's values and ethics – that is precisely what a theodicy should do, in order
to place *humanity* on the hook in God's place. Blame *does* need to be taken off
God because it is humanity that perpetrates the evil.

He was a big man; a pillar of church and community. He was the man you
went to if you had problems with education for your children, or disputes
over farmland. Mr Gacumbitsi was the man who preserved order in the
crowded hills. Who kept a signed blessing from the Pope on the walls of
his home. His was the face of authority. So when he appeared at the church
on the first morning of the slaughter, Flora was completely taken aback.

And then the Mayor began shouting out instructions, urging the killers
into action. The hundreds of terrified refugees, who had fled to the church
at Nyarubuye, were surrounded. Slowly, the killers worked their way
through the crowd, Mayor Gacumbitsi allowing them to break for lunch
and go home in the evenings.

The task of killing was undertaken during normal working hours. But
as one of the mob told me later, 'It was exhausting work. Very difficult.'
To ensure that none of their intended victims could escape during the
night, the killers slashed the tendons of their feet.

It is not clear if Mr Gacumbitsi literally steeped his own hands in the
blood that flowed over the four long days of killing. But Flora clearly
remembers that he ferried the killers to and from the village in his pickup
truck and that he supplied the machetes and clubs which were used to hack
and beat and gouge. More than anything, she remembers his voice,
bellowing words of murder. It rose above the dull sounds of clubbing and
hacking; above the cries of the dying and the pleas for mercy.

A month or so later, I tracked Gacumbitsi to a refugee camp in Tanzania
where he had fled with thousands of other Hutu …. Not surprisingly, when
I confronted the Mayor with evidence of his crimes, he denied all responsibility. 'The Tutsis are the ones who say this. I am a Hutu. Do you think
they like me?' he said.

It was without doubt the most frustrating encounter of my journalistic
career. Gacumbitsi was clearly implicated in a monstrous crime against
humanity, and yet he was able to smirk at the allegations, confident that he
had escaped justice.[92]

Who was it that committed these acts, then, smirking, denied all responsibility
for them? And what would it do for this man's sense of responsibility to hold
God accountable, to speak as Roth does of 'human justice and compassion' in
protest against 'divine injustice'? 'Justifying' God in a theodicy, therefore, is an
important *practical* first step – not a self-gratifying 'theoretical' exercise. This
is because it rules out recourse to God's negligence or injustice as an excuse for
human misbehaviour. So long as God is to blame, we are acquitted and need do
nothing but complain to or about God; like Gacumbitsi, we can refuse to

examine our own action and selves, and instead smirk and deny all responsibility. Protesting theodicies, like Roth's or Sontag's, try to remove human responsibility, though they don't think so; the apposite question is not 'Why does God allow it?', but 'Why do we do it'? Secondly, the protest *against* theodicy, like Surin's and Tilley's, can obscure the crucial and practical question of responsibility for evil. In this context, I think – precisely for the sake of its own ends and values – the protest against theodicy is misguided. If no theodicy is possible, either a good and powerful God does not exist, or God is to blame – and therefore there is no reason whatever for human beings to take responsibility and become engaged with the world in an effort to transform it.

The justice of *which* God?

The task of theodicy is the task of creating the proper context in which to *view* evil, and where possible to *understand* it, and above all to *respond* appropriately to it. This contextualisation is in part the fruit of experience, in part the fruit of reflection such as is done in theodicy, and it is also an affirmation of faith: to affirm the ultimacy of good, not evil.

What of Flew's challenge to this belief?

> Someone tells us that God loves us as a father loves his children. We are reassured. But then we see a child dying of inoperable cancer of the throat. His earthly father is driven frantic in his efforts to help, but his Heavenly Father reveals no obvious sign of concern. Some qualification is made – God's love is 'not a merely human love' or it is 'an inscrutable love', perhaps – and we realize that such sufferings are quite compatible with the truth of the assertion that 'God loves us as a father (but, of course ...)'. We are reassured again. But then perhaps we ask: what is this assurance of God's (appropriately qualified) love worth, what is this apparent guarantee really a guarantee against?[93]

In Gareth Moore's opinion, this misses the point of what Christians say about the love of God. Flew wants to know what such a love is a guarantee against; Moore wonders why love must be taken as a 'guarantee'. One who says that 'God loves me' does not thereby claim certain things cannot happen; 'for he may say it when every conceivable misfortunate *has* afflicted him.' In fact, he may say it precisely *because* such things have happened.

> To one who trusts in God, one who says things like 'God loves me', what actually happens to him is irrelevant to the love of God for him. He has confidence in God, but that is not because he has learned by experience that God is loving, trustworthy and solicitous for his welfare. To say that God is loving is an expression of confidence in God, and so of a disposition to live in a certain way – not to despair, take to drink or commit

suicide, in the face of adversity. While he has that confidence, nothing is going to count as evidence of God's not loving him .... And to say that is not to convict him of irrationality; it is to make a comment on the meaning, that is the use, of the phrase 'the love of God'.[94]

The reason Flew's challenge cannot be answered on its own terms, Moore suggests, is because it falsely construes the love of God as being just like the love of a human being; Flew's challenge is really a challenge to his own false conception of the love of God. Rather than to look and see how religious believers actually use the sentence and therefore to understand what it means, Flew has assumed he knows what it means because he thinks God is logically the same as a human being.

> Hence he wants to say that one of the central and typical situations in which talk of the love of God is used – comforting people in great anguish – is one where it is not to be used at all. But this is like saying that it is illegitimate to use a hammer to bang nails ....
>
> To continue to believe in God means still to see a certain way of life as possible, and one who is that badly hurt may be unable to see it as possible. But if that is so, he has not been swayed by evidence; he has been affected, by what has happened in his life. A man may lose faith because of the death of his son; he is not likely to lose faith over the death of a stranger thousands of miles away ..., for it does not enter his life in the same way .... Belief in the love of God is not based on evidence, and so neither is the loss of that belief.[95]

The religious believer is not merely entitled but compelled to question the existence of God; and not just that but more, the *conception* of God that she has. This is where the incoherence in the theist's belief in the face of evil may lie. If God is conceived as a divine social worker who constantly intervenes to prevent us from doing harm, then either that God is incompetent, or apathetic, or non-existent. But is that the inescapable conclusion? Or does it rather suggest that such a notion of divine action is fundamentally misconceived?

10. Endless Suffering

Specific issues raised by massive or 'dysteleological' suffering

One can still 'believe' in a God who allowed those things to happen, but how can one still speak to Him?[1]

As we have seen, some argue that God could not have created a world with *certain* goods in it if that world did not contain *certain* evils; and they claim that it is a greater good for these goods to exist than not, so evil is redeemed, outweighed, or justified. But the most testing challenge to any greater good defence is the existence of gratuitous evil, or 'dysteleological suffering' as Hick named it. This is evil or suffering which leads to no good, or is so overwhelming that it far outweighs the good that is produced; evil no good can 'justify'.[2] How much compassion or courage or forgiveness or transformation would have to arise from the horrors of the twentieth century to justify such an appalling quantity of suffering? The existence of apparently gratuitous, out-of-scale evil that seems to lead to no good, or not enough good, threatens to undermine any 'greater good' style of argument. In the fact of horrendous suffering, such arguments appear more like 'lesser good' defences.[3] Even if one attempts to justify God with an appeal to an imagined outcome, one can still complain that God ought to at least offer some comfort: 'Given inscrutable evil, His failure to manifest Himself and His love is all the more striking.'[4] William Rowe argues: 'when God permits horrendous suffering for the sake of some good, if that good is *beyond our ken*, God will make every effort to be consciously present to us during our period of suffering, will do his best to explain to us why he is permitting us to suffer, and will give us special assurances of his love and concern during the period of the suffering.'[5]

One response to the problem of dysteleological evil, as we have seen, is to abandon the doctrine of scrupulous or meticulous providence: that God remains in charge of every detail of the world and history, that each situation evokes his attention, concern, and response. Instead, we might imagine that God maintains a general, concerned, interest in the world, but does not become involved in every situation and every detail, and therefore it is not God's job to try to sort out every problem that arises in history. For some, meticulous providence is an important part of their faith; and to give up the idea that God is listening and might answer every petition in a direct and involved way is tantamount to giving up faith in God altogether. But for some, it makes sense, and does not lessen God's greatness, to see Him as one who delegates responsibility to us. Perhaps God is like a mother who lets her small child dress himself, with predictably haphazard results, realising that her child's development and self-esteem in being responsible for himself are more important than getting the shoe on the right foot at the first attempt (or at all). So although some theists would reject this view, some might actually see it as a wiser form of divine love than smothering love of the over-protective parent. Thus something like a greater-good line can be spun out of the abandonment of the doctrine of meticulous providence.

If one copes with the philosophical problem of dysteleological evil by conceptualising a more laid-back or hands-off Providence, however, a difficulty arises. If God does not intervene to *ensure* that good comes out of this or that or all evil situations, what basis do we still have for claiming the good *does* outweigh evil, or will in the long run? In other words, how does good come out of evil if God does not *make* it? Do we have to imagine that it happens somehow automatically, or that God has somehow built it into the nature of things that good comes out of evil in the end? One solution might be to opt for the traditional Muslim and Christian notion of a final reckoning or Last Judgement. If things have not been rectified by then, they will be at the end of time. This response however will not do for the eschatologically squeamish. So one would have to deploy one's defences with the understanding that they only claim a loose or ultimate 'outweighing', and may not stand up to a specific accounting undertaken and balanced like a cheque book each month.

The ratchet objection

In observing that God supposedly maintains the world in being, we can ask why God does not withdraw being from the worst evildoers. Why did God not have Hitler die of diphtheria in childhood? Why does God not prevent evils, at least the worst evils, from happening, or intervene before they deteriorate beyond a certain point? Why doesn't God intervene to offset at least the worst effects of abused free will, permitting the freedom but ameliorating the worst results? Parents may well let their toddling offspring fall when learning to walk; but most would intervene to prevent a fall down a long flight of concrete stairs, reasoning that such a fall would not be best described as 'all part of the learning process'. Is God less caring and concerned than the average parent? Then why doesn't God build some kind of ratchet into the natural world, to prevent the worst evils from happening? Robert McKim, like Boër, has mounted such a challenge; God could have created a world in which 'we can inflict considerable harm on each other, but we cannot destroy each other'.[6]

Swinburne argues that God *has* set limits on suffering. 'There is a temporal limit constituted by death to the amount a given man can suffer. And there is also presumably a limit to the intensity of possible suffering, set by the constitution of the brain through which suffering comes to man.'[7] Dilley writes, the limits McKim proposes look quite like those limits which the orthodox theist would accept as being *presently operative* in the real world .... God does put limits on the damage that can be done to us, the believer might say .... God allows evil-wishers to harm the flesh, but God does not allow the essential person, the spirit, to be slain by evil-doers.[8]

The point that the length of time that one can suffer is limited by death or the onset of unconsciousness is not particularly consoling; nor is the observation that the amount of evil a human being can inflict is limited by their life-span. But the logical point, as it were, remains: in a finite world, suffering cannot be infinite. Nevertheless, I do not feel that this observation really addresses the issue. The complaint is not that suffering is infinite; but rather that though finite, the upper limit on suffering is set at too high a level. What can be said about that?

Perhaps God *has* built a ratchet into the system; perhaps He continually intervenes to ameliorate situations. *If so, we would not know it.* Not seeing a possible future which will never be realised, and never knowing for sure what would have been the case but isn't, we could never know what God may actually have prevented. We can imagine that a genocidal leader worse than Hitler or Stalin might arise, but we would never know that the child whose early death that we mourned would actually have been such a person. Therefore we cannot object that God does not prevent the worst possible evils, for in fact He may be doing so all the time without our realising it. We could at most object that He doesn't prevent the worst of the evils that remain, and can object to the point at which He decides to take matters into his own hands.

So God knocked off the would-be dictator who would have been worse than Stalin or Hitler; why did God not take them at an early age too? And if He did, why did He not miscarry Milosevic and Sadam Hussein while He was at it? – It is clear from following this line of reflection that pain and vice form a kind of continuum; from scuffed knees to AIDS; from fibbing to genocide. The fact that suffering exists in a continuum means that a God who intervened would not so much 'eliminate the worst evils' in a general sort of way, as draw the line at a particular point.

If suffering, then, is a kind of continuum, human perceptions are relative to other points on the continuum. 'The worst' is not a separate category or different group of evils, but the furthest point on a continuous scale of our experience. We can ask why God does not eliminate a particular evil thing; but to eliminate 'The Worst' would be as incomprehensible as asking God to eliminate the largest number. It is a task that could never be completed. If God had prevented the existence of Hitler and AIDS, we would demand of Him why He did not prevent those villains or diseases which would now be the worst on our scales of evil and of physical suffering. We would eventually reach the point at which dysteleological objectors would demand to know why God had permitted the existence of the American hero and founding father George Washington, who it is alleged supported the genocide of peoples of the First Nations.[9] Meanwhile, others would be arguing that the existence of tummy aches, or their least favoured politicians, are dysteleological evils and as such disprove the existence of God.

In the end, this objection reduces to the initial question of why is there evil at all. To fix on any point in the continuum of evils is going to be seen as arbitrary and arguable to those who would want to have it fixed two notches further. We can always haggle over the price.

Mesle does not agree, and responds to a similar argument by Hick, which speaks of a 'slippery slope', by saying that there is a right place to stop: 'There is a stopping place on the slippery slope …, and that is the kind of world best suited for raising children so as to be loving, trustworthy, and sympathetic people.'[10]

Mesle's suggestion might sound appealing as a rhetorical utterance – who wants to speak out against an environment that would produce loving, trustworthy, and sympathetic children? To try to actually *conceive* it concretely leads one to doubt that it makes any kind of sense, however. It is undermined first and foremost by the phenomenon of human diversity, which makes it look hopelessly simplistic to assert that there is one 'right' balance between fruitful hardship and lack of suffering. Mesle may be confident in knowing what the *world* best suited for child-raising consists in; I am not confident in proclaiming what such a *household* would consist in. Even if I were not frequently confounded by my own children as to what is the 'correct' balance between strictness and indulgence, ease and challenge, I would hesitate to assert that the best way to raise my child to be loving and sympathetic is the best way for everyone else's children. Experience has taught me rather that what works for one child is ineffective or inappropriate with another; what functions as a productive challenge for one is an insupportable burden for another. The same is also true for adults. To create an environment which did not crush some while leaving others insufficiently stimulated would require the ironing out of individual differences. Moreover, a sameness of life-experiences might also be necessary. An event that challenges and stimulates an adult, and from which she can draw greater good, might damage or destroy a child. So there would need to be metaphysical controls on certain events, like the death of parents, to prevent them occurring at the wrong time. What we must envision to make sense of Mesle's proposal is not 'an environment' designed to be supportive and beneficial, but a totally controlled and determined life-course for each individual. One could dispute that this is unquestionably the greatest good for human existence.

A best possible world?

In Islamic philosophy, the notion of God's justice was taken by some to imply that God is *obliged* to provide the best for us. The details of this claim were disputed. The school of Basra restricted itself to the relatively modest claim that this applied only to religious matters, and the optimum that God is obliged to provide is defined in terms of 'benefit'. The Baghdad school made the rather more ambitious claim that God must lay on the best, not only in spiritual affairs but also in worldly situations – according to His wisdom and providence.[11]

Yet the founder of the Baghdad school, Bishr ibn al-Mu'tamir, did declare: 'It is not obligatory for God to do the best of things for man; indeed, this is absurd because there is no end and no term to the beneficence which God can perform.'[12] And here he has made a point lost on some modern Western commentators. Many object that this is not the best of all possible worlds and imply that God should have created a better one: one with people who could do no wrong, with no natural dangers, or one with a different built-in 'stopping point' on the continuum of suffering. Others, Plantinga, Adams and Aquinas[13] among them, believe that the notion of a 'best possible world' is about as coherent as 'the largest possible prime number'. One can always push the frontiers back. Dream up the best of all possible worlds; now add a few more chocolates. You've now got a better best possible world. Now add one more act of gratuitous kindness. Your 'best possible world' is no longer the best. And so on.

But, says the ratchet objector, I do not demand the *best* possible world; I just want a better world than this one. Aquinas maintained, in unconscious accord with al-Mu'tamir, that as an important affirmation of God's omnipotence, whatever world is actual, God *could* always have created a better one. Aquinas felt it would be a compromise of God's power to claim that God could not, so to speak, outdo himself. The result of this, paradoxical for God's omnipotence, is that *precisely because* God is omnipotent, he can never create a 'best of all possible worlds'. To Mesle's boast that he can conceive of a better world than this for God to create,[14] Aquinas might have responded dryly, 'So can God.'

If this point is accepted, one could formulate a kind of mini-theodicy out of it: God cannot be blamed for not creating a best of all possible worlds, for that is logically impossible. No matter how good the world and our natures were, so long they were not perfect, human beings could (and probably would) always complain about such evil as existed. The relativity inherent in human perceptions and reactions to our experience means that we would find any evil or lack of a possible good to be something worth complaining about. And if the world, and we, were perfect, we would be God.

The end-justifies-the-means principle and the doctrine of double effect

Stewart observes that, just as many defences have a greater-good core, all of these in turn work with an end-justifies-the-means (EJM) principle.[15] It is necessary now to consider some of the aspects of this issue.

The EJM principle claims that one is justified in permitting or creating a less than desirable state of affairs for the sake of a good end. Obviously there must be some limits and conditions to this: the means must be causally necessary or, for an omnipotent being (who is not bound by ordinary causality), logically necessary. If one could achieve the same end without using that undesirable means, one is not justified in using it.[16] One might also add that the means must be proportionate to the goodness of the end. I may be justified in displeasing or angering my child in the course of raising him to be a moral and considerate person; but I am not justified in abusing him to attain the same end.

However, some find it inescapably distasteful to apply the EJM principle to God. D.Z. Phillips has phrased the objection this way:

> What then are we to say of the child dying from cancer? If this has been *done* to anyone, it is bad enough, but to be done for a purpose, to be planned from eternity – that is the deepest evil. If God is this kind of an agent, He cannot justify His actions, and His evil nature is revealed.[17]

In other words, it is bad enough that God *allows* evil to happen. If we suggest that God willingly makes use of evil to achieve His aims, the moral implications for the Divine Being are even worse. But does the greater good defence have that inescapable implication?

To say that good comes from evil does not require us to think that God acts to create an evil state of affairs, in order to then act in bringing a good state of affairs out of it. The theist as well as the atheist might reject that as absurd. All that is required is to maintain that God *allows* evil states of affairs to exist, without God being the one to *commit* the evil. The sceptic might retort that it amounts to the same thing. But does it? Even my small child can understand the difference between me inflicting something on him to teach him a lesson, and me responding to a self-inflicted or negligent accident by saying 'Well, you've learned not to do that again, haven't you!' Allowance of something regrettable that arises from other causes, knowing that something good can come of it, is not morally the same as deliberately inflicting the state of affairs for the purpose of instruction or any other purpose.[18]

It may be more useful to consider these questions under the doctrine of 'double effect'. An act may have two results, one good and one bad; it may be acceptable in some cases to perform that act to bring about the good result and suffer the bad, while it would have been unacceptable to create the bad result directly and as an end in itself. Thus, some people who are morally opposed to abortion in general are prepared to accept a medical procedure necessary to save a woman's life but which may result in the death of her foetus.

Trau puts forward the doctrine of double effect as part of a solution to the problem of evil. The free will defence (see next chapter) speaks of evil results as a double effect of free will, while natural evils can be a double effect of some natural good. The primary effect should not, she cautions, be seen as an 'aim' or an 'end', but rather as something that must occur if the universe is to exist as it is.

> If it is true that there could be no other material universe, that this universe could not function any other way, and that it is better that this universe

exist than it not, we can make this claim: the existence of the universe is a natural good and has positive value. Because the existence of the universe is a natural good and has positive value, the events involved in its existence also have positive value. If natural evils are necessary double effects of those events, then the double effects have positive value.[19]

The doctrine of double effect should be distinguished from the simpler claim that something evil can have positive value if it has sufficient *instrumental* goodness; this might be true, but would only apply to certain cases. The double effect doctrine goes further, in her view: 'If we can show that evil exists as a double effect of the necessary condition for the existence of goodness, then we can show that all evil has positive value.' 'The doctrine of the double effect allows us to make the claim that because the possibility of the existence of evil is *necessary* for the existence of free will and moral goodness, the positive value of evil can exceed its negative value, even when evil retains all its intrinsic badness.'[20]

To succeed as a justification, however, it must be the case that the bad effect is really unavoidable, and that the desired good result cannot be obtained in any other way. A sceptic might question whether this can ever be the case for an omnipotent God, whose ways and means ought not to be so constrained. Trau's view is that such limits lie in the nature of things, and not in God's power to realise other possible worlds. God could have realised other material worlds without the laws of this one, but they would be very different worlds. God could not actualise *this* world with *different* natural laws; that is impossible.

> Thus, if this material universe is a great natural good, if we prefer that it exist, and if certain natural evils are necessary double effects of its existence, we cannot ask God to eliminate those evils. To eliminate the evils is to eliminate the natural goods. Thus another underlying claim is that it is a good thing that this world exists.[21]

Some might be willing to accept this account for most evil and suffering, but might balk at the suggestion that genocide might be an unavoidable means to a desirable end. Can such reasoning help the problem of dysteleological suffering?

Does size matter?

Eliezer Berkovits, in dealing with the Holocaust, makes the point that the death of one innocent person is no less morally or theologically problematic than the death of millions. Oliver Leaman summarises: 'The only difference between the Holocaust and previous disasters lies in the size of the former, and there is little theological significance in size. The issues surrounding the death of just one innocent person are the same as in the case of six million.'[22]

There are at least two ways that one can interpret this suggestion. 'The death of six million is no worse than the death of one'? That would misconstrue

Berkovits, who intends something more like: 'One must be held accountable for a single murder no less than for genocide.' We may feel that a serial murderer has done something worse than one who has committed a single murder; nevertheless we do not say to the murderer, 'It was only one death, not many; so you needn't be tried for it.' We hold the murderer to account, whether he has killed one or twenty. By analogy, then, if it is proper to hold God to account for human deaths, He needs to be theodicially justified for the death of one person, not less than for millions. The question is one of accountability, not of the qualitative or quantitative difference between horrible events, or the difference in emotional and psychological impact between single bereavements and atrocities.

The import of this issue, as I see it, is whether a *different* theodicial manoeuvre or piece of reasoning is required for 'dysteleological' evils than has been encountered already. The effect of Berkovits' claim would be to say that in principle 'dysteleological' evil does *not* ultimately require a different sort of theodicial justification than a single death.

Nevertheless, the impact of massive evils on our reflection is different. It does force a different kind of consideration. As Arthur Cohen writes, 'The death camps are a reality which, by their very nature, obliterate thought and the human programme of thinking.'[23]

The epistemological assumptions of 'dysteleological' objections

How do we make the claim that something is *dysteleological*? What do we do, when we say: 'No good can ever come of this,' or 'No good can ever outweigh or redeem this evil'? How do we arrive at that conclusion? How do we *know*?

We might identify a good that has come out of a terrible situation, but find it trivial in comparison to the evil. Or we might operate on an intuitive sense of proportion, and just declare or decree that no good can be as big as this evil. Both are natural things to do, but there are nevertheless philosophical problems with both if they are more than a heartfelt exclamation. Can you rule out in advance that something that is logically possible will or indeed can happen? Can you know with certainty that all the results and evidence are in, and that it is time now to make a final judgement that the good has not, in fact, outweighed the evil? And can that be done at any point before 'the end of history'? Consider the assertion: 'History refutes more than it confirms God's providential care.'[24] If this is really meant as an assertion, not a cry of anguish, one wonders what kind of method or historical analysis can ever support this judgement.

First and most fundamentally, *all* such styles of reasoning, whether for or against religious belief, require the quantification of what can in no way be 'objectively' quantified: the extent and intensity of suffering and evil, on the one side, and on the other side the value of human existence and human freedom and the existence of the natural world as we know it. Plantinga coins the term 'turp' to signify a unit of evil, and Stewart the term 'ben' for a unit of goodness; but both seem to have some awareness of the absurdity of doing this. For how do you measure a turp, or allocate turps to acts of moral cruelty as compared to degrees of physical pain? Do pleasures and virtues rate equally on the ben scale?

The business becomes even more difficult when you come to the point of weighing turps against bens to see which is greater. How many bens cancel out one turp and thus justify God? Can you cash in bens more than once in wiping out turps, if in fact that good arose from both those evils? How closely do the turp and the ben have to be connected in order to pay off one with the other?

To make these puzzles concrete, consider Roth's claim that nothing can ever outweigh the Holocaust. How do you 'measure' the suffering of the Holocaust to reach this conclusion? What goods, which joys and pleasures of existence, and *whose* existence, are allowed to count as relevant in the comparison between the good and the evil?

The implication that goods and evils can be placed in a scale and compared, in order to see if God is justified or not, begs the question of the right context in which to make one's 'numerical' or 'quantitative' comparison. This is both a diachronic and a synchronic question; that is, a question of duration in time, and of breadth of relevance. First of all, how do you decide which good results are relevant for your consideration? Must every suffering be outweighed in the life of each individual? This overlooks the common experience of learning and benefiting from the experience of others. The sum total of outweighing goods might not manifest themselves in the lives of those individuals immediately involved and affected. May not the impact of something on many millions of people throughout history be included in the reckoning? As a result of the sufferings of the Jews in the Second World War, there might be millions more who are deterred from racism and anti-Semitism; or who draw back from espousing or tolerating a violent nationalism or totalitarianism. How much anti-Semitism might have continued festering in Germany if she had not embarked on a radical denazification and anti-racist programme, still sufficiently successful that fifty years later far more Germans (including the Chancellor) than Britons (*not* including the then Prime Minister) came out on demonstrations against racism?

Secondly, there is the question of the appropriate cut-off point. Every story can have a happy ending, or a sad one; it all depends on whether you stop the narrative after a happy bit or a sad bit and call that 'The End'. In the same way, is it plausible to fix a deadline for all resulting goods to have occurred, in order to be considered in the reckoning of the results of a particular evil? 2,000 years later, we are still learning from the example and teachings of Jesus; we are still learning from the example and teachings of Socrates and Buddha and Mahavir, who lived even longer ago, and people today still moderate their behaviour according to the teachings and examples of all four of these people. Perhaps 2,000 years from now, people might still be learning good moral lessons from the horrors and evils of the twentieth century, modifying their behaviour and thus preventing evils that might otherwise have occurred.

Next, there are also problems of interpretation, not least in deciding what is good and what is evil to start with. Alcohol, dancing and making love are considered by some to be some of life's blessings, and by others to be some of life's evil temptations. An act that furthers one person's interests and damages another's will certainly be differently construed. Secondly, there is an obvious degree of debatable interpretation involved in deciding whether or not a good 'resulted from' an evil, whether it could have been achieved any other way (which involves 'middle knowledge', the certain knowledge of 'what if' cases) and thus whether the evil was 'justified' or not.

Perhaps 'theodicies' are in part explanation, part justification; after all, the meaning or use of these two words is not always distinct. Both explanation and justification can occur on different levels. Let us create a rather gruesome analogy.

Imagine a forensic psychologist saying to a serial killer: 'Why did you kill twenty women?' The man answers: 'Well, I killed the first victim because she was a prostitute and so she deserved to die, and the second one because she reminded me of my mother, and the third because I didn't like her hairstyle' and so on. In this way he 'accounts' for each individual murder on its own. Would it make sense for the psychologist to respond, 'Yes, but you haven't told us why you killed all twenty of them – you've only given a particular explanation for each, but not for the series of twenty.' Does the phenomenon of 'a series of twenty' need its own justification, over and above the account given of each?

Or alternatively: let us say that the whole series of twenty murders is 'accounted for' by the man's psycho-pathological hatred of women. Beyond that, he can't say why he killed this woman rather than that one; or killed on this night, but not on another. Have the deaths not been accounted for in the general explanation, or do we need to explain the man's behaviour with reference to each individual woman: some explanation maybe that derives from the woman's own characteristics, and not his?

These questions are intended to bring out the fact that different accounts can be given of the same phenomenon, when it is considered under different aspects: on its own, or as part of category or classification which we create. A murder could be considered as the murder of one individual, or as one of a series of murders (and this interpretation might affect the detectives' investigation); it might require an explanation as one of a psychotic person's acts, or as part of a growing trend in 'violent crime', or as a 'sex attack', or as an example of misogyny and violence against women – and quite different accounts may be given of it under those different headings.

So when we create new headings, do they require a new kind of justification? Let us suppose the forensic psychologist, reading the latest figures and statistics on crime, returned to the serial murderer and asked him to explain why he had participated in a growing trend towards violent crime. Do we expect the serial murderer give a different answer to this question than to the earlier ones?

So for anyone trying to provide a theodicy for dysteleological evils or for anyone contending that it cannot be done, the question arises: on which level must an account be provided? We can ask for explanations to be given at every level or under every classification we can create. (This is especially informative when a new insight or critique is developed: feminist critique now allows one to re-examine history and a number of other disciplines and ask questions that have never before been answered. The answers to these questions bring new revelations.) Considering genocide, we can ask why one particular individual was unable to escape, and examine the question on the level of personal biography. We can ask for the historical, social or cultural reasons for the hatred of that group by another. We can ask for psychological explanations of one person's willingness to be a perpetrator, and ask group psychology for an explanation for the willingness of a whole group to commit brutal acts. We can ask why the politics or government of that country allowed these events, or ask why the international community failed to respond or intervene promptly and effectively.

But when it is no longer of humanity and its world that we require explanations, but ask for God's justification, does God need to be justified or explained on each of these levels? For example, must God be 'justified' for each individual's death within the framework of their own biography, and justified again for that death viewed as one piece of a major historical event? Must God be 'justified' for human racism, and then provide for Himself a different theodicy to cover the economic conditions that facilitated that group violence?

Let us imagine that on Judgement Day God is made to account to us for all His evil deeds. The prosecutor asks about His justification for the Holocaust. Imagine that God gives a greater good defence, but purely on an individual, case-by-case basis. He does so successfully, in that the total amount of good 'outweighs' the total amount of evil. At the end of this, however, the prosecutor replies: 'Yes, but you still haven't accounted for the Holocaust itself.' Is that true? If he has accounted for each individual death, has he accounted for the Holocaust? Or, reversing the situation, if God can account for the 'the Holocaust' as a whole, in terms of its long-term impacts on human history and attitudes, has He 'accounted for' the death of each individual? Does everything need at least two justifications, on the level of the individual evil and the aggregate of evils?

But what is an aggregate of evils? The sense that 'massive' evils are something over and above the individual evils and tragedies they embody is what some would call 'a human construct'. By this I do not mean that it is 'untrue'. Rather, we do not see the deaths in Nazi Germany or Stalin's Soviet Union as random events; rather, we link together certain events as meaningfully belonging together. For example, in talking about the Holocaust, we frequently refer to the deaths of the 'six million'. But more than six million were victims of the Nazi atrocities; a further estimated five million were killed whom we often do not include in the figure of Nazi victims because they were not Jewish. Meanwhile, more than six million Jews died in those years. Many other Jewish people around the world, including soldiers from Jewish communities in the Allied countries, also died in the war, yet their deaths are not included in the figure of the six million, because the circumstances of their deaths were different. *Certain* people in *certain* circumstances are joined in our mind as a meaningful group. Depending on the interpretative grid one lays over the events, different group- ings could arise. One can divide up and group together individual persons or events in different ways.

It is a natural hermeneutical tendency of ours to gather events and look for explanations and causes not just of the individual events, but of the whole group we have marked out. But this is *our* interpretative activity, and it may not have a further divine justification. Let us consider six million traffic accident victims, or six million people who died by choking: God 'allowed' all these people to suffer and die too. But we do not see these as massive, dysteleological evils, because we do not see them as a single event. We do not require a special theodicy for these (asking why God lets *all* road traffic accident victims die; how can God be justified for allowing the creation of automotives?) – unless the combined individual cases have for us a special identity, or special tragic aspect: AIDS has what we might call a 'dysteleological identity', while cardiac failure does not. 'The death of children' is more likely to provoke a dysteleological reaction than 'the death of everyone who is 68'.

There seems to me to be no way that the measurement, definition, contextu- alisation and interpretation of good and evil can be put on a universally agreed and public footing (made objective, in other words), in such a way as to justify a claim of 'dysteleological' suffering. To be more than a mere assertion, it would require a God's eye view at the end of history. Perhaps, if we were strictly logical, we would consider all human death as a dysteleological evil. God allows everyone to die someday in any case, and perhaps God is no less 'guilty of mass- murder' in virtue of the fact that He allows billions of people to die peacefully of natural causes. God is either 'justified' or not for all human deaths. Certainly atrocities raise questions and demands explanations that natural or accidental death does not. But is it of *God* that we require the explanation? Is it not *human action* that marks the profound moral difference between accidental death and genocide, not God's apparent allowance of evil? Is it not of ourselves then that we should seek the explanations?

It is not so much God's ways that are inscrutable, then, as humanity's. It is less relevant to say that God is unjustified in allowing massive evils in His creation, as it is to say that humanity is unjustified in perpetrating them. Evils and sufferings *can* be utilised by ourselves and by nature to transform hardship or wickedness into better states of affairs. This is not an excuse or justification for evil human action. The good may not 'outweigh' the evil in the life of the individual sufferer. It may not 'redeem' the situation, if this is understood as effecting a great transformation of the immediate state of affairs. And I do not think myself that belief in God's existence should be seen as a guarantee that good will always come from evil. However, I say this not from scepticism or pessimism, but rather because such a guarantee removes human responsibility and initiative. It is up to *us* to make sure that no evils are or become 'dysteleo- logical'; not up to God to eliminate this 'category' of evil. If good comes from such events, it is not a conjuring trick of God's, or some automatic mechanism that has been placed in the workings of the universe. 'Good comes from evil' should not be seen, or expected, as a phenomenon that can be passively observed. Rather, it should be seen as an inspiration, an exhortation, even a command. 'Good comes from evil' *because people make it*; whether the good outweighs the evil or not cannot be decided in a piece of moral or historical bookkeeping. To affirm this is to be determined to take good as the overarching context for evil, not evil for good. For one who believes in a just, good, and powerful God, this holds open the possibility that good, and still more good, may yet come from a tragedy or atrocity – better still, 'may yet be *made* to come from evil'. This attitude does not dismiss or minimise the horror of evil: what it does is to create room for the action required to make this affirmation true. The judgement that 'no good can ever come from this' or 'nothing can outweigh this evil' is the prescription for doing nothing. The contrary affirmation, that good can yet come from evil, fuels the determination to 'storm and strive' against all odds, even against the impossible, to *make* it do so. It is the decision not to feed on the carrion comfort of despair. The zest, the edge, the ecstasy that Hopkins describes only exists with this possibility of action.

Modern theodicy, for both the sceptic and the traditional philosopher of religion, has taken on the air of a court-room, with its language of evidence in favour, evidence against, guilt, justification. It is as if writers have misunderstood the meaning of the word 'theodicy'. The task of theodicy is not to 'justify evil'; the word 'theodicy' refers rather to the 'justice of God'. In my view the believer should not seek to 'justify evil'. And to ask if God is 'justified' in allowing massive evils is a category mistake. My own conviction is that humanity, not divinity, must be put in question and called to account in 'theodicy'. We must be challenged as to the origin, persistence, and certainly the extent and intensity of evil. We must also be challenged to respond, and any theological or philosophical reflection that encourages responsibility and prudent action is to be preferred, all else being equal, to one that does not. To echo Fackenheim,[25] we must not grant posthumous victories to Nazism, or any other evil force or event. To decide that God is evil, weak, necessarily non-existent, temporarily unavailable, and to decide that the world is pointless and senseless, human beings irredeemably cruel, is precisely to give the victory to what we profess to despise.

11. The Perfect Law of Freedom

Ways of considering freedom or free will in discussions of the problem of evil

Bound or free?

Arjuna, seated in the chariot, took up his bow and prepared to shoot his arrows. After looking at the sons of Dhrtarastra drawn in military array, Arjuna then spoke to Lord Krishna these words: 'O infallible one, please draw my chariot between the two armies so that I may see those present here, who desire to fight, and with whom I must contend in this great trial of arms.' Lord Krishna drew up the fine chariot in the midst of the armies of both parties.

There Arjuna could see, within the midst of the armies of both parties, his fathers, grandfathers, teachers, maternal uncles, brothers, sons, grandsons, friends, and also his fathers-in-law and well-wishers. Arjuna said: 'My dear Krishna, seeing my friends and relatives present before me in such a fighting spirit, I feel the limbs of my body quivering and my mouth drying up. My whole body is trembling, my hair is standing on end, my bow is slipping from my hand, and my skin is burning. I am now unable to stand here any longer. I am forgetting myself, and my mind is reeling. I see only causes of misfortune, O Krishna. I do not see how any good can come from killing my own kinsmen in this battle, nor can I, my dear Krishna, desire any subsequent victory, kingdom, or happiness. When teachers, fathers, sons, grandfathers, maternal uncles, fathers-in-law, grandsons, brothers-in-law and other relatives are ready to give up their lives and properties and are standing before me, why should I wish to kill them, even though they might otherwise kill me? Alas, how strange it is that we are preparing to commit greatly sinful acts. Driven by the desire to enjoy royal happiness, we are intent on killing our own kinsmen. Better for me if the sons of Dhrtarastra, weapons in hand, were to kill me unarmed and unresisting on the battlefield.'

Arjuna, having thus spoken on the battlefield, cast aside his bow and arrows and sat down on the chariot, his mind overwhelmed with grief.[1]

In the previous chapters we saw how much of the evil and suffering in the world has been accounted for by religious believers: by attributing it to human action.

What of this human action itself? Are we free and sovereign beings, possessing something called a 'free will'? Or are we bound by fate, or determined by our circumstances, our genes, our predestined end?

Freedom west and east

Monotheists have formalised free will into a 'defence' against the sceptic's challenge to the existence of God.[2] Observing that much of the evil in our world is due to human action, the Free Will Defence (hereafter FWD) argues that for God to have prevented all these evils, He would have to have created human beings without free will. The freedom to choose between good and evil is itself a 'good' – so good, in fact, that it justifies God in allowing us the scope to go wrong.

The idea that we have a free will is, of course, contested in Western philosophy, and not only by philosophers but also by scientists. Theologians also dispute the freedom of humanity. For some Protestant Christians and some Ash'arite Muslims, for example, God's omnipotence and God's omniscience imply a doctrine of predestination: that God knows in advance and wills in advance who is to be saved; and there is nothing we can do about it.[3] The Ash'arite position affirmed God's omnipotence so strongly that it denied human free will.

Other Muslims, with as much support from the Qur'an as their opponents,[4] ascribed the responsibility for evil to human action. Al-Hasan al-Basrī asserted that we have free will, above all to prevent any accusation that God was unjust, in willing someone's sin then punishing him for it. 'Our God is too just and too fair to blind a man and then say to him, "See! or else I shall punish you", or to deafen him and then say, "Hear! or I shall punish you," or to strike him dumb and then say, "Speak! or else I shall punish you." '[5] Indeed, the Qadarīya school who defended free will were also known as 'the party of justice', since an insistence on divine justice was one of their main concerns in asserting free will. God 'does no wrong nor does He choose it, nor does He fail to fulfill what is obligatory upon Him, and all His acts are good.'[6]

So those monotheists who espouse the notion of free will view it as a necessary ingredient in humanity, personhood, and moral agency. Human freedom, then, is a sign of God's goodness – and as the Islamic debate suggests, God's justice.

The East also had its debates on free will. One such debate lies at the beginnings of Buddhism. A contemporary of the Buddha, Gosāla Maskariputra, advocated a kind of extreme determinism, the absence of any free will or moral responsibility. Against this challenge the Buddha asserted the reality of free action, and with it, moral responsibility. And yet the second Buddha, Vasubandhu, believed that all actions of the body or speech depend on the mind, and the mind wholly depends on causes and conditions. We will return to this apparent contradiction between free action and causality later.[7]

The doctrines of saṃsāra and karma do not only serve to explain the origin of evil as we have already seen, but also have major repercussions on the conception of the human being as basically bound or basically free. Paradoxically, this 'bound' condition results from a freedom of action. '... Karma is the intellectual statement of the attitude of a bound man.'[8] And yet, these circumstances 'thrust upon us' are in fact the consequences of our own action; we are 'bound' insofar as we cannot escape the consequences – of our own *free* action. Meanwhile, the Buddhist doctrine of Dependent Origination asserts that all the miseries of existence ultimately depend on ignorance – a matter in which we have some say. So although human agency alone cannot arrange karmas and their consequences as we would wish, there is a dialectic of freedom and bondage.

> The pride and confidence borne by the West in its will, resoluteness and power were alien to the Indian spirit, inasmuch as it never discriminated right actions from the wrong ones on any ground other than the ledger of everyone's foregone lives. The general Western attitude towards the universe is one of challenge to the given order of events; it is heavily charged with industriousness, by which it wants to harness everything for the welfare of man. For Indians, on the contrary, until the karmas are paid off, the individual has to surrender to whatever he is destined to get and has to stay bound to the world.[9]

However, 'freedom' in Indian philosophy is not primarily discussed as an aspect of will, but is viewed primarily as 'freedom from suffering', freedom from the misery of the world. As such, it is not a starting-point so much as a desired end. Whether in the world or beyond it,[10] this liberty (or liberation) is a goal, for which we must strive. Both freedom and suffering are understood more broadly than in purely moral terms; both in fact are most often viewed as the fruits of knowledge and ignorance than wickedness and goodness.

What emerges is a Western picture of freedom as an entitlement, and an Eastern notion of freedom as an achievement. Whereas the West maintains (or disputes) that 'freedom' is what we are born with, in the 'Upaniṣadic world-view' we are born into a state of bondage to the world and to existence. 'Freedom' is something we cannot take for granted, but must work towards ourselves – arduously. As Sinari puts it, we 'live *unto* freedom'.

The dialectic of freedom and bondage in Indian religion demonstrates, however, that 'freedom' is a complex notion, not simply a question of the timing of our freedom or how it is acquired. The fundamental difference is in what really counts as 'freedom', and what merits discussion in the scope or restriction of human action.

The Freely Impeccable People objection

Objections have been raised to both these conceptions of the limits of human action. Cārvāka was almost unique in rejecting the notions of karma, saṃsāra, of merit and demerit altogether. There is no transcendental justification for the injustices of life. There is no reward and punishment – there is not even evil or good action itself.

However, in their advocacy of hedonism, the Cārvāka thinkers implicitly left scope for the possibility of choice in human action. Quite different then is the challenge made by the sceptic Antony Flew, who disputed the central claim of the FWD: that God could not have made people free without running the risk of them misbehaving.[11] God *could* have created human beings who, while still free, always freely chose to do good. But God did not do this, therefore the FWD fails: either God is not good, or God does not exist.

Flew's challenge was subsequently taken up and expounded by J.L. Mackie:

> If God has made men such that in their free choices they sometimes prefer what is good and sometimes what is evil, why could he not have made men such that they always freely choose the good? If there is no logical impossibility in a man's freely choosing the good on one, or on several, occasions, there cannot be a logical impossibility in his freely choosing the good on every occasion. God was not, then, faced with a choice between making innocent automata and making beings who, in acting freely, would sometimes go wrong: there was open to him the obviously better possibility of making beings who would act freely but always go right. Clearly, his failure to avail himself of this possibility is inconsistent with his being both omnipotent and wholly good.[12]

I shall dub this objection the 'Freely Impeccable People' objection (FIP for short; while a fip is a freely impeccable person).

Transworld depravity or: What can God do about it?

Alvin Plantinga deals with the FIP objection with the ludic conjecture that someone might suffer from 'transworld depravity'.[13] In any possible world in which she was significantly free, she would always go wrong in some respect. If there is just one person suffering from this condition, then any possible world with that person in it which God might create, would include that person's tendency to go wrong. It would in fact be logically impossible for God to create a world in which that person did not go wrong, because to do so would involve a contradiction.[14] If it is at least *possible* that one person suffers from transworld depravity, Plantinga claims, then, necessarily God *could* not have created a world with free beings and no moral failings. 'What is important about the idea of transworld depravity is that if a person suffers from it, then it wasn't within God's power to actualise any world in which that person is significantly free but does no wrong – that is, a world in which he produces moral good but no moral evil.'[15]

Translating this argument out of its modal language,[16] it is possible that human beings are such that it is inevitable that they will go wrong in at least one respect so long as they are free. If human beings are so constituted, then by definition God could not have created a world in which they existed, were free, and never went wrong. Plantinga's transworld depravity rebuttal carries the day, however, only within the narrow limits he has set himself: to demonstrate that it is *possible* to imagine a state of affairs that makes beliefs in God's good attributes consistent with the existence of evil. He maintains that this minimal defence is all that is required to acquit the theist of contradiction. Nevertheless, FIP objectors could maintain against Plantinga that an omnipotent God could in theory actualise *any* world that we can imagine. It is surely up to an omnipotent God whether he creates the freely impeccable or the transuniversally depraved.

Mackie, for example, rejects the idea that people might have properties or essences that an omnipotent God would just have to put up with. Omnipotence means God is not limited by anything beyond logical impossibility, and he like Flew asserts that fips are logically possible.[17] So free will defenders must entertain the possibility that even an omnipotent God can *choose* to limit Himself, or delegate some power over moral events to us.

This understanding of God's use of power can be marketed as, in fact, a superior state of affairs in itself:

> I see no reason why God must, in order to be sovereign, retain control over all power. That notion has been rejected as incompatible with the idea that God brings into existence creatures who are genuine agents with power to act freely. That God could and so might bring into existence such creatures might be a greater attestation to his power and confidence in his sovereignty, than not doing so.[18]

Thus it can function as a codicil to the FWD.

How far is God Himself bound by the structures of the moral universe? This question was explored in greater depth in the East than in the West. Does the notion of karma and saṃsāra require the idea of a God, or not? The Nyāya, Yoga, and Vedāntin traditions all maintained that the divine existed and is the controller of karma. But Sāṅkhya and Pūrva Mīmāṃsā philosophies both disputed the existence of God. The Pūrva Mīmāṃsā thinkers, pre-eminently Jaimini and Kumārila, argued that if there is something like karma or adṛṣṭa administering justice on the basis of merit or demerit, there is no need for a god to do so. Or, if God also is subject to the universal law of karma, God is not omnipotent. It is better to understand karma as operating by its own necessity. Every act carries the potency of producing its own effect. As Sinari observes, a self-subsistent principle like this has no need of a God; but even if a God exists, the principle need not come under His influence but can enjoy a kind of independence or even transcendence.[19] Non-theistic traditions of Buddhism clearly understand the cycle of saṃsāra and the workings of karma to operate without any form of divine assistance, as does Jainism, which also rejects the idea of a deity.

Von Glasenapp examines the place of 'gods' in Buddhism, which he likens to Christian or Muslim saints in many respects. Where they differ from the gods of other religions is that they too are subject to birth and death, karma and saṃsāra. This, he suggests, is not an exclusively Buddhist idea but a 'general Indian view'.[20] (I suppose it does depend on what you consider a 'god.')

> Like all other beings, the Buddhist gods are subject to the karmic law of cause and effect, and natural law sets a beginning and an end for their status as gods. They are neither almighty nor omniscient, nor can they grant liberation. In all this they take second place to the Buddha, and even after the more advanced of his disciples.[21]

The possibility of doing evil: kinds of possibility

In defence of fips, Mackie observes that there is no logical impossibility involved in freely choosing the good on every occasion; and indeed there is not. There is also no *logical* impossibility in tossing a pair of dice 1,000 times and seeing two sixes come up every time. But logically possible or not, if the dice did behave in such a fashion, we would soon come to wonder whether they were loaded.

The FIP objection equivocates on the crucial question of what sort of possibility is involved in the fip's choice. Arabic logic has a distinction between 'conceptual possibility' and 'actual possibility'. Conceptual possibility is found when the mind forms an idea of something that could be, regardless of whether or not it is concretely possible: 'It is possible that I could run a mile in four minutes.' 'Actual possibility' is reserved for things that can be done or achieved in practice: 'It is *not* possible for me to run a four-minute mile.' So for me to run a mile in four minutes is 'possible' in one sense of the word 'possible', but 'not possible' in another.

The question then, is what kind of 'possibility' is ascribed to the fip choosing evil? Conceptual possibility, certainly. We can imagine the fip choosing evil though she will never do so, just as I can imagine being able to breathe under water, though I will never do so. But conceptual possibility does not entail actual possibility; something can be conceptually possible and actually impossible.

So how do we in fact determine what is actually possible?

Which kind of possibility does the fip require for the FIP objection to have teeth? Mackie would say merely conceptual possibility; for as long as the notion is logically possible, an omnipotent God should be able to actualise it. Conceptual possibility, or the absence of contradiction, might indeed be all that is necessary for an omnipotent God to create such a being. But that point is not in dispute; the point is the moral status of such beings. For if something cannot be realised, like a fip choice for evil, then it is 'actually impossible'. Since a fip is defined as one that always chooses good, in practice, it is part of the definition of a fip that choosing evil is actually impossible. So it has to be 'conceptually possible' but 'actually impossible' for a fip to do evil. Is simultaneous actual impossibility and conceptual possibility sufficient for 'freedom'?

Does freedom require an alternative?

Let us imagine that, after my husband goes to work, I reluctantly get out of bed. It is a grey and miserable day. I am tired and I feel a cold coming on, and I do not want to go out in the London rain to college. I decide to stay home and read in bed. So inclement is the weather that I do not leave the house all day, not to post a letter, buy a newspaper, or walk the dog. Staying in is what I want to do, and so I consider that I have chosen to do this freely.

That day, unbeknownst to me, my husband absent-mindedly took my keys and double-locked the front door. So even if I had wanted to leave the house, I *couldn't* have. Although I couldn't have done otherwise, I freely chose to do what I did.

In recent years, there has been some discussion of whether one can be described as 'free' when one is not 'able to do otherwise', which is precisely the fips' situation.[22] Can one be described as responsible for one's actions when one could not have done otherwise?

It is usually supposed that, in order to describe someone as 'free' and to ascribe to them moral responsibility for an action, there must be some alternative to that action. If someone has no choice but to do what they do, then they are not really free in that situation and therefore do not bear (full) moral responsibility for their act. This assumption – and the 'Principle of Alternate Possibilities' that underlies it – was challenged by Harry Frankfurt.[23] Frankfurt proposed that we abandon the traditional view that moral responsibility requires 'freedom to do otherwise'. In some situations, an agent lacks the possibility of doing other than she does, and yet still bears moral responsibility for what she does. Frankfurt suggested counter-examples designed to illustrate situations where someone freely chose something to which there was no alternative.[24] One can freely choose the tarte tatin at a restaurant, not realising that they have run out of the creme caramel anyway. And one still bears the moral responsibility for choosing and eating the tarte.

The mark of freedom, on this view, is doing something *because one really wants to*, not because there are a variety of options. The fact that one couldn't do otherwise in Frankfurt situations plays no role in the decision and action taken. For Frankfurt, 'acting freely' in this sense is all that is required for moral responsibility; not even 'freedom of will' (being undetermined in one's choice) or 'freedom of action' (being able to actualise a different situation).[25]

So perhaps Frankfurt's scenario could be used to assert the coherence of the fip idea. Fips 'act freely', but possess very little 'freedom of action'. However, insofar as they do act freely, they bear moral responsibility for their actions. So the FWD fails.

And yet the Frankfurt situations help the FIP objector less than might be supposed, even though the fip 'acts freely' while enjoying neither freedom of choice nor freedom of action. This is because there are two different ways in which one can have no alternative but to do what one does. Either one can be forced to do something, by compulsion or by a lack of choice, or the alternative can have some intrinsic obstacle that prevents its realisation. All the Frankfurt examples which succeed in showing that an agent *is* morally responsible fall into the latter category. They don't force choice, they just predetermine the end result, they prevent the alternative from being realised should one choose it. (Typically, the scenarios involve a mad neuroscientist implanting a device in someone's brain to prevent them from acting out an alternative choice.) So Frankfurt examples do not demonstrate how 'free choice' itself can be compelled yet remain free. They demonstrate how one can 'freely' choose something when the alternative turns out to be impossible.[26] It is fair to say that in Frankfurt counterexamples, one couldn't have *done* otherwise, but one could have *chosen* otherwise (and been prevented from acting upon it). We don't in fact have an argument or even an example here for how the act of choice itself can be compelled and yet remain free, which the fip's condition requires. Frankfurt examples allow for the possibility of cips: comparatively impotent people, who could choose evil but not enact it; but not fips: people who *must* always choose the good and yet deserve full credit for so doing.

Could one adapt the structure of Frankfurt's examples somehow and use that as a way to defeat the FWD? Rather than the notion of fips, which focuses on choice, one could imagine God preventing the realisation of evil choices that we make. Is that more coherent than the FIP objection? Steven Boër has argued that the FWD does not justify the existence of moral evil, since God could always act to prevent the actual *results* of the evil action from occurring. Thus, one could enjoy all the benefits of free choice while suffering none of the consequences. 'In short, freedom of the will is freedom of opportunity: it is a licence to choose and try, not a warranty of success.'[27] Seeking to ward off the suggestion that this would make the world a chaotic place and that this might create cognitive difficulties, he suggests that God's intervention could be in the form of 'coincidence miracles', so that they appeared as coincidences to us: 'far from being chaotic, [the world in question] would be exactly like our own except that evil machinations would never result in harm to any innocent party.'[28]

Frank Dilley has argued in response that this makes a nonsense of the whole business of trying to do good or evil. Never to accomplish evil, to have good always result from one's acts or intentions, whether virtuous or vicious, indeed, to decouple intentions and their consequences makes a nonsense not just of moral responsibility but also 'cuts the heart out of the notion of the creation of a community of interacting beings'.[29] This is a parallel argument to the one we have already examined in relation to the integrity of the natural world and our epistemic need for consistency.

So it seems that the free will defender can see off Frankfurt situations without damaging the FWD. Anyway, Frankfurt's attempt to dissociate moral responsibility from freedom and control has not been uncontroversial. Peter van Inwagen, for example, claims that in all Frankfurt-style situations one can more precisely distinguish aspects of the state of affairs for which one is responsible from aspects for which one is not. Aspects for which one can be held responsible in Frankfurt situations, he claims, are always those aspects for which one does have an alternative.[30] 'So', one could say: fips deserve credit for 'choosing good', if they freely embrace their only possibility; however, they do not deserve credit for 'not choosing to do evil'. The two are not always the same. 'Choosing to be pregnant' and 'choosing not to have an abortion' may both refer to an ongoing pregnancy, but do not necessarily describe the same emotional state of affairs.

The one truth in the FIP objection is that freedom in a basic sense of 'being able to do whatever one wants', and 'choice' are not the same. As some Frankfurt examples show, one can be 'free' in the sense that one can do what one wants without having any choice in the matter if the only route available to you happens to be the route you desire. Similarly, one can have a choice and yet be unfree, in my view. A woman who decides not to struggle against the rapist who threatens to kill her if she does, possesses a choice between two courses of action but is hardly 'free to do what she wants'.

So which is the mark of freedom in the Bhagavad-Gītā – choice or the satisfaction of desire?

Arjuna, when caught in *his* moral dilemma, is in the enviable position of having a god to give him advice. Does Krishna advise him to throw down his arms, prevent war, and save thousands of lives? – No; Krishna advises him to go into battle. If, as many have, you find Krishna's moral reasoning repellent, then perhaps you can find it easy to understand the revolt that Buddhism and Jainism represent; when Buddhism urges compassion (*karuna*) and Jainism advocates non-violence (*ahimsā*) as overriding principles for action.

Arjuna feels himself caught between two courses of action, both of which will result in sorrow. No Frankfurt situation; he has a choice, but is not free. There is no third option. For Krishna, however, there *is* a third option. Or better, there is a different choice: which is not to consider and care about the result of one's action in making the decision. The choice could be to choose between *attachment* or *non-attachment* to the results of one's own action. For the true mark of freedom for Krishna is *not* found in 'having lots of choices', nor in 'really wanting to'. Real freedom is found in detachment from the consequences of one's action. Only by the exercise of self-discipline in non-attachment can Arjuna grow into greater freedom. 'Krishna's position is simply that ultimate values do not rest in the fruits of actions, on results such as the winning or losing of wars or the killing or nonkilling of people, but rather in freedom alone, which is not a result at all but an attitude.'[31]

Causality

The 'bound' element in the theory of saṃsāra and karma is not like the FIP notion; it is not compulsion of action. It is clear that Arjuna is both undetermined and responsible for his choice of action, whether to go into battle or not. The lack of freedom as Hinduism, Buddhism and Jainism conceive it is located in the inescapability of the consequences of our action.

> Even a flight in the air cannot free you from suffering,
> after the deed which is evil has once been committed.
> Not in the sky nor in the ocean's middle,
> Nor if you were to hide in cracks in mountains,
> Can there be found on this wide earth a corner
> Where karma does not catch up with the culprit ...
> Whatever deeds a man may do, be they delightful, be they bad,
> They make a heritage for him; deeds do not vanish without trace ...
> The iron itself creates the rust,
> Which slowly is bound to consume it.
> The evil-doer by his own deeds
> Is led to a life full of suffering.[32]

The focus of the debate over the feasibility of fips, however, has centred on the question of whether one can be 'caused' and still 'free'.[33]

Flew's argument for a determinist account of freedom runs as follows: 'acting freely', 'being free to choose', and so on do not require that acts be unpredictable or uncaused. There is no contradiction involved in saying that a particular decision or act was '*both* free, and could have been helped, and so on; *and* predictable, or even foreknown, and explicable in terms of caused causes'.[34] From this, he suggests that 'it really is logically possible for an action to be both freely chosen and yet fully determined by caused causes'.[35]

For Flew and Mackie, to be compelled by one's nature does not constitute unfreedom,[36] and indeed they claim that something like this is already the case for human beings. Therefore, God should be able to cause us to act freely, so the FWD is vanquished by the FIP objection.

Many free will defenders, on the other hand, will be 'incompatibilists' – that is, they say that freedom and determinism (being caused to act as one does) are incompatible. So they will argue that being *so constructed*, like fips, as to always freely choose good, amounts to being *caused* to always freely choose good and thus is incompatible with freedom, even if always *opting* to freely choose good is not. Therefore, greater goodness attends on the possession of the freedom to do wrong.

The discussion in Flew and Mackie is a little brisk to give confidence that the complexities of human motivation and behaviour have been adequately accounted for. Reflecting on our existence, both the claim that *all* our action is *totally* determined, and the claim that *none* is seem false and extreme. It is particularly unsatisfactory to abstract the philosophical question from our situation of being in the world, as if it were an issue to be decided in the context of 'human nature' and 'the will' alone.

Nevertheless, the FIP objection as a rejection of the FWD has found an unexpected supporter in a religious believer, the Dominican philosopher of religion Brian Davies:[37] 'As far as I can see, God could have made a world in which people, angels, or any other creatures ... always act well.'[38] Using a Thomist account of God's causing, he believes all states of affairs to be caused by God, though we still remain free. This leads him to reject the FWD: 'I have rejected the free will defence since it rests on the assumption that human free choices are not caused by God.'[39]

> [T]heists cannot view human free choices as not caused to be by God. In that case, however, the Free Will Defence is of no avail to them. It is useless as a way of defending God's moral integrity – even supposing that God has any moral integrity to defend. That is because it denies that humans acting freely are caused to act as they do by God. It conceives of human free actions as events which God must somehow stand back from and learn about as an oberver. Effectively, it conceives of them as uncreated.[40]

At this point it looks as if Davies has either misunderstood Thomism or the FWD. Certainly the FWD does not require one to see human free choices as independent of God's fundamental causal action in maintaining the universe in being. Above all from the Thomist standpoint, this locates God's causation on the wrong plane. Davies asserts that the FWD is wrong to deny that 'humans acting freely are caused to act *as they do* by God' (emphasis mine). But the Thomist too surely would deny that people are caused to act *as they do* by God. For a Thomist could say quite happily: 'God causes the state of affairs to be in which I choose freely.' A Thomist ought not to say: 'God causes me to make *this particular choice*.' The former utterance, in which God is seen as the ultimate cause of all that exists *as* it exists, is perfectly compatible with the FWD; by creating me with free will, God has caused me to freely choose. But this does not mean God has caused me to choose a particular option. And Aquinas would deny that too, particularly as it applies to sin. The way to put it in logical jargon is that the 'God causes' bit is an external modal operator, not an internal one.

As Davies clearly has a firm grip on Aquinas' view of God's causal activity, perhaps he is working with a very narrow understanding of the FWD. For in fact he goes on himself, still following Aquinas, to affirm the reality of human moral freedom; and later he argues that God does not 'do' the evil which humans do. Thus he affirms the essential claims of a FWD: that humans have moral freedom to make decisions for which they are morally responsible; that God does not make humans do evil; and that therefore God is not morally responsible for human wickedness. The FWD does not entail the specific understanding of God's causality that Davies rejects; and I would say that a mainstream version of the FWD is essentially what Davies offers.

The Indian picture of intertwined determinism and freedom, however, is more complex and equivocal than most contributions to the Western FW debate. The 'bound' element in the theory of saṃsāra and karma is not like the FIP or the Frankfurt notions; it is not *compulsion of action*. The lack of freedom is located first and foremost in the inescapability of the *consequences* of our action. Thus in Indian systems even *lack of freedom* is made to support notions of human responsibility. But, more subtly, lack of freedom also arises in the habits and compulsions that *result from our own free choices*. Even our own success can be a source of bondage and unfreedom, because it leads us to habitually restrict our habits and options to what worked last time.

In Indian metaphysics, the problem of freedom and determinism is located within the depiction of causality in the universe as a whole. The urge to understand causality, and with it both 'freedom-from' and 'freedom-to', characterises all the great Indian philosophical systems; so that, as Karl Potter suggests, the problem of causation is the fundamental philosophical problem in Indian thought, and ontology and epistemology are only introduced to support these causal accounts.[41]

[T]he Indian mind exhibits a twofold approach to reality. On the rational plane it asserts the supremacy of a universal and necessary order, a kind of cosmic *norma*; yet on the transcendental plane it trusts that absolute freedom (*mokṣa*) is realizable. The gap between these two planes has always remained unbridged.[42]

Indian philosophers maintained that a causal order existed, while denying that the spiritual and transcendental aspects of human life were wholly contained within it. For the possibility of breaking out of the deterministic causal chain, of attaining *mokṣa*, always exists.

The urge for absolute freedom can act against the whole domain of moral causation and bondage, and throw the exit to *mokṣa* open. Man's being in the bound world is conceived as a causally explicable phenomenon, an event in accordance with a universal order; but it is not denied that considering the prospective free choice he is capable of making, the bound existence will some day be annulled.[43]

The apparent Buddhist 'contradiction' can be resolved here. For the Buddha repudiates determinism and asserts the reality of free will and responsibility. He also, like his follower Vasubandhu, asserts the inescapability, the necessity of causal laws. This is found above all in the chain of 'Dependent Origination'. But for the Buddhist, necessity is not something fixed – all is transient. Necessity is constant change; so are we. Buddhist epistemology and ontology, which insist on the transience of everything, support a notion of causality as inescapable yet always moving toward a particular end. And with insight, we can break the chain of Dependent Origination to achieve release.

This suggests a complexity that reflects human existence in all its contradiction. We *are* compelled; above all, we are compelled when we do not consider the possibility that we might be otherwise. When we do – when we gain insight into our lack of freedom and the causes of it, a new space does open up for wider possibilities of action. The compulsion was not false; nor is the freedom we can realise.

What does it mean 'to do good'?

Although it is the notion of freedom that has attracted all the attention in the FWD debate, perhaps the notion of freedom is the least of the problems associated with the FIP objection. For the FIP objection speaks, in a blithe sort of way, about always 'doing good'; but the fip must be able to identify the good in order to do it.

What is it that makes an action good or bad, so that the fip, or we, for that matter, can readily identify it? The FIP proposal implies that goodness is intrinsic to actions. Acts are intrinsically good or bad, and the fip impeccably chooses the former. Is goodness really something intrinsic and inseparable from the act itself, however? Quite often, actions might be neutral in themselves and it is only the context, purpose or the result of the action that confers on the act its moral status. Indeed, an act normally considered intrinsically good might sometimes be a bad moral choice to make if it led to a bad result. Informing on a drug dealer might not be a morally good thing to do if the result is that a corrupt police force will torture and murder him.

But this suggests that the same action can be either good or bad, depending on the circumstances. So the fip cannot be pre-programmed always to feed the hungry, because it would be a harmful thing to feed someone who was about to undergo general anaesthesia.

The Islamic Basrian school had a different view of what goodness or badness comes from. The Basrian view was that an agent's ability has as its object not individual actions but classes of actions. The power to do something refers to an indefinite number of actions, not a single unique action. If one has the power to use a knife to slice, one can use a knife to slice cabbages or throats. One cannot have 'the ability to cut cabbages but not throats', or 'to slice tomatoes but not my finger'. All the moral attributes an action may have come from its performance by a certain agent with certain intentions, how it is done, why, when, in what context – but not from the mere kind of activity it is. My ability to slice is neither good nor bad. A slicing-event which I enact derives its goodness or badness from my intentions, what I slice, the context, and so on. But the ability to perform such acts is not restricted to its performance under certain conditions. One who can do something can do it in circumstances that are ethically good or ethically bad. In Indian philosophy, good is likewise not an intrinsic quality of the act, inseparable from the human's action. On this view of good action, wherever the constraints on the fip lie, it cannot be in the area of the ability to perform actions.

The abilities to do good

What is required to do good is not the ability to recognise some moral markers intrinsic to acts, if the Basrians are even remotely right about the many conditions that determine the goodness of an act. It requires an accurate reading of *situations* to know whether in these circumstances it is good or bad to do something. Moreover, it requires foreknowledge of the consequences; whether it is a good thing to intervene in a certain way depends in a large part on the results of one's intervention.

All too often, our experience is not that we know what is right but find it difficult to do. Rather, in a moral dilemma what one feels is: 'What on earth is the right thing to do here? I'd gladly do it, if only I knew!' The problem of choosing to do the right thing, then, is often not a problem of 'will' but of *knowledge*.

So there are epistemological problems with fips. For the FIP objection to succeed in depicting a world without evil that God should have created, it is not enough for the humans always reliably to *do their best given their state of knowledge at the time*. More is required: they must be *correct and infallible* in their moral choices. They do not simply need always to choose what they *think* is best; they need in addition to be right that that *is* the best. Otherwise there would still be evil in the world as the result of well-meaning but misguided choices; and there is no reason to think that that possible world would be a better one than ours, in which we might suffer more, but also enjoy a greater degree of liberty.

Does the ability to *always* freely choose to do good mean that this faculty is present and fully developed from birth? It seems so. For if the human person needed to learn, develop, mature morally in order to become reliably good, then there would still be evil in the world – even if not in the form of consciously malicious decisions, at least as the result of immature or mistaken moral choices. But then even if God *had* created humans as fips, evil would still not be eliminated. So to succeed, the FIP objection needs to postulate that humans would always freely choose to do good from birth. Teething infants would not bite their mothers' breasts, for even if this is morally blameless, few women consider this a *good* action. Toddlers would not snatch each others' toys. Unlike any other faculty or ability then – unlike even eating and elimination, as basically natural as you can get, but which both require many moments and aspects of learning, maturation and self-control – no development in the human person is necessary or even possible in the moral sphere. The free will defender is entitled, in my view, to question whether a world in which there was no possibility of development or improvement is really a better world. The inhabitants of such a world are never permitted to improve themselves, which does not seem what an omnibenevolent God should be obliged to choose.

So the FIP proposal, to be functional and therefore successful as a theodicial challenge, requires that human beings are created with perfect moral judgement in assessing situations and contexts; and furthermore, that we are able always to foresee with perfect accuracy what the result of a number of different actions would be, in order to accurately choose the best. It requires the ability to know what would be the actual outcome of all future conditionals in any situation – a form of foreknowledge, in short, that some do not even ascribe to an omniscient God. Kenny, for example, thinks it incredible that a God could have foreknowledge of the future free actions of human beings in order to know in advance which is the best possible world.[44] How much more incredible is it that *human beings* could have such 'middle knowledge' in order to know in advance which is the best possible course of action?

Indeed, more may be required for competent fips. If they do possess such foresight, they might well be able to see and desire good states of affairs which they do not have the power to carry out. 'Choosing' may mean more than a mental act of selecting a preference; choosing in most people's minds means execution as well. It could be argued that if one cannot swim, one cannot really 'choose' to swim to the rescue of a person drowning in deep water. Even if the possible world of fips existed, therefore, they themselves might object that an omnipotent and omnibenevolent God had not created the *best* possible world. Despite their formidable moral and epistemological abilities, they might object that they were not sufficiently empowered to effect the best in every situation. And no matter how powerful they were created to be, as long as their powers of action were finite, they would have scope to complain that if only they were still more powerful, they could achieve still more in the moral sphere. Nothing short of omnipotence, as well as virtual omniscience and omnibenevolence, would be sufficient for fips to feel that even their impeccable moral choosing and action was as good as it could be.

To bed fips into a world even remotely as we know it as an imaginative experiment reveals another little difficulty. The FIP proposal presupposes a 'human nature' which causes us to act as we do. Do we really have such a thing? To postmodern ears, the notion sounds quaint, though admittedly it is making a comeback in a much altered form in evolutionary psychology. But let us suppose that we *are* governed by a 'human nature'; God ought to have designed us (and our environment as well) so that those who always do good have a considerable advantage and thus would succeed in the evolutionary drama. Or perhaps God ought to have designed us with a gene for doing good, that never mutated or was missing or damaged.

However, even if we grant a human nature or contraints on human DNA, there are clearly great differences between one person and another. We seem to vary according to a number of different factors, genetic, biological, cultural, environmental. Even aspects of human behaviour as fundamental as eating or sex reveal this: one might say that if anything is fundamental to human nature, it is to eat. Yet not only does eating vary considerably throughout the world in what is eaten, how, and under what circumstances; human beings cannot even always be relied upon to eat in order to survive. Some choose to starve themselves. Likewise, the sex drive, which is indispensable to our species, can be overridden by other choices or also satisfied in situations where reproduction is impossible. Whatever goes to make up people's sexual preferences and activities, something more than a universal fundamental 'nature' is involved. Moreover, do not different cultures, systems of law and ethics differ in what is considered good, such as the role and behaviour of women? Might not there be legitimate differences in perception and judgement even within a shared ethic and culture, so that people with a good will and the same religious background may nevertheless strongly disagree on what is the 'good' thing to do in a given situation?

The final anthropological challenge to the FIP objection, then, is the fact of human diversity. For God to construct us so that we always do good it is not only necessary that each person's behaviour is unvaryingly good; it is also necessary that what is seen and chosen as good does not vary from person to person. Yet it is difficult to believe that culture, history, religion, class, education, gender, and sexual preferences play no role in influencing any behaviour that is morally significant. They influence sexual behaviour, for a start, which is usually a prime area for moral scrutiny. So either God would have to iron out the cultural and other differences in the world[45] (including the difference between two sexes? What a less-good-world!) or else the world and humanity would have to be redesigned so that all these individual differences play no part in moral judgement and action. But this implies that all of human existence can be neatly divided into two spheres: a moral realm which remains unaffected by cultural or religious values, and a colourful but trivial world of 'culture' which somehow escapes moral import. One might imagine 'culture', if it were to consist only of matters like food and dress, to be of no moral importance. But in a time of BSE, factory farming, environmental damage resulting from the way food is produced, controversies over genetically modified food crops, obsessive eating in some countries and widespread starvation in others, it is clear that 'eating' contains some of the most contentious and problematic ethical issues we face today. So perhaps 'eating', along with sexual activity, would have to come under the category of moral behaviour, rather than culture. But then neither can it vary significantly throughout the world or between individuals. And that is not much fun.

A world for fips

As long as the fip species retained many points of contact with ourselves as we are, it is difficult even to imagine that it could be realised. The FIP objection does not merely require a transformation of human beings into morally perfect, virtually omniscient and indeed perhaps omnipotent (but boringly identical) beings. It also requires a very different world than the one in which we live.

In many situations, it appears to us that there *is* no perfectly good choice.

There may not even be a 'lesser of two evils' – the two (or more) choices might all be equally undesirable or harmful, while refraining from making the choice would have an even worse result. A well-known novel and film described the agonising position that was 'Sophie's choice': a woman was forced by a Nazi concentration camp guard to choose which of her two children would be killed and which spared.[46] If she refused to choose, both would be killed. It cannot be said that there was a 'good' choice among her three options, nor was choosing one child to survive even a 'lesser evil' than choosing the other. A fip *could* not then choose 'good' in any situation where there was no good to be chosen, and the notion of a person who always chooses rightly is self-refuting therefore in any situation of that structure.

Indeed, even if one were to object that in a fip world there could be no moral dilemmas arising from human evil, there are many situations that arise from the structure and limitations of the natural world. There are obstetric situations where the best interests of the mother and of the unborn baby are not the same, and may even be opposed: what is good for the foetus is bad for the mother, or vice versa.

Moreover, natural resources are limited. Daily some parents face the decision of whom to feed; or whether to choose to share the inadequate amount of food out equally amongst all, and thereby run the risk of all dying from starvation. In a natural disaster, one might be able to rescue some, but not all. In this world, human interests sometimes inevitably conflict, even when this is not the result of human aggression or hostility.

In some situations, there *is* no perfectly good moral choice; yet the act of choosing does not thereby lose its moral status. Sophie had to make a decision of moral importance. In order for there always to be a good course of action for a fip to choose, then, we need to imagine a different world from ours, one in which there is never a legitimate conflict of interests, not even between species, if one takes an ecological perspective. Pregnancy and childbirth pose no risks to women, what is advantageous to one never disadvantages another, natural resources are infinite, and all animals are vegetarian.

The FIP objection is not the focused defeat of the FWD that its proponents imagined. What it requires is such a radical reconception not merely of ourselves, but of our world, that it is impossible to compare it to this one to decide which is preferable. We cannot even decide between them on the basis of pleasure, let alone moral achievement.

Is it worth it?

Is freedom worth the disadvantages? Can the goodness that free will adds to the world possibly compensate for the evil that results from the ability to choose bad which is the side effect of free will? If not, it would have been a better world if we hadn't had the choice. Mesle has lodged a complaint against the value of freedom:

> We do not really value the 'freedom' to become drug addicts and child molesters, murderers or concentration camp guards .... Freedom can be meaningful even when it is 'limited' to choices which are good, loving, creative, and enriching .... It is the choice between goods that we value, not the temptation to abuse our children in the night.[47]

Mesle may be right that freedom to be evil is not something that moral people treasure. However, freedom in choosing only between good choices is commonly referred to as 'taste', which indeed 'can be meaningful' but has little moral import. Mesle tells us that he did not value the 'freedom' to abuse his child when his child exasperated him almost beyond endurance. The question is, did he value the fact that he did *not*? His mistake is to think that the FWD has to argue that the possibility of doing evil is a value in itself. The FWD claims rather that the freedom to choose good is a value in itself, but that this is inseparable from the freedom *not* to. Mesle seems to assume that the freedom to be a child molester is a different item from the freedom not to be; but this hypostasising language is misleading. We do not possess two different and separated *things*, one for good and a different one for evil, different 'freedoms' to use his word, in this or any situation. We are able to choose a number of different responses or actions in our relations with children. 'Freedom' refers to a way of being, not to a thing we can possess.

Suppose Mesle had a certain strong view about how he wanted to raise his child: what beliefs and values he wanted the child to respect, what kind of schooling system he wanted, or what sports or potentially risky activities he thought the child might be allowed to engage in for her own benefit. Let us suppose Mesle's opinions were rather controversial; Mesle is the member of a new religious movement, or does not want to send his child to school, or wants to allow the child to go parachuting. Suppose an over-zealous, interfering health professional disagreed with his judgement and decided that Mesle must be prevented from 'abusing' his child in this way: he cannot raise the child in the framework of the religion of his choice, cannot educate his child at home, and so on. Wouldn't Mesle object that this was an infringement on his freedom? Doesn't Mesle value the freedom to make his own decision as to *what constitutes* good child-raising and to carry it out with his child, even if a differently-minded person thinks it 'abusive'? Doesn't this example suggest that the freedom we are discussing goes beyond a simplistic opposition of 'knowingly doing good' and 'knowingly doing evil', and that to object that one does not 'value the freedom to do evil' has no real bearing on the case?

> For if freedom is possible, then men have it in their power to be concerned for each other lovingly yet disciplinedly, spontaneously yet responsibly. If freedom is worthwhile everyone has a stake in everyone else's advancement, for to help another become more concerned for yourself is at the same time to help yourself become more concerned for him.[48]

What is the point of freedom?

Mackie claims that any objection to his and Flew's determinist conception of fippish freedom implies that freedom must mean 'complete randomness or indeterminacy, including randomness with regard to the alternatives good and evil, in other words that men's choices and consequent actions can be "free" only if they are not determined by their characters'. But he wonders: 'What value or merit would there be in free choices if these were random actions which were not determined by the nature of the agent?'[49]

He may be right in claiming that moral freedom, if it is considered to be so precious, must consist in something more than sheer randomness. But it is disingenuous to suggest that the libertarian view of freedom consists in sheer randomness. The libertarian does not maintain that one is only free if one has no preference whatsoever between two options. She claims that there is a difference in significance – moral significance above all – between situations in which we choose between two options, and situations in which we happily go along with our only possibility.

We do in practice make such distinctions in our assessment of other people's decisions and morals. If our friend Trismegistus, when offered a choice of drinks first thing in the morning, chose to drink beer, we might feel this was an important indicator of his propensity to drink alcohol. But we would not see the same significance in his choice to drink beer for breakfast if we greeted him in the morning with 'Unfortunately the water's been cut off, and there's no juice either; it's beer or nothing, I'm afraid.' In these circumstances, we would have as little grounds for thinking Trismegistus is an alcoholic as we would have for calling a fip 'morally admirable' in a FIP world.

It is this kind of freedom the FWD hangs its argument upon. Even if one were to reject the libertarian view of freedom as romantic, unrealistic, or just untrue: the FWD claims that there is a virtue to be found in choosing what is good. That virtue does not just derive from the goodness of the result, but also from the chooser's choice: not just to choose a particular good state of affairs, but to choose to choose goodness itself. Only then does it possess maximal moral value. It seems to me that the FIP objection hypothesises that our natures could be so constructed that moral choices have the same sort of pattern of liberty and constraint that breathing does for us now: something we can control, but not fully choose not to do. But it is not insignificant that breathing, for us, is *not* an ethical issue.

The fundamental drive *and* the final goal

In the end, however, there is something unsatisfying about the fixation on 'free will' in the monotheists' debates. 'Free will' is far too narrow a concept in which to consider the question of human moral freedom. It reifies both 'freedom' and 'will' in a way reminiscent of the eighteenth-century language of 'faculty psychology';[50] these become *things* we have, whose nature is in dispute. Such language suggests a possession that we have and control – perhaps a characteristically 'First World' attitude – rather than a way of being, which freedom more truly is. Perhaps it even betrays a desire for self-sufficiency and independence from God or whatever is more ultimate than we are; an attempt to gain control over the events in our lives, to justify – or dignify – our bad behaviour as 'a legitimate exercise of freedom'. But allocating blame for evil, or justifying ourselves in the face of our moral hideousness, is not the best purpose to which reflection on freedom can be put.

The doctrines of karma and saṃsāra have several strengths, compared to the notion of free will as normally deployed. They are not focused exclusively on 'the will' as our one free spot; they are not focused on our own abilities or constraints. Moreover, they insist that doing good actually has *agency*, *power*, first and foremost in its impact on one's own life. Good and bad actions are efficacious; they impact on our lives, and are not mere tokens of good or evil intent. Furthermore, liberation has an epistemological overtone, as we see above all in Śankara, for whom freedom *is* illumination or knowledge.[51] As our discussion of fips revealed, one of the greatest constraints on our moral action is not a petty will but restricted epistemological horizons.

Although 'free will' in the Western monotheisms and 'freedom from suffering' in the Indian religions appear to be quite different, it is questionable whether they should be separated. Bondage to suffering and the tribulations of existence restrict our ability to discern, to choose, to act. What we undergo affects our ability to be good and compassionate, as can be witnessed in the cycles of abuse that tragically are handed down from one human generation to another. 'Suffering' and 'morality' are not separate issues for one who looks on humanity with a compassionate eye. What is required, then, to shed more light and less heat in theodicy debates is a broader, but also more dynamic notion of freedom: something that embraces both the joyous and the tragic aspects of our participation in the world and human existence; and as something that pertains both to our action and our being acted upon. Above all, we need a notion of freedom as something that is only our starting-point insofar as we realise it, and something that is our goal only insofar as we actualise it.

Hamann wrote: 'Without the freedom to be evil there is no merit and without the freedom to be good no ascription of any guilt, yes, no recognition of good and evil itself.'[52] He was aware that the issue is not so much a 'free will' that can choose between good and evil options, but that the very ability to discern the good from the bad presupposes freedom in a deeper sense.

Freedom, he tells us, 'is the maximum and minimum of all our natural powers and the fundamental drive as well as the final purpose of their entire direction, development and return'. Without freedom we are not fully human; it is the indispensable starting-point for all our activity. And yet it is also the end, the purpose of all our drives and powers, a final accomplishment. Thus he unites both of the perspectives we have contrasted: the view of freedom as a given, and the perception of freedom as an achievement, the goal of fulfilment.

Freedom is also the ground and context for all our activities; all our mental powers, like consciousness, attention, or reflection, he describes as 'energies of our freedom'. In this he echoes Aristotle; and thereby suggests that all that we are and can do is united in the entelechy[53] of freedom. But at this point, Hamann moves the discussion of freedom into a new dimension. Freedom immediately brings with it a moral responsibility. 'Freedom' is not merely a question of our own inner being; it is not only our 'undetermined powers' which belong to freedom; but also something that Hamann portrays not as an entitlement but as a privilege: the privilege of 'being able to contribute to our destiny'. This – not fippish impeccability, not human self-sufficiency and entitlement – is the ability that human freedom is.

In this passage Hamann implicitly suggests that one danger in being obsessed with 'freedom' as an inner state, a condition of some faculty we have, is that the wider, social, indeed, political dimension of freedom is ignored. For Hamann, political freedom and autonomy cannot be separated from 'inner freedom'. The two are in a reciprocal relationship. The privilege of contributing to our destiny carries with it the obligation to contribute to others' future in a way that is good, not evil.

Finally, Hamann grounds freedom in a relationship to God, by alluding to a passage from the Letter of James: those that look to the 'perfect law of freedom' will be blessed in their doing.[54] The 'perfect law' of religious liberation is contrasted with the unjust political regime under which Hamann lived. Although a 'law', it is a not a system of oppressive regulations, but is that order and harmony of our being that makes action ('doing') possible and fruitful.

What is fundamentally at issue in the question of freedom and evil is moral responsibility; and what best fosters our awareness of it. We should no longer think in terms of a 'Free Will Defence' but rather of a 'Moral Responsibility Understanding': greatest goodness exists in relationships between God and human beings, and between human beings themselves, who bear a maximal degree of moral responsibility. Perhaps we should also cease to think of an entity called free will operating in situations in the world, and replace it with an understanding of desire. Desire is what sets us in motion, to realise our 'maximum' from our 'minimum' of freedom; desire is what guides us to our ultimate fulfilment. With the twin ideas of desire and responsibility our reflection on human freedom in action might take a different direction.

Conclusion

The question for theodicy then is really what relationship we bear to God. This is the proper context in which to examine questions like free will; and to take one's model as a relationship, not a court-room or a ledger-book, transforms the nature of the debate. One does not ask if God was justified in allowing us free will, with the somewhat begrudging implication that we are doing God a favour in being free. One does not try to construct human natures with or without an item called a free will and total up the goods and the evils occurring in the experimental and the control groups of creatures to see which is better.

In the context of a relationship, acts are *gifts*: neither pieces of evidence nor units of currency. In the context of a relationship, what one does has meaning; it is *significant* for the other, what I do *means something* to him. So in dealing with the issues of human action and freedom, the profound questions are not 'what would outweigh' or 'what would justify'; the questions are: in what circumstances, in what conditions do my acts have the most meaning and value? And here, using human relationships as a heuristic model, we find that acts have a range of meanings and imports. In situations of *maximal choice*, our decisions have *maximal importance*; they also bring with them *maximal responsibility*. They reveal the most of us, they reflect our discernment, our judgement, our willingness to will good – at the very least, they reveal our taste. The freedom offered by alternatives from which we may choose allows scope for our self-expression, self-revelation, as well as self-realisation. It allows our desire to reveal who we are and decide what we become.

One can therefore maintain that evil can only be understood in the context of our relationship to God; and in this framework, the existence of evil signifies God's respect for us. It signifies not only our desire, but *God's* desire, for our action to have as much meaning and importance as possible. It is misleading to brandish the Free Will Defence and maintain that evil is a side effect which somehow escapes an omnipotent God's control. Rather, the Moral Responsibility Understanding maintains that God desires to be in a relationship with creatures who are morally responsible rather than not. Such creatures possess power and scope for discernment, decision and action; their decisions and actions therefore are meaningful and significant. They are beings who create and reveal themselves in their decision and action; beings who possess autonomy, authority, and agency; beings who, apparently, are being treated with more respect than they sometimes want.

All is divine, and the question of the origin of evil turns in the end on a play on words and scholastic chatter. Everything divine, however, is also human. This is a fundamental law and the principle key of all our knowledge and the entire visible economy.[55]

The Call of the Real

'How did you know that the call was the call of the real?'

   'Because he annihilated me, then encompassed me, and it was as if all the hairs on my body were speaking from all sides about the call, and were themselves on their own power responding to the call! When the lights of awe encompassed me and the lights of majesty ... addressed me, I knew that I was being addressed on the part of the truth.'[1]

Human existence as the experience of the real is an experience of both enjoyment and distress, sometimes banal, sometimes intense. Especially when intense, the temptation to move beyond the material sphere as the sphere of meaning and interpretation of our experience is irresistible for some, although it will always be inexplicable for others.

   As Jakob Boehme wrote, 'The being of beings is a wrestling power.' Those who are drawn to intimacy with it have not only found peace, tranquillity, joy, but also torment, inner violence – a refiner's fire.

   Some of this discomfort is not only psychological, or spiritual, but also philosophical, or epistemological. To make sense of one's experience, consider whether it is delusion and fantasy, explain it, and justify it to oneself is arduous; to do so to another is a hideous embarrassment. The mystic is perhaps more acutely aware of the possibility of being deceived in her thinking than the logician is.

'How did you know that the call was the call of the real?'

'Mr Waller, what *is* jazz?' a woman once asked Fats Waller. He replied: 'Lady, if you have to ask, you'll never know.'

   This is a fair statement of our ultimate problem. It is known to philosophers as the 'Meno paradox', after the Platonic dialogue of the same name.[2] How can you ever learn something? For this requires you to recognise the answer to your question, which presupposes that you already know the answer; how else could you recognise it?

   This is the problem alluded to earlier, in relation to the knowledge of God. To identify the divine as the 'object' of an experience, we need first to know it; but how can we know it before we have experienced it?

   This problem was raised with a special linguistic twist by Maṇḍana. Maṇḍana maintains that Brahman can only be known through language. What could be a *pramāṇa*, a mode of knowledge, for Brahman? The sentences of the Upaniṣads cannot be, because the ability of a sentence to communicate presupposes the hearer's knowledge of the object of speech. This is turn presupposes some previous knowledge of the object in question. You must know something about the topic of discussion to understand what is said about it. So speech cannot reveal new knowledge about Brahman. The object of knowledge then must be known by another mode of knowledge. So neither words nor sentences can give knowledge of Brahman – although Maṇḍana has said that Brahman can *only* be known by the *pramāṇa* of language. On the other hand, if Brahman can be known by other modes of knowledge, then the words of scriptures are redundant.[3]

So we must know about the unknown in order to learn anything about it; moreover, we must talk about what we do not know, although we can have nothing to say about it.

Plato attempts to answer this problem by invoking the knowledge from past lives, or the period spent disembodied between lives. All knowledge is recognition; we recognise what we knew previously.

I suggest another solution to the problem. Take an everyday example. You are looking for a birthday present for your aunt, but finding it difficult. The shop assistant helpfully asks you what you are looking for. You respond: 'I don't know, but I'll know it when I see it.'

How will you know it when you see it, how will you recognise it if you don't even know what it is? Not by some extraordinary form of pre-knowledge. This doesn't really solve anything; it's like the 'pre-wash' on a washing machine (if it isn't washing, what is a 'pre'-wash *doing* to my clothes?) You recognise it, not because you *knew* it but because you *wanted* it. Knowledge itself cannot break open the vicious circle; but *desire* can.

The beginning of learning and understanding is not knowing, but wanting. Hamann understood this well: 'Human beings learn ... because they can learn, must learn and indeed truly want to learn .... But despite the fact that every apprentice co-operates with his instruction to learn according to his inclinations, abilities, and opportunities; learning is nevertheless in a real sense as little invention as mere re-cognition.'[4]

In Hamann's picture, learning is not solitary. The apprentice learns from another. The experience of desire is also not solitary.

> ... it is desire that is given the responsibility for that minimum connexion with ancient knowledge that the subject must retain if truth is to be immanent in the realization of knowledge. [The] 'cunning of reason' means that, from beginning to end, the subject knows what he wants.
>
> [This] reopens the junction between truth and knowledge .... In this respect: that desire becomes bound up with the desire of the Other, but that in this loop lies the desire to know.[5]

These somewhat cryptic words from Lacan remind us that it is desire that connects us with knowledge; and without this we are excluded from the truth.

Desire also guides our learning – even our 'reason'; perhaps that is reason's 'cunning'. But Lacan also goes on to assert that desire for knowledge and desire for the other cannot be separated. The legend of Odysseus and the sirens has already hinted as much to us.

Desire to know the real, then, is what nullifies the philosopher's vicious circle of knowledge. It is the *pramāṇa* for Brahman – *even* within the tradition of Indian religious philosophy, which seeks enlightenment through the overcoming of desire.

Still greater darkness

Into blinding darkness enter those who worship ignorance and those who delight in knowledge enter into still greater darkness, as it were.[6]

This sentence from the Iśa Upaniṣad articulates the paradox of knowing: that the ascending pathway of deep longing is the ascent to greater light, and greater darkness still.

It is as it was for St Theresa: you have only to go to Rome and see Bernini's statue, to understand at once that she is, without doubt, in the act of enjoying. And what does she enjoy? It is clear that the essential testimony of mystics consists in saying that they experience it, but do not know anything about it.[7]

Yet it is the mystics who *do* know about it.

In this late text from Lacan, he considers that his account of 'jouissance' (enjoyment which includes suffering) as 'phallic' may be missing something.[8] Perhaps there is 'another jouissance', 'the jouissance of the Other'? A jouissance that is ineffable?

Here Lacan stands baffled before the spectacle of women and mystics enjoying themselves.

In the unknown enjoyment of the woman there must be an unknown truth, which resembles the mystical experience of ecstasy – as if the woman, in going beyond phallic enjoyment and not being totally submitted to its limitations, acquires something *more* which, as with the mystics, puts her in touch with God …. This enjoyment of the woman can be compared to the culminating moment of a relationship with God. It involves an unknown knowledge, in so far as it does not belong to the human sphere but to divine knowledge, which, in ecstasy, appears to overlap with divine enjoyment.[9]

In the Lacanian framework, the Other Jouissance, feminine and non-phallic, is not in the realm of the symbolic but in the real. This means, in Lacanian algebra, that it resists speech. God, associated with the Other Jouissance and with woman, also resists speech – and is therefore associated with the real. This leads the atheist Lacan to the logical consequence (it could even be put in a syllogism) that 'A God is something that one encounters in the real, inaccessible'; 'the gods are real'.

I would simply point out that within Lacan's framework, while the real resists speech, it does not escape metonymy. If the object of desire is always deferred, as we are told (which is why desire is a metonymy); then God as the Real remains present in speech as metonymy, though God will always escape linguistic and epistemological capture.

Some readers will no doubt be allergic to this style of thinking and its assumptions. (And women may like [metonymically] to shift the 'phallic' off the position of being the subject and into the role of the one who is the *Other* one.) I am simply using the Lacanian framework and ideas as a kind of metonymy itself for the problems of philosophy of religion; above all, the need to have one's cake while eating it too, or to contradict oneself, which have been persistent if tacit themes in the analyses and discussions of this book. The Lacanian problem is an analogy for the philosopher's problem of knowing and speaking about the divine: to know without being able to know, to speak without being able to articulate. It resolves the paradox of the philosopher's conflicting desires: to insist that God transcends knowledge and language, and nevertheless to write a great deal about the subject.

It does so by suggesting an epistemology that recognises the cunning of reason's desire, that allows us to know what we cannot know;[10] because knowledge consists in a proper relationship to the truth, and relationships are constituted by desire. It also suggests an account of religious language which avoids problems of reference and effability, by recognising that speaking about the inexpressible and the absent is precisely what language is *for*. It also, tacitly, suggests a theology: the God who annihilates but encompasses; the God who always goes before you and thus will always elude you, but is in the canoe with you seeking your new home.

'The tavern's door is open'

I am not suggesting that we replace philosophy of religion with mysticism. The best mystics in the religious traditions that have them were philosophers as well. Illogical or irrational some might declare them, but so much the worse then for logic and rationality, because such mystics are some of the most critical thinkers, and possess the sharpest, most insightful intellects.

It is not a question of opposing understanding, reason and rationality to desire, longing and passion. Responsible reflection on religion is a question of bringing *all* one's powers to bear in analysis and critique. Attempts to separate a non-thing called reason from emotions, passions, longings and desires is not only disabling, it is self-deceiving. It obscures the truth. Such a 'quest for the truth' ironically becomes a 'defence of the faith' – the faith in 'rationality'. Why not instead have faith in the legitimacy of being as we *really* are, when we reflect?

Those who are wary about the sublation of 'objectivity' because they are anxious about 'subjectivism' can be reassured that one sublates *both* objectivity and subjectivity in inter-subjectivity. Those who are rightly concerned about blindness, bias and prejudice can set 'neutrality' aside for what it is that you really desire in trying for it: openness to change, willingness to be shown to be wrong, acceptance of being 'other' and different, and never unquestionably justified.

Socrates conducted much of his philosophy in the marketplace, because he did not write books alone in his study. His philosophy consisted in asking questions and having conversations. Most of us do not have ecstatic experiences of self-forgetfulness. Most of us are not in studies writing books, or in monasteries as mystics or privileged clerics. Most of us are actually excluded from these places. No matter. Reflection on religious questions happens most fruitfully in conversations, wherever they take place.

> The drunkard who is ruined in the path of Love,
> his sweet drunkard's dreams are like praying.
> Since they would not let me in the monastery last night,
> I went to the tavern's door, but lo … the door was so high …
> Then out of the tavern a song rose up:
> 'Oh, *find yourself*, for the tavern's door is open!'[11]

Notes

Invocation

1. From a chant in praise of Pele, which begins 'O kaua a Pele i hakā i Kahiki'. Hawaiian text and a translation in Nathaniel B. Emerson, *Pele and Hiiaka* (Charles Tuttle, 1982; first edition 1915), p. 130. My translation is indebted to his but differs slightly.

2. 'Hawaii' nowadays denotes the whole chain of islands, whereas the proper form 'Hawai'i' is denotes the specific island whose name was taken for the whole.

3. An interesting example is found in Quinn and Taliaferro's *Companion to Philosophy of Religion* (Blackwell, 1997). The piece on 'Being', a topic of immense importance in twentieth-century German and French philosophy, deals almost exclusively with specific logical points about existence as a predicate. The final paragraph tells us: 'I pass over in silence works of other philosophers entitled [here are named the major works of European philosophy on the subject]. Of them, and the whole tribe of existentialists, the less said the better. Those who have understood what I have said of Frege will understand why.'

4. Shaikh Fakhruddin Ebrahim Hammedani (Eraqi) in an unublished translation by Mehri Niknam.

1. All at Sea

1. F. Nietzsche, *The Gay Science*, translated by Walter Kaufmann (Vintage Books, 1974), §18, §125.

2. I. Kant, *The Critique of Pure Reason*, translated by Norman Kemp Smith (Macmillan, 1987), p. 257, B294-5, A235-6.

3. John E. Smith, 'Faith, Belief, and the Problem of Rationality in Religion' in C.F. Delaney (ed.), *Rationality and Religious Belief* (University of Notre Dame Press, 1979), pp. 42-64, see pp. 42ff.

4. Ibid., pp. 44ff.

5. Brian Davies, *Introduction to the Philosophy of Religion* (Oxford University Press, 1993), p. 1.

6. Cf. Richard Rorty's (somewhat critical) description of philosophy: it 'sees itself as the attempt to underwrite or debunk claims to knowledge made by science, morality, art or religion. It purports to do this on the basis of its special understanding of the nature of knowledge and the mind. Philosophy can be foundational in respect to the rest of culture because culture is the assemblage of claims to knowledge, and philosophy adjudicates such claims.' Rorty, *Philosophy and the Mirror of Nature* (Princeton University Press, 1980), p. 3.

7. Hans Blumenberg has done an entire study of the image of the shipwreck and its spectators. H. Blumenberg, *Schiffbruch mit Zuschauer* (Bibliothek Suhrkamp, 1979).

8. Ibid., pp. 10f.

9. P. Anderson, *A Feminist Philosophy of Religion* (Blackwell, 1998), pp. xi-xii, 11ff., 215f.

10. Abridged from Homer, *The Odyssey*, translated by E.V. Rieu (Penguin Books, 1946).

11. I have discussed this in 'The Roots of the Great Fig-Tree', in Herman Browne and Gwen Griffith-Dickson (eds), *A Passion for Critique* (Ecumenical Publishing House, 1997): 'Either "there is a world of objective reality that exists independently of us and that has a determinative nature or essence that we can know ... knowledge is achieved when a subject correctly mirrors or represents objective reality" or "we must therefore make trial whether we may not have more success in the tasks of metaphysics, if we suppose that objects must conform to knowledge." Either Truth is something that exists independent of human reasoning, language, and existence, to which these latter should strive to approximate (realism; correspondence theory of truth) or "Truth" is entirely relative to a particular culture or system, varies therefore between systems, does not exist outside systems and cannot be compared between systems (relativism; coherence theory of truth). Either the goal of inter-pretation is to recover the specific meaning of the author which is placed in the text or meaning is what is created by the reader: meaning, like beauty, is in the eye of the beholder. Either language is a passive instrument, a mode of transport for thoughts; its purpose is to represent reality, and its meaning consists in designation; words have meaning because they signify things; *or* language is almost, to paraphrase Heidegger, the prison of being; it is a bubble in which we live from which we cannot escape; nothing lies outside it and it entirely controls and determines the way we think and perceive the world. Human beings either have a fixed and determinative essence or nature, independent of their place in history or their culture – or they have none, selves do not exist. Finally, *either* God is a being-thing out there, or else he is an inner presence, not reified, but not real either' (pp. 50f.). I suggest that there is an alternative to these opposed positions.

12. Note that I am not using this word in the sense that it is often colloquially used: as one who does not believe in God.

13. *The Odyssey*, ed. cit., p. 200.

14. W.K. Clifford, *Lectures and Essays* (1879), reprinted in various places, including B. Brody, *Readings in the Philosophy of Religion* (Prentice Hall, 1991), pp. 241ff.

15. Ibid., p. 246.

16. W. James, *The Will to Believe*, given as a lecture, first published in 1896. Reprinted in Brody, op. cit., pp. 247ff.

17. Ibid., pp. 261f.

18. Mark McLeod examines arguments put forward by Alston and Plantinga which suggest a parity between the formation of religious beliefs and other beliefs, such as beliefs based on sense perception. Finding both flawed, he puts forward his own which is 'holistic'. The others fail because of a 'lack of recognition of the necessary role of an epistemic base – a set of background beliefs – in the formation and justification of certain kinds of belief.' Mark S. McLeod, *Rationality and Theistic Belief: An Essay on Reformed Epistemology* (Cornell University Press, 1993), p. 9.

19. Michael Scriven, *Primary Philosophy* (Hutchinson, 1966), p. 103. Plantinga complains that Scriven is not treating 'God exists' and 'God does not exist' in the same way. If there is no evidence for the first, we must believe the second; but he does not say, if there is no evidence for the second, we must believe the first; why this lack of parity? It is 'merely arbitrary intellectual imperialism'. Alvin Plantinga, 'Reason and Belief in God' in A. Plantinga and N. Wolterstorff (eds), *Faith and Rationality: Reason and Belief in God* (University of Notre Dame Press, 1983), pp. 27f.

20. Stephen T. Davis, *Faith, Skepticism, and Evidence. An Essay in Religious Epistemology* (Associated University Presses, 1978), p. 9, see also the extended examination of James' essay in Part II.

21. Ibid., p. 211.

22. Ibid., p. 225.

23. W. Donald Hudson, 'The Rational System of Beliefs' in A. Loades and L.D. Rue (eds), *Contemporary Classics in Philosophy of Religion* (Open Court, 1991), pp. 33-58.

24. In this 'Rational System', the beliefs fall into two categories: beliefs about what is the case (propositions), and beliefs about what is appropriate to do (principles). They have two features: they regulate what it makes sense to say or do, and general assent is given to them. Some propositions within this system play a special role: they may be fundamental to our world-view, or to an academic discipline, as 'Nature is uniform' is fundamental to

natural science and 'The earth existed long before I was born' is indispensable for a study of history. Or they may be propositions that are widely taken for granted in our society. When changes come about to this rational system of beliefs, Hudson argues, they do not come about (at least, not solely) through the application of the criteria of rationality, proof, evidence, and so on. People can lose interest in them, or exercise free choice in beliefs. There is a perpetual tension between the propositions which are established, and those which are emerging. Conformity with the rational system also means being open to revision and re-thinking.

25. D.Z. Phillips, *Faith After Foundationalism* (Routledge, 1988), p. 3.

26. A. Plantinga, 'Is Belief in God Rational?', op. cit., see especially p. 26.

27. Kenneth Konyndyk claims that evidentialism is a surprising principle for Christians to adopt, as faith is incompatible with it. His interpretation of Aquinas and Calvin suggests that faith, which is rational and which has some evidences for its content, nevertheless goes beyond evidence of this life, and that holding belief does not get its certainty from evidence. Faith requires a certainty not rooted in sensory experience. Yet neither Aquinas nor Calvin thought the believer irrationalist. Kenneth Konyndyk, 'Faith and Evidentialism' in R. Audi and W. Wainwright (eds), *Rationality, Religious Belief, and Moral Commitment: New Essays in the Philosophy of Religion* (Cornell University Press, 1986), pp. 82-108.

28. Plantinga, 'Reason and Belief in God', op. cit., p. 17.

29. See 'Reason and Belief in God', op. cit., pp. 90-1. Cf. also Alvin Plantinga, 'Coherentism and the Evidentialist Objection to Belief in God' in R. Audi and W. Wainwright (eds), *Rationality, Religious Belief, and Moral Commitment: New Essays in the Philosophy of Religion* (Cornell University Press, 1986), pp. 109-38.

30. K.J. Clark, *Return to Reason: A Critique of Enlightenment Evidentialism and a Defense of Reason and Belief in God* (Eerdmans, 1990), p. 97.

31. Alvin Plantinga, *God and Other Minds* (Cornell University Press, 1967).

32. Clark, *Return to Reason*, op. cit., p. 121.

33. 'Belief in God is rationally accepted *immediately*. It is a fundamental belief which one reasons *from* not *to*. It does not require arguments or evidence in order to be rationally accepted or maintained – the theist has a perfect right to believe without the evidential support of an argument. In fact, the evidentialist demand for evidence is perverse, obdurate, or improper.' Ibid., p. 122.

34. Norman Kretzmann, 'Evidence Against Anti-Evidentialism' in K. Clark (ed.), *Our Knowledge of God: Essays on Natural and Philosophical Theology* (Kluwer Academic Publishers, 1992), pp. 17-38.

35. David B. Burrell, 'Religious Belief and Rationality' in C.F. Delaney (ed.), *Rationality and Religious Belief* (University of Notre Dame Press, 1979), pp. 84-115, p. 105.

36. Ibid., p. 109.

37. Gareth Moore, *Believing in God* (T. & T. Clark, 1988), p. 17.

38. Ibid., p. 17.

39. Ibid., p. 41.

40. N. Wolterstorff, 'Is Reason Enough?' in R.D. Geivett and B. Sweetman (eds), *Contemporary Perspectives on Religious Epistemology* (Oxford University Press, 1992), pp. 142-9, see p. 149.

41. Plantinga, 'Reason and Belief in God', op. cit., pp. 59-61.

42. Ibid., pp. 78-80.

43. R. Pargetter, 'Experience, Proper Basicality, and Belief in God' in R.D. Geivett and B. Sweetman (eds), *Contemporary Perspectives on Religious Epistemology*, op. cit., pp. 150-67, see p. 151.

44. N. Wolterstorff, 'Can Belief In God Be Rational If It Has No Foundations?' in A. Plantinga and N. Wolterstorff (eds), *Faith and Rationality: Reason and Belief in God*, op. cit., p. 176.

45. R. Pargetter, 'Experience, Proper Basicality, and Belief in God', op. cit., pp. 155-7.

46. S.C. Goetz, 'Belief in God Is Not Properly Basic' in R.D. Geivett and B. Sweetman (eds), *Contemporary Perspectives on Religious Epistemology*, op. cit., pp. 168-77.

47. Robert Audi, 'Direct Justification, Evidential Dependence, and Theistic Belief' in R. Audi and W. Wainwright (eds), *Rationality, Religious Belief, and Moral Commitment: New Essays in the Philosophy of Religion*, op. cit., pp. 139-66.

48. See E. Husserl, *Cartesian Meditations: An Introduction to Phenomenology*, translated by D. Cairns (Martinus Nijhoff, 1973).

49. A. Kenny, *What is Faith?* (Oxford University Press, 1992), pp. 44f.

50. Cf. this is its 'strong form': 'in order to have a properly basic theistic belief, one that is both rational and not based on any evidence beliefs, S must meet a certain rational standard. He must have, or be able to construct, either an adequate argument against certain putative reasons to believe that God does not exist or at least an adequate argument for the view that there are no sufficient reasons for believing that he does not exist ...'; a view Audi characterises as 'argumentalism'. 'It shares with evidentialism the view that theistic beliefs are justificatorily dependent, since it takes them to depend for their justification (and rationality) on that of other beliefs; but it seems more plausible. It is, however, also quite inimical to experientialism of the kind that conceives certain theistic beliefs as justificatorily independent.' The weak form: 'in order to have properly basic theistic beliefs, S must be such that, given his circumstances and beliefs, he is justified in believing, even if he in fact does not believe, propositions that would at least neutralize any plausible antitheistic considerations of which he is aware or may reasonably be expected to be aware.' Even if this weaker version is true, then direct theistic beliefs are justificatorily dependent. Robert Audi, 'Direct Justification, Evidential Dependence, and Theistic Belief', op. cit., p. 157.

51. K.E. Yandell, *The Epistemology of Religious Experience* (Cambridge University Press, 1993), p. 143. Yandell adds: 'This arises from the facts (or alleged facts) that S's lacking grounds that epistemically favor P does not appear among the conditions of improper basicality, that a belief that is basic to S but not improperly basic to S is properly basic to S, and that a basic belief for which I has no grounds is one that S is irrational in having.' Ibid.

52. David Hume, *An Enquiry Concerning Human Understanding* (Oxford University Press, 1979).

53. Beware of those who would tell you that 'Hume didn't believe in causality'. 'Believing' in causality is precisely what he did; his point was that reason was useless to *prove* it, and one had to take it on faith – as with many other crucial structural beliefs. The point of his critique was not to prove that causality did not exist, but to challenge the power of reason as capable of proving even something so universal and indispensable as causality. This interpretation of Hume may be a minority one, but it is convincing. See Galen Strawson, *The Secret Connexion: Causation, Realism and David Hume* (Clarendon, 1989).

54. L. Wittgenstein, *On Certainty* (Blackwell, 1969), §166.

55. N. Malcolm, 'The Groundlessness of Belief' in R.D. Geivett and B. Sweetman (eds), *Contemporary Perspectives on Religious Epistemology*, op. cit., pp. 92-103.

56. Wittgenstein, *On Certainty*, op. cit., §160.

57. N. Malcolm, 'The Groundlessness of Belief', op. cit., p. 92.

58. Wittgenstein, *On Certainty*, op. cit., §192.

59. N. Malcolm, 'The Groundlessness of Belief', op. cit., p. 94. See Wittgenstein, *On Certainty*, op. cit., §163.

60. Malcolm, 'The Groundlessness of Belief', op. cit., p. 95.

61. Ibid., p. 98.

62. Ibid., p. 99.

63. D.Z. Phillips, 'Faith, Skepticism, and Religious Understanding' in R.D. Geivett and B. Sweetman (eds), *Contemporary Perspectives on Religious Epistemology*, op. cit., pp. 81-91, p. 83.

64. Malcolm, 'The Groundlessness of Belief', op. cit., p. 99.

65. Ibid., p. 100.

66. John E. Smith objects to this Wittgensteinian, functionalist view of religion: 'It does no good to say that a person has this belief always before him in unshakeable form regulating for all his life, unless there is some difference between the belief itself and the regulating function. That is to say, the belief means that there is a judge, a persona, an all-encompassing center of knowledge capable of making the judgment, and I fail to see how the belief could perform its function of guidance in the life of the individual unless he or she believed in the reality of that judge. Whatever the regulating function is and means, it cannot take the place of the belief itself .... The main reason for the inadequacy of all the practicalistic and fideistic solutions to the dilemma of religious knowledge since Kant is found in their tendency to identify the belief content with the function it has to perform and thus to evade the issue of what validity is to be attached to the belief itself.' J.E. Smith, 'Faith, Belief, and the Problem of Rationality in Religion' in C.F. Delaney (ed.), *Rationality and Religious Belief*, op. cit., p. 55. Gary Gutting identifies three elements in this stance: 'a methodological injunction to examine religious discourse from the inside; without the imposition of external (e.g. scientific, philosophical) criteria of meaning and truth'; 'a fundamental epistemological point (most prominent in *On Certainty*) that all justifications must be based on "framework principles" that define the context in which questions of justification may be raised and for which the question of justification cannot be properly raised'; and 'an analysis of the nature of religious language ... showing that fundamental religious beliefs are framework principles.' Wittgensteinians try to get away with raising the first or second points; but what is really required to show that justification of beliefs is inappropriate or unnecessary is the third task: an analysis of religious language to show that religious beliefs really do function as framework principles exempt from evidence or argument. He does not feel that any such systematic account has been offered, let alone succeeded. Moreover, to represent religion as a 'form of life' is insufficient to the 'great' religions. 'Such religions do not constitute our basic forms of life but rather criticize and transform them. Primitive religions, like that of the Zande, may be inextricable elements of their society and so perhaps cannot be evaluated by those within that society. But such religions are entirely *naturalistic* in the sense that they represent no truths or values beyond those fundamental for the society in which they function. By contrast, Christianity, Buddhism, Hinduism, etc. articulate systems of truths and values designed to challenge and transform their societies. Of course, they call us to new "forms of life" in some sense, but this is a matter of *reform* within a way of life ....' *Religious Belief and Religious Skepticism* (University of Notre Dame Press, 1982), p. 77. Gutting's portrayal of 'primitive' religions as 'entirely naturalistic' does serious injustice to the complexity of many traditional societies and the function of their religious world-views, which carry within themselves their own traditions of dissent and transformation.

67. Phillips, 'Faith, Skepticism, and Religious Understanding', op. cit., p. 83.

68. Malcolm, 'The Groundlessness of Belief', op. cit., p. 100.

69. M. Williams, *Groundless Belief: An Essay on the Possibility of Epistemology* (Blackwell, 1977), p. 179.

70. 'There is a sense in which the no-foundations view amounts to a defence of direct realism; for I should certainly want to hold that non-inferential knowledge of acts about physical objects is possible, though this knowledge is not non-inferential in the sense required by phenomenalistic theories of knowledge.' Ibid.

71. O. Neurath, 'Protokollsätze' in *Erkenntnis* III (1932-3), pp. 204-14. According to Blumenberg, however, the first source of the metaphor was Emil du Bois-Reymond. *Schiffbruch*, op. cit., p. 78f.

72. P. Anderson, *A Feminist Philosophy of Religion*, op. cit., passim.

73. Williams, *Groundless Belief*, op. cit., p. 180.

74. The programme of Logical Positivism in eradicating 'metaphysics' is discussed in the next chapter.

75. See the discussion in Blumenberg, *Schiffbruch*, op. cit., pp. 78-83.

76. Cited in ibid., p. 82.

77. Ibid., p. 83.

78. Cited in Gwen Griffith-Dickson, *Johann Georg Hamann's Relational Metacriticism* (Walter de Gruyter, 1995), p. 272.

79. Johann Georg Hamann, 'Metacritique of the Purism of Reason' in ibid., p. 522.

80. Johann Georg Hamann, *Briefwechsel*, vol. 4 (edited by Ziesemer and Henkel), Nr. 646, 376: 16-19. My translation.

81. Johann Georg Hamann, 'Philological Ideas and Doubts', N III, 39:14-19, in G. Griffith-Dickson, *Johann Georg Hamann's Relational Metacriticism*, op. cit., p. 479.

82. Ibid., 39: 28-30.

83. See the Invocation, p. 2.

84. She has both theological and, as it were, geological grounds for doing so. Theologically, in the Hawaiian conception, as all creation, 'inanimate' and animate, are descended from the same origin, all are kin. Geologically, Hi'iaka is the sister of Pele, the volcano goddess, who is the ultimate source for volcanic rock.

85. Goethe: to Lavater 6 March 1776.

86. F. Nietzsche, *The Gay Science*, op. cit., § 'The Horizon of the Infinite'.

87. Ibid., §289, 'Aboard ship!'

88. From Lt. King's journal, here cited and paraphrased by Marshall Sahlins, *How 'Natives' Think. About Captain Cook, For Example* (University of Chicago Press, 1995), p. 73.

89. Samwell's journal on 16 February, Beaglehole 1967: 1210; Sahlins, ibid., p. 243.

90. Lt. King's journal, Sahlins, ibid., p. 56.

91. Lt. King's journal, Beaglehole 1967: 625; cf. Cook and King 1784, 3:131. Sahlins, ibid., p. 250.

92. See Karl Barth, *Church Dogmatics*, vol. 1/2, *The Doctrine of the Word of God*, translated G.T. Thomson and H. Knight (T. & T. Clark, 1956), pp. 280, 297-300, 309f., 325-7, 388, 353f.

93. See Karl Rahner, 'Anonymous Christians' in K. Rahner, *Theological Investigations*, vol. 6 (Helicon Press, 1969), pp. 390-8.

94. Michael Barnes, 'Religious Pluralism', forthcoming, edited by J. Hinnells.

95. See Marshall Sahlins, *Historical Metaphors and Mythical Realities: Structure in the Early History of the Sandwich Island Kingdom* (University of Michigan Press, 1981) and Marshall Sahlins, 'The Apotheosis of Captain Cook' in Michel Izard and Pierre Smith (eds), *Between Belief and Transgression* (Chicago University Press, 1982), in particular pp. 73-102.

96. Gananath Obeyesekere, *The Apotheosis of Captain Cook. European Mythmaking in the Pacific* (Princeton University Press, 1992).

97. Ibid., p. 3.

98. Sahlins, *How 'Natives' Think*, op. cit., p. 6.

99. Ibid., p. 148.

100. 'Maita'i', or modern 'maika'i', means 'splendid, excellent, well done!'

101. See Obeyesekere, *The Apotheosis of Captain Cook*, op. cit., p. 68. See also Sahlins, *How 'Natives' Think*, op. cit., p. 244.

102. We don't know how the temple Hikiau caught fire.

103. Hans Blumenberg, *Work on Myth*, translated by R.M. Wallace (MIT Press, 1985), p. 163.

104. Diogenes Laertius VII, 1, 2 in J. von Arnim (ed.), *Stoicorum Veterum Fragmenta* (Teubner, 1964).

105. L. Wittgenstein, *Tractatus Logico-Philosophicus*, translated by D.F. Pears and B.F. McGuinness (Routledge & Kegan Paul, 1961), p. 151, §6.54.

106. Johann Georg Hamann, 'Socratic Memorabilia' in G. Griffith-Dickson, *Johann Georg Hamann's Relational Metacriticism*, op. cit., p. 379.

107. In relation to the difficult thought of Heraclitus.

108. Heinrich Zimmer, *Philosophies of India*, edited by J. Campell (Routledge & Kegan Paul, 1969), p. 352.

109. Letter to Herder, 8 May 1785. In Johann Georg Hamann, *Briefwechsel*, vol. 5, edited by W. Ziesemer and A. Henkel (1955-1975), Nr. 833, 432: 29-36. This is in the context of a discussion of Kant.

110. Letter to Jacobi, 27 April to 3 May 1787. In ibid., vol. 7, Nr. 1060, 165: 33-7.

111. In S. Radhakrishnan and C.A. Moore (eds), *A Source Book in Indian Philosophy* (Oxford University Press, 1957), p. 265.

112. For a discussion of this phenomenon in the context of philosophical method see Griffith-Dickson, 'The Roots of the Great Fig-Tree', op. cit. For its origins in Freud, see *Die Verneinung* (1925) in *Gesammelte Schriften* XI, 3-7 or in *Gesammelte Werke* XIV, 11-15. In the Standard Edition of Freud's works, it is entitled 'On Negation'; Standard Edition XIX, 235-9. For a discussion of Lacan's concept see B. Benvenuto and R. Kennedy, *The Works of Jacques Lacan* (Free Association Books, 1988). For a Hegelian discussion in the context of a Lacan seminar, see Jean Hippolyte, 'Commentaire parlée sur la *Verneinung* de Freud', *La Psychanalyse* 1 (1956), pp. 29-40. Reprinted in English translation in Jacques Lacan, *The Seminar of Jacques Lacan* Book I, translated by John Forrester (Cambridge University Press, 1975), pp. 289-97, 291.

113. Anderson, *A Feminist Philosophy of Religion*, op. cit., p. 68.

114. Ibid., p. 74.

115. See Sandra Harding, *Whose Science? Whose Knowledge? Thinking from Women's Lives* (Open University Press, 1991), pp. 120-33, 249f.

116. Anderson, *A Feminist Philosophy of Religion*, op. cit., p. 76.

117. Ibid., p. 79.

118. Ibid.

119. Johann Georg Hamann, 'Socratic Memorabilia' in G. Griffith-Dickson, *Johann Georg Hamann's Relational Metacriticism*, op. cit., p. 381. N II, 63: 34-7.

120. Ibid. N II, 63: 31-4.

121. Ibid., p. 379. N II, 61: 7-9.

122. See Hans-Georg Gadamer, *Truth and Method*, translated by W. Glen-Doepel, second revised edition (Sheed & Ward, 1989).

123. Johann Georg Hamann, 'Socratic Memorabilia' in G. Griffith-Dickson, *Johann Georg Hamann's Relational Metacriticism*, op. cit., p. 381. N II, 63: 14-20.

124. See R. Rorty, *Philosophy of the Mirror of Nature*, op. cit., p. 7.

125. Anderson, *A Feminist Philosophy of Religion*, op. cit., p. 241.

126. Chāndogya Upaniṣad VII.1.9.1, in *The Principal Upaniṣads*, translated by S. Radhakrishnan. Emphasis mine.

127. Nietzsche, *The Gay Science*, op. cit., I, §46.

128. See the related discussion in Blumenberg, *Schiffbruch*, op. cit., pp. 26f.

129. Nietzsche, *The Gay Science*, op. cit., §18. I have taken a slight liberty with the sentence order.

2. The Tincture of Speech

1. Augustine, *De Magistro*. English translations include: Augustine, *Earlier Writings*, selected and translated by John H.D. Burleigh, Library of Christian Classics (SCM, 1953); *The Greatness of the Soul. The Teacher*, translated and annotated by J.M. Colleran, Ancient Christian Writers. The Works of the Fathers in translation (Newman Press, 1950).

2. Virgil, *Aeneid* II, 659. These words are spoken in the midst of the sack of Troy by the Greeks, with the subversive Trojan horse. I don't know why Augustine chose this sentence. Perhaps the context has no import and he just struggled to find a sentence that opened with a succession of three 'empty' words to fox Adeodatus.

3. L. Wittgenstein, *Tractatus Logico-Philosophicus*, translated by D.F. Pears and B.F. McGuinness (Routledge & Kegan Paul, 1961), from the Preface.

4. See Simon Blackburn, *Spreading the Word: Groundings in the Philosophy of Language* (Clarendon Press, 1984), pp. 3-5.

5. It is a neat scheme. Each corner of the triangle has a philosophical discipline that deals with it: 'psychology' deals with the speakers; 'metaphysics' deals with the world, and 'meaning' is the philosophical issue of language. Next, each side of the triangle, or each relationship between each of the three, has a theoretical discipline. The relationship between speakers and the world is the domain of the 'theory of knowledge'; between speakers and language, 'theory of meaning'; and between language and the world, 'theory of truth'. The history of philosophy has shown varying emphases on one or another corner of this triangle. The European tradition from Descartes until now has emphasised the individual and his or her capacities for experience and reasoning. The aim of metaphysics then is to attain a conception of the world which would enable the individual to know something about it. The nature of the mind then determines what kind of language this individual can speak; and Locke and Kant's prime investigations therefore have been into what kind of mind the individual has. In the nineteenth and twentieth centuries, philosophy has been dominated by 'scientific naturalism': the conviction that the science of psychology would provide only real advance in our understanding of logic, language, and thought. The same attitude persists in much empiricist philosophy of language this century, he argues; although which discipline is thought to bring the best understanding of language shifts: from psychology, to formal logic, to formal semantics, to structural linguistics. The really notable change has been the shift to concentration upon language itself, to give it priority over the other elements of the triangle.

6. Ibid.

7. *Taittirīyopaniṣadbhāsyavārtikka*, p. 9. See Karl Potter (ed.), *Encyclopedia of Indian Philosophies: Advaita Vedānta up to Śankara and His Pupils* (Princeton University Press, 1981), p. 525.

8. Ibid., p. 54.

9. John Macquarrie, *God-Talk: An Examination of the Language and Logic of Theology* (SCM, 1967), p. 17.

10. S. McFague, *Metaphorical Theology* (Fortress Press, 1982).

11. Augustine, *De Magistro*, op. cit. Cf. the discussion in §7-18.

12. Wittgenstein, *Tractatus Logico-Philosophicus*, op. cit., 4.01.

13. According to Wittgenstein, propositions represent the existence and non-existence of states of affairs [4.1]. The totality of true propositions is the whole of natural science (or the whole corpus of the natural sciences) [4.11]. Philosophy is not one of the natural sciences [4.111]. Philosophy aims at the logical clarification of thoughts. Philosophy is not a body of doctrine but an activity. A philosophical work consists essentially of elucidations. Philosophy does not result in 'philosophical propositions', but rather in the clarification of propositions [4.112]. Philosophy sets limits to the much disputed sphere of natural science [4.113]. It must set limits to what can be thought; and in doing so, to what cannot be thought [4.114]. It will signify what cannot be said, by presenting clearly what can be said [4.115]. Its task is therefore 'elucidation' – the process of clarifying our thought and our talk. It is *not* to add a body of doctrines or true statements to our knowledge – that is a matter for the natural sciences.

14. Ibid., 6.522.

15. Important members were Moritz Schlick, Otto Neurath, Rudolf Carnap, as well as Friedrich Waismann, Herbert Feigl, Viktor Kraft, Philipp Frank, Kurt Gödel, Hans Hahn.

16. See Alfred J. Ayer, *Language, Truth and Logic* (Penguin Books, 1978).

17. They found two broad ways to speak about the unspeakable when they wanted to. One was the naturalistic route: ethics could be understood as statements about what is or is not conducive to human happiness – a kind of Utilitarianism. Schlick in *Fragen der Ethik* suggests that ethics is about what human beings want, and how these desires are to be satisfied. In this way 'ethics' becomes a matter of the social sciences, and is decided on the basis of psychology, sociology, anthropology. Another route for discussing ethics is to see it either as a form of imperative statement, so that ethical statements are not not fact-stating, a matter of truth or falsity (Carnap); or to see them as emotive statements, expressions of feelings (Ayer). Both these sorts of statements were permitted by the Logical Positivists.

18. In an interview with Brian Magee.

19. There are further problems. Something which could not possibly be verified 100 years ago, and therefore was meaningless, we might now accept as scientific truth. Was it meaningless 700 years ago that the world was round, and now true? Schlick sought to find a way to make the Verification Principle independent of the current state of affairs in scientific knowledge. He attempted this by saying a statement is meaningless if it is 'unverifiable in principle', 'logically impossible'. So the VP judges matters on *logical* grounds, not empirical ones? Schlick tried to harmonise the two, by saying there was no conflict between logic and experience, and that every logician must be an empiricist; but this position is not convincing to many.

To avoid some of these problems, Neurath reached the conclusion that we can never measure up sentences against reality or 'the facts' to see if the one fits the other. Sentences can only be compared with sentences. Therefore verification is a relation between sentences, not between sentences and experiences. Sentences are verified by 'protocol sentences'. These are direct reports of experience. These reports are translatable into 'the language of physics' – my experience of seeing red might be translated into medical statements about the activity of certain nerves or my retina. Experience can also be translated behaviouristically, so that my experience of pain can be translated into a statement about my writhing and moaning. – It may be possible to *postpone* the connection between the sentence and experience in this way, but it is difficult to see how it can be *prevented* – as long as the sentences still claim to be 'empirical'. Someone must be observing the activity of the retina or the moaning.

This leads to a third area of difficulty. In the end, something can only be verified by someone having an experience of some kind – seeing and feeling if it is raining, checking the reading on a laboratory instrument, etc. Usually, this comes down to someone's sensory perceptions; and this (following Russell) boils down to someone experiencing or having sense-data. But sense-data are ultimately private. We may all look at the same object and all utter the same description, but we cannot swap our sense-data. The ultimate result will be that the verification of a statement can only be checked by the person whose experience it is. And on this, it could be argued, a person must be infallible. You cannot be wrong that you are experiencing what you are experiencing, even if your judgments and assessments about the situation are. Certainly no one else can tell. Either such statements of personal experience are 'incorrigible', as Carnap thought; which amounts to (as he admitted) a kind of 'solipsism' (though he tried to pass it off as merely 'methodological.' Or else they are not, as Neurath thought. This means not only that we have to allow the possibility that we can be wrong about what we are in fact experiencing, it also seems to subvert the very possibility of 'verifying' anything. But either position leads to a problem in the total 'privacy' that it maintains. All statements boil down to a purely personal experience that can never be checked or confirmed by another human being. Even the existence of other human beings translates into my experience of seeing other objects, and nothing more. And yet what Logical Positivism was attempting to do was provide a philosophy of *science*, a public objective and verifiable discourse. How do you make a transition from private experience to the public world within this framework? Schlick first attempts to solve this problem with a distinction between 'structure' and 'content'; like a colouring-book, where the structure is the outline, the content is the colouring. We all have the same colouring-book, which each of us colours in for ourselves. We cannot communicate the 'content', the actual experience, to any one else. But if we cannot communicate *content*, we can observe that our two different worlds share the same *structure*. I can observe that when I look at this card I say 'red', and when you look at the same card you say 'red' too, though I cannot see what you are seeing to know if you see the same thing. I can see that when you say you are in pain you wince and cry 'Ow!' just as I do, although I cannot feel your pain. This is all we need to communicate with each other. But is this distinction permissible, and what would pure structure be? Neurath and Carnap rejected this position. The fundamental verifiable statements must be intersubjective and somehow refer to public physical events. Neurath's move is to espouse 'physicalism', or 'behaviourism', that translates human experiences into observable behaviour. Carnap attempts to solve this problem in *The Unity of Science* (1934) by suggesting that all empirical statements can be expressed in a single 'language', which is the language of physics. So every statement of personal experience can be translated into a statement of my body: which can be physically tested in some way. 'I am seeing red' = 'Body G was told to push the button if she saw red, and on being shown the red-coloured card she pushed the button.' But do these two sentences *mean* the same thing? Carnap maintained that they did; any difference between them was one of purely personal associations. They are logically equivalent, therefore they mean the same thing. (But imagine 'I am in pain' being taken as identical to pain behaviour; then imagine someone faking.)

20. See the discussion in Karl Potter (ed.), *Encyclopedia of Indian Philosophies*, op. cit., pp. 56ff.

21. See the discussion in Maṇḍana Miśra, *Brahmasiddhi*, particularly at I.26. For a paraphrase, see Potter (ed.), *Encyclopedia of Indian Philosophies*, op. cit., p. 362.

22. See Antony Flew, R.M. Hare, and Basil Mitchell, 'Theology and Falsification: A Symposium' in B. Mitchell (ed.), *The Philosophy of Religion* (Oxford University Press, 1971), p.13.

23. S. Davis, *Faith, Skepticism and Evidence: An Essay in Religious Epistemology* (Associated University Presses, 1978). See the argument concluding pp. 210-21.

24. Ludwig Wittgenstein, *Philosophical Investigations*, translated by G.E.M. Anscombe (Blackwell, 1993), §30.

25. Ibid., §33.

26. Wittgenstein alludes to a passage in Augustine's *Confessions*, I. 8. Ironically, he seems unaware of *De Magistro*. As I have discussed elsewhere, this foreshadows Wittgenstein's later critique: 'Are you inclined still to call these words "names of objects"?' (*Philosophical Investigations*, §27). This is ironic, since the view that Augustine rejects in *De Magistro* is the view which Wittgenstein attributes to him, precisely in order to reject it on the same or similar grounds. See Gwen Griffith-Dickson, ' "Outsidelessness" and the "Beyond" of Signification', *Heythrop Journal* 37 (1996), pp. 258-72.

27. Augustine, *De Magistro*, op. cit., §33.

28. Gerard O'Daly, *Augustine's Philosophy of Mind* (Duckworth, 1987), p. 172, observes that the pointing in ostension is a sign as much as a word is.

29. Augustine, *De Magistro*, op. cit., §32.

30. *Brahmasiddhi* I.15.

31. Jacques Lacan, *The Seminar of Jacques Lacan I*, edited by Jacques-Alain Miller (Cambridge University Press, 1988), p. 259.

32. Ibid., p. 253.

33. Ibid., p. 262.

34. Anatole France, *The Garden of Epicurus*; cited in R. Rorty, *Philosophy and the Mirror of Nature* (Princeton University Press, 1980), p. 368.

35. Indian philosophers took a variety of stances on the question of the particular and the universal, and how it interacts with form. The Mīmāṃsakas held that the universal is the primary meaning; the logicians of the Nyāya and Vaiśeṣika traditions that the particular is, although it is characterised by the universal and by the form. Since the Buddhists reject universals they required a different theory. This and other theories will be alluded to later. For an introduction to these issues, see Potter (ed.), *Encyclopedia of Indian Philosophies*, op. cit., p. 55.

36. Carl Henry, *God, Revelation, and Authority*, vol. 3 (Crossway Books, 1999), p. 364.

37. Moses Maimonides, *Guide of the Perplexed*, translated by S. Pines (University of Chicago Press, 1963), see III.20.

38. Bṛhad-āraṇyaka Upaniṣad IV.4.22, in Radhakrishnan's translation, *The Principal Upaniṣads*, p. 279.

39. Bṛhad-āraṇyaka Upaniṣad III.8.8, in Radhakrishnan's translation, *The Principal Upaniṣads*, p. 232.

40. *Brahmasiddhi* I.26.

41. Cf. the discussions in David Burrell, *Analogy and Philosophical Language* (Yale University Press, 1973), and James Ross, *Portraying Analogy* (Cambridge University Press, 1981).

42. Aquinas grounds this similarity and difference in two ways: in 'attribution' and 'proportion'. To illustrate the analogy of 'attribution', I'll adapt Aquinas' example and speak of people and a diet as 'healthy'. One possesses the attribute 'formally', the other causally: the diet is 'healthy' because it causes people to be healthy. One can also possess the attributes to a different degree or 'proportion'.

43. Barry Miller, *A Most Unlikely God: A Philosophical Enquiry* (University of Notre Dame Press, 1996), see ch. 8.

44. Ibid., pp. 9f.

45. Ibid, p. 10

46. Ibid.

47. Ibid., p. 152.

48. Ibid., p. 153.

49. Law in James Law (ed.), *The Early Identification of Language Impairment in Children* (Chapman & Hall, 1992), p. 49. See the seminal work by Brown, *A First Language: The Early Stages* (Penguin Books, 1973) in opposition to Chomsky's suggestion that the parent's style of speech is a defective model for language learning. Brown demonstrated that 'motherese' differs from other speech styles consistently and predictably.

50. See Griffith-Dickson, *Johann Georg Hamann's Relational Metacriticism* (Walter de Gruyter, 1995), pp. 209f. et passim. This is from a letter to Herder, in Johann Georg Hamann, *Briefwechsel*, edited by Ziesemer and Henkel, vol. 2, Nr. 350, 415: 22-33.

51. See Ian Ramsey, *Religious Language* (SCM, 1957), ch. 2.

52. Hamann calls Berkeley (and Hume) to his support. See Berkeley, *Principles of Human Knowledge*, edited by R. Woolhouse (Penguin, 1988), Introduction, §18ff. Berkeley is often called an 'idealist'. Beware of this misunderstanding. Berkeley is in fact a realist of a rigorously empiricist persuasion. He believes that everything that is real is perceived. This does *not* mean that once you leave the room, the objects in it cease to exist. It is not *our perception that confers reality and existence to things*. God too is a perceiver; and since God continually perceives all, everything is held in being by God's consciousness. The chairs and tables in the room you leave are not endangered by your absence.

53. See Johann Georg Hamann, 'Metacritique of the Purism of Reason' in Gwen Griffith-Dickson, *Johann Georg Hamann*, op. cit., pp. 517-25, see in particular p. 520.

54. Johann Georg Hamann, *Sämtliche Werke*, edited by Josef Nadler (Verlag Herder, 1949-1957), vol. II, 136: 3-4. Translation mine.

55. 'Aesthetica in Nuce' in ibid., 211: 5-13; see Griffith-Dickson, *Johann Georg Hamann*, op. cit., p. 425.

56. Aristotle says that poetry is truer than history in *Poetics* 9, 1451b5-10.

57. Nelson Goodman, *Languages of Art* (Hackett, 1976), p. 69.

58. See Janet Martin Soskice's chapter 'Metaphor Amongst Tropes' for an examination of metaphor alongside its 'near relations', in Soskice, *Metaphor and Religious Language* (Clarendon, 1985), pp. 54-66. This work is the most useful and comprehensive study of the topic.

59. See ibid., p. 25.

60. Thomas Hobbes, *Leviathan*, edited by R. Tuck (Cambridge University Press, 1997), part I ch. 4, p. 26.

61. For a discussion of the 'emotivist' theory of metaphor, in which metaphor is seen as lacking in cognitive content, but having an emotional impact or import, and for a discussion of Donald Davidson's complex theory of metaphor, see Soskice, *Metaphor and Religious Language*, op. cit., pp. 26-30.

62. Ibid., p. 25.

63. This is sometimes referred to as the 'Incremental' view. See Soskice for lucid descriptions of its varieties and exponents, such as Monroe Beardsley's controversion theory, Max Black's interactive theory, the interanimation theory of I.A. Richards. Soskice, ibid., pp. 31-53.

64. John Middleton Murry, *Countries of the Mind* (Oxford University Press, 1931).

65. 'The whole of science is shot through and through with metaphors, which transfer and link one part of our experience to another, and find likenesses between the parts. All our ideas derive from and embody such metaphorical likenesses.' Jacob Bronowski, *The Visionary Eye* (MIT Press, 1978). See also Soskice, *Metaphor and Religious Language*, op. cit.; Mary Hesse, *Revolutions and Reconstructions in the Philosophy of Science* (Indiana University Press, 1980); and Ian Barbour, *Myths, Models and Paradigms: The Nature of Scientific and Religious Language* (SCM, 1974).

66. Jacques Lacan, *The Seminar of Jacques Lacan I*, op. cit., p. 238.

67. Hans Blumenberg, *Paradigmen zu einer Metaphorologie* (Suhrkamp, 1998, second edition 1999), p. 25.

68. Ibid., pp. 8f.

69. Paul Tillich, 'Symbols of Faith' from *Dynamics of Faith*, vol. 10 (Harper Torchbooks, 1958), p. 41. See also pp. 41-54.

70. Randall, *The Role of Knowledge in Western Religion* (University Press of America, 1986).

71. Paraphrased from Paul Ricoeur, *Freud and Philosophy*, translated by D. Savage (Yale University Press, 1970), p. 527.

72. Ibid., p. 530.

73. Ibid., p. 531. See also pp. 524-31.

74. Dan R. Stiver in *The Philosophy of Religious Language: Sign, Symbol & Story* (Blackwell, 1996), pp. 123f., and Soskice, *Metaphor and Religious Language*, op. cit., p. 55, hint as much. See also the work of Langdon Gilkey, who understands 'symbol' very broadly: Jesus, the Exodus, creation, incarnation, redemption etc. are all 'symbols'. The purpose of theology is to reflect on this symbolic system. Langdon Gilkey, *Message and Existence: An Introduction to Christian Theology* (Seabury Press, 1979).

75. See Rudolf Bultmann, 'New Testament and Mythology' (1941) in H.W. Bartsch (ed.), *Kerygma & Myth* (2 vols. SPCK, 1969 and 1964) and *Jesus Christ and Mythology* (SCM, 1960).

76. Note what Bultmann is *not* saying: 'The purpose of demythologizing is not to make religion more acceptable to modern man by trimming the traditional Biblical texts, but to make clearer to modern man what the Christian faith is. He must be confronted with the issue of decision.' 'Such an attempt does not aim at reassuring modern man by saying to him: "You no longer have to believe this and that" ...; not by showing him that the number of things to be believed is smaller than he had thought, but because it shows him that to believe at all is qualitatively different from accepting a certain number of propositions.' Rudolf Bultmann, 'The Case for Demythologizing: A Reply' (1953), in H.W. Bartsch (ed.), *Kerygma & Myth*, op. cit., vol. 2, pp. 182f.

77. In a letter to Karl Barth, 11-15th November 1952, Bultmann declared: 'Naturally it is easy to argue against me from the statements of the NT, but only because the christological statements of the NT are clothed in the language of mythology which I want to strip off.' *Karl Barth – Rudolf Bultmann: Letters 1922-1966*, edited by B. Jaspert (T. & T. Clark, 1982), p. 93.

78. See Charles W. Kegley (ed.), *The Theology of Rudolf Bultmann* (SCM, 1966), for an excellent selection of critical essays on Bultmann's work as well as a reply by Bultmann. Also see Anthony C. Thiselton, *The Two Horizons: New Testament Hermeneutics and Philosophical Description with Special Reference to Heidegger, Butlmann, Gadamer, and Wittgenstein* (The Paternoster Press, 1980), passim.

79. In *Metaphorologie*, op. cit.

80. Odo Marquard, 'Lob des Polytheismus' in Hans-Joachim Höhn (ed.), *Krise der Immanenz. Religion an den Grenzen der Moderne* (Fischer, 1996), pp. 154-8.

81. *Arbeit am Mythos*; ET as *Work on Myth*. References are to the English translation.

82. A starting-point for this was Cassirer's *The Myth of the State* (Oxford University Press, 1946).

83. See the introduction to Blumenberg, *Work on Myth*, op. cit., pp. xxivff.

84. Ibid., p. 629.

85. Anderson, *A Feminist Philosophy of Religion*, ch. 5.

86. See ibid., p. 137.

87. Johann Georg Hamann, 'Aesthetica in Nuce' in *Sämtliche Werke*, edited by Josef Nadler, op. cit., vol. II, 206:16-19. Translation mine; see Griffith-Dickson, *Johann Georg Hamann's Relational Metacriticism*, p. 420.

88. Jacques Lacan, *The Seminar of Jacques Lacan I*, op. cit., p. 178.

89. Ibid., p. 243.

90. John R. Searle, *Meaning* (Center for Hermeneutical Studies in Hellenistic and Modern Culture, 1983), p. 44.

91. See Terence Tilley, *The Evils of Theodicy* (Georgetown University Press, 1991), particularly ch. 3.

92. Ian Ramsey's 'Christian Existentialism' similarly asserted that there are certain situations in which religious language that is not propositional makes sense. These are characterised by 'discernment' and 'commitment'. Discernment is used in situations where we recognise an important insight, which he calls 'disclosure situations'. This is what religious language is currency for. Commitment means that one sees one's whole life in terms of an insight. There is a point at which argument stops: some actions are self-justifying, and at such times we use phrases like: 'Duty is duty'. Although in analytical terms these appear to be empty and uninformative, they are 'significant tautologies' – *not* an assertion, but a significant tautology which points to a commitment. 'God is love' is such a tautology.

93. J.L. Austin, *How to do Things with Words*, 2nd edition (Oxford University Press, 1976), passim.

94. See above, Chapter 1.

95. Cf. D.B. Zilberman, *The Birth of Meaning in Hindu Thought* (D. Reidel Publishing Co., 1988), p. 71.

96. Ludwig Wittgenstein, *Philosophical Investigations*, op. cit., p. 27.

97. Maṇḍana Miśra, *Brahmasiddhi*, I.22, I.25; see also III.41; for convenience see the paraphrases in Potter (ed.), *Encyclopedia of Indian Philosophies*, op. cit., pp. 360-2, 399.

98. Wittgenstein, *Philosophical Investigations*, op. cit., p. 23.

99. Ibid., p. 24.

100. 'We said that the sentence "Excalibur has a sharp blade" made sense even when Excalibur was broken in pieces. Now this is so because in this language game a name is also used in the absence of its bearer.' Ibid., p. 44.

101. R.B. Braithwaite, 'An Empiricist's View of the Nature of Religious Belief' in B. Mitchell (ed.), *The Philosophy of Religion*, op. cit., pp. 72-91.

102. Gareth Moore, *Believing in God* (T. & T. Clark, 1998), pp. 147f.

103. Jacques Lacan, *The Seminar of Jacques Lacan I*, op. cit., p. 178.

104. Ibid.

105. Jacques Lacan, 'The Agency of the Letter' in Jacques Lacan, *Écrits: A Selection* (Routledge, 1997), p. 150.

106. Jacques Lacan, *The Seminar of Jacques Lacan I*, op. cit., p. 238, cf. also pp. 247f.

107. Cf. the complex discussion in Jacques Lacan, 'The Agency of the Letter', op. cit. The specific reference here is to p. 164.

108. Ibid., p. 157.

109. As my example shows, this structure of language mirrors the structure that Freud and Lacan imagine for the unconscious, and the Freudian theory of dream interpretation operates in this fashion. Lacan translates his terms into Freud's: 'condensation' is the superimposition of signifiers, in other words, metaphor; 'displacement' is metonymy.

110. Metaphor or metonymy? Or *kaona*?

111. Lacan, 'The Agency of the Letter', op. cit., p. 150.

112. Wittgenstein, *Philosophical Investigations*, op. cit., §13.

113. See Don Cupitt, *After All: Religion Without Alienation* (SCM, 1994), passim. See also *Life Lines* (SCM, 1986) and *The Long-Legged Fly* (SCM 1987).

114. Lacan, *The Seminar of Jacques Lacan I*, op. cit., p. 248.

115. Ibid., p. 259.

116. Ibid., p. 243.

117. Lacan, 'The Agency of the Letter', op. cit., p. 154.

118. Lacan, *The Seminar of Jacques Lacan I*, op. cit., p. 263.

119. See Aristotle, *Politics* (Cambridge University Press, 1988), I.2.

120. Lacan, *The Seminar of Jacques Lacan I*, op. cit., p. 243.

121. Ibid., p. 262. Italics mine.

122. Ibid., p. 174.

123. Rgveda R.V., X.71.2. Cited in Zilberman, *The Birth of Meaning in Hindu Thought*, op. cit., 93.

124. *Taittirīyopaniṣadbhāsyavārtikka*; cf. Potter (ed.), *Encyclopedia of Indian Philosophies*, op. cit., pp. 595-614.

125. Jean-Luc Marion argues something like this in *God Without Being* (University of Chicago Press, 1991); though on the behalf of polytheists and idolaters I would want to dissociate myself from some of his tacit assumptions (especially about idols).

126. 'Metacritique of the Purism of Reason'. See the translation, notes and discussion in Griffith-Dickson, *Johann Georg Hamann*, op. cit.

127. See Maṇḍana Miśra, *Brahmasiddhi*, op. cit., I.17 et passim.

128. 'Śabda is described … as a slight vibration or disturbance in the field of Reality. It is conducive to the everlasting self-revelation of Reality as its first and ceaseless vexation. Vāc, Speech, is every ready to express some-thing and relate it to some-body.' Zilberman, *The Birth of Meaning in Hindu Thought*, op. cit., pp. 75ff.

129. Hamann, 'The Last Will and Testament of the Knight of the Rose-Cross', N III, 32: 21-8; Griffith-Dickson, *Johann Georg Hamann*, op. cit., p. 468.

130. Zilberman, *The Birth of Meaning in Hindu Thought*, op. cit., p. 76.

131. *Parā Vāc*, 'Transcendent Speech', is reality in itself. It is then manifested as *Paśyantī Vāc*, 'Visualised Speech', its cosmic manifestation, in potential, but before any of us witness it. *Madhyamā Vāc*, 'Mediating Speech', communication, is the objectivation of *Paśyantī Vāc*. This is finally linked to *Vaikharī Vāc*, 'Vocally Expressed Speech', which is what we actually say. 'The more this subject-mattered objectivation of speech progresses, the looser and less demanding are the correlations between words and things. The sense-hunting intentions, as it were, exhaust themselves in objects. In the parā, or "transcendent" state, words and things are indiscernible, as there is nothing to speak about, and no one to listen to their references and relations'. At Paūyantī level, word and its target (name and referent) are not differentiated in expression but are discernible in content. Zilberman, *The Birth of Meaning in Hindu Thought*, op. cit., pp. 76f.

132. See the discussion in Potter (ed.), *Encyclopedia of Indian Philosophies*, op. cit., p. 56.

133. Maṇḍana Miśra, *Brahmasiddhi*, op. cit., I.16

134. Lacan, *The Seminar of Jacques Lacan I*, op. cit., p. 178.

135. Ibid., pp. 247f.

3. Going Mad

1. This question posed to the experimental subjects is known as 'Hardy's question'. Cf. D. Hay, *Exploring Inner Space* (Penguin, 1982). Cf. Hay and Morisy, 'Reports of Esctatic, Paranormal, or Religious Experience in Great Britain and the United States – A Comparison of Trends', *Journal for the Scientific Study of Religion* 17 (1978), 3, p. 259.

2. Other studies include: Andrew Greeley, asking about the experience of a 'powerful spiritual force', with a total positive response of 35%; Glock and Stark, 1965, 'Have you ever as an adult had the feeling that you were somehow in the presence of God?'; Back and Bourque, 1970, 'Would you say that you ever had a "religious or mystical experience;" that is, a moment of sudden religious insight or awakening?' receiving 20.5% the first time and 41.2% the second time; Wuthnow 1976, 'Have you ever felt you were in close contact with something sacred?' with a positive response of 50%. For further discussion of these studies, see Hay and Morisy, *Journal for the Scientific Study of Religion* or J.-P. Valla and R.H. Prince, in *Altered States of Consciousness and Mental Health: A Cross-Cultural Perspective*, ed. Coleen A. Ward (Sage Publications, 1989), pp. 149f.

3. Morgan Research, 1983, Australia, 44% positive response; Alistair Hardy Research Centre (Gallup), 1985, UK, 33%, in USA 43%; Hay and Heald (Gallup), 1987, 48%.

4. When Hay and Morisy first encountered this surprisingly large positive response, they checked to see if perhaps they had over-represented groups that were likely to respond positively, whether groups of age, sex, education or class. Finding that the sample was indeed balanced, they finally concluded that that was the true response rate; theorising that the difference was the style of investigation, which encouraged more confidence and trust in the people than does a poll. The subsequent experience of other researchers confirms this idea. Hay discusses the reluctance of people to confide such experiences in his 1994 paper 'On the Biology of God', p. 11.

5. Wayne Proudfoot, *Religious Experience* (University of California Press, 1985), pp. 196f.

6. See Karl Jaspers, *General Psychopathology*, translated by J. Hoenig and M.W. Hamilton (Manchester University Press, 1963).

7. Just to give a few examples, Michel Foucault has suggested that not merely the arts but also the sciences are culturally constructed, that is, not simply objective reflections of the way things are but are affected by cultural values. See in particular Michel Foucault, *Madness and Civilization: A History of Insanity in the Age of Reason* (Routledge, 1989). Paul Feyerabend has subjected the 'persistent fog of objectivism' in science to repeated critique. Paul Feyerabend, *Against Method* (Verso, 1988 revised edition); *Farewell to Reason* (Verso, 1987); *Realism, Rationalism and Scientific Method* (Cambridge University Press, 1981). Littlewood advocates an 'ironic simultaneity' of 'understanding' and 'explanation'. Neither understanding nor explaining is completely true, nor completely false. Littlewood, 'Psychopathology, Embodiment and Religious Innovation: An Historical Instance', note 3, in Dinesh Bhugra (ed.), *Psychiatry and Religion: Context, Consensus and Controversies* (Routledge, 1996). See also Roland Littlewood, *Pathology and Identity: The Work of Mother Earth in Trinidad* (Cambridge University Press, 1993).

8. Or perhaps it is too much to ask of something as complex as a belief system that it be completely unified and well-organised and utterly lacking in contradiction; so the fact of a lack of coherence is just par for the course. Or perhaps truth itself is not coherent and harmonious, but paradoxical, and cannot be adequately captured and contained in a congruent epistemic system, as we have considered in the first chapter? Or maybe even God is like that?

9. Keith E. Yandell, *The Epistemology of Religious Experience* (Cambridge University Press, 1993), p. 182.

10. See D. Hay and A. Morisy, 'Reports of Esctatic, Paranormal, or Religious Experience in Great Britain and the United States – A Comparison of Trends', op. cit., pp. 255-68.

11. Jerome I. Gellman, *Experience of God and the Rationality of Theistic Belief* (Cornell University Press, 1997), pp. 37-9.

12. 'Our consciousness of all existence ... belongs exclusively to the unity of experience; any alleged existence outside this field, while not indeed such as we can declare to be absolutely impossible, is of the nature of an assumption which we can never be in a position to justify.' Immanuel Kant, *Critique of Pure Reason*, translated by Norman Kemp Smith (Macmillan, 1978), p. 506 [A 601; B 609].

13. Georg Wilhelm Friedrich Hegel, *Lectures on the Philosophy of Religion*, vol. 1, ed. Peter C. Hodgson, translated by R.F. Brown, P.C. Hodgson, J.M. Stewart (University of California Press, 1984), p. 258.

14. Martin Buber, 'Autobiographical Fragments', p. 24. Cited in N. Lash, *Easter in Ordinary: Reflections on Human Experience and the Knowledge of God* (SCM, 1988), p. 203.

15. C. Glock and R. Stark, *Religion and Society in Tension* (Rand McNally, 1965).

16. Caroline Franks Davis, *The Evidential Force of Religious Experience* (Clarendon, 1989), pp. 33-65.

17. Yandell, *The Epistemology of Religious Experience*, op. cit., pp. 25-30.

18. See P.C. Almond, *Mystical Experience and Religious Doctrine: An Investigation of the Study of Mysticism in World Religions* (Mouton, 1982).

19. So Otto, Stace, and Smart. Otto divides experiences into theistic and mystical (subdivided into 'inward' and 'outward' way), R. Otto, *Mysticism East and West: A Comparative Analysis of the Nature of Mysticism*, translated by B.L. Bracey and R.C. Payne (Theosophical Publishing House, 1987); Stace into extravertive and introvertive, W.T. Stace, *Mysticism and Philosophy* (Macmillan, 1961); Smart into numinous and mystical, Ninian Smart, 'Interpretation and mystical experience', *Religious Studies* 1 (1965) pp. 75-87; Zaehner into panenhenic ('all-in-one'), monistic, theistic, *Mysticism, Sacred and Profane* (Oxford University Press, 1961). See also the discussion in Margaret Poloma, 'The Sociological Context of Religious Experience', in *Handbook of Religious Experience*, ed. Ralph W. Hood Jr. (Religious Education Press, 1995), pp. 167f.

20. Stace, *Mysticism and Philosophy*, op. cit., p. 36, cited Peter Donovan, *Interpreting Religious Experience* (Sheldon Press, 1979), p. 27. Cf. also 'There is reason to suppose that what are basically the same experiences have been differently interpreted by different mystics.' W.T. Stace, *Mysticism and Philosophy*, op. cit., p. 18.

21. See Steven T. Katz, *Mysticism and Philosophical Analysis* (Sheldon, 1978).

22. C.F. Davis, *The Evidential Force of Religious Experience*, op. cit., pp. 171f.

23. This challenge and responses to it will be discussed in 'Being Eminently Rational' (Chapter 5).

24. Lash maintains that: 'it is not the case that all experience of God is necessarily religious in form or content and, on the other hand, that not everything which it would be appropriate to characterize, on psychological or sociological grounds, as "religious" experience would thereby necessarily constitute experience of God.' N. Lash, *Easter in Ordinary*, op. cit., p. 7.

25. *Bṛhad-āraṇyaka Upaniṣad* V. 7. 1 translated by S. Rahdakrishnan, *The Principal Upaniṣads*, pp. 294f., in S. Radhakrishnan and C.A. Moore (eds), *A Source Book in Indian Philosophy* (Oxford University Press, 1957).

26. John Hick, *An Interpretation of Religion* (Macmillan, 1988), p. 240; see esp. ch. 14.

27. C.F. Davis., *The Evidential Force of Religious Experience*, op. cit., p. 85.

28. Donovan, *Interpreting Religious Experience*, op. cit., p. 80.

29. Ibid., p. 82.

30. Proudfoot, *Religious Experience*, op. cit., p. 108.

31. Davis calls it the 'vicious circle challenge', and observes: 'Such a narrowly empiricist and foundationalist position is rarely found now outside discussions of religious experience.' *The Evidential Force of Religious Experience*, op. cit., p. 143.

32. A. Flew, *God and Philosophy* (Hutchinson, 1966), p. 139.

33. Yandell, *The Epistemology of Religious Experience*, op. cit., p. 186.

34. Ibid., p. 188.

35. Donovan, *Interpreting Religious Experience*, op. cit., pp. 28-30.

36. Katz, *Mysticism and Philosophical Analysis*, op. cit.

37. Proudfoot, *Religious Experience*, op. cit., p. 43.

38. Ibid., p. 219.

39. William P. Alston, *Perceiving God: The Epistemology of Religious Experience*

(Cornell University Press, 1991), pp. 37f.

40. Donovan, *Interpreting Religious Experience*, op. cit., p. 28.

41. Ibid.

42. William P. Alston, 'Is Religious Belief Rational?' in Ann Loades and Loyal D. Rue (eds), *Contemporary Classics in Philosophy of Religion* (Open Court, 1991), p. 150. Yandell lodges a similar complaint, using an analogy with sense perception: 'Why should it not be true of a scientist who has been trained to run a certain sort of experiment, is devoted to a theory that says that a certain event will occur under certain experimental conditions, and knows that her theory is false if that event does not occur, that she will have an experience in which that event at least seems to occur once she has created the relevant experiential conditions?' Yandell, *The Epistemology of Religious Experience*, op. cit., p. 203.

43. Davis, *The Evidential Force of Religious Experience*, op. cit., p. 144.

44. Norman Ballantyne, in a private communication.

45. Davis, *The Evidential Force of Religious Experience*, op. cit., pp. 49-51.

46. Lash cites the understanding of experience put forward by Jean-Pierre Jossua, identifying four features: that 'experience is a matter of our *relationships* with ourselves, and others, with the world – and with God'; that 'to speak of experience is to speak of relationships constituted by *real* (and not merely notional) participation in an event – of love, or political struggle ... or whatever'; that 'such relationships only form part of our experience in the measure that they are *refracted* in consciousness', rather than just passively mirrored, so that 'all talk of experience needs to be critically alert to a sense of the limits within which we are ever able to bring experience to speech', and finally that 'the refraction of experience in consciousness is not a mechanical or automatic process, but the work of human agents: it is a matter of *deciphering* our circumstance, of *interpreting* the events and relationships in which we participate.' See Lash, *Easter in Ordinary*, op. cit., pp. 173f.

4. Seeing God or Seeing Snakes?

1. Bertrand Russell, *Religion and Science* (Oxford University Press, 1935), p. 188.

2. The situation is not improved for one who does not hold a correspondence theory of truth. The pragmatist could argue that if evidence exists that religious experience is harmful or a close parity can be demonstrated between religious and pathological experience, the validity of religious experience is undermined. Meanwhile, if a coherent and adequate explanation of religious experience can be provided without recourse to religious values or explanations, religious or spiritual factors can be made redundant. The coherence of the experience with the rest of the subject's mindset could even be taken as evidence that the experience was created by the subject, as a form of wish-fulfilment.

3. Alston, 'Is Religious Belief Rational?', in A. Loades and L.D. Rue (eds), *Contemporary Classics in Philosophy of Religion* (Open Court, 1991), pp. 139-55.

4. 'Personalistic and naturalistic paradigms are not altogether contradictory. At certain points they slide into each other .... This conventional distinction between the naturalistic and the personalistic has been eroded in twentieth-century physics and cognitive science, ... whilst the epistemological claims of natural science to directly reflect reality have been challenged as themselves culturally constructed.' Roland Littlewood, 'Psychopathology, Embodiment and Religious Innovation: An Historical Instance' in Dinesh Bhugra (ed.), *Psychiatry and Religion: Context, Consensus and Controversies* (Routledge, 1996), pp. 178f.

5. Raymond H. Prince, 'Religious Experience and Psychopathology: Cross-Cultural Perspectives' in John F. Schumaker (ed.), *Religion and Mental Health* (Oxford University Press, 1992), p. 281. The general conclusion of the piece is that what is regarded as normal or as pathological in experience varies from one culture to another.

6. So Spiro, see M.E. Spiro, 'Culturally Constituted Defense Mechansisms', in M.E. Spiro (ed.), *Context and Meaning in Cultural Anthropology* (Free Press, 1965), p. 100.

7. A. Ellis, 'The Case Against Religion: A Psychotherapist's View', in B. Ard (ed.), *Counseling and Psychotherapy: Classics on Theories and Issues* (Science and Behavior Books, 1975), p. 440.

8. W. La Barre, *The Ghost Dance: Origins of Religion* (Allen & Unwin, 1970).

9. Roland Littlewood, 'Psychopathology, Embodiment and Religious Innovation: An Historical Instance', op. cit., pp. 180, 182. His detailed case study makes use of the example of Sabbatai Svi, a seventeenth-century rabbi who Gerschom Scholem has suggested lies at the roots of Hasidism. Littlewood suggests he was manic-depressive (others have suggested paranoid schizophrenia). He was proclaimed Messiah by Nathan of Gaza and attracted a considerable following, despite some outrageous acts, teaching, and practices (particularly sexual), before 'converting' to Islam under pain of death.

10. J.L. Mackie, *The Miracle of Theism* (Clarendon Press, 1982), p. 180.

11. As Eyseck and Claridge each suggest for neurosis and for psychosis. See, for example, H. Eysenck and S. Eysenck, *Psychoticism as a Dimension of Personality* (Hodder and Stoughton, 1976); and G. Claridge, *Origins of Mental Illness* (Basil Blackwell, 1985). On problems of conceptualisation of religiosity, religious experience and mental health, see Leslie J. Francis, 'Religion, Neuroticism, and Psychotism' in John F. Schumaker (ed.), *Religion and Mental Health* (Oxford University Press, 1992), pp. 149-60.

12. C.-D. Batson and W.L. Ventis, *The Religious Experience: A Social Psychological Perspective* (Oxford University Press, 1982).

13. L. Francis, 'Religion, Neuroticism, and Psychotism', op. cit., p. 156, using Eysenck's models of neuroticism and psychoticism.

14. C.F. Davis, *The Evidential Force of Religious Experience* (Clarendon, 1989), pp. 213f.

15. M. Jackson, 'Divine Madness: A Study of the Relationship between Psychotic and Spiritual Experience'. Unpublished doctoral dissertation, Oxford, 1991.

16. Peter Fenwick, 'The Neurophysiology of Religious Experience' in Dinesh Bhugra (ed.), *Psychiatry and Religion: Context, Consensus and Controversies*, op. cit., p. 171.

17. Arthur J. Deikman, 'Deautomatization and the Mystic Experience' in Charles A. Tart (ed.), *Altered States of Consciousness: A Book of Readings* (John Wiley & Sons, 1969), p. 43.

18. Ibid.

19. Arnold M. Ludwig, 'Altered States of Consciousness', in ibid., p. 18. The sole religious maladaptive expression that he identifies is 'symbolic acting-out of unconscious conflicts', which can be represented by demoniacal possession or bewitchment. The adaptive expressions are investigated in greater detail, and comprise healing, avenues of new knowledge or experience, and social functions. See ibid., pp. 19-21.

20. See Valla and Prince in C.A. Ward (ed.), *Altered States of Consciousness and Mental Health: A Cross-Cultural Perspective* (Sage Publications, 1989), p. 154.

21. David Hay, ' "The Biology of God": What is the Current Status of Hardy's Hypothesis?', *International Journal for the Psychology of Religion* 4 (1), 1994, pp. 1-23. Abstract p. 1.

22. W.N. Pahnke, 'Drugs and Mysticism: An Analysis of the Relationship between Psychedelic Drugs and the Mystical Consciousness'. Unpublished doctoral dissertation, Harvard University, 1963.

23. William Sargant, *Battle for the Mind* (Heinemann, 1957).

24. Ibid., p. 25.

25. See, for example, Don Gibbons and James de Jarnette, 'Hypnotic Suggestibility and Religious Experience', *Journal for the Scientific Study of Religion* 11 (1972), pp. 152-6; Benjamin Beit-Hallahmi and Michael Argyle, *The Social Psychology of Religion* (Routledge & Kegan Paul, 1975); and Geoffrey Scobie, *Psychology of Religion* (Batsford, 1975).

26. Davis, *The Evidential Force of Religious Experience*, op. cit., p. 202.

27. Gibbons and De Jarnette, 'Hypnotic Susceptibility and Reported Religious Experience', Psychological Reports 33 (1973). Their study selected 23 students who scored either very low or very high on a test for suggestibility, and asked them six questions concerning their religious orientation, their church attendance, whether they had changed denomination, whether their mother and their father were perceived as religious, and whether they had had a conversion experience.

28. Ibid., p. 155.

29. Ibid., p. 154.

30. Ibid., p. 155.

31. One study distinguishes 'primary' suggestibility, which governs the effects of placebos and 'social' and 'prestige' suggestibility (people more readily change their opinions according to social influences); from 'secondary' suggestibility, which is the ease with which someone falsely 'perceives' or 'recalls' things suggested by another. The study found that religious people are more suggestible in the primary sense, but not the secondary one. So religious people are more likely to respond to placebos and social pressures. They are *not* more likely to perceive things that aren't there or recall things that aren't true. So if religious experiences arise from a sort of placebo effect, or a desire for social acceptability or prestige, then perhaps religious experiences simply arise from suggestibility. But an ability to perceive things that aren't there on suggestion cannot explain religious experiences, because people who have spiritual experiences are no more suggestible in this respect than anyone else.

Gellman observes that in fact what you can induce a hypersuggestible to believe he is experiencing is rather limited. You can get him to think he sees a glow in the dark, which is the kind of test usually employed in tests of suggestibility. It is quite another matter to get him to think he is seeing a skyscraper in front of him where there isn't one, or to believe that the table in front of him has suddenly burst into flames. He suggests that thinking that one is experiencing God when one isn't is more like seeing a delusory skyscraper or seeing the table burst into flames, than a plausible or innocuous percept like a glowing spot. Gellman, op. cit., p. 130.

32. See, for example, E.R. Guthrie, *The Psychology of Learning* (Harper & Row, 1952). G.B. Vetter, *Magic and Religion: Their Psychological Nature, Origin and Function* (Philosophical Library, 1958). See also H. Newton Malony, 'Behavioral Theory and Religious Experience', in *Handbook of Religious Experience*, op. cit., p. 388.

33. Stuart Linke, *Psychological Perspectives on Traditional Jewish Practices* (Jason Aronson Inc., 1999).

34. Ibid., p. 119.

35. Davis, *The Evidential Force of Religious Experience*, op. cit., p. 221.

36. See also the discussion of these in ibid., pp. 204-10.

37. Sigmund Freud, 'A Religious Experience' (1928), in S. Freud, *Works* XXI, pp. 169-72.

38. See Sigmund Freud, *Civilisation and its Discontents* (Hogarth Press, 1929).

39. Augustine, *Confessions*, IV, 1, 1.

40. J. Kristeva, *In the Beginning Was Love: Psychoanalysis and Faith* (Columbia University Press, 1987), p. 24. Cf. an abridged version: J. Kristeva, 'In the Beginning was Love: Psychoanalysis and Faith', in Ivan Ward (ed.), *Is Psychoanalysis Another Religion? Contemporary Essays on Spirit, Faith and Morality in Psychoanalysis* (Freud Museum, 1993).

41. Cf. 'The Significance of the Father in the Destiny of the Individual' (1909), in Carl G. Jung, *The Collected Works of C.G. Jung* (20 vols), vol. IV for his early views. Jung's middle-period views can be found in *The Psychology of the Unconscious. Symbols of Transformation* (1911-12), in *Works* V and *Two Essays on Analytical Psychology*, in *Works* VII.

42. *Analytical Psychology*, pp. 181f. See also *On the Nature of the Psyche*, VIII 115.

43. See Carl G. Jung, *Psychology and Religion* (1937), in vol. XI of *The Collected Works of C.G. Jung* (20 vols), edited by H. Read, M. Fordham, and G. Adler (Princeton University Press, 1953-1979).

44. On 29.10.59.

45. On 21.1.60.

46. Benjamin Beit-Hallahmi, 'Object Relations Theory and Religious Experience', in *Handbook of Religious Experience*, op. cit., p. 261.

47. Winnicott, *The Maturational Process and the Facilitating Environment* (Hogarth Press, 1965). Lewin, *The Psychoanalysis of Elation* (International Universities Press, 1950). Prince and Savage, 'Mystical States and the Concept of Regression', *Psychedelic Review* 8 (1966) pp. 69-75.

48. J. Masson, 'The Psychology of the Ascetic', *Journal of Asian Studies* 35 (1976) pp. 611-25.

49. See the work of D. Aberbach, 'Grief and Mysticism', *International Review of Psychoanalysis* 14 (1987), pp. 509-26.

50. Lee A. Kirkpatrick, 'Attachment Theory and Religious Experience', in *Handbook of Religious Experience*, op. cit., p. 454.

51. 'An individual might well be able to invent or reinvent his or her perceived relationship with God in secure terms without inadvertently undermining the process through previously established, counterproductive patterns of behavior.' Ibid., p. 455.

52. See D. Hay, ' "The Biology of God": What is the Current Status of Hardy's Hypothesis?', op. cit. Hay and Morisy found a significant correlation between reporting religious experience and psychological well-being, as measured by the Bradburn Balanced Affect Scale. Greeley's study confirms this result; people who had frequent religious experiences were most likely to be optimistic and least likely to be authoritarian or racist. In a later study he found that people who prayed frequently were more likely to have happier marriages, and people who prayed most frequently and had sex most frequently had the happiest relationships of all. (I hope the reader's course of action is clear.) Wuthnow's study found that those who reported frequent religious experience were significantly more likely than others to find life meaningful, to have a purpose, and to be self-assured; were less materialistic, less status conscious, and had more social concern. Ralph Hood, in assessing a new measure for reported mystical experience, reports on four studies correlating this with other factors, and finds a positive correlation between such experience and openness to experience, intrinsic religious orientation (as opposed to religious commitment driven by 'extrinsic' factors, such as social acceptance). 'What tentatively emerges from these data is a reasonably consistent picture of a person who from a posture of openness to experience in fact experiences the world atypically and who, if he is devoutly oriented, identifies these experiences as sacred and joyful.' (R. Hood, 'The Construction and Preliminary Validation of a Measure of Reported Mystical Experience', *Journal for the Scientific Study of Religion* 1975, p. 40.) Poloma and Pendleton found that 'peak' and prayer experiences correlated positively with subjective perceptions of well-being. (M. Poloma and B. Pendleton, *Exploring Neglected Dimensions of Religion in Quality of Life Research*, Mellen Press, 1991.) Cf. also D. Lindskoog and R.E. Kirk, 'Some Life-History and Attitudinal Correlates of Self-Actualization among Evangelical Seminary Students', *Journal for the Scientific Study of Religion*, 14, 1975, pp. 51-5; R. Hood, 'Psychological Strength and the Report of Intense Religious Experience', *Journal for the Scientific Study of Religion*, 13, 1974, pp. 65-71; M. Jackson, 'Divine Madness: A Study of the Relationship between Psychotic and Spiritual Experience', op. cit.; L.E. Thomas and P.E. Cooper, 'Incidence and Psychological Correlates of Intense Spiritual Experiences', *Journal of Transpersonal Psychology* 12 (1980), pp. 75-85.

53. W. James, *The Varieties of Religious Experience* (Fontana, 1960).

54. See Abraham Maslow, *Religions, Values and Peak Experiences* (Ohio State University Press, 1964) and *Towards a Psychology of Being* (Litton Educational Publishing, 1968). On the question of the relation between science and religion, see *Religions, Values and Peak Experiences*, ch. 2, 'Dichotomized Science and Dichotomized Religion'.

55. A. Maslow, *Toward a Psychology of Being*, op. cit., p. 24.

56. Ibid., p. 91.

57. Ibid., ch. 3.

58. See the useful summary in Linke, *Psychological Perspectives on Traditional Jewish*

Practices, op. cit., pp. 69-71. Ken Wilber is a popular exponent of this approach; cf. *The Spectrum of Consciousness* (Quest Books, 1977), *The Atman Project: a Transpersonal View of Human Development* (Quest Books, 1980), *Up From Eden: A Transpersonal View of Human Evolution* (Routledge & Kegan Paul, 1981). Cf. also 'Ontogenetic Development: Two Fundamental Patterns', in *Journal of Transpersonal Psychology* 13 (1981) 1.

59. Kristeva, *In the Beginning Was Love: Psychoanalysis and Faith*, op. cit., p. 44.

60. Anthony DeLuca, *Freud and Future Religious Experience* (Littlefield, Adams & Co., 1977), p. 237.

61. Ibid., p. 235.

62. M.P. Carroll, 'Praying the Rosary: The Anal-Erotic Origins of a Popular Catholic Devotion', *Journal for the Scientific Study of Religion* 26 (1987), pp. 486-98.

63. Proudfoot argues that while beliefs can normally be assessed without attention to their origin or cause, beliefs that include a claim about the cause must be an exception: perceptual beliefs and judgements, to give his examples. To put it in a way that he does not, if someone claims that God imparted an experience of Herself to him, the cause or origin of the belief most certainly does become an important question. For someone to identify an experience as religious 'assumes an embedded causal claim; consequently the experience has an epistemic quality, as in the case of sense perception' (W. Proudfoot, *Religious Experience* (University of California Press, 1985), p. 178). *Certain* religious experiences do make causal claims or have causal implications; however, others do not. A number of the religious experiences which are reported do not involve an analogy with visual perception. Some are rather felt to involve an emotion, or a changed understanding or awareness. A causal model is too simplistic for such experiences; the causal implications of experiences are more varied for religious experiences than Proudfoot allows for here.

64. As Bruno Bettelheim observes, 'most important psychological phenomena are over-determined', i.e. have more than one cause or explanation. Bettelheim, *A Good Enough Parent* (Pan Books, 1988), p. 192.

65. Bhikku Khantipalo, *Calm and Insight* (Curzon Press, 1981), pp. 106f.

66. Jacques Lacan, *The Seminar of Jacques Lacan I*, edited by Jacques-Alain Miller (Cambridge University Press, 1988), p. 165.

67. Wilhelmus Luijpen, *Phenomenology and Atheism*, translated by Walter van de Putte (Duquesne University Press, 1964), pp. 336f.

5. Being Eminently Rational

1. See William Wainwright, 'Mysticism and Sense Perception', *Religious Studies* 9 (1973), pp. 257-78; and ch. 3 of W. Wainwright, *Mysticism* (University of Wisconsin Press, 1981).

2. 'Doxa' means belief or opinion in Greek.

3. W.P. Alston, *Perceiving God: The Epistemology of Religious Experience* (Cornell University Press, 1991). Cf. pp. 42-50 for his rebuttal of reasons for rejecting mystical experience as a mode of perception, and ch. 5 for his refutation of objections to religious doxastic practice.

4. Ibid., p. 183.

5. For the following citations, see K.E. Yandell, *The Epistemology of Religious Experience* (Cambridge University Press, 1993), pp. 207-9.

6. Alston would rejoin: The exponent of the rationality of religious doxastic practice, however, could provide other modes of religious 'input' to test the 'output' of a religious experience; indeed, the traditions of discernment in the long-established religions are teeming with ways of testing one's outputs against other people's, and the tradition. Thus the doxastic practice based on religious experience could be confirmed by other kinds of religious doxastic practice, in the way that visual doxastic practice can be confirmed by auditory doxastic practice.

7. Alston argues that it is rational to engage in Christian doxastic practice not because it is analogous to sensory doxastic practice, but because it is socially established, and there is insufficient reason to think it unreliable. Alston, *Perceiving God*, op. cit., pp. 223f.

8. Basil Mitchell, *The Justification of Religious Belief* (Macmillan, 1973), p. 112.

9. Richard Swinburne, *The Existence of God* (Clarendon Press, 1979), pp. 247f.

10. Ibid., p. 254.

11. Burhenn argues that Swinburne's position is only possible because of the more general critique of empiricism as theory of knowledge that has taken place since the mid-century. 'But if we reject that sort of foundationalism, then we are led to recognize that our whole picture of our world depends on our trusting many kinds of experience and also on our trusting the reports of others. Religious experience and reports about such experiences are among the items to which we must grant initial credibility since there are no valid general reasons for rejecting the evidential value of this kind of experience.' Herbert Burhenn, 'Philosophy and Religious Experience', in *Handbook of Religious Experience*, ed. Ralph W. Hood Jr. (Religious Education Press, 1995), p. 154.

12. Swinburne, *The Existence of God*, op. cit., p. 254.

13. Ibid., p. 272.

14. Ibid., p. 271.

15. Gary Gutting, *Religious Belief and Religious Skepticism* (University of Notre Dame Press, 1982), p. 148. He provides a counter-example in supposing that he walks into his study and seems to see his recently deceased aunt. He seems to me to be right in judging that the PC should not warrant the acceptance of this experience as veridical; but wrong I think in using this to rebut Swinburne; it would seem to be overridden by Swinburne's third 'special consideration', 'that on background evidence it is probable that X was not present' (Swinburne, op. cit., p. 261). Gutting rules out the applicability of this third consideration, claiming that he knows 'nothing at all about the habits or powers of the dead, so I have no reason to think that my aunt could not now be in my study or, if present, could not be seen by me.' (Ibid., p. 148). I think Gutting claims too much ignorance of the habits of the dead.

16. C.F. Davis, *The Evidential Force of Religious Experience* (Clarendon, 1989), p. 93.

17. Ibid., p. 100.

18. Yandell, *The Epistemology of Religious Experience*, op. cit., p. 274.

19. Gellman, *Experience of God and the Rationality of Theistic Belief* (Cornell University Press, 1997).

20. His version allows for another person more experienced than the subject of the event to interpret it authoritatively; he speaks of a 'best explanation' of an experience rather than speaking about what is 'probable' (which avoids the problems of calculating the 'probability' of God as a hypothesis). BEE only applies to what is phenomenally present, not to hunches or inner conviction. It creates a presumption for O's existence, thus is evidence; but it can be defeated by countervailing factors, so it does not speciously claim to be self-validating. Finally, the effect of saying 'everything else being equal' is to place the burden of proof on one who argues everything else is not equal.

21. Verbatim: 'If a person, S, has an experience, E, which seems (phenomenally) to be of a particular object, O (or of an object of kind, K), then our belief that S's having experienced O (or an object of kind K) is the best explanation (everything else being equal) of E, is strengthened in proportion to the number of purported experiences of O there are and in proportion to the variability of circumstances in which such experiences occur.' Ibid., pp. 52f.

22. 'If a person, S, has an experience, E, in which it seems (phenomenally) that a partic-ular object, O (or of an object of kind, K), has a property, P, then everything *else being* equal, the best explanation of S's having E is that S has (truly) experienced O (or an object of kind, K) possessing P.' Ibid., p. 54.

23. I am indebted to Mary Weston for this exasperated acronym.

24. Davis, *The Evidential Force of Religious Experience*, op. cit., p. 218.

25. Gellman, *Experience of God and the Rationality of Theistic Belief*, op. cit., pp. 128-

36; cf. also p. 133: 'We therefore conclude that in the various forms of it that we have considered, we have been given no reason to think that a person who is in a pathological condition and who seems to perceive God is not really perceiving God.'

26. Michael Martin, *Atheism: A Philosophical Justification* (Temple University Press, 1990), p. 170, 'the negative principle of credulity'. See also Michael Martin, 'The Principle of Credulity and Religious Experience', *Religious Studies* 22 (1986) pp. 79-93.

27. B. Russell, *Religion and Science* (Oxford University Press, 1935), p. 187.

28. Gellman, *Experience of God and the Rationality of Theistic Belief*, op. cit., p. 59; on this point generally, see ch. 3, 'On Not Experiencing God', pp. 57-89.

29. Gellman, *Experience of God and the Rationality of Theistic Belief*, op. cit., p. 63.

30. Davis argues similarly: 'Where the very existence of an entity is at issue, then, a failure to perceive it is not by itself prima facie evidence for its nonexistence, whereas an experience of its presence is itself prima facie evidence for the entity's existence.' *The Evidential Force of Religious Experience*, op. cit., p. 98.

31. For an interesting hands-on discussion of this experience, see the work of Ruth Burrows, e.g. *Guidelines for Mystical Prayer* (Sheed & Ward, 1976) or *To Believe in Jesus* (Sheed & Ward, 1978) or her treatment of John of the Cross, whose *Dark Night of the Soul* addresses this issue: *Ascent to Love* (Darton, Longman and Todd, 1987).

32. Antony Flew, *God and Philosophy* (Hutchinson, 1966), pp. 124-39.

33. Alston, 'Is Religious Belief Rational?', in Loades and Rue (eds), *Contemporary Classics in Philosophy of Religion* (Open Court, 1991), pp. 151f.; cf. also *Perceiving God*, op. cit., p. 278.

34. Swinburne, *The Existence of God*, op. cit., p. 266.

35. Davis, *The Evidential Force of Religious Experience*, op. cit., p. 178.

36. Ibid., pp. 174f. The common core, in my summary of her description, is: mystics generally agree that the ordinary world is not the ultimate reality, nor the everyday self the deepest self. Ultimate reality is holy, and however it is described, all descriptions are inadequate. Some form of union with ultimate reality is our highest good. See pp. 190f.

37. Gellman, *Experience of God and the Rationality of Theistic Belief*, op. cit., p. 95.

38. Ibid., p. 96.

39. Ibid., p. 102.

40. Ibid., pp. 103f.

41. Ibid., p. 105.

42. Ibid., p. 118.

43. A. Flew, *God and Philosophy*, op. cit., p. 129.

44. Russell, *Religion and Science*, op. cit., p. 178.

45. William Rowe, 'Religious Experience and the Principle of Credulity', *International Journal of the Philosophy of Religion* 13 (1982), pp. 90f.

46. Davis, *The Evidential Force of Religious of Experience*, op. cit., pp. 116ff.

47. As in the case of the small schoolboy who complained to my brother-in-law, a headmaster, that he had been 'kicked in the testaments'. There are rational grounds for doubting this proposition, while allowing the injured party a degree of incorrigibility about his experience.

48. 'The proposition O *has* A comes within the scope of polar disconfirmation if and only if there is some condition C such that O's not being experienced in C is evidence in favor of O *does not* exist.' Yandell, *The Epistemology of Religious Experience*, op cit., p. 245.

49. Ibid., pp. 250ff.

50. Or, in Yandell's formulation, 'The proposition O has A comes within the scope of lateral disconfirmation if and only if it is logically possible that there be an experience that provides evidence for O* *has* B (where, of course, O* is different from O) and the truth of O* *has* B is evidence against the truth of O *has* A.' Ibid., p. 246.

51. Yandell's version is: 'What I took to be O turns out to lack A; O* has B, and if so then there cannot be an O that has A; O* has some of the properties of O, but lacks a property O

must have, and it is not likely that there be two things with the properties that O has.'
See the discussion in Yandell, ibid., pp. 250-5.
52. Ibid., p. 266.
53. Ibid., p. 268.
54. Ibid., p. 269.
55. Gutting, *Religious Belief and Religious Skepticism*, op. cit., p. 152.
56. Davis, *The Evidential Force of Religious Experience*, op. cit., pp. 76f.
57. Ibid., p. 77.
58. Yandell, *The Epistemology of Religious Experience*, op. cit., p. 267.
59. Ibid., pp. 267f. Gellman's 'STING' argument (see above) is also an attempt to harness the question of confirmation in religious experience to the advantage of the religious believer. Gellman, *Experience of God and the Rationality of Theistic Belief*, op. cit., pp. 52f.

6. Or Maybe Not?

1. A reader of this passage in draft called my attention to the following: 'I'm frigid I think, and they tell me. And I don't know what to *try* for. It's like any serious experience: hardly anyone can describe them: they simply bore you by going on about whatever it is being unique.' From Elizabeth Jane Howard, *Odd Girl Out* (Jonathan Cape, 1972), p. 87.

2. We do not arrive at the knowledge that our friends exist through a process of inference, but rather through direct encounter. We feel we know 'intuitively' that the persons we meet are conscious subjects and agents – we do not consciously base that belief on other beliefs. Many features of an 'I-Thou' relationship and many aspects of the 'Thou' which we apprehend in that relationship are practically impossible to put into words. Just as humans reveal something of themselves through behaviour, speech, and other external signs, so God is said to reveal himself through the created world, through the effects of the holy spirit in individuals, and so on. Further, 'getting to know' a person is not some mysterious telepathic penetration into the person's 'essence', even in the case of a non-physical person. But it also is not – as the personal encounter analogy stresses – a matter of collecting facts about a person. Theists generally rate experience of God far above knowledge about him. This perspective also allows 'faith' to mean trust, as a personal response, rather than mere cognitive assent to religious doctrines. Against the charge that this perspective is too parochial, limited only to monotheistic or Western religions, Davis observes that it can allow for the validity of other types of religious experience, since God reveals Herself in other ways and other aspects. C.F. Davis, *The Evidential Force of Religious Experience* (Clarendon Press, 1989), pp. 78f.

3. Ibid., p. 82.

4. The 'Personalists' who wrote in German were Ferdinand Ebner, Franz Rosenzweig, and Martin Buber. Not many of their works are available in English, with the exception of Buber. A good source for readings and extracts is Maurice Friedman (ed.), *The Worlds of Existentialism. A Critical Reader* (Humanities Press International, Inc., 1994).

5. Buber, *I and Thou*, edited and translated by W. Kaufmann (Charles Scribner's, 1970), p. 27. Cf.: '*Real* existence, that is, real man in his relation to his being, is comprehensible only in connexion with the nature of the being to which he stands in relation.' Buber, *Between Man and Man* (Routledge & Kegan Paul, 1949), p. 164. 'Only in the discovery of a "Thou" is it possible to hear an actual "I", an "I" that is not self-evident but emphatic and underlined.' F. Rosenzweig, *Star of Redemption* (University of Notre Dame Press, 1985), II, p. 112.

6. F. Rosenzweig, *The New Thinking* (Syracuse University Press, 1999), p. 179.

7. F. Ebner, *Das Du und die geistige Realitäten* (Brenner-Verlag, 1921), p. 24. Reprinted in F. Ebner, *Fragmente, Aufsätze, Aphorismen. Zu einer Pneumatologie des Wortes*, edited by Franz Seyer (Kösel Verlag, 1963). Translation mine.

8. Rosenzweig, *Star of Redemption*, op. cit., II, pp. 143f.

9. Buber, *I and Thou*, op. cit., p. 75. Cf. also: 'God [is] the absolute Person, i.e. the Person who cannot be limited. It is as the absolute Person that God enters into direct relation with us. The contradiction yields deeper knowledge. As a Person God gives personal life, he makes us as persons become capable of meeting with him and with one another. But no limitation can come upon him as the absolute Person, either from us or from our relations with one another; in fact we can dedicate to him not merely our persons but also our relations with one another. The man who turns to him therefore need not turn away from any other *I-Thou* relation; but he properly brings them to him, and lets them be fulfilled "in the face of God." ' Ibid., p. 136.

10. Ibid., p. 103.

11. Cf. Ebner, *Schriften* II, p. 243; I, p. 115; cf. II, p. 274.

12. Ebner, op. cit., I, p. 653.

13. Ibid., I, p. 86, p. 258, p. 913; II, p. 27, p. 47.

14. Ibid., I, p. 281; II, p. 36.

15. Ibid., I, p. 438. Translation mine.

7. Problems of Evil

1. An ancient Babylonian poem, '*Ludlul bêl nemeqi*', 'I will praise the Lord of Wisdom', II, 36-42, 48 (W.G. Lambert, *Babylonian Wisdom Literature* (Oxford University Press, 1960), p. 41). See the discussion of the ancient Mesopotamians' problem of evil in Georges Roux, *Ancient Iraq* (Pelican, 1980), pp. 103-5. The ancient Sumerian text which lies behind this, 'Sumerian Job', is even older (*c.* 2000 BCE).

2. R.A. Sinari, *The Structure of Indian Thought* (Charles C. Thomas, 1970), p. 4.

3. Ibid., p. 11.

4. Ibid., p. 13.

5. H. Zimmer, *Philosophies of India* (Routledge & Kegan Paul, 1952), p. 351.

6. Alvin Plantinga, 'Epistemic Probability and Evil', in Daniel Howard-Snyder (ed.), *The Evidential Argument from Evil* (Indiana University Press, 1996), p. 69.

7. Ibid.

8. Of course it is possible to formulate ethics from an atheist position. For an account of an atheist ethical programme, see Kai Nielsen, *Ethics Without God* (Prometheus Books, 1990).

9. Johann Herder in a letter to Hamann. In J.G. Hamann, *Briefwechsel* ed. Walther Ziesemer and Arthur Henkel, from vol. 4 on edited by Henkel alone (Insel Verlag, 1955-1975), vol. 2, no. 349, 408-15. See Gwen Griffith-Dickson, *Johann Georg Hamann's Relational Metacriticism* (Walter de Gruyter, 1995), pp. 196ff.

10. See Frederick Kumar, *The Philosophies of India: A New Approach* (Edwin Mellen Press, 1991) and Sinari, *The Structure of Indian Thought*, op. cit.

11. See Marquis de Sade, *The Passionate Philosopher*, ed. Margaret Crosland (P. Owen, 1991); T. Airaksinen, *The Philosophy of the Marquis de Sade* (Routledge, 1995); D. Allison, M. Roberts, A. Weiss, *Sade and the Narrative of Transgression* (Cambridge University Press, 1995); P. Klossowski, *Sade My Neighbour* (Northwestern University Press, 1991), P. Kondylis, *Die Aufklärung im Rahmen des neuzeitlichen Rationalismus* (Ernst Klett, 1981).

12. See the interesting discussion of this progression of nihilism in Kondylis, ibid.

13. As Airaksinen argues in *The Philosophy of the Marquis de Sade*, op. cit., p. 169.

14. See *Justine*. Or better, don't.

15. See Hume's satiric comments about the world as a 'rude essay of an infant Deity' in *Dialogues Concerning Natural Religion* (Hackett Publishing Company, 1980).

16. See A. Plantinga, *God, Freedom and Evil* (Allen & Unwin, 1975, first published Harper & Row, 1974), pp. 12-24.

17. K.E. Yandell, *The Epistemology of Religious Experience* (Cambridge University Press, 1993), pp. 322-8.

18. Plantinga, *God, Freedom and Evil*, op. cit., pp. 23f.

19. Ibid., pp. 24-9.

20. *Jātaka Stories,* translated by E.B. Cowell et al., 6 vols (Cambridge, 1895-1913), cited in Helmuth von Glasenapp, *Buddhism – A Non-theistic Religion* (Allen & Unwin, 1970), p. 152.

21. Allegedly spoken by the Bodhisattva, cited in von Glasenapp, ibid., p. 154.

22. Antony Flew, 'Theology and Falsification', in Flew and MacIntyre (eds), *New Essays in Philosophical Theology* (SCM Press, 1955), pp. 98f.

23. Ibid., p. 97.

24. A thorough examination of different senses of probability and how they might be used, including Bayes' Theorem, is provided by Melville Stewart, in *The Greater Good Defence: Essay on the Rationality of Faith* (Macmillan, 1992), pp. 7-14.

25. David Conway rejects the division into two problems, the logical (or deductive) and the evidential (or probabilistic). For him, the problem rests on the claim that evil could be prevented. The question is not whether this is a necessary proposition (the logical problem) or a contingent one (the evidential problem) but whether or not it is *true*. D. Conway, 'The Philosophical Problem of Evil', *International Journal for Philosophy of Religion* 24 (1988), pp. 35f.

26. According to Bayes' Theorem, the probability that a hypothesis is true given the evidence and the relevant background information is calculated using the following variables: A: the prior probability that the hypothesis is true, given the evidence; B: the probability of the background information given the evidence and that the hypothesis is true; C: the prior probability that the hypothesis is false, given the evidence (i.e. the opposite of A); D: the probability of the background information, given the evidence and that the hypothesis is false (i.e. the opposite of B). According to Bayes' Theorem the probability of a hypothesis is:

$$\frac{A \times B}{[A \times D] \times [C \times D]}$$

Now, if the hypothesis is that God exists, the variables would be filled in as follows: A: the probability that God exists, given the evidence (which will include evil); B: the probability that the world would be as it is if God existed; C: the probability that God *does not* exist, given the evidence; D: the probability that the world would be the way it is if God *didn't* exist. So the theorem would calculate the probability of God's existence, given what we know about the world and the evil in it. Splendid! But first one needs to be able to assign values to each of these variables, A to D. How, for example, does one assign a number to the probability of God's existence, given the existence of evil (A)? That is precisely the point being contested. The approach might style itself as objective or logical, claiming for itself all the logic and objectivity of mathematics; but to put it into practice requires a bravura display of subjective interpretation and potential bias. What states of affairs will be allowed in as evidence? Who is to decide how the world is? How is it for you? The problem is first and foremost the question of determining the 'prior probabilities' – the very point at issue – and the sophistication of any subsequent calculations ought not to disguise the fact that the argument is circular.

27. J.L. Mackie in *The Miracle of Theism* (Clarendon Press, 1982) and R. Swinburne in *The Existence of God* (Clarendon Press, 1979).

28. M. Martin, 'Is Evil Evidence against the Existence of God?', *Mind* 87 (1987), pp. 429-32; reprinted in M. Peterson (ed.), *The Problem of Evil: Selected Readings* (University of Notre Dame Press, 1992), pp. 135-9. David Basinger unearths two assumptions of this argument: that an omnipotent, omniscient, wholly good God can create any logically possible state of affairs, and that God could intervene to reduce greatly the amount of evil in our world. Basinger finds sufficient grounds to refute these assumptions, and so to reject Martin's argument. D. Basinger in 'Evil as Evidence against God's Existence', *Modern Schoolman* 58 (1981), pp 175-84; reprinted in Peterson (ed.), *The Problem of Evil: Selected Readings*, op. cit., pp. 141-52.

29. 'No statement, theological or otherwise, should be made that would not be credible in the presence of burning children.' I. Greenberg, 'Cloud of Smoke, Pillar of Fire: Judaism, Christianity, and Modernity after the Holocaust', in E. Fleischner (ed.), *Auschwitz: Beginning of a New Era* (Ktav, 1977), pp. 9f.

30. Zimmer, *Philosophies of India*, op. cit., p. 349. Cf.: 'Suffering, therefore, is only a problem so long as it appears to be a final and inescapable truth. But when it is realised that the self is not bound for ever to the transient world of suffering, but rather that it is *Brahman*, then suffering can no longer occur', p. 214. J. Bowker, *Problems of Suffering in Religions of the World* (Cambridge University Press, 1970), pp. 207ff., for an overview.

31. In portraying Augustine's treatment of the nature of evil in the *Enchiridion*, Tilley writes: 'Never, after his conversion to Christianity, did Augustine deny the fundamental equation of being with goodness'. T. Tilley, *The Evils of Theodicy* (Georgetown University Press, 1991), p. 118.

32. 'Therefore, every entity, even if it is defective, is good insofar as it is an entity and evil insofar as it is defective.' Augustine, *Enchiridion* 13. Quoted in Tilley, *The Evils of Theodicy*, op. cit., p. 119.

33. Martin Buber, *Between Man and Man* (Routledge & Kegan Paul, 1949), p. 78.

34. Martin Buber, *Images of Good and Evil* in M. Buber, *Good and Evil: Two Interpretations* (Scribner's, 1953).

35. See Mordecai Kaplan, *The Meaning of God in Modern Jewish Religion* (Behrman House, 1947) and *Judaism without Supernaturalism* (Reconstructionist Press, 1958).

36. E. Berkovits, *Major Themes in Modern Philosophies of Judaism* (Ktav, 1974), p. 161.

37. Eric Ormsby, *Theodicy in Islamic Thought* (Princeton University Press, 1984), p. 264.

38. Ibid.

39. Moses Maimonides, *The Guide of the Perplexed*, translated by S. Pines (University of Chicago Press, 1963), III, 23, p. 496.

40. Ibid., p. 497.

41. B. Davies, *Thinking About God* (Geoffrey Chapman, 1985) and *Philosophy of Religion: A Guide to the Subject* (Cassell, 1998).

42. In *Thinking About God*, Davies provides three reasons why God is not a moral agent. First, God is changeless, whereas those who are subject to moral duties and obligations must be changeable, and have the chance of becoming something different as a result of their response to their duty. Secondly, to be a moral being depends on being a human being with the ability to choose between alternative courses of action. But God is not a human being, therefore He cannot be a moral being. Finally, with humans, one has moral obligations in a certain context: as a parent, as a doctor, and these differ. But God creates *ex nihilo*, which means there is no context or background against which God's act of creating can be evaluated. So God does not have duties and obligations. – The argument could be better grounded. God, on a Thomist understanding such as Davies espouses, cannot be subject to some pre-existing moral code or list of obligations. God cannot be subject to anything, because He is omnipotent and exists in absolute freedom. A moral code is, in a sense, something higher than the one who is bound by it. Nothing, however, is higher than God, to which He must be bound; the whole notion is nonsensical. Secondly, God cannot be obligated to some moral code because God Himself precedes anything and everything, temporally and ontologically, and cannot be made to conform to some prior moral code.

43. Davies, *Thinking About God*, op. cit., p. 212.

44. Davies, *Philosophy of Religion: A Guide to the Subject*, p. 185.

45. Aquinas, *Summa Theologiae* I, 4, 1; cited in Davies, ibid., p. 186.

46. Ibid., p. 187.

47. Ibid., p. 189.

48. Ibid., p. 186.
49. Ibid., p. 182.
50. Zimmer, *Philosophies of India*, op. cit., p. 350.

8. Origins of Evil

1. Al-Ash'arī, *al-Ibānah 'an uṣul al-diyānah* (Cairo, 1977), p. 23, cited in E. Ormsby, *Theodicy in Islamic Thought* (Princeton University Press, 1984), p. 24.

2. Oswald Bayer, 'Poetological Theology', translated by Gwen Griffith-Dickson, *International Journal of Systematic Theology* 1 (1999), p. 165.

3. N.N. Glatzer (ed.), *The Dimensions of Job: A Study and Selected Readings* (Schocken Books, 1969), p. 221.

4. This is the name for God transcendent in the Kabbala, that is, God-in-God's-self as opposed to God's manifestations.

5. G. Scholem, 'Kabbalah', in *Encylopedia Judaica*, vol. 10, cols 588-601, col. 589. See also: A. Steinsaltz, *The Thirteen Petalled Rose*, translated by Yehuda Hanegbi (Basic Books, 1980), p. 37: 'The world becomes possible only through the special act of Divine withdrawal or contraction. Such Divine non-Being or concealment, is thus the elementary condition for the existence of that which is finite.'

6. Moses Maimonides, *Guide of the Perplexed*, translated by S. Pines (Chicago University Press, 1963), p. 444. Bk. III, ch. 12 (employing the principle of plenitude that every genuine possibility must at some time be instantiated).

7. P. Vardy, *The Puzzle of Evil* (Fount/HarperCollins, 1992), p. 28.

8. R.W. Kropf, *Evil and Evolution: A Theodicy* (Fairleigh Dickinson University Press, 1984), p. 41.

9. Ervin Staub, *The Roots of Evil: The Origins of Genocide and Other Group Violence* (Cambridge University Press, 1989).

10. John Hick, *Evil and the God of Love* (Macmillan, 1990). The theodicy itself will be examined in the next chapter.

11. Tilley takes objection to this: the account Hick gives as 'Augustinian' is not Augustine's account; it is an amalgamation of various ideas taken out of context from Augustine's various writings, taking no account of the shift in his views from early to late writings. His own theological position varied greatly depending on the polemical context. 'Augustine's positions are too inconsistent to yield a coherent position.' T. Tilley, *The Evils of Theodicy* (Georgetown University Press, 1991), pp. 116f. 'What theodicists treat as "Augustinian theodicy" is part of a discourse system for dealing with evil that arose in the Constantinian church. Its central concept is the bondage of the will in Original Sin brought about by the Fall of humanity, a concept Augustine moved to the center of the Christian story. Its acceptance means that humans radically need ultimately to be redeemed by Christ, to be restrained forcibly by political and ecclesial authorities, and to be retrained completely to overcome the evil that has infected them. The latter proximate implications of the bondage of the will theologically legitimate the political and spiritual domination of established (male) authorities.' Ibid., p. 116.

12. See Bruce Reichenbach, *Evil and a Good God* (Fordham University Press, 1982), and 'Evil and a Reformed View of God', *International Journal for Philosophy of Religion* 24 (1988), pp. 67-85.

13. R. Swinburne, *The Existence of God* (Clarendon Press, 1979), p. 211.

14. Ibid., p. 210.

15. Ibid., pp. 210f.

16. D. Basinger, 'Evil As Evidence against God's Existence', in M. Peterson (ed.), *The Problem of Evil: Selected Readings* (University of Notre Dame Press, 1992), pp. 146-8.

17. D. Birnbaum, *God and Evil: A Unified Theodicy/Theology/Philosophy* (Ktav

Publishing House, 1989), p. 97 and p. 144.

18. Basinger, 'Evil as Evidence against God's Existence', op. cit., p. 147.

19. Ibid.

20. These points can still be defended by those who believe that God does sometimes intervene in the course of human history. Extraordinary and rare interventions ('miracles'), or God's action as a response to human prayer, would not have the same confusing effect. We can be occasionally confounded without having our sense of the intelligibility of things destroyed.

21. Eleonore Stump, 'Knowledge, Freedom, and the Problem of Evil' in M. Peterson (ed.), *The Problem of Evil: Selected Readings*, op. cit., p. 321.

22. Cited in E. Ormsby, *Theodicy in Islamic Thought*, op. cit., p. 26.

23. Basinger concludes that atheologians have not established that the relatively specific modifications that they demand to the natural order would result in a significant improvement in the world. He doubts whether such an undertaking could be done, and whether it would not represent a significant reduction in the integrity of human freedom. 'He or she must demonstrate that, in the context of the entire world system of which it would be a part, such modification would actually result in a significant increase in the net amount of good in comparison to the actual world.' Basinger, 'Evil as Evidence against God's Existence', op. cit., p. 147.

24. G. Roux, *Ancient Iraq* (Pelican, 1980), p. 103.

25. Wendy Doniger O'Flaherty, 'Karma and Rebirth in the Vedas and Purāṇas' in W.D. O'Flaherty (ed.), *Karma and Rebirth in Classical Indian Traditions* (University of California Press, 1980), p. 29.

26. Gananath Obeyesekere, 'Rebirth Eschatology and its Transformations: A Contribution to the Sociology of Early Buddhism', in O'Flaherty (ed.), *Karma and Rebirth in Classical Indian Traditions*, op. cit., pp. 137-64; this list is on pp. 139f.

27. Ibid., p. 146.

28. Principal sources for this doctrine of *paticca-samuppāda* are the *Samyutta Nikāya* 2.1-133, and the *Dīgha Nikāya* 2.55-71.

29. *Samyutta Nikāya*, 22, 90. This version is my arrangement of the text.

30. 'The fact that various spokesmen in the *Mahābhārata* designate first one then another factor as the cause of events would seem to indicate that they did not feel that the total complexity of forces at work in the world could be accounted for by reference to a single principle or agent.' Long, in O'Flaherty (ed.), *Karma and Rebirth in Classical Indian Traditions*, op. cit., p. 47. Both Long and O'Flaherty provide numerous textual examples.

31. See the discussion in Halbfass, in O'Flaherty (ed.), *Karma and Rebirth in Classical Indian Traditions*, op. cit., pp. 286f.

32. Ibid., p. 287.

33. For two illuminating discussions of this problem, see R. Sinari, *The Structure of Indian Thought* (Charles C. Thomas, 1970), pp. 140ff., and K.H. Potter, *Encyclopedia of Indian Philosophies: Advaita Vedānta up to Śankara and His Pupils* (Princeton University Press, 1981), pp. 78ff.

34. Although, according to Nayak, explaining the origin of the universe was not Śankara's interest or intention; he thought this was not the business of philosophy. See G.C. Nayak, *Philosophical Reflections* (Motilal Banarsidass, 1987), p. 50.

35. Ibid., p. 53.

36. Nayak sighs, 'The entire programme of Śankara, to my mind, has been seriously misunderstood by and misrepresented at the hands of his own followers, not to speak of his opponents.' Ibid., p. 50.

37. *Jīva*, not *ātman*.

38. Nayak, *Philosophical Reflections*, op. cit., p. 49.

39. In the *Naiṣkarmyasiddhi*, presuming Sureśvara is its author (authorship of the work is uncertain and disputed).

40. Sinari's reading, see Sinari, *The Structure of Indian Thought*, op. cit., p. 141.

41. Herder's question to Hamann. In Hamann, J.G., *Briefwechsel* edited by Walther

Ziesemer and Arthur Henkel, from volume 4 on edited by Henkel alone (Insel Verlag, 1955-1975), vol. 2, no. 349, 408-15. See Gwen Griffith-Dickson, *Johann Georg Hamann's Relational Metacriticism* (Walter de Gruyter, 1995), pp. 196ff.

42. *Mahābhārata* 3.179-221; see the discussion in J. Bruce Long, 'Karma and Rebirth in the *Mahābhārata*', in O'Flaherty (ed.), *Karma and Rebirth in Classical Indian Traditions*, op. cit., pp. 49-52.

43. See A. Plantinga, *God, Freedom and Evil* (George Allen & Unwin, 1975), pp. 57-9, and P. Vardy, *The Puzzle of Evil*, op. cit., pp. 56-60, respectively.

44. Cf. E. Pagels, *Adam, Eve and the Serpent* (Weidenfeld & Nicolson, 1988).

45. Abū al-Qāsim al-Shābbī (1909-1934), *Dīwān* (Beirut, 1972), pp. 342-3, cited in Ormsby, *Theodicy in Islamic Thought*, op. cit., p. 265.

46. Ibid., p. 223.

47. Ibid., pp. 223f.

48. Presumably Mackie is unaware of it, as one hardly falls over al-Jāḥiẓ in Anglo-American philosophy of religion.

49. J.L. Mackie, 'Evil and Omnipotence' reprinted in M. McCord Adams and R. Merrihew Adams (eds), *The Problem of Evil* (Oxford University Press, 1990), p. 32.

50. Ibid.

51. Ibid., p. 29.

52. Ibid., p. 30.

53. al-Ghazālī, *Iḥyā IV,* 111, line 7ff. Cited in Ormsby, *Theodicy in Islamic Thought,* op. cit., p. 255.

54. Mackie, 'Evil and Omnipotence', op. cit., pp. 33-6.

55. Ibid., p. 30.

56. C.R. Mesle, *John Hick's Theodicy: A Process Humanist Critique* (Macmillan, 1991), p. 43.

57. T.B. Yoma, 69b. My paraphrase of H.M. Schulweis' paraphrase in *Evil and the Morality of God* (Hebrew Union College Press, 1984), p. 137.

58. H. Zimmer, *Philosophies of India* (Routledge & Kegan Paul, 1952), p. 350.

59. From the unfinished poem, 'St Winifred's Well'. Gerard Manley Hopkins, *The Poems of Gerard Manley Hopkins*, edited W.H. Gardner and N.H. MacKenzie (Oxford University Press, 4th edition, 1980), p. 191.

60. Thomas Aquinas, *Summa Theologica* Ia25,6, ad 3.

61. Ormsby, *Theodicy in Islamic Thought*, op. cit., pp. 221-5, 259-65, *et passim*.

62. In a work available to me only after this work had been submitted to the publisher, David O'Connor maintains that this ability [claimed ability, I would say] to compare possible worlds is the foundation of the debates on evil in current analytical philosophy of religion. See David O'Connor, *God and Inscrutable Evil: In Defense of Theism and Atheism* (Rowman & Littlefield, 1998), p. 41 and the preceding and succeeding pages.

63. A useful briefing on this question is found in A.C. Grayling, *An Introduction to Philosophical Logic* (Duckworth, 1990), pp. 68ff. The criticisms he reports and mounts of possible worlds talk is more damning as well as more complex than my humble puzzlement, reported here.

64. David Hume, *Dialogues Concerning Natural Religion* (Hackett Publishing Company, 1980), Part XI, pp. 67-8.

65. Ibid., Part II, p. 21.

66. al-Jāḥiẓ, *Kitab al-ḥayawān* I, p. 206.

67. Ibid.

68. Ormsby, *Theodicy in Islamic Thought*, op. cit., p. 224.

69. al-Jāḥiẓ, *Kitab al-ḥayawān* I, p. 206.

70. From the chant 'Aia lā o Pele i Hawai'i', in my translation, slightly expansive or explanatory for the sake of clarity. This chant is also cited at the beginning of this book.

9. The Ends of Suffering

1. M. Stewart, *The Greater Good Defence: Essay on the Rationality of Faith* (Macmillan, 1992), p. 56.

2. See ibid., ch. 3.

3. Thus Hick, defending himself against Mesle, insists that despite the enormous amount of evil which we would be better off without, nevertheless the world will finally fulfil God's purpose for it, in a 'limitlessly good end-state'. Hick in C.R. Mesle, *John Hick's Theodicy: A Process Humanist Critique* (Macmillan, 1991), pp. 130f.

4. Mesle uses Griffin's distinction of '*prima facie*' and 'genuine' evil. See D. Griffin, *God, Power and Evil: A Process Theodicy* (Westminster, 1976), p. 22.

5. Mesle, *John Hick's Theodicy*, op. cit., p. 39.

6. Hick, in Mesle, ibid., pp. 130f.

7. J.M. Trau, 'The Positive Value of Evil', *International Journal for Philosophy of Religion* 21 (1988), pp. 21-33.

8. For a thorough discussion of Saadia's philosophy and theology, see Israel Efros, *Studies in Medieval Jewish Philosophy* (Columbia University Press, 1974).

9. Cf. Philo, *De decalogo*, §§ 176-8, in *Works*, edited and translated by F. Colson, G. Whitacker and R. Marcus, 12 vols. Loeb Classical Library (Harvard University Press, 1929-62); see also the discussion in Oliver Leaman, *Evil and Suffering in Jewish Philosophy* (Cambridge University Press, 1995), pp. 37f.

10. Moses Mendelssohn, *Jerusalem or on Religious Power and Judaism*, translated by A. Arkush (University Press of New England, 1983), p. 62.

11. See the articles by E. Dressler (p. 26), Y. Hutner (p. 39), and M. Gifter (p. 56) reprinted in N. Wolpin, *A Path through the Ashes* (Masorah Publications, 1986).

12. D. Landau, *Piety and Power: The World of Jewish Fundamentalism* (Hill & Wang, 1993), p. 141.

13. For example, Norman Lamm calls it 'massively irrelevant, impudent, and insensitive'; *The Face of God* (New York: Yeshiva University, 1982), sec. 2. Cited in D. Birnbaum, *God and Evil: A Jewish Perspective* (Ktav, 1989), pp. 26f..

14. Cf. Job where God is portrayed as rejecting this theodicy in 42.7-8.

15. I. Maybaum, *The Face of God After Auschwitz*. Cited in L. and D. Cohn-Sherbok, *A Short History of Judaism* (Oneworld, 1994), p. 118.

16. Wendy Doniger O'Flaherty suggests that this psychological explanation for sin is primarily a Buddhist tendency, whereas in Hindu texts, past sins are the starting-point for explaining present evil and suffering. W.D. O'Flaherty (ed.), *Karma and Rebirth in Classical Indian Traditions* (University of California Press, 1980), p. xxiii.

17. Ibid.

18. *Mahābhārata Vanaparva* 207.19f.

19. M. Stoeber, *Evil and the Mystics' God: Towards a Mystical Theodicy* (Macmillan, 1992), p. 189.

20. Saadia Gaon, *Book of Theodicy: Translation and Commentary on the Book of Job*, translated by S. Rosenblatt (Yale University Press, 1988), pp. 125f. See also Efros, *Studies in Medieval Jewish Philosophy*, op. cit., pp. 96-100.

21. For an interesting examination of the history of Jewish interpretation of this passage, see Seymour Feldman, 'The Binding of Isaac: A Test-Case of Divine Foreknowledge', in Tamar Rudavsky (ed.), *Divine Omniscience and Omnipotence in Medieval Philosophy. Islamic, Jewish and Christian Perspectives* (Reidel, 1985) pp. 105-33.

22. Kierkegaard's early work *Fear and Trembling* (Penguin, 1986) uses the story of Abraham as a way of exploring these ideas.

23. Feldman, 'The Binding of Isaac: A Test-Case of Divine Foreknowledge', op. cit., p. 124.

24. D. Birnbaum, *God and Evil: A Jewish Perspective* (Ktav, 1989), p. 34.

25. Moses Maimonides, *The Guide of the Perplexed*, translated by S. Pines (Chicago University Press, 1963), III.24, p. 498.

26. See H. Cohen, *Religion of Reason: Out of the Sources of Judaism* (F. Ungar, 1972), and the discussion of Cohen's views in Leaman, *Evil and Suffering in Jewish Philosophy*, op. cit., pp. 157-64.

27. Cohen, *Religion of Reason*, op. cit., p. 18.

28. Ibid., p. 19.

29. M. Stewart, *The Greater Good Defence*, op. cit., p. 145.

30. Cited in Hans Küng, *Judaism Between Yesterday and Tomorrow* (Crossroad, 1992), pp. 585f.

31. M. Stoeber, *Evil and the Mystics' God: Towards a Mystical Theodicy* (Macmillan, 1992).

32. Ibid., p. 188.

33. Ibid., p. 189.

34. Maimonides, *The Guide of the Perplexed*, op. cit., p. 628.

35. From a poem by Eraqi, which begins, 'The instrument of the joy of Love, who knows it?'; in an unpublished translation by Mehri Niknam.

36. Ja'far al-Ṣādiq's commentary on the Qur'anic Moses, in *Early Islamic Mysticism. Sufi, Qur'an, Mi'raj, Poetic and Theological Writings*, edited and translated by M.A. Sells (Paulist Press, 1996), p. 82.

37. J. Hick, *Evil and the God of Love* (Macmillan, 1977).

38. Ibid., pp. 257-9.

39. R.W. Kropf, *Evil and Evolution: A Theodicy* (Fairleigh Dickinson University Press, 1984).

40. Ibid., p. 108.

41. Ibid., p. 109.

42. Ibid., pp. 124f.

43. Ibid., p. 125.

44. Ibid., p. 136.

45. Ibid., p. 159.

46. Birnbaum, *God and Evil*, op. cit., p. 54.

47. Ibid., p. 61.

48. Ibid., p. 65.

49. Cf. Deut. 31.17-18, Isa. 1.12, 8.15, 45.14, 54.8, 57.15, 59.1, 64.10, Job 34.29, 23.3.

50. See the citation from J.B. Soloveitchik in A.R. Besdin, *Reflections of the Rav* (World Zionist Organisation, Department of Torah Education and Culture in the Diaspora, 1979), p. 36. Cited in Birnbaum, *God and Evil*, op. cit., p. 124.

51. Birnbaum cites Eliezer Berkovits in his support: 'In the presence of God, there is no freedom. No one who stands in God's presence can deny him.' Berkovits, *Major Themes in Modern Philosophies of Judaism* (Ktav, 1974), p. 116. See Birnbaum, *God and Evil*, op. cit., p. 134.

52. Ibid., p. 141.

53. Ibid., p. 146.

54. Ibid., p. 148.

55. Ibid., p. 159.

56. Ibid., p. 145.

57. Hans Küng, *Judaism Between Yesterday and Tomorrow* (Crossroad, 1992), pp. 593f.

58. See Griffin, in S.T. Davis (ed.), *Encountering Evil: Live Options in Theodicy* (T. & T. Clark, 1991).

59. L. Ford, in M. Peterson (ed.), *The Problem of Evil: Selected Readings* (University of Notre Dame Press, 1992), p. 249.

60. Griffin, in Davis (ed.), *Encountering Evil*, op. cit., p. 114.

61. Ford, in Peterson (ed.), *The Problem of Evil*, op. cit., p. 257.

62. Madden and Hare in Peterson, ibid., p. 267.

63. R. Rubenstein, *After Auschwitz*: *Radical Theology and Contemporary Judaism* (Bobbs-Merrill, 1966), p. 153.

64. Ibid., p. 46.

65. J.K. Roth, 'A Theodicy of Protest', in Davis (ed.), *Encountering Evil*, op. cit., p. 11.

66. Ibid., p. 14.

67. Ibid., p. 16.

68. Ibid., p. 15.

69. E. Wiesel, *The Oath*, translated by M. Wiesel (Random House, 1973), p. 78.

70. E. Wiesel, *Messengers of God*, translated by M. Wiesel (Random House, 1976), p. 235.

71. Roth, 'A Theodicy of Protest', op. cit., p. 18.

72. Frederick Sontag, 'Anthropodicy and the Return of God', in Davis (ed.), *Encountering Evil*, op. cit., pp. 148f.

73. David R. Griffin, 'Critique of Roth', in Davis (ed.), *Encountering Evil*, op. cit., p. 28.

74. Birnbaum in relating a tale of the early Hasidic master Levi Yitzhak of Berdiczez. See Birnbaum, *God and Evil*, op. cit., p. 31.

75. Cited in Küng, *Judaism Between Yesterday and Tomorrow*, op. cit., p. 605.

76. Leaman, *Evil and Suffering in Jewish Philosophy*, op. cit., p. 190.

77. I. Greenberg, 'Cloud of Smoke, Pillar of Fire: Judaisim, Christianity, and Modernity after the Holocaust', in E. Fleischner (ed.), *Auschwitz*: *Beginning of a New Era*? (Ktav, 1977), pp. 9f.

78. K. Surin, *Theology and the Problem of Evil* (Basil Blackwell, 1986), p. 147.

79. Ibid., p. 149.

80. Surin's own conviction is: 'The principle that the self-revelation of God on the cross of Christ is the self-justification of God is integral to the "practical" approach to the theodicy-problem. In the face of this divine self-justification the attempt by the *human* thinker to justify God vis-à-vis the fact of evil (which of course is what theodicy essentially is) becomes super-fluous. The Christian who takes the atonement seriously has no real need for theodicy.' Ibid., p. 142.

81. T. Tilley, *The Evils of Theodicy* (Georgetown University Press, 1991), p. 3.

82. Ibid., p. 229.

83. Surin, *Theology and the Problem of Evil*, op. cit., p. 51.

84. Tilley, *The Evils of Theodicy*, op. cit., p. 232.

85. James Wetzel, 'Can Theodicy be Avoided? The Claim of Unredeemed Evil', *Religious Studies* 25 (1989), pp. 1-13. Reprinted in Peterson (ed.), *The Problem of Evil*, op. cit., p. 361.

86. Ibid., p. 363.

87. Ibid., p. 362.

88. One surely cannot judge the depth or intensity of the suffering a person has experi-enced simply by a consideration of the events of their life. 'O the mind, mind has mountains; cliffs of fall / Frightful, sheer, no-man-fathomed. Hold them cheap / May who ne'er hung there.' G.M. Hopkins, *The Poems of Gerard Manley Hopkins*, edited by W.H. Gardner and N.H. MacKenzie (Oxford University Press, 1980), p. 100. (First line: 'No worst, there is none. Pitched past pitch of grief.')

89. Eleanor Stump, in a wise observation, cites Tilley: 'Theodicies construct consoling dreams to distract our gaze from real evils', and responds: 'everything depends on what you take to be dream and what you take to be reality'. Stump, in 'Aquinas on the Sufferings of Job', in Daniel Howard-Snyder (ed.), *The Evidential Argument from Evil* (Indiana University Press, 1996), p. 64.

90. Surin, in Peterson (ed.), *The Problem of Evil*, op. cit., p. 343.

91. See Surin, *Theology and the Problem of Evil*, op. cit., pp. 51f.

92. Fergal Keane, 'The day I met a mass killer – and he smirked, knowing he'd escape justice', *Independent*, Saturday 20 June 1998.

93. Antony Flew, 'Theology and Falsification', in Flew and MacIntyre (eds), *New Essays in Philosophical Theology* (SCM Press, 1955), pp. 98f.

94. Gareth Moore, *Believing in God* (T. & T. Clark, 1988), p. 127.
95. Ibid., pp. 128f.

10. Endless Suffering

1. M. Buber, 'The Dialogue between Heaven and Earth' cited in E.L. Fackenheim, *To Mend the World* (Schocken, 1982), p. 196.

2. David O'Connor has recently published a book-length treatment of this issue, which was available to me only after my own work here was completed. It is not given sufficient treatment in what follows, therefore. O'Connor's overall conclusion is that '*both* sides [theism and atheism] are sustained, and that the issue of God and evil remains unsettled, and arguably cannot be settled' (pp. 225-6) and he calls for a 'détente'. David O'Connor, *God and Inscrutable Evil: In Defense of Theism and Atheism* (Rowman & Littlefield, 1998).

3. Stewart observes that Hick, Yandell, and Peterson, all of whom offer defences that have a 'greater good' element, all seem to agree that there is such a thing as gratuitous evil; that is, evil that cannot be justified by any apparent good result. And yet, when their writings are examined, all three nevertheless seem to offer justifications for this allegedly unjustifiable evil. Peterson, for example, has a three-fold justificatory scheme that includes free will, natural law and soul-growth defences. The point is even excessive suffering tends to be taken up into greater good justificatory patterns. M. Stewart, *The Greater Good Defence: Essay on the Rationality of Faith* (Macmillan, 1992), pp. 80f.

4. Daniel Howard-Snyder, 'The Argument from Inscrutable Evil', in D. Howard-Snyder (ed.), *The Evidential Argument from Evil* (Indiana University Press, 1996), p. 307.

5. William Rowe, 'The Evidential Argument from Evil: A Second Look', in Howard-Snyder (ed.), *The Evidential Argument from Evil* (Indiana University Press, 1996), p. 276.

6. Robert McKim, 'Worlds Without Evil', *International Journal for Philosophy of Religion* 15 (1984), pp. 161-70: p. 164. He is supporting the line of argument put forward by Steven E. Boër, 'The Irrelevance of the Free Will Defence', *Analysis* 38.2 (1978), pp. 110-12.

7. R. Swinburne, *The Existence of God* (Clarendon Press, 1979), p. 219.

8. Frank Dilley, 'The Free-Will Defence and Worlds without Moral Evil', *International Journal for Philosophy of Religion* 27 (1990), p. 6. His parodistic citation is of McKim, 'Worlds Without Evil', op. cit., p. 164.

9. George Washington's 'immediate objectives were "the total destruction and devastation of their settlements. It will be essential to ruin their crops in the ground and prevent their planting more".' Brian Masters, *The Evil that Men Do* (Doubleday, 1996/Black Swan edition, 1997), p. 258.

10. C.R. Mesle, *John Hick's Theodicy: A Process Humanist Critique* (Macmillan, 1991), p. 64.

11. E. Ormsby, *Theodicy in Islamic Thought* (Princeton University Press, 1984), p. 21.

12. Al-Ash'arī, *Maqālāt al-islāmīyīn* (ed. Ritter; Istanbul, 1929-33) I, 246. Cited in Ormsby, *Theodicy in Islamic Thought,* op. cit., p. 22.

13. Plantinga writes: 'What is the reason for supposing that *there is* such a thing as a best of all possible worlds?' A. Plantinga, *God, Freedom and Evil* (Allen & Unwin, 1975), p. 34. Aquinas also implicitly rejects the idea, thinking it an important affirmation of God's omnipotence that for every world God creates, he could create a better one. See *Summa Theologica*, vol. I, qn. 25, art. 6, translated by the Fathers of the English Dominican Province; cf. Stewart, *The Greater Good Defence*, op. cit., pp. 57f., and F. Copleston, *A History of Philosophy: Medieval Philosophy*, vol. 2, part II (Doubleday & Company, 1962), p. 89.

14. See, for example: 'An omnipotent God with values like mine would have created us with better natures, a better environment and better freedoms', Mesle, *John Hick's Theodicy*, op. cit., p. 43.

15. Stewart, *The Greater Good Defence*, op. cit., pp. 65f.

16. Stewart's suggestion, ibid., pp. 65-9. There is an immediate logical problem: for almost any necessary evil means that leads to a good end, we can identify a different evil situation that could achieve the same result; therefore no *one particular* evil means could ever be logically necessary. Stewart deals with this objection by adding 'of equal negative value' to the specification.

17. D.Z. Phillips, *Concept of Prayer* (Routledge & Kegan Paul, 1965), p. 93.

18. Yandell argues that allowing something does not entail doing it. It can be wrong to do it, but not wrong to allow it. Moreover, it might not be wrong for *God* to allow something, even though it would be wrong for us to allow it, because God has more power to overcome evil than we do. It might not be negligent for Him, so to speak (this is my phrase, not Yandell's). K.E. Yandell, *The Epistemology of Religious Experience* (Cambridge University Press, 1993), pp. 326f.

19. J.M. Trau, 'The Positive Value of Evil', *International Journal for Philosophy of Religion* 21 (1988), p. 32.

20. Ibid., p. 29.

21. Ibid., p. 31.

22. Oliver Leaman, *Evil and Suffering in Jewish Philosophy* (Cambridge University Press, 1995), p. 191. See Eliezer Berkovits, *Faith after the Holocaust* (Ktav, 1973).

23. Arthur Cohen, *The Tremendum: A Theological Interpretation of the Holocaust* (Crossroad, 1981), p. 1.

24. John K. Roth, 'A Theodicy of Protest', in S.T. Davis (ed.), *Encountering Evil: Live Options in Theodicy* (T. & T. Clark, 1981), pp. 7-22; p. 17.

25. Emil Fackenheim formulated the famous 614th commandment (so called because traditional Jews believe that the number of commandments given by God in scripture is 613). Fackenheim's 614th commandment reads: 'We are, first, commanded to survive as Jews, lest the Jewish people perish. We are commanded, second, to remember in our very guts and bones the martyrs of the holocaust, lest their memory perish. We are forbidden, thirdly, to deny or despair of God, however much we may have to contend with Him or with belief in Him, lest Judaism perish. We are forbidden, finally, to despair of the world as the place which is to become the kingdom of God lest we help make it a meaningless place in which God is dead or irrelevant and everything is permitted. To abandon any of these imperatives, in response to Hitler's victory at Auschwitz, would be to hand him yet other posthumous victories.' Emil L. Fackenheim, 'Transcendence in Contemporary Culture: Philosophical Reflections and a Jewish Theology', in *Transcendence*, edited by Herbert W. Richardson and Donald R. Cutler (Beacon Press, 1969), p. 150.

11. The Perfect Law of Freedom

1. From the first chapter of the Bhagavad-Gītā, verses 20-46, abridged.

2. God's omnipotence is construed by most free will defenders not to entail that God is able to act in ways that are logically impossible, or even self-contradictory. If they are right, this implies that God cannot create person *Y* if person *Y*'s creation would involve a logical contradiction. Now, free will defenders claim that it would involve a logical contradiction to create free beings who lacked the moral freedom to make mistakes. That is, it would be logically impossible to create beings who were free to choose rightly but not free to choose wrongly. Therefore, so the argument goes, God could not have created free moral creatures who lacked the possibility of sin. There is a necessary connection, it is said, between human personality and moral freedom to go wrong; to make us as we are but without this freedom, that is, not free to choose wrongly as well as rightly would be self-contradictory. Therefore, God could not have created free moral creatures without the possibility of sin.

3. See H.A. Wolfson, *The Philosophy of the Kalam* (Harvard University Press, 1976).

4. Qur'an 3:165, 4:79.

5. Cited in E. Ormsby, *Theodicy in Islamic Thought* (Princeton University Press, 1984), p. 19.

6. Cited in ibid., p. 21.

7. For a discussion of Buddhist conceptions of causality and free will, see the interesting discussion in F.Th. Stcherbatsky, *Buddhist Logic* (Dover, 1962), vol. 1, pp. 131-4.

8. R. Sinari, *The Structure of Indian Thought* (Charles C. Thomas, 1970), p. 17.

9. Ibid., p. 19.

10. It is a misconception frequently met with that Indian philosophy entails a withdrawal from or a negation of the world, although that tendency may be more evident in Indian Buddhism than the various philosophies and traditions lumped together as 'Hinduism'. Nayak, in his discussion of Vidyāraṇya's *Pancadaśī,* writes: 'The enlightened one, like an expert who knows and understands two languages, is conversant with both the bliss of Brahman and the worldly joys, and does not see any conflict between the two. The idea of mukti as something mystical and otherworldly is thus entirely ruled out by *Pancadaśī.* It is as if someone has mastery over two different languages; as there is no incongruity here, similar is the case with one having philosophical illumination continuing to be conversant with the worldly affairs. This dispels once and for all the deep-rooted misconception about Indian philosophy that in mukti one is transferred as it were from the mundane existence to a supra-mundane plane of reality, so that the worldly awareness is gone forever. Enlightenment consists in mastering a technique, a philosophical technique, so to say, and this has no conflict with our normal awareness. What is important to note in this connection is that the enlightened person is not affected or disturbed by the pleasure or pain ...; thus and only in this sense he is a free man. The only difference between the enlightened who is free and the unenlightened who is in bondage is that the former remains undisturbed and patient through all his afflictions ..., whereas the latter is impatient and suffers on account of this. This is the sense in which the metaphysical or philosophical concept of freedom in Indian thought, instead of remaining confined to the conceptual level alone, is seen to have a definite bearing on our practical day-to-day life.' G.C. Nayak, *Philosophical Reflections* (Motilal Banarsidass, 1987), pp. 76f. In fact, the enlightened one is in a better position to do good in the world.

11. A. Flew, 'Divine Omnipotence and Human Freedom' in A. Flew and A. MacIntyre (eds), *New Essays in Philosophical Theology* (SCM, 1955), pp. 144-69; cf. on this point pp. 149ff.

12. J.L. Mackie, 'Evil and Omnipotence' reprinted in M. McCord Adams and R. Merrihew Adams (eds), *The Problem of Evil* (Oxford University Press, 1990), p. 33.

13. See A. Plantinga, *The Nature of Necessity* (Clarendon Press, 1974), and *God, Freedom and Evil* (Allen & Unwin, 1975).

14. To create her in such a way that she didn't correspond to her nature is a logical contradiction; so it would be as impossible as making a square circle.

15. Plantinga, *God, Freedom and Evil*, op. cit., p. 48.

16. Some have rejected the possible-worlds-ontology that Plantinga deploys. Kenny raises several critical questions, such as that of what God needs to know in advance in creating an allegedly best possible world. (See, for example, A. Kenny, *The God of the Philosophers* (Clarendon, 1979), pp. 65ff.) For God to create the best possible world, he needs to know in advance which possible world this is; and in order to do this he must know all the counterfactuals: he must, so to speak, know the truth about what isn't true, but what could have been. Stewart suggests that if possible worlds talk is disallowed, Plantinga's defence collapses. However, Plantinga himself gives clear indications that he sits lightly to any 'ontology' of possible worlds; far from claiming as his defence that God has made the best of all possible worlds, he makes it clear that he repudiates such a notion. *God, Freedom and Evil*, op. cit., p. 34. In this case, Kenny's objections that God could not know in advance which is the best possible world in order to create it is entirely misplaced as a refutation of Plantinga. Plantinga also makes it clear that God does not create *any* possible world: '... God does not, strictly speaking, *create* any possible worlds or states of affairs at all. What He creates are the heavens and the earth and all that they contain. But He has not created states of affairs.' Ibid., p. 38. In Plantinga's conception, God creates the theatre but does not write the script; so problems concerning God's foreknowledge of which play ought to be produced therefore are quite irrelevant.

17. J.L. Mackie, *The Miracle of Theism* (Clarendon Press, 1982), pp. 153 and 174.

18. M. Stewart, *The Greater Good Defence: Essays on Rationality and Faith* (Macmillan, 1992), p. 113.

19. Sinari, *The Structure of Indian Thought*, op. cit., p. 50.

20. See H. von Glasenapp, *Buddhism – A Non-Theistic Religion,* trans. I. Schloegel (George Allen & Unwin Ltd., 1970), p. 23.

21. Ibid., p. 30.

22. This discussion has taken place in the context of the debates about causal determinism and moral responsibility, but is clearly relevant here – even if, curiously, these debates from 'mainstream' philosophy have not been raised in the context of theodicy.

23. Harry Frankfurt, 'Alternate Possibilities and Moral Responsibility', *Journal of Philosophy* 66 (December 1969) pp. 828-39. This and a number of related articles are reprinted in John Fischer (ed.), *Moral Responsibility* (Cornell University Press, 1986). A further collection of articles on the question was published by Fischer and Mark Ravizza (eds.), *Perspectives on Moral Responsibility* (Cornell University Press, 1993). These two volumes should be consulted by anyone who wants to investigate the debate in more detail and depth.

24. The general structure of such Frankfurt situations is that one can choose, as one thinks, between two options – while unbeknownst to one, conditions exist that would actually prevent the alternative from being realised, should one choose it.

25. The theological correlate to the FWD/FIP dispute is the question of predestination in Christianity and Islam. Those Christians who believe in predestination may suggest a notion of freedom as 'the liberty of spontaneity' rather than 'the liberty of indifference', as is seen in debates between Luther and Erasmus. The liberty of spontaneity holds that one is free in a choice so long as one wills it, whether or not one had an alternative choice. To use an example from Duns Scotus, even after jumping off a cliff, one's falling is still 'free' (although causally necessary) as long as one continues to wish to fall while doing so. The liberty of indifference holds that freedom is only real where there is a genuine possibility of realising either course of action.

26. Mackie writes: 'one would not be directly aware of any antecedent causes of one's choosing, and equally, therefore, one could not be directly aware of the absence of antecedent causes. Contra-causal freedom, or the lack of it, simply is not the sort of thing of which we could have any "sense", any immediate introspective evidence.' *The Miracle of Theism*, op. cit., p. 167. So in cases where no fully determining causes can be found or experienced, the determinist must assert the existence of determining forces of which we are completely unaware and for which we have no evidence. If there is no evidence of such forces, however, what justification can there be for overriding the testimony of experience – the experience of the *absence* of any such forces or compulsion? It may indeed be the case that we are often caused or determined by unconscious or physiological forces of which we are unaware. But in such cases our experience of our behaviour is most often not so much one of total liberty, as of total inexplicability: 'I don't know why, I just couldn't help myself.' The person suffering from a compulsion to wash her hands repeatedly may be unaware of what compels her. What this means, however, is not that she is unaware of being compelled, but rather that she is unaware of the cause. What she certainly does not say is that she has freely chosen to wash her hands thirty times today.

27. Steven E. Boër, 'The Irrelevance of the Free Will Defence', *Analysis* 38.2 (1978), pp. 110-12; p. 111.

28. Ibid., pp. 111f.

29. Frank Dilley, 'Is the Free Will Defence Irrelevant?', *Religious Studies* 18 (1982), pp. 355-64, p. 357.

30. In Fischer (ed.), *Moral Responsibility*, op. cit., pp. 153ff. In my locked house scenario, one might say that I was not morally responsible for staying at home; for that, there was no alternative. However, I do bear moral responsibility for not trying to leave, even if unsuccessfully.

31. Karl Potter, *Presuppositions of India's Philosophies*, Prentice-Hall, Englewood Cliffs, NJ, 1963, p. 19.

32. Sanskrit *Dharmapada*, *Karmavarga* vi. 4-5, 8, 19, trans. Conze.

33. The philosophical debate may be inextricable from the scientific disputes over freedom and determinism, but there is no clear agreement here either.

34. A. Flew, 'Divine Omnipotence and Human Freedom', op. cit., p. 151.

35. Ibid., p. 153. Mackie, in his later attempt to expand on this issue, locates the dispute between the incompatibilist and the determinist in one understanding of what it means that 'A can do X and A can do Y': the incompatibilist accepts and the determinist rejects that it can mean 'that there is nothing at all that excludes either possibility, in particular, no set of antecedent sufficient causes for his doing X rather than Y, or vice versa.' Mackie, *The Miracle of Theism*, op. cit., p. 167.

36. It is interesting to compare the Flew/Mackie position to the Kantian view of freedom, according to which human beings are only really free when they choose the good; on a Kantian scenario, then, fips would indeed be paragons of 'freedom'. However, this view seems counter-intuitive when contrasted to the ways in which human freedom is usually construed.

37. B. Davies, *Philosophy of Religion: A Guide to the Subject* (Cassell, 1998), discussion of this topic is found on pp. 182-5, 190-2.

38. Ibid., p. 197.

39. Ibid., p. 190.

40. Ibid., p. 184.

41. Potter, *Presuppositions*, op. cit., p. 105.

42. Sinari, *The Structure of Indian Thought*, op. cit., p. 38.

43. Ibid., p. 51.

44. See the discussion in A. Kenny, *The God of the Philosophers*, op. cit., pp. 67-71.

45. There would either have to be no differences, or else the different cultures, religions and so on would all have to be unanimous on any moral question.

46. William Styron, *Sophie's Choice* (Picador, 1992).

47. C.R. Mesle, *John Hick's Theodicy: A Process Humanist Critique* (Macmillan, 1991), pp. 42f.

48. Potter, *Presuppositions*, op. cit., p. 19.

49. Mackie, 'Evil and Omnipotence', op. cit., p. 34.

50. An approach which describes a number of different 'faculties' we have such as 'reason', 'will', 'passions' and handles them as if they were separate objects in our minds.

51. So argues Nayak, *Philosophical Reflections*, op. cit., p. 73. See the Brahma-Sutras, 1.1.4.

52. See Gwen Griffith-Dickson, *Johann Georg Hamann's Relational Metacriticism* (Walter de Gruyter, 1995), p. 478, and the discussion on pp. 194-8.

53. The realisation or actualisation of something, as opposed to potential, in Aristotle's system.

54. James 1.25.

55. Abridged from J.G. Hamann, 'The Knight of the Rose-Cross', N III 27:2-14; in Griffith-Dickson, *Johann Georg Hamann's Relational Metacriticism*, op. cit., p. 463.

The Call of the Real

1. Ja'far al-Ṣādiq's commentary on the Qur'anic Moses, in M.A. Sells (ed. and trans.), *Early Islamic Mysticism. Sufi, Qur'an, Mi'raj, Poetic and Theological Writings* (Paulist Press, 1996), p. 81.

2. Plato, *Meno*, in Plato, *Protagoras and Meno*, translated by W. Guthrie (Penguin Books, 1979).

3. *Brahmasiddhi* IV.1.

4. J.G. Hamann, 'Philological Ideas and Doubts', in Gwen Griffith-Dickson, *Johann Georg Hamann's Relational Metacriticism* (Walter de Gruyter, 1995), p. 481.

5. Jacques Lacan, 'The Subversion of the Subject and the Dialectic of Desire in the Freudian Unconscious', in Jacques Lacan, *Écrits: A Selection* (Routledge, 1997), p. 301. I have omitted references to Hegel and Freud.

6. *Iśa Upaniṣad* 9, in Radhakrishnan's translation.

7. Jacques Lacan, *Encore. On Feminine Sexuality: The Limits of Love and Knowledge*, translated with notes by Bruce Fink (Norton, *c.* 1998), p. 71.

8. Maybe it isn't women who are 'missing something', as Freudian accounts tend to assert?

9. Bice Benvenuto and R. Kennedy, *The Works of Jacques Lacan* (Free Association Books, 1988), pp. 191f.

10. Recall the end of our poem from Eraqi: 'Even more strange, is that though I see your radiant Beauty, yet, I don't know what I perceive, so ignorant am I, – I don't know. All I know, is that the world is bright, day and night, from your Face, but are you the sun or the iridescent moon? – I don't know. Fettered am I in Eraqi, a prisoner of your separation, will I be released from this captivity? – I don't know.'

11. Another poem by Eraqi, which begins, 'The instrument of the joy of Love, who knows it?'; in an unpublished translation by Mehri Niknam.

Glossary

ad hominem. A form of argument in which one attempts to disprove a person's views by attacking the person. Or arguing in a way that does not advance matters unless one holds a particular set of beliefs.

Advaita Vedānta. A tradition of Vedānta, sometimes said to have begun with Gauḍapāda. Its principal thinker was Śankara (Śamkara) (eighth century CE). Of the three 'ways' to salvation, it places greatest emphasis on the way of knowledge (see Three Ways). The purpose of philosophy is to lead to liberation from the bondage of our existence. This bondage arises from ignorance, and therefore liberation is achieved by its removal. True knowledge reveals that Brahman is Ultimate reality, absolute and unchanging. All that seems to be other than Brahman, whether objects in the world or individual selves, is appearance. Brahman as absolute can be with attributes or without them. Ultimate reality is Brahman without attributes: nirguna. It is unconditioned, indescribable (not an abstraction or nothing); eternal Being, pure consciousness. It assumes different forms because it is its nature to express itself, but it is beyond name or form; it cannot be separated into itself and its attributes (e.g. doesn't 'have consciousness'). Nirguṇa is logically prior, indeterminate and absolute; 'saguṇa' is determinate, called Īśvara. It is a relational reality, a mode of Brahman's expression which makes the empirical world possible. This is what makes it possible to know Brahman by many names and forms; which ultimately themselves are unreal. This manifold however is to be transcended in ultimate knowledge. Īśvara is immanent in the world, the inner self, 'inner ruler', judge of individual souls and gives reward, according to laws of karma. The self, ātman, is Brahman. The apparent differences are due to ignorance; there is no ontological difference between them. Therefore *real* knowledge is beyond the dualism of subject-object, of knower and known. This division, like all others, is false.

Ahimsā. The Jain doctrine of non-violence, non-hurting.

al-Ash'arī, Abu'l-Ḥasan (873 or 874-935 or 936) Islamic theologian who reacted against the Hellenisation of Islamic thought. Founder of the Ash'arite school, often uncompromising on questions relating to predetermination and God's powers.

al-Basrī, Ḥasan (d. 728) and Basrīan school. Ascetic and Islamic philosopher, an influence on the Mu'tazilite school. His circle was perhaps first centre of discussions in Islamic philosophy and theology, initially in raising debates on freewill and predestination. He believed in human free will in order to defend God's justice.

al-Fārābī, Abū Naṣr (*c.* 870-950). Islamic Aristotelian philosopher. He imported Aristole's logic into Islamic thought. He was also influenced by neo-Platonism, portraying creation as an emanation. See *The Virtuous City*.

al-Ghazālī, Abū Ḥāmid Muhammad (1059-1111). Islamic Ash'arite theologian who taught at Baghdad, he eventually abandoned theology for a life of contemplation. He was a notorious critic of the claims of Aristotelian philosophers; emphasising intuition above reason. See his *The Incoherence of the Philosophers*.

al-Jāḥiẓ, Abū 'Uthman 'Amr ibn Bakr al-Basrī (766-868). Born in Basra to a working-class family, his mother recognised his academic potential and encouraged him to become a writer – successfully, for he wrote 200 works on a variety of subjects from science to philosophy, poetry, grammar and zoology. He was one of the first to write on such subjects accessibly for the non-specialist. He asserted the importance of evil as well as good in

282

creation, particularly in stimulating our thought and inspiring trust in God. Everything in creation is ultimately beneficial and shows the signs of Allah.

al-Kindī, Yaqub ibn Isḥāq (d. after 866). An early Islamic philosopher who taught at Baghdad. He introduced neo-Platonic and Aristotelian thought into Islamic philosophy, himself translating the works of Aristotle and Plotinus. He tended to emphasise faith over reason.

al-Ma‘arī, Abū al-‘Alā’ (973-1057). Syrian poet, one of the greatest in the Arabic tongue, and something of a sceptic, who declared that there is no imam but reason. He was also a vegetarian and an exponent of animal rights.

al-Mu‘tamir, Bishr ibn (d. 825). Muslim thinker who established the Baghdad school of *kalam*.

al-Naẓẓām, Ibrāhīm ibn Sayyār (d. 835 to 845). Basrian Mu‘tazilite theologian, who advocated the use of sceptical method in philosophy to move beyond faith to true knowledge.

al-Ṣādiq, Ja‘far (702-765). One of the twelve Imams of the early Shi’ite movement in *kalam*. He was among the masters of the members of the House of the Prophet; highly respected for his truthfulness, generosity, spirituality and wisdom.

Anselm, St. (1033-1109) Christian medieval philosopher; born in Aosta, archbishop of Canterbury 1093-1109. Most famous for using the concept of God as ‘that than which nothing greater can be conceived’ in order to prove that this God must exist – the so-called ‘Ontological Argument’. See *Monologion, Proslogion*.

Aquinas, Thomas (1225-74). Christian Dominican philosopher and theologian. He attempted a synthesis of Christian doctrine and the philosophy of Aristotle. He is famous for propounding Five Ways in which the existence of God can be demonstrated. He wrote the multi-volume works *Summa contra Gentiles* and *Summa Theologica*.

Arama, Isaac ben Moses (*c.* 1420-94). Spanish Jewish thinker. Author of the influential *Akedat Yizhak* (*Binding of Isaac*). He wrote on the relation between faith and reason, arguing that reason should not be the judge of faith. He was a critic of the rationalism of Maimonides.

Aristotle (384-322 BCE). Greek philosopher. Pupil of Plato and teacher of Alexander the Great. Invented the discipline of logic and pioneered ethics and physics. He stressed empiricism and natural science. Many traditional theological concepts derive from Aristotle, substance, for example.

Ātman. The soul or self in Hinduism, Buddhism, Jainism.

Augustine of Hippo (354-430). Christian theologian. A convert from Manichaeanism to Christianity. His most famous works are his autobiography, *The Confessions* and *The City of God*.

Averroës, see Ibn Rushd

Avicenna, see Ibn Sīna

Barth, Karl (1886-1968). Swiss Protestant theologian, whose thinking is variously described as ‘dialectical theology’ (because it sees not a continuity but a contradiction or a ‘dialectic’ between God and humanity) or ‘Neo-Orthodoxy’. A critic of the Enlightenment and of nineteenth-century Neo-Protestantism and Liberal Protestant Theology, his early work on the *Epistle to the Romans* established his reputation. His huge, many-volumed *Church Dogmatics* was not completed before his death. He emphasised the central place of God’s self-revelation in Scripture; his focus was not on human experience or ‘religion’, but on God’s revelation.

Berkeley, George (1685-1753). Bishop in Ireland, of English descent. Principal philosophical work is *Principles of Human Knowledge*. One of the ‘British empiricists’, he is commonly viewed as an idealist because of his doctrine that ‘to be is to be perceived’, leading some to suppose that he believes that all perceptions are really just ideas in the mind. However, because he believes that God perceives all and all is dependent on God, it seems more accurate to suppose him to be a realist who believes that things are independent of the human mind (though not God’s).

Berkovits, Eliezer (1900-92). A Transylvanian Jew who lived in Germany and England before emigrating to Australia and then the United States. His work is an attempt to provide a theological response to the Holocaust.

Boethius, Anicius Manlius Torquatus Severinus (480-524). Christian philosopher. His most famous book, *The Consolation of Philosophy*, is an attempt to show how the soul can reach the vision of God through philosophy.

Brahman. Ultimate, unconditioned Reality; (variously) the divine being.

Buber, Martin (1878-1965). A Viennese Jew who grew up in Poland. He was a member of the Zionist movement and an advocate of Hebrew Humanism (working for reconciliation with the Arab people of Palestine. He is well-known for his religious philosophy of dialogue, set out in *I and Thou*. He was also involved in fostering Jewish-Christian understanding.

Bultmann, Rudolf (1884-1976). German New Testament scholar. He was a pioneer of form criticism and an advocate of historical research. He used Heidegger's existentialist philosophy to interpret the Bible. He is most famous for his attempts to 'demythologise' the New Testament.

Calvin, John (1509-64). French Christian reformer. His most influential book is *Institutes of the Christian Religion*, which became a standard reading for Protestants. He is well-known for his views on predestination.

Cārvāka. (Pronounced 'Charvaka'). An early materialist philosophy, atheistic, sceptical and hedonistic in nature. Said to be founded by the thinker Cārvāka, an Indian sage who was mentioned in the Mahābhārata, castigated in the *Bhagavad Gītā*. Matter alone is real. There is no God, soul, life after death; nor even good and evil, right and wrong merit and demerit. Only perception yields knowledge; thus its epistemology is positivist in nature. What is imperceptible has no existence. See Lokāyata materialism.

Cohen, Arthur (1928-86). Jewish theologian most famous for his work on post-holocaust theology. See *Tremendum*. He proposed that human beings, rather than God, should be held responsible for the holocaust.

Cohen, Hermann (1842-1918). German Jewish neo-Kantian philosopher. He developed a form of moral argument for the existence of God, conceived as an idea; the idea of God is the only ground for believing that moral obligations can be fulfilled. In *Religion of Reason out of the Sources of Judaism* he attempted to redefine the core features of the Jewish faith in accordance with reason.

Crescas, Hasdai (1340-1412). Spanish Jewish theologian and statesman. As a statesman, he was concerned with combating Christian propaganda against the Jews. As a theologian, he was critical of Aristotelianism and the work of Maimonides.

Dharma. Fundamental concept in Indian philosophy. It refers to the order which makes life and the universe possible.

Daud, Abraham ben (1110-80). Jewish philosopher, physician, historian and astronomer. Born in Cordoba and lived in Spain until his death. His most important philosophical work is, *Exalted Faith* (*Emunah Ramah*), which addresses the problems of determinism and free-will.

Descartes, René (1596-1650). French philosopher and mathematician. One of the principal founders of modern philosophy. He advocated methodological doubt – abandoning all one's prior assumptions in order to reach certainty. With the proposition 'I think, therefore I am', Descartes believed he had found certainty. See *Discourse on Method* and *Meditations*.

Duns Scotus, John (*c.* 1266-1308). Scottish Christian theologian. After becoming a Franciscan he taught in London and Paris. He was a prominent critic of the philosophy of Aquinas, arguing that faith cannot be rationally established and thus must be kept separate from philosophy. He wrote *Treatise on the First Principle*.

Ebner, Ferdinand (1882-1931). Austrian Catholic thinker, a school teacher, who wrote an early work *The Word and the Spiritual Realities* and a journal later published in several volumes. None of his work has been translated into English except in isolated passages. One of the personalists, or early thinkers in the 'dialogical philosophy', the heart of his thinking was the I-Thou relationship: not merely between human persons, but also between humanity and God. Language and dialogue play a central role. Influential on philosophers like Buber as well as theologians like Emil Brunner.

Epicurus. (431-270 BCE). Greek philosopher who proposed that the aim of philosophy is to enable us to live well.

Erasmus, Desiderius (*c*. 1466/9-1536). Influential Catholic Dutch humanist, scholar and statesman. He wrote *On the Freedom of the Will* against Luther, and *In Praise of Folly* against evils in the contemporary church and state.

Eschatology. That part of theology which is to do with the 'end times' or 'last things'.

Fackenheim, Emil (b. 1917). German Jewish Reform rabbi. He is best known for his later theological work in which he explored the religious implications of the holocaust.

fip. A freely impeccable person (Griffith-Dickson coinage, not in common parlance).

Gaon, Saadia ben Joseph (882-942). The earliest Jewish philosopher of the medieval period. Influenced by the Mu'tazalite kalām philosophers, he wrote treatise on a number of subjects. His most important philosophical work is *The Book of Beliefs and Opinions*. In an attempt to refute the claims of Christians, Muslims and Zoroastrians, he argued that there are four sources of knowledge: sense experience, intuition of self-evident truths, logical inference and reliable tradition.

Gersonides [Levi ben Gershom] (1288-1344). Jewish philosopher, halakhist and scientist. Gersonides rejected the view of the Aristotelian philosophers that the existence of God, as Prime Mover, could be deduced from motions within the universe. Instead he proposes a form of the argument by design – a proof of the existence of God is based on the orderly processes that take place within the world. He argues that the regularity of certain processes implies that they are caused by an intelligence. His most famous book is *The Wars of the Lord*.

Hamann, Johann Georg (1730-88). German Lutheran theologian and philosopher. He pioneered a holistic approach, attacking the dualism (for example, reason/passion) of many prominent Enlightenment philosophers.

Hegel, Georg Wilhelm Friedrich (1770-1831). One of the most influential of Western philoso-phers, although very difficult to understand. Principal themes include the importance of history, 'dialectic' and alienation. Came to believe that all reality is ultimately mental, hence espoused a form of idealism, which conceived of history as the process of Absolute Mind realising itself in history.

Heidegger, Martin (1889-1976). Student of Husserl, therefore schooled in phenomenology, using philosophical method to analyse immediate experience; also influenced by Kierkegaard. Heidegger's work is one of the foundations of existentialism. His large early work, *Being and Time*, attempts to analyse human existence or being in the world (*Dasein*). Later work increasingly focused on the nature of language.

Herder, Johann Gottfried von (1744-1803). German Lutheran philosopher and historian. An influential figure on the German romantic movement. He dissented from the typical Enlightenment stress on universal laws, emphasising instead history and culture. One of the first philosophers, following Hamann, to link reason and language.

Hester Panim. Hebrew term meaning 'the hiding of the face'.

Hume, David (1711-76). Scottish empiricist philosopher and historian. Notorious for his crit-icisms of Christian beliefs, for example, belief in miracles and in life after death. See *Essay Concerning Human Understanding* and *Dialogues Concerning Natural Religion*.

Ibn Rushd [Averroës] (1126-98). A highly influential Islamic Aristotelian philosophers. Most of his works were commentaries on Aristotle. His aim was to rescue Aristotle's work from the corruption of Platonic notions. Against the rationalism of al-Ghazālī, he wrote *Incoherence of the Incoherence*.

Ibn Sīnā [Avicenna] (980-1037). Islamic neo-Platonist philosopher. Born in Bukhara, a wandering court scholar who died in Isfahan. He popularised a neo-Platonic version of Aristotelianism, which had a huge influence on thirteenth-century Christian scholasticism.

Irenaeus (*c*. 115-90). Christian church father, born in Asia Minor. He wrote at length against Gnosticism. He is well known for his theory of recapitulation – people who lived prior to Christ could still be saved through Christ.

Kabbala [cabbala]. Hebrew term meaning 'that which is handed down'. The term first referred to the books of the Jewish scriptures other than the Pentateuch; around 1200 its use was extended to cover the oral tradition of the Mishnah and Talmud. It combines angelology, cosmology, gnosticism and magic and has become a esoteric mystical tradition of interpreting the Jewish scriptures.

Kalām. Arabic term for 'speech'. The term is used to refer to a variety of Muslim theological schools existing between the eighth and the eleventh century. These schools used philosophical proofs to justify religious doctrines. It has a similar role in Islam to the role of scholasticism in Christian theology. The practitioners of *kalām* were referred to as the *Mutakallimūn*. Mu'tazalite scholars emphasised that rational argument had a vital role to play in religious matters, and they attempted to employ Greek philosophy in the service of their faith.

Kant, Immanuel (1724-1804) German philosopher. In later life, wrote three 'Critiques' which have been extremely influential on Western philosophy: *Critique of Pure Reason* (1781), *Critique of Practical Reason* (1788), and *Critique of Judgement* (1790). The first Critique is concerned with knowledge, what can be known by pure reason and without experience. The second is concerned with action, especially moral action. The third is concerned with aesthetic and teleological judgements. He called his stance transcendental or critical idealism.

Kaplan, Mordecai (1881-1983). Jewish theologian. A Lithuanian Jew who emigrated to the United States as a child. Kaplan's work, *Judaism as a Civilisation*, is the foundation of the Reconstructivist movement within Judaism. He proposed a naturalistic conception of religion, with Judaism being seen as an evolving religious civilisation. Accusations of atheism and heresy led to his excommunication.

Karma. Literally meaning action, then the effects of action, it refers more specifically to the doctrine in Hinduism, Buddhism and Jainism that the conditions of one's present existence are the effects of acts committed in previous existences.

Kierkegaard, Søren Aaby (1813-55). Danish Lutheran philosopher and theologian. Famous for the declaration that 'truth is subjectivity'; emphasising that faith implies a decision, he is known as one of the most prominent modern exponents of fideism. See *Concluding Unscientific Postscript*.

Leibniz, Gottfried Wilhelm (1646-1716). German philosopher. Produced one of the great rationalist systems of the seventeenth century. Responsible for the notion that this is the best of all possible worlds. See his *Discourse on Metaphysics, Theodicy, and Monadology*.

Lokāyata Materialism. The earliest form of atheistic materialism in India. The earliest mentioned thinker is Brihaspati Lanka, who is mentioned in the Rgveda; he believed that matter was the ultimate reality, and did not believe in God, the immortality of the soul, or an afterlife. Other thinkers and important texts include Brigu, Parsvanatha (eighth century BCE), Kautsa, Purāna Kāsyapā, Makkhali Gosala, Ajita Kesa Kambalī. See also Cārvāka.

Luria, Isaac (1534-1572). Jewish kabbalist. Grew up in Egypt, moving to Safed, Israel, where he lived until his death. He studied the early Jewish mystical tradition and developed this into a doctrine of his own. Luria conceived of creation as a negative act. The infinite had to bring into being an empty space by removing the divine light, so that there was a space for creation to take place in. This divine contraction was termed *Tsimtsum*, a form of divine exile.

Luther, Martin (1483-1546). German Christian. One of the principle reformers. Famous for the doctrine of justification by faith; a doctrine which led him to deny the need for a priesthood and reject the idea that the church was a mediator between people and God. His famous Ninety-Five Theses attacked current catholic abuses, notably the practice of granting indulgences. He was tried in Augsburg in 1518, he finally broke with the catholic church and was excommunicated. His writings include *To the Christian Nobility of the German Nation* and *The Freedom of the Christian*.

Madhva (thirteenth century CE). Founder of a dualist form of Vedānta. God is one, but the world and individual selves are also ultimately real, but are dependent on God. He has a 'realist' epistemology: things can be known as they are, and sense-perception is valid. Against Śankara, he believes that God is never free from attributes. God's attributes and actions are the same as God himself.

Mādhyamika (second century CE). 'Middle School' of Buddhism, also known as Śūnyavāda (śūnya = empty). No object of intellectual knowledge is real. Genuine insight into Being cannot be delivered by the intellect. Reality is completely nonaccessible to reason. See also Nāgārjuna. Other thinkers include Arya Deva (third century CE), Buddhapalita (fifth century CE), Chadrakirti (seventh century CE).

Mahābhārata. One of the two major epics of Indian scriptures, the other being the *Rāmāyana*.

Mahāvīr, Mahāvīra (*c*. 599-527 BCE). Indian ascetic and wandering preacher. Regarded by Jains as the greatest teacher in their tradition.

Mahāyāna. One of the two major traditions of Buddhism, literally the 'greater vehicle'.

Maimonides, Moses [Moses ben Maimon] (1135-1204). Spanish Jewish philosophical theologian. He fled Spain during a period of persecution, settling in Fez and then Cairo where he became head of the Jewish community. He attempted to reconcile Jewish thought with the philosophy of Aristotle. He was concerned with the relation between reason and faith, writing *Guide of the Perplexed* to show how they could be reconciled. His work influenced Aquinas.

Maṇḍana Miśra. Indian Advaita Vedānta philosopher probably of the eighth century CE; although not only the details but even the basic facts about his life and identity are uncertain. According to tradition, he was a pupil of Kumārila, and wrote several works in the Bhaṭṭa Mīmāṃsā tradition. Sent with his wife to debate with Śankara, he ended up being converted by him to Śankara's vision of Advaita Vedānta. He is the author of the *Brahmasiddhi*, a very important work in the Advaita Vedāntin tradition.

Marcel, Gabriel (1889-1973). French catholic existentialist. He proposed a mid-way between scholasticism and atheistic existentialism. See *Being and Having* and *The Mystery of Being*.

Māyā. A term used in Indian philosophy referring to delusion or illusion.

Maybaum, Ignaz (1897-1976). Jewish rabbi and theologian. Born in Vienna, moving to Berlin and then London. He developed a very influential post-Holocaust theology, the focal point of which is the idea of God's covenant with Israel. See *The Face of God after Auschwitz*.

Mendelssohn, Moses (1729-1786). German Jewish enlightenment philosopher. He was concerned to modernise Jewish life, to this end he translated the Pentateuch into German. He wrote a number of philosophical works arguing for the existence of God, and defending the role of reason *vis-à-vis* faith.

Mīmāṃsā. Sometimes divided into Pūrva Mīmāṃsā and Uttara Mīmāṃsā. Arising around the fourth century BCE, a non-theistic school of Vedānta. It was suggested by its first thinkers, Jaimini in Mīmāṃsā *Sūtra* and Kumārila Bhaṭṭa in *Ślokavārtikka* that karma and the universal order need not presuppose the existence of a divine being. If karma is under the rule of God, it is a tautological category; if God is subordinate to the universal law of karma, God is not almighty and transcendent. Pūrva Mīmāṃsā heavily emphasised the rituals and practices of Vedic religion. Other thinkers include Prabhākāra, Parthasarathi. In their metaphysics, the empirical world is real, and not dependent on the knower. Their epistemology is realist; all knowledge is self-valid.

Mokṣa, Moksha. Liberation. Ultimate salvation in Indian religions, especially Hinduism.

Mullā Sadr al-Dīn, Muhammad ibn Ibrāhīm Shīrāzi [Mullā Sadrā] (1571-1640). Shi'ite philosopher, born in Iran. He was concerned to reconcile Islam with Aristotelian philosophy and Gnostic systems. The controversial nature of his work forced him into frequent exile. See *The Four Journeys*.

Mutakallimūn. See *Kalām*.

mutatis mutandis. Latin term used in philosophy to mean 'with the necessary changes';

adapted as necessary to the present case.

Mu'tazilite. See *Kalām*.

Nāgārjuna. A philosopher of the second century CE of the Buddhist Mādhyamika school. Author of the *Mādhyamika Karika*. Ultimate reality cannot be known by the intellect. Reality is ultimate emptiness; both being and nothingness, neither being nor nothingness. The empirical world is unreal.

Nietzsche, Friedrich (1844-1900). German philosopher, controversial both on political grounds (scornful of democracy and egalitarianism, hostile to women) and on his philosophical importance (an influential philosopher or a mere aphorist and essayist?) His work can be interpreted in many ways, which has contributed to the diverse influence he has on twentieth-century philosophy, e.g. on existentialism and postmodernism. Raised critical and subversive questions about the possibility and nature of knowledge, morality, objectivity, rationality, 'facts' and truth; as well as the relationship between language and thought. Bitterly critical of religion and metaphysics.

Nirvāṇa, nibbāna. Release from existence, liberation, enlightenment in Buddhism.

Nyāya. 'Right reasoning'. An Indian philosophical school, the most concerned with epistemology and logic. Its metaphysics and epistemology are 'realist'; things and the world are real and independent of our mind or spirit. They are not all aspects of one reality; hence Nyāya philosophy is also 'pluralist'. Nature includes both nature, or matter, and spirit. Both are independent and real. Consciousness is partly a matter of spirit and not simply a function of the material body. God is one; omniscient, omnipotent, by which he guides the universe, directs souls inspiring them to act in accordance with their karma. Arguments were put forward to prove the existence of God.

Otto, Rudolf (1869-1937). German protestant theologian. Famous for his analysis of religious feelings which he viewed as potentially valid experiences of the transcendent. See *The Idea of the Holy*.

Patañjali. Principal exponent of Yoga, wrote *Yoga Sūtras*.

Philo (25 BCE – 50 CE). Alexandrian Jewish philosopher. Philo's writings are the fullest source of knowledge available about the philosophy of this crucial period. Philo himself combined Hellenistic philosophy and Alexandrian Judaism.

Plotinus (*c.* 205-270 CE). Neoplatonist philosopher in Alexandria, later taught in Rome. His writings were later gathered into the *Enneads*. Ultimately all derives from The One, which is The Good. Mind emanates from the One, and Soul emanates from Mind; and thereafter the material world comes from Soul. Our ultimate goal should be to return to The One through contemplation.

Radhakrishnan, Sarvepalli. Twentieth-century Indian philosopher and scholar.

Rahner, Karl (1904-84). German catholic theologian, instrumental in Vatican II. He attempted to reformulate traditional Thomist theology through the influence of Heidegger. He proposed that theology must start from human experience, particularly transcendental experience. See *The Foundations of Christian Faith*.

Rāmānuja (eleventh century CE). Rāmānuja's Vedānta is a 'qualified non-dualism' as compared to Śankara. Rāmānuja agrees with Śankara that the absolute has the nature of consciousness, is foundation of all. Unlike Śankara, he considers God to be personal. Religiosity can find no meaning in an absolute with no qualities and no feeling, thought, will. It doesn't meet our deepest needs, especially for fellowship and communion with an other. The Supreme Other must be a personality. His view is 'identity in and through and because of difference' (in Radhakrishnan's words). Individual existence is not illusory but real; liberation involves a gain of knowledge and bliss, not identification with God, and this comes about from continual remembrance of God.

Rāmāyana. One of the two major epics of Indian scriptures, the other being the *Mahābhārata*.

Rosenzweig, Franz (1886-1929). Jewish philosopher, like Ebner and Buber a 'personalist' or dialogical philosopher. Wrote *The Star of Redemption, Understanding the Sick and the Healthy* and 'The New Thinking'. His work, critical of mainstream philosophy and its attitudes to thought, time and totality, proposes instead a dialogical or narrative philosophy, whose starting point is the triad God-World-Humanity.

Rubenstein, Richard (b. 1924). Jewish theologian and Conservative rabbi. His most important work is *After Auschwitz*. Rubenstein argues that it is impossible to hold a traditional view of God after Auschwitz. He proposes that a form of mystical Jewish paganism or nature worship would be the most appropriate expression of piety for today.

Saadia, Saadya. See Gaon.

Saṃsāra. In Indian religions and philosophy, the cycle of birth, death, rebirth.

Śankara, Śamkara [Śankaracarya] (*c*. 788-820). Indian religious philosopher. One of the most influential thinkers in the history of Indian religions.

Sāṇkhya or Sāmkhya. An Indian philosophical school, largely non-theistic. It emphasises the reality of the empirical world. The world has no beginning or end; it has its origins in an uncaused cause, and it continues to unfold and develop. The whole of the physical universe has its origin in prakṛti, 'nature' or 'matter'. 'Spirit' or 'consciousness', puruṣa is different; matter is not an aspect of it. The mental, the intellect, is identified with prakṛti not puruṣa. Puruṣa is formless, freedom, independent of qualities, pure consciousness, inactive, free from change, free from attachments. Puruṣa is plural: we are not all part of the same puruṣa. Each spirit is independent. Puruṣa is distinguished from the 'empirical self' (jīva). Jīva is temporal, changing, acting, whereas puruṣa is not. Jīva is the self as determined by the body. It experiences pain, pleasure, has other mental modes, unlike puruṣa. See yoga.

Satori. Zen state of enlightenment.

Sautrānika. One of two main schools of Theravāda Buddhism, the other being Vaibhāṣika. It arose around the fourth century CE. It holds that the external world is real and perceptible, but still accepts the momentariness of reality central to Buddhism.

Schleiermacher, Friedrich Daniel Ernst (1768-1834). German Christian reformed theologian and preacher. A core member of the romantic movement in Berlin. He argued that religion was principally a matter of feeling and intuition, not dogma. He famously defined religion as 'the feeling of absolute dependence'. He is often regarded as the father of modern Protestant theology. See *On Religion: Speeches to its Cultured Despisers* and *The Christian Faith*.

Spinoza, Baruch [Bendict de Spinoza] (1632-77). A Dutch Jewish thinker, one of the earliest representatives of the Jewish Enlightenment. At the age of twenty-three he was excommunicated from the Jewish community for his heretical beliefs. Spinoza denied both creation and freedom, arguing that God is the totality of all bodies in the physical universe. He proposed that religion had to do with ethics, whereas philosophy had to do with truth.

Soloveitchik, Joseph (1903-93). Polish Jewish Talmudic expert and rabbi.

Śūnya, śūnyatā. A particular concept of emptiness in Buddhism. See Mādhyamika.

Sureśvara. See also Maṇḍana Miśra; traditions say that the two are the same, Maṇḍana taking the name Sureśvara after his conversion to Śankara's teaching, although some scholars doubt this. Indian Advaita Vedāntin philosopher. It is said that Śankara gave him the task of commenting on two of his own works. Works attributed to him most reliably include commentaries on Śankara's commentaries on several important Upaniṣads: the *Brhadāranyakopaniṣadbhāsyavārtikka* – long in content as well as in name – the *Taittirīyopanisadbhāsyavartikka, Naiskarmyasiddhi;* he is also credited with authorship of the *Dakṣināmurtivartikka* (or *Mānasollāsa*) and the *Pañcīkaranavārtikka* (or *Pranavavārtikka)*.

Sūtra. A saying or aphorism, it also refers to the collection of sayings of Indian sages.

Svatantra-Vijñānavāda. See also Vijñānavāda. A school of Buddhist logic arising within the Vijñānavāda school of Mahāyāna Buddhism. Outstanding exponents were Diṇnāga (sixth century CE), Dharmakīrti (seventh century CE), Santaraksita and Kamalasila (eighth century CE). In addition to the 'idealist' aspect of the Vijñānavāda school, it emphasises the 'momentariness' of reality as taught by Buddhism: knowledge only reflects moments of existence; there is no permanence in anything that is an object of knowledge or consciousness. An object of knowledge is not the same from one moment to the next.

Tathāgata. An honorary name for the Buddha, Gautama Siddhārtha; it means 'thus gone.'

Tathāta. 'Thusness' or 'suchness'; used by Aśvaghosa to speak of 'non-self'.

Teilhard de Chardin, Pierre (1881-1955). French catholic theologian and palaeontologist. His reputation is based on the book *The Phenomenon of Man*, where he argued that God is part of the evolutionary process. Christ is portrayed as the centre of the evolutionary process which is moving towards the Omega Point. His general attempt to unify science and theology has been more influential than the details of his theory.

Tertullian (*c.* 160-225). From Carthage, converted to Christianity in his thirties. One of the Church Fathers of the Western (Latin) Church. Insisted on the sufficiency of the Bible as opposed to secular philosophy for the knowledge of God.

Theodicy. A term first used in its modern form by the philosopher Leibniz in 1710. The term goes back to a Greek word for 'justification of God'.

Theravāda. Literally 'The Teaching of the Elders'. One of two main traditions of Buddhism, also referred to as 'Hīnayāna' (the lesser vehicle). The other is Mahāyāna.

Three Ways. A Hindu tradition that there are three ways to salvation: of knowledge (jñana-marga), of devotion (bhakti-marga), and of action (karma-marga). These are not in opposition to each other, but are there for the sake of different types of people. Nyāya, Sānkhya, Yoga, Advaita Vedānta, Buddhist and Jain systems all favour the way of knowledge; bhakti by is favoured Rāmānuja, Madhva, Nimbarka, Vallabha, Mahaprabhu Chaitanya, and Pūrva Mīmāmsā and other traditions of popular practice favour action and ritual.

Tillich, Paul Johannes (1886-1965). German Lutheran philosopher and theologian. He portrayed God as the ground of Being, who can be known through ultimate concern. See his three-volume *Systematic Theology*.

Tochācha. A Jewish concept based on Lev. 26 and Deut. 28. Essentially it is the idea that humans not God cause evil. This concept was important in early mediaeval Jewish philosophical theology (particularly in the work of Saadia ben Joseph Gaon), and has been used in more recent times with reference to the Holocaust.

Tsimtsum. Divine contraction. See Luria.

Upanisads. Literally, 'the final parts of the Vedas'. Sections of philosophical reflections added to the Vedas, the Hindu scriptures. See Vedas.

Vaibhāṣika. One of two main schools of Theravāda Buddhism, the other being the Sautrāntika school. It arose around the second century CE and its outlook was one of straightforward realism. Objects are real, external to the mind, and lasting (cf. Svatantra-Vijñānavāda).

Vaiśesika. A school of Hinduism which arose between the sixth and third centuries BCE. It developed independently from Nyāya, but because of the similarities of views it is often assimilated to Nyāya and referred to as Nyāya-Vaiśesika. Its founder was Kaṇada. The Vaiśesika system is realist in its epistemology and metaphysics, and 'pluralist', in that objects and selves are independently real, not just appearance or illusion.

Vedas. The oldest Hindu religious texts. The Vedic period runs from approximately 1500 to 700 BCE. The Rgveda was composed perhaps as early as 1500 BCE; the other Vedas are the Sāmaveda, Yajurveda, and Atharvaveda. The Upanisads are attached as conclusions to the Vedas, and are speculations and reflections of a philosophical nature, whereas much of the rest of the Vedas are hymns to the gods and instructions for ritual, sacrifice, etc. The Epic period runs from 800 BCE to 200 CE. The two principal collections of epic literature are the *Mahābhārata*, which contains the *Bhagavad-Gītā*, and the *Rāmāyana*. The Sūtra period extended from 400 BCE to 500 CE. The Sūtras are aphorisms of the various Indian philosophical traditions (including Buddhism and Jainism). The Commentary period runs from 400 to 1700 CE, and contains the reflections and commentaries of the great thinkers on the Vedas and Sūtras.

Vedānta. Literally, the last parts of the Vedas. A tradition of Indian philosophy, with important differences between schools, which based itself firmly on the Upaniṣads. In many ways, it is an attempt to reflect philosophically on certain passages which suggest an identity between Brahman and ātman, that underlying reality is one. This issue was handled differently by three main schools, the 'non-dualist', 'qualified non-dualist', and 'dualist' views. See also Advaita Vedānta, Śankara, Rāmānuja, Madhva.

veridical. Truthful. Veridical perceptions represent things as the genuinely are. Non-veridical or un-veridical perceptions are illusory.

Vijñānavāda. Also Yogācāra. A major school of Mahāyāna Buddhism, idealist in its epistemology and metaphysics. Everything inside and outside the mind has its origin in Universal Mind, or Cosmic Consciousness. The empirical world is not there; it arises from thought. Thus empirical knowledge can never be certain; true and ultimate knowledge is the point at which enlightenment breaks in. The founder of the school is said to be Maitreyanatha (fourth century CE); followers include Asanga and his brother Vasubandhu (fifth century CE), Diṇṇāga (sixth century CE), Dharmakīrti (seventh century CE), Santaraksita and Kamalasila (eighth century CE).

Wiesel, Elie (b. 1928). A Jewish writer, born in Romania and a survivor of Auschwitz. Famous for his autobiographical novel, *Night*, in which he portrays the development of his doubts about the existence and character of God as a response to the experience of the Nazi death-camps. His later works develop the theme of religious protest.

Wittgenstein, Ludwig (1889-1951). Wrote an early, massively influential work, *Tractatus Logico-Philosophicus* (1921) which deals with the possibilities and limits of language and how it represents and depicts the world. Later he turned against his own 'picture theory' of meaning as too simplistic, and decided that meaning is best discovered by examining the uses to which words are put. In *Philosophical Investigations* and later works (many published posthumously from notes) he views language as diverse, using the analogy of a 'tool' or as widely differing 'games' that can only be understood with reference to the life and community in which they are played. His later view saw philosophy as a therapeutic endeavour.

Yoga. Not a mere system of exercise. It has the same fundamental metaphysics as Sānkhya, but is theistic. The world is real, and there is a real plurality of selves, they are not aspects of or modifications of God. God is the creator, but is coeternal with prakṛti and puruṣa. God directs evolution, in particular, in making the impact of merit and demerit, karma, be realised. God is conceived as personal, perfect, impassible. Ten qualities are ascribed to God: knowledge, detachment, lordship, austerity, veracity, forgiveness, patience, creative power, self-knowledge, superintendence. The foremost exponent of Yoga is Patañjali. See Sānkhya.

Yogācāra. See Vijñānavāda.

Zen. A tradition of Buddhism, principally identified with Japan, also practised in China and Korea.

Zeno (b. *c.* 490 BCE). Ancient Greek philosopher famous for his 'paradoxes' about motion. In one, he argues that an arrow in flight is in fact at rest. In another, he argues that since space is infinitely divisible, a runner in a stadium can never finish the course. Before he can reach the end, he must reach the half-way point; and before he can reach the quarter-way point, he must reach the eighth; and so on indefinitely. Since finite distances consist of an infinite series of points, and one can never complete an infinite series, one can never reach the end of the course.

Bibliography

Introductions and readers

Anderson, P.S., *A Feminist Philosophy of Religion* (Blackwell, 1998)

Brody, B. (ed.), *Readings in the Philosophy of Religion* (Prentice Hall, 1st ed., 1974; 2nd ed., 1991)

Cahn, S. & D. Shatz (eds), *Contemporary Philosophy of Religion* (Oxford University Press, 1982)

Charlesworth, M.J., *Philosophy of Religion: The Historic Approaches* (Herder & Herder, 1972)

Churchill, J. & D. Jones (eds), *An Introductory Reader in the Philosophy of Religion* (SPCK, 1979)

Copleston, F.C., *Religion and Philosophy* (Gill & Macmillan, 1974)

Davies, B., *An Introduction to the Philosophy of Religion* (Oxford University Press, 1993)

Ferré, F., *Basic Modern Philosophy of Religion* (G. Allen & Unwin, 1968)

Ferré, F., J.J. Kockelmans & J.E. Smith (eds.), *The Challenge of Religion: Contemporary Readings in Philosophy of Religion* (Seabury Press, 1982)

Flew, A., *God and Philosophy* (Hutchinson, 1966)

Flew, A. & A. MacIntyre (eds), *New Essays in Philosophical Theology* (SCM, 1955)

Hartshorne, C. & W. Reese (eds), *Philosophers Speak of God* (University of Chicago Press, 1963)

Hick, J., *Philosophy of Religion* (Prentice Hall, 4th ed. 1989)

Hick, J. (ed.), *Classical and Contemporary Readings in the Philosophy of Religion* (Prentice Hall, 3rd ed. 1990)

Hick, J., *Faith and the Philosophers* (Macmillan, 1964)

Hudson, Y. (ed.), *The Philosophy of Religion* (Mayfield, 1991)

Kolakowski, L., *Religion* (Oxford University Press, 1982)

Lewis, H.D., *Philosophy of Religion* (English Universities Press, 1965)

Loades, A. and L.D. Rue (eds), *Contemporary Classics in the Philosophy of Religion* (Open Court, 1991)

Mackie, J.L., *The Miracle of Theism* (Clarendon Press, 1982)

McPherson, T., *Philosophy and Religious Belief* (Hutchinson, 1974)

Mitchell, B. (ed.), *Philosophy of Religion* (Oxford University Press, 1971)

Morris, T.V. (ed.), *The Concept of God* (Oxford University Press, 1987)

Peterson, M., W. Hasker, B. Reichenbach & D. Basinger (eds), *Philosophy of Religion: Selected Readings* (Oxford University Press, 1995)

Phillips, S.H., *Philosophy of Religion: A Global Approach* (Harcourt Brace, 1996)

Pojman, L. (ed.), *Philosophy of Religion: An Anthology* (Wadsworth, 2nd ed. 1994)

Quinn, P.L. & C. Taliaferro (eds), *A Companion to the Philosophy of Religion* (Blackwell, 1997)

Rowe, W. & W.J. Wainwright (eds), *Philosophy of Religion: Selected Readings* (Harcourt Brace Jovanovich, 1989)

Sherry, P. (ed.), *Philosophers on Religion: A Historical Reader* (Chapman, 1987)

Smart, N., *Reasons and Faiths: An Investigation of Religious Discourse, Christian and Non-Christian* (Routledge & Kegan Paul, 1958)

Smart, N., *Philosophers and Religious Truth* (SCM Press, 1969)

Smart, N., *The Phenomenon of Religion* (Macmillan, 1973)

Smart, N., *The Religious Experience* (Prentice Hall, 1996)

Swinburne, R., *The Existence of God* (Clarendon Press, 1979)

Taliaferro, C., *An Introduction to Contemporary Philosophy of Religion* (Blackwell, 1998)

Tilghman, B.R., *An Introduction to the Philosophy of Religion* (Blackwell, 1994)

Vardy, P., *The Puzzle of God* (Fount, 1990)

Wainwright, W., *Philosophy of Religion* (Wadsworth, 1988)

Metacritical issues

Alston, W.P., *Perceiving God*: *The Epistemology of Religious Experience* (Cornell University Press, 1991)

Anderson, P.S., *A Feminist Philosophy of Religion* (Blackwell, 1998)

Appleby, P., 'Reformed Epistemology, Rationality and Belief in God', *International Journal for Philosophy of Religion* 24 (1988), pp. 129-42

Aristotle, *Poetics I*, tr. with notes by Richard Janko (Hackett Publishing Co., 1987)

Askew, R., 'On Fideism and Alvin Plantinga', *International Journal for Philosophy of Religion* 23 (1988), pp. 3-16

Audi, R. & W. Wainwright (eds), *Rationality, Religious Belief and Moral Commitment*: *New Essays in the Philosophy of Religion* (Cornell University Press, 1986)

Audi, R., 'Direct Justification, Evidential Dependence, and Theistic Belief', in R. Audi & W. Wainwright (eds), *Rationality, Religious Belief and Moral Commitment*: *New Essays in the Philosophy of Religion* (Cornell University Press, 1986)

Audi, R., *The Structure of Justification* (Cambridge University Press, 1993)

Austin, J., *How to Do Things with Words* (Harvard University Press, 2nd ed. 1981)

Ayer, A.J., *Language, Truth and Logic* (Dover, 2nd ed. 1946)

Barbour, I., *Myths, Models and Paradigms*: *The Nature of Scientific and Religious Language* (SCM, 1974)

Basinger, D., 'Plantinga, Pluralism and Justified Belief', *Faith and Philosophy* 8 (1991), pp. 67-80

Beaty, M. (ed.), *Christian Theism and the Problems of Philosophy* (Notre Dame, 1990)

Benvenuto, B. & R. Kennedy, *The Works of Jacques Lacan* (Free Association Books, 1988)

Bernstein, R.J., *Beyond Objectivism and Relativism*: *Science, Hermeneutics, and Praxis* (Basil Blackwell, 1983)

Blackburn, S., *Spreading the Word*: *Groundings in the Philosophy of Language* (Clarendon Press, 1986)

Blumenberg, H., *Paradigmen zu einer Metaphorologie* (Suhrkamp, 1st ed. 1998; 2nd ed. 1999)

Blumenberg, H., *Schiffbruch mit Zuschauer* (Suhrkamp, 1979)

Blumenberg, H., tr. Robert M. Wallace, *Work on Myth* (MIT Press, 1985)

Blumenberg, H., *Work on Myth*, tr. R.M. Wallace (MIT Press, 1985)

Braithwaite, R.B., 'An Empiricist's View of the Nature of Religious Belief' repr. in J. Hick (ed.) *The Existence of God* (Macmillan, 1964)

Brody, B. (ed.), *Readings in the Philosophy of Religion* (Prentice Hall, 1991)

Bronowski, J., *The Visionary Eye* (MIT Press, 1978)

Brown, R.W., *A First Language*: *The Early Stages* (Penguin Books, 1973)

Brown, H., 'Alvin Plantinga and Natural Theology', *International Journal for Philosophy of Religion* 30 (1991), pp. 1-19

Brown, S.C., *Reason and Religion* (Cornell University Press, 1977)

Browne, H.B. & G. Griffith-Dickson (eds.), *Passion for Critique*: *Essays in Honour of F.J. Laishley* (Sit, 1997)

Bultmann, R., 'New Testament and Mythology' in H.-W. Bartsch (ed.) *Kerygma and Myth* (2 vols SPCK, 1969 and 1964)

Bultmann, R., *Jesus Christ and Mythology* (SCM Press, 1960)

Burrell, D., *Analogy and Philosophical Language* (Yale University Press, 1973)

Burrell, D., 'Religious Belief and Rationality', in Delaney, C.F. (ed.), *Rationality and Religious Belief* (Notre Dame, 1979)

Cell, E., *Language, Existence, and God: Interpretations of Moore, Russell, Ayer, Wittgenstein, Wisdom, Oxford Philosophy, and Tillich* (Humanities Press, 1971)

Charlesworth, M.J., *The Problem of Religious Language* (Prentice Hall, 1974)

Clark, K.J., *Return to Reason: A Critique of Enlightenment Evidentialism and a Defense of Reason and Belief in God* (Eerdmans, 1990)

Clark, K. (ed.), *Our Knowledge of God: Essays on Natural and Philosophical Theology* (Kluwer Academic Publishers, 1992)

Clifford, W.K., 'The Ethics of Belief', repr. in 1st ed. of B. Brody (ed.), *Readings in the Philosophy of Religion* (Prentice Hall, 1991); original ed., *Lectures and Essays* (Macmillan, 1886)

Crownfield, D., C.A. Raschke & E. Wyschogrod (eds), *Lacan and Theological Discourse* (State University of New York Press, 1989)

Davis, S.T., *Faith, Skepticism, and Evidence: An Essay in Religious Epistemology* (Associated University Presses, 1978)

Delaney, C.F. (ed.), *Rationality and Religious Belief* (Notre Dame, 1979)

Donovan, P., *Religious Language* (Hawthorn Books, 1976)

Emerson, N.B., *Pele and Hi'iaka* (Charles Tuttle, 1982; 1st ed., 1915)

Evans, C.S. & J. Westphal (eds), *Christian Perspectives on Religious Knowledge* (Eerdmans, 1993)

Evans, S.C., 'Kierkegaard and Plantinga on Belief in God', *Faith and Philosophy* 5 (1988), pp. 25-39

Ferré, F., *Language, Logic and God* (University of Chicago Press, 1961)

Flew, A. & A. MacIntyre (eds), *New Essays in Philosophical Theology* (SCM, 1955)

Flew, A., *God and Philosophy* (Hutchinson, 1966)

Flew, A., *The Presumption of Atheism* (Barnes & Noble, 1976)

Flew, A, 'The Presumption of Atheism', in R.D. Geivett & B. Sweetman (eds), *Contemporary Perspectives on Religious Epistemology* (Oxford University Press, 1992)

Flint, T. (ed.), *Christian Philosophy* (Notre Dame, 1990)

Gadamer, H.-G., *Truth and Method* (Continuum, 1989)

Geivett, R.D. & B. Sweetman (eds), *Contemporary Perspectives on Religious Epistemology* (Oxford University Press, 1992)

Gill, J., *On Knowing God: New Directions for the Future of Theology* (Westminster, 1981)

Gill, J., 'Wittgenstein and Religious Language', *Theology Today* 21 (1964), pp. 59-72

Goodman, N., *Languages of Art* (Hackett, 1976)

Goetz, S., 'Belief in God is not Properly Basic', in R.D. Geivett & B. Sweetman (eds), *Contemporary Perspectives on Religious Epistemology* (Oxford University Press, 1992)

Gowen, J., 'Foundationalism and the Justification of Religious Belief', *Religious Studies* 19 (1983), pp. 393-406

Grene, M., *The Knower and the Known* (Faber & Faber, 1966)

Griffith-Dickson, G., *Johann Georg Hamann's Relational Metacriticism* (Walter de Gruyter, 1995)

Grigg, R., 'The Crucial Disanalogies between Properly Basic Belief and Belief in God', *Religious Studies* 26 (1990), pp. 389-401

Grigg, R., 'Theism and Proper Basicality: A Response to Plantinga', *International Journal for Philosophy of Religion* 14 (1983), pp. 123-7

Gutting, G., 'The Catholic and the Calvinist: A Dialogue on Faith and Reason', *Faith and Philosophy* 2 (1985), pp. 236-56

Gutting, G., *Religious Belief and Religious Skepticism* (Notre Dame, 1982)

Hanink, J., 'Some Questions about Proper Basicality', *Faith and Philosophy* 4 (1987), pp. 13-25

Hatcher, D., 'Plantinga and Reformed Epistemology: A Critique', *Philosophy and Theology* 1 (1986), pp. 84-95

Hatcher, D., 'Some Problems with Plantinga's Reformed Epistemology', *American Journal of Philosophy and Theology* 10 (1989), pp. 21-31

Heidegger, M., tr. J. Macquarrie & E. Robinson, *Being and Time* (SCM Press, 1962)

Henry, C., *God, Revelation and Authority* (2nd ed., Crossway Books, 1999)

Hepburn, R., 'Demythologising and the Problem of Validity' in A. Flew & A. MacIntyre (eds), *New Essays in Philosophical Theology* (SCM Press, 1955)

Hick, J., *Faith and Knowledge* (Cornell University Press, 1966)

Hick, J., *God and the Universe of Faiths*: *Essays in the Philosophy of Religion* (St Martin's Press, 1973)

Hick, J., *An Interpretation of Religion*: *Human Responses to the Transcendent* (Macmillan, 1989)

Hobbes, T., *Leviathan* (J.M. Dent & Sons, 1914)

Höhn, H.-J. (ed.), *Krise der Immanenz*: *Religion an den Grenzen der Moderne* (Fischer, 1996)

Homer, *The Odyssey*, tr. E.V. Rieu (Penguin Books, 1946)

Hoitenga, D.J., *Faith and Reason from Plato to Plantinga*: *An Introduction to Reformed Epistemology* (SUNY, 1991)

Hudson, W.D., 'The Rational System of Beliefs', in A. Loades & L.D. Rue (eds), *Contemporary Classics in the Philosophy of Religion* (Open Court, 1991)

Husserl, E., *Cartesian Meditations*: *An Introduction to Phenomenology*, tr. D. Cairns (Nijhoff, 1960)

Ihara, C. & J. Runzo (eds), *Religious Experience and Religious Belief*: *Essays in the Epistemology of Religion* (University Press of America, 1986)

James, W., 'The Will to Believe', in 1st ed. of Brody, B. (ed.), *Readings in the Philosophy of Religion* (Prentice Hall, 1991)

Jeffner, A., *The Study of Religious Language* (SCM Press, 1972)

Johnson, B.C., *The Atheist Debater's Handbook* (Prometheus, 1983)

Kant, I., *Critique of Pure Reason*, tr. Norman Kemp Smith (Macmillan, 1987)

Kenny, A., *What is Faith?* (OUP, 1992)

Kerr, F., *Theology After Wittgenstein* (Blackwell, 1986; SPCK, 1997)

Konyndyk, K., 'Faith and Evidentialism', in R. Audi R. & W. Wainwright (eds), *Rationality, Religious Belief and Moral Commitment*: *New Essays in the Philosophy of Religion* (Cornell University Press, 1986)

Kretzmann, N., 'Evidence Against Anti-Evidentialism', in Clark, K.J. (ed.), *Our Knowledge of God*: *Essays on Natural and Philosophical Theology* (Kluwer Academic Publishers, 1992)

Lacan, J., *Écrits*: *A Selection* (Routledge, 1997)

Law, J., *The Early Identification of Language Impairment in Children* (Chapman & Hall, 1992)

Lewisohn, L., *Beyond Faith and Infidelity*: *The Sufi Poetry and Teachings of Mahmud Shabistari* (Curzon Press, 1995)

Loades, A. & L.D. Rue (eds), *Contemporary Classics in the Philosophy of Religion* (Open Court, 1991)

Long, A.A. & D.N. Sedley, *The Hellenistic Philosophers*, vol. 1 (Cambridge University Press, 1987)

Mackie, J.L., *The Miracle of Theism* (Clarendon, 1982)

Maimonides, M., *Guide of the Perplexed*, tr. S. Pines (Chicago, 1963)

Malcolm, N., 'The Groundlessness of Belief', in R.D. Geivett & B. Sweetman (eds), *Contemporary Perspectives on Religious Epistemology* (OUP, 1992)

Marion, J.-L., *God Without Being* (University of Chicago Press, 1991)

Martin, C.B., *Religious Belief* (Cornell University Press, 1959)

Martin, M., *Atheism*: *A Philosophical Justification* (Temple University Press, 1990)

Mascall, E.L., *Existence and Analogy* (London, 1966)

McFague, S., *Metaphorical Theology* (Fortress Press, 1982)

McLeod, M.S., *Rationality and Theistic Belief, An Essay on Reformed Epistemology* (Cornell University Press, 1993)

McLeod, M., 'The Analogy Argument for the Proper Basicality of Belief in God', *International Journal for Philosophy of Religion* 21 (1987), pp. 3-20

McLeod, M., *Meister Eckhart. Teacher and Preacher*, ed. & tr. by B. McGinn (Paulist Press, 1986)

Miller, B., *A Most Unlikely God: A Philosophical Enquiry into the Nature of God* (University of Notre Dame Press, 1996)

Miller, J.-A. (ed.), *The Seminar of Jacques Lacan. Book 1. Freud's Papers on Technique 1953-1954*, tr. J. Forrester (Cambridge University Press, 1988)

Moore, G., *Believing in God: A Philosophic Essay* (T. & T. Clark, 1989)

Murry, J. M., *Countries of the Mind* (Oxford University Press, 1931)

Nash, R.H., *Faith and Reason: Searching for a Rational Faith* (Zondervan, 1988)

Nielsen, K., 'Religion and Groundless Believing', in C.K. Ihara & J. Runzo (eds.), *Religious Experience and Religious Belief: Essays in the Epistemology of Religion* (University Press of America, 1986)

Nielsen, K., *Ethics Without God* (Prometheus Books, 1989)

Nielsen, K., *God, Skepticism and Modernity* (Ottawa University Press, 1989)

Nielsen, K., *Philosophy and Atheism: In Defence of Atheism* (Prometheus, 1985)

Nielsen, K., 'Does Religious Skepticism Rest on a Mistake?', in R.D. Geivett & B. Sweetman (eds), *Contemporary Perspectives on Religious Epistemology* (OUP, 1992)

Nietzsche, F., *The Gay Science*, tr. Walter Kauffmann (Vintage Books, 1974)

Obeyesekere, G., *The Apotheosis of Captain Cook: European Mythmaking in the Pacific* (Princeton University Press, 1992)

Palmer, H., *Analogy* (London, 1973)

Pargetter, R., 'Experience, Proper Basicality, and Belief in God', in R.D. Geivett & B. Sweetman (eds), *Contemporary Perspectives on Religious Epistemology* (Oxford University Press, 1992)

Parker, F., *Reason and Faith Revisited* (Marquette, 1971)

Penelhum, T., *God and Skepticism* (Reidel, 1983)

Penelhum, T., *Religion and Rationality* (Random House, 1971)

Peterson, M., W. Hasker, B. Reichenbach & D. Basinger (eds), *Reason and Religious Belief: An Introduction to the Philosophy of Religion* (OUP, 1991)

Phillips, D.Z., 'Faith, Skepticism, and Understanding', in R.D. Geivett & B. Sweetman (eds), *Contemporary Perspectives on Religious Epistemology* (OUP, 1992)

Phillips, D.Z., *Faith after Foundationalism* (Routledge & Kegan Paul, 1988)

Phillips, D.Z., *Faith and Philosophical Enquiry* (Routledge & Kegan Paul, 1971)

Phillips, D.Z. (ed.), *Religion and Understanding* (Blackwell, 1967)

Plantinga, A. 'Coherentism and the Evidentist Objection to Belief in God', in R. Audi & W. Wainwright (eds), *Rationality, Religious Belief and Moral Commitment: New Essays in the Philosophy of Religion* (Cornell University Press, 1986)

Plantinga, A. & Wolsterstorff, N., *Faith and Rationality: Reason and Belief in God* (Notre Dame, 1983)

Plantinga, A., 'Advice to Christian Philosophers', *Faith and Philosophy* 1 (1984), pp. 253-71

Plantinga, A., 'Is Belief in God Rational?' in C.F. Delaney (ed.), *Rationality and Religious Belief* (Notre Dame, 1979)

Plantinga, A., 'Is Theism Really a Miracle?', *Faith and Philosophy* 3 (1986), pp. 109-34

Plantinga, A., 'Justification and Theism', *Faith and Philosophy* 4 (1987), pp. 403-26

Plantinga, A., 'Reason and Belief in God', in A. Plantinga & N. Wolsterstorff, *Faith and Rationality: Reason and Belief in God* (Notre Dame, 1983)

Plantinga, A., 'The Foundations of Theism: A Reply', *Faith and Philosophy* 3 (1986), pp. 298-313

Plantinga, A., 'Is Belief in God Properly Basic?', in A. Loades & L.D. Rue (eds), *Contemporary Classics in the Philosophy of Religion* (Open Court, 1991)

Plantinga, A., *Warrant: The Current Debate* (OUP, 1993)

Plato, *Protagoras and Meno*, tr. W. Guthrie (Penguin Books, 1979)

Polanyi, M., *Personal Knowledge* (Routledge & Kegan Paul, 1958)

Polanyi, M., *Personal Knowledge: Towards a Post-Critical Philosophy* (Routledge & Kegan Paul, 1958)

Porter, S. (ed.), *The Nature of Religious Language* (Sheffield Academic Press, 1996)

Potter, K.H. (ed.), *Encyclopedia of Indian Philosophies: Advaita Vedānta up to Śankara and his Pupils* (Princeton University Press, 1981)

Pseudo-Dionysius: The Complete Works, tr. C. Luibheid (Paulist Press, 1987)

Quinn, P.L., 'In Search of the Foundations of Theism', *Faith and Philosophy* 2 (1985), pp. 469-86

Radcliffe, E.S. & C.J. White (eds), *Faith in Theory and Practice: Essays on Justifying Religious Belief* (Open Court, 1993)

Radhakrishnan, S. & C.A. Moore (eds), *A Source Book in Indian Philosophy* (Oxford University Press, 1957)

Ramsey, I., *Religious Language* (SCM Press, 1957)

Randall, J.H., *The Role of Knowledge in Western Religion* (University Press of America, 1986)

Reynolds, F. & D. Tracy (eds), *Discourse and Practice* (State University of New York Press, 1992)

Richmond, J., 'Religion without Explanation: Theology and D.Z. Phillips', *Theology* 83 (1980), pp. 34-43

Ricoeur, P., *Freud and Philosophy: An Essay on Interpretation*, tr. D. Savage (Yale University Press, 1970)

Ricoeur, P., *Hermeneutics and the Human Sciences: Essays on Language, Action, and Interpretation*, ed. and tr. John Thompson (Cambridge University Press, 1981)

Robbins, J.W., 'Is Belief in God Properly Basic?', *International Journal for Philosophy of Religion* 14 (1983), pp. 241-9

Robbins, W.J., 'Does the Existence of God Need Proof?', *Faith and Philosophy* 2 (1985), pp. 272-86

Rorty, R., *Philosophy and the Mirror of Nature* (Princeton University Press, 1980)

Ross, J., *Portraying Analogy* (Cambridge University Press, 1981)

Runzo, J., 'World-Views and the Epistemic Foundations of Theism', *Religious Studies* 25 (1989), pp. 31-51

Sahlins, M., *Historical Metaphors and Mythical Realities: Structure in the Early History of the Sandwich Island Kingdom* (University of Michigan Press, 1981)

Sahlins, M., 'The Apotheosis of Captain Cook' in Michel Izard & Pierre Smith (eds) *Between Belief and Transgression* (University of Chicago Press, 1982), pp. 73-102

Sahlins, M., *How 'Natives' Think. About Captain Cook, For Example* (University of Chicago Press, 1995)

Scriven, M., *Primary Philosophy* (Hutchinson, 1966)

Searle, J.R., *Speech Acts* (Cambridge University Press, 1984)

Sells, M.A. (ed. & tr.), *Early Islamic Mysticism: Sufi, Qur'an, Mi'raj, Poetic and Theological Writings* (Paulist Press, 1996)

Sessions, W., 'Plantinga's Box', *Faith and Philosophy* 8 (1991), pp. 51-66

Sherry, P., *Religion, Truth and Language Games* (Barnes & Noble, 1977)

Sinari, R.A., *The Structure of Indian Thought* (Charles C. Thomas, 1970)

Smith, J.E., 'Faith, Belief and the Problem of Rationality in Religion' in C.F. Delaney (ed), *Rationality and Religious Belief* (Notre Dame, 1979)

Soskice, J.M., *Metaphor and Religious Language* (Clarendon, 1987)

Stein, G. (ed.), *An Anthology of Atheism and Rationalism* (Prometheus, 1980)

Stiver, D., *The Philosophy of Religious Language: Sign, Symbol and Story* (Blackwell, 1996)

Strawson, G., *The Secret Connexion: Causation, Realism, and David Hume* (Clarendon Press, 1989)

Swenson, J. 'Treating God as Real', *Theology Today* 45 (1984), pp. 446-50
Swinburne, R., *The Coherence of Theism* (Clarendon Press, 1977)
Thiselton, A., *New Horizons in Hermeneutics* (Zondervan, 1992)
Thiselton, A., *The Two Horizons* (Paternoster Press, 1980)
Tilley, T., *Talking of God*: *An Introduction to Philosophical Analysis of Religious Language* (Paulist Press, 1978)
Tilley, T., *The Evils of Theodicy* (Georgetown University Press, 1991)
Tillich, P., 'Symbols of Faith', in *Dynamics of Faith* vol. 10 (Harper Torchbooks, 1958)
Trigg, R., *Rationality and Religion* (Blackwells, 1998)
Van Inwagen, P. & J. Tomberlin (eds), *Alvin Plantinga* (Reidel, 1985)
von Arnim, J. (ed.), *Stoicorum Veterum Fragmenta* (Teubner, 1964)
Ward, K., *Holding Fast to God* (SPCK, 1982)
Westphal, J. (ed.), *Certainty* (Hackett Publishing Co., 1995)
Williams, M., *Groundless Belief*: *An Essay on the Possibility of Epistemology* (Blackwell, 1977)
Wisdo, D., 'The Fragility of Faith: Toward a Critique of Reformed Epistemology', *Religious Studies* 24 (1988), pp. 365-74
Wittgenstein, L., *Lectures and Conversations on Aesthetics, Psychology and Religious Belief* ed. C. Barrett (Basil Blackwell, 1970)
Wittgenstein, L., *On Certainty* (Blackwell, 1969)
Wittgenstein, L., *Philosophical Investigations* (Macmillan, 1968)
Wittgenstein, L., *Tractatus Logico-Philosophicus* (Routledge & Kegan Paul, 1961)
Wolterstorff, N., 'Can Belief in God be Rational if it has no Foundations?', in A. Plantinga & N. Wolsterstorff, *Faith & Rationality*: *Reason and Belief in God* (Notre Dame, 1983)
Wolterstorff, N., *Reason within the Bounds of Religion* (Eerdmans, 1984)
Wolterstorff, N., 'Is Reason Enough?', in R.D. Geivett & B. Sweetman (eds), *Contemporary Perspectives on Religious Epistemology* (Oxford University Press, 1992)
Zagzebski, L. (ed.), *Rational Faith*: *Catholic Responses to Reformed Epistemology* (Notre Dame, 1993)
Zeis, J., 'A Critique of Plantinga's Theological Foundationalism', *International Journal for Philosophy of Religion* 28 (1990), pp. 173-89
Zilberman, D.B., *The Birth of Meaning in Hindu Thought* (D. Reidel Publishing Co., 1988)
Zimmer, H., *Philosophies of India* (Routledge & Kegan Paul, 1952)

Religious experience

Aberbach, D., 'Grief and Mysticism', *International Review of Psychoanalysis* 14 (1987), pp. 509-26
Almond, P.C., *Mystical Experience and Religious Doctrine*: *An Investigation of the Study of Mysticism in World Religions* (Mouton, 1982)
Alston, W.P., *Perceiving God*: *The Epistemology of Religious Experience* (Cornell University Press, 1991)
Alston, W.P., 'Is Religious Belief Rational?' in Ann Loades & Loyal D. Rue (eds), *Contemporary Classics in Philosophy of Religion* (Open Court, 1991)
Alston, W.P., 'Religious Experience and Religious Belief' in R.D. Geivett & B. Sweetman (eds), *Contemporary Perspectives on Religious Epistemology* (Oxford University Press, 1992), pp. 295-303
Ard, B. (ed.), *Counseling and Psychotherapy*: *Classics on Theories and Issues* (Palo Alto, Science & Behavior Books, 1975)
Back, K.W. & L.B. Bourque, 'Can Feelings be Enumerated?', *Behavioural Science* 15 (1970), pp. 487-96
Batson, C.D. & W.L. Ventis, *The Religious Experience*: *A Social Psychological Perspective*

(Oxford University Press, 1982)

Beit-Hallahmi, B. & M. Argyle, *The Social Psychology of Religion* (Routledge & Kegan Paul, 1975)

Beit-Hallahmi, B. & M. Argyle, 'Object Relations Theory and Religious Experience', in R.W. Hood Jr. (ed.), *Handbook of Religious Experience* (Alabama, Religious Education Press, 1995)

Bettelheim, B., *A Good Enough Parent* (Pan Books, 1988)

Bhugra, D. (ed.), *Psychiatry and Religion*: *Context, Consensus and Controversies* (Routledge, 1996)

Buber, M., *I and Thou*, ed. & tr. W. Kaufmann (Charles Scribner's, 1970)

Bufford, R.K. *The Human Reflex*: *Behavior Psychology in a Biblical Perspective* (Harper & Row, c. 1981)

Bultmann, R., *Faith and Understanding*, tr. L. Pettibone Smith (SCM Press, 1969)

Burhenn, H., 'Philosophy and Religious Experience', in R.W. Hood Jr. (ed.), *Handbook of Religious Experience* (Religious Education Press, 1995)

Burrows, R., *Guidelines for Mystical Prayer* (Sheed & Ward, 1976)

Burrows, R., *To Believe in Jesus* (Sheed & Ward, 1978)

Burrows, R., *Ascent to Love* (DLT, 1987)

Byrnes, J., *The Psychology of Religion* (Macmillan, 1984)

Carroll, M.P., 'Praying the Rosary: The Anal-Erotic Origins of a Popular Catholic Devotion', *Journal for the Scientific Study of Religion* 26 (4) (1987), pp. 486-98

Claridge, G., *Origins of Mental Illness* (Basil Blackwell, 1985)

Crapps, R., *An Introduction to Psychology of Religion* (Mercer University Press, 1986)

Davis, C.F., *The Evidential Force of Religious Experience* (Clarendon, 1989)

Deikman, A.J., 'Deautomatization and the Mystic Experience' in C.A. Tart (ed.), *Altered States of Consciousness*: *A Book of Readings* (John Wiley & Sons, 1969)

DeLuca, A., *Freud and Future Religious Experience* (Littlefield, Adams & Co., 1977)

Donovan, P., *Interpreting Religious Experience* (Sheldon Press, 1979)

Ebner, F., *Schriften*, ed. Franz Seyr (München, vol. 1, 1963; vol. 2, 1963; vol. 3, 1965)

Ebner, F., *Das Du und die geistige Realitäten* (Brenner-Verlag, 1921), repr. In F. Ebner, *Fragmente, Aufsätze, Aphorismen. Zu einer Pneumatologie des Wortes*, ed. Franz Seyer (Kösel Verlag, 1963)

Ellis, A.,'The Case Against Religion: A Psychotherapist's View', in B. Ard (ed.), *Counseling and Psychotherapy*: *Classics on Theories and Issues* (Palo Alto, Science & Behavior Books, 1975)

Eysenck, H. & S. Eysenck, *Psychoticism as a Dimension of Personality* (Hodder & Stoughton, 1976)

Fenwick, P., 'The Neurophysiology of Religious Experience' in D. Bhugra (ed.), *Psychiatry and Religion*: *Context, Consensus and Controversies* (Routledge, 1996)

Feyerabend, P., *Against Method* (Verso, 1988 rev. ed.)

Feyerabend, P., *Farewell to Reason* (Verso, 1987)

Feyerabend, P., *Realism, Rationalism and Scientific Method* (CUP, 1981)

Flew, A., *God and Philosophy* (Hutchinson, 1966)

Foucault, M., *Madness and Civilization*: *A History of Insanity in the Age of Reason* (Routledge, 1989)

Francis, L.J., 'Religion, Neuroticism, and Psychotism' in John F. Schumaker (ed.), *Religion and Mental Health* (Oxford University Press, 1992), pp. 149-60

Freud, S., *The Future of an Illusion* (Hogarth Press, 1927)

Freud, S., *Civilisation and its Discontents*, (Hogarth Press, 1929)

Friedman, M., *The Worlds of Existentialism*: *A Critical Reader* (Humanities Press International, Inc., 1994)

Geivett, R.D. & B. Sweetman (eds), *Contemporary Perspectives on Religious Epistemology* (Oxford University Press, 1992)

Gellman, J.I., *Experience of God and the Rationality of Theistic Belief* (Cornell University Press, 1997)

Gibbons, D. & J. de Jarnette, 'Hypnotic Suggestibility and Religious Experience', *Journal for the Scientific Study of Religion* 11 (1972), pp. 152-6

Gibbons, D. & J. de Jarnette, 'Hypnotic Susceptibility and Reported Religious Experience', Psychological Reports 33 (1973), pp. 549-50

Glock, C.Y. & R. Stark, *Religion and Society in Tension* (Rand McNally, 1965)

Greeley, A., *The Sociology of the Paranormal: A Reconnaissance* (Sage, 1975)

Guthrie, E.R., *The Psychology of Learning* (Harper & Row, 1952)

Gutting, G., *Religious Belief and Religious Skepticism* (University of Notre Dame Press, 1982)

Hay, D., *Exploring Inner Space* (Penguin, 1982)

Hay, D., ' "The Biology of God": What is the Current Status of Hardy's Hypothesis?', *IJPR* 4 (1994), pp. 1-23

Hay, D. & A. Morisy, 'Reports of Esctatic, Paranormal, or Religious Experience in Great Britain and the United States – A Comparison of Trends', *Journal for the Scientific Study of Religion* 17 (1978), pp. 255-68

Hegel, G.W.F., *Lectures on the Philosophy of Religion*, vol. 1, ed. P.C. Hodgson, tr. R.F. Brown, P.C. Hodgson & J.M. Stewart (University of California Press, 1984)

Hick, J., *God and the Universe of Faiths: Essays in the Philosophy of Religion* (St Martin's Press, 1973)

Hick, J., *An Interpretation of Religion: Human Responses to the Transcendent* (Macmillan, 1989)

Hood, R.W. Jr. (ed.), *Handbook of Religious Experience* (Religious Education Press, 1995)

Hood, R.W. Jr., 'Psychological Strength and the Report of Intense Religious Experience', *Journal for the Scientific Study of Religion* 13 (1974), pp. 65-71

Howard, E. J., *Odd Girl Out* (Jonathan Cape, 1972)

Jackson, M., 'Divine Madness: A Study of the Relationship between Psycotic and Spiritual Experience'. Unpublished doctoral dissertation, Oxford, 1991

James, W., *The Varieties of Religious Experience* (Fontana, 1960)

Jaspers, K., *General Psychopathology* Eng. tr. of 7th ed. of *Allgemeine Psychopathologie* (Berlin, Springer, 1963)

Jung, C.G., *The Collected Works of C.G. Jung*, ed. Sir Herbert Read *et al.* (Princeton University Press, 1970)

Kant, I., *Critique of Pure Reason*, tr. Norman Kemp Smith (Macmillan, 1978)

Katz, S.T., *Mysticism and Philosophical Analysis* (Sheldon, 1978)

Kirkpatrick, L.A., 'Attachmment Theory and Religious Experience', in R.W. Hood, Jr. (ed.) *Handbook of Religious Experience* (Religious Education Press, 1995)

Kristeva, J., *In the Beginning Was Love: Psychoanalysis and Faith* (Columbia University Press, 1987)

La Barre, W., *The Ghost Dance: Origins of Religion* (Allen & Unwin, 1970)

Lacan, J., *Seminar I*, ed. Jacques-Alain Miller (Cambridge University Press, 1988)

Lacan, J., *Écrits: A Selection* (Routledge, 1997)

Lantenari, V., *The Religions of the Oppressed: A Study of Modern Messianic Cults* (Knopf, 1963)

Lash, N., *Easter in Ordinary: Reflections on Human Experience and the Knowledge of God* (SCM, 1988)

Lewin, I.M., *Ecstatic Religion* (Penguin, 1971)

Lewin, I.M., *The Psychoanalysis of Elation* (International Universities Press, 1950)

Lindskoog, D. & R.E. Kirk, 'Some Life-history and Attitudinal Correlates of Self-actualization among Evangelical Seminary Students', *Journal for the Scientific Study of Religion* 14 (1975), pp. 51-5

Littlewood, R., 'Psychopathology, Embodiment and Religious Innovation: An Historical

Instance' in D. Bhugra (ed.), *Psychiatry and Religion: Context, Consensus and Controversies* (Routledge, 1996)

Littlewood, R., *Pathology and Identity: The Work of Mother Earth in Trinidad* (Cambridge University Press, 1993)

Loades, A. & L.D. Rue (eds), *Contemporary Classics in Philosophy of Religion* (Open Court, 1991)

Ludwig, A.M., 'Altered States of Consciousness', in C.A. Tart (ed.), *Altered States of Consciousness: A Book of Readings* (John Wiley & Sons, 1969)

Luijpen, W., *Phenomenology and Atheism*, tr. Walter can de Putte (Duquesne University Press, 1964)

Malony, H.N., 'Behavioral Theory and Religious Experience', in R.W. Hood, Jr. (ed.), *Handbook of Religious Experience* (Religious Education Press, 1995)

Martin, M., *Atheism: A Philosophical Justification* (Temple University Press, 1990)

Martin, M., 'The Principle of Credulity and Religious Experience', *Religious Studies* 22 (1986), pp. 79-93

Marx, K. & F. Engels, *On Religion* (Progress Publishers, 1957)

Maslow, A., *Religions, Values and Peak Experiences* (Ohio State University Press, 1964)

Maslow, A., *Towards a Psychology of Being* (Litton Educational Publishing, 1968)

Masson, J., 'The Psychology of the Ascetic', *Journal of Asian Studies* 35 (1976), pp. 611-25

Mitchell, B., *The Justification of Religious Belief* (Macmillan, 1973)

Otto, R., Mysticism *East and West: A Comparative Analysis of the Nature of Mysticism*, tr. B.L. Bracey and R.C. Payne (Theosophical Publishing House, 1987)

Pahnke, W.N., 'Drugs and Mysticism: An Analysis of the Relationship between Psychedelic Drugs and the Mystical Consciousness'. Unpublished doctoral dissertation, Harvard University, 1963

Phillips, D.Z., *The Concept of Prayer* (Routledge & Kegan Paul, 1965)

Poloma, M., 'The Sociological Context of Religious Experience', in R.W. Hood, Jr. (ed.), *Handbook of Religious Experience* (Religious Education Press, 1995), pp. 167-8

Poloma, M. & B. Pendleton, *Exploring Neglected Dimensions of Religion in Quality of Life Research* (Mellen Press, 1991)

Prince, R.H., 'Religious Experience and Psychopathology: Cross-cultural Perspectives' in John F. Schumaker (ed.), *Religion and Mental Health* (OUP, 1992)

Prince, R. & C. Savage, 'Mystical States and the Concept of Regression', *Psychedelic Review* 8 (1966), pp. 69-75

Proudfoot, W., *Religious Experience* (University of California Press, 1985)

Rahner, K., *Foundations of Christian Faith*, tr. W. Dych (Darton, Longman & Todd, 1978)

Rosenzweig, F., *Star of Redemption* (University of Notre Dame Press, 1985)

Rosenzweig, F., *The New Thinking* (Syracuse University Press, 1999)

Russell, B., *Religion and Science* (OUP, 1935)

Sargant, W., *Battle for the Mind* (Heinemann, 1957)

Schumaker, J.F. (ed.), *Religion and Mental Health* (OUP, 1992)

Scobie, G., *Psychology of Religion* (Batsford, 1975)

Smart, N, 'Interpretation and Mystical Experience', *Religious Studies* 1 (1965), pp. 75-87

Spiro, M.E., 'Culturally Constituted Defense Mechansisms', in M.E. Spiro (ed.), *Context and Meaning in Cultural Anthropology* (Free Press, 1965)

Stace, W.T., *Mysticism and Philosophy* (Macmillan, 1961)

Swinburne, R., *The Existence of God* (Clarendon Press, 1979)

Tart, C.A. (ed.), *Altered States of Consciousness: A Book of Readings* (John Wiley & Sons, 1969)

Thomas, L.E. & P.E. Cooper, 'Incidence and Psychological Correlates of Intense Spiritual Experiences', *Journal of Transpersonal Psychology* 12 (1980), pp. 75-85

Valla, J.-P. & R.H. Prince, 'Religious Experiences as Self-Healing Mechanisms', in C.A. Ward (ed.), *Altered States of Conciousness and Mental Health: A Cross-Cultural Perspective* (Sage Publications, 1989), pp. 149f.

Vetter, G.B., *Magic and Religion: Their Psychological Nature, Origin and Function* (Philosophical Library, 1958)

Wainwright, W., 'Mysticism and Sense Perception', *Religious Studies* 9 (1973), pp. 257-78

Wainwright, W., *Mysticism* (University of Wisconsin Press, 1981)

Ward (ed.) *Altered States of Consciousness and Mental Health: A Cross-Cultural Perspective* (Sage Publications, 1989) pp. 149f.

Wilber, K., *The Spectrum of Consciousness* (Quest Books 1977)

Wilber, K., *The Atman Project: A Transpersonal View of Human Development* (Quest Books, 1980)

Wilber, K., *Up From Eden: A Transpersonal View of Human Evolution* (Routlege & Kegan Paul, 1981)

Wilber, K., 'Ontogenetic Development: Two Fundamental Patterns', in *Journal of Transpersonal Psychology* 13 (1981), 1

Winnicott, D.W., *The Maturational Process and the Facilitating Environment* (Hogarth Press, 1965)

Wuthnow, R., 'Peak Experiences: Some Empirical Tests', mimeographed paper, cited in David Hay & Ann Morisy, 'Reports of Esctatic, Paranormal, or Religious Experience in Great Britain and the United States – A Comparison of Trends', *Journal for the Scientific Study of Religion* 17 (1978), pp. 255-68

Yandell, K.E., *The Epistemology of Religious Experience* (Cambridge University Press, 1993)

Zaehner, R.C., Mysticism, *Sacred and* Profane*: An Inquiry into some Varieties of Praeternatural Experience* (Clarendon Press, 1957)

Evil

Airaksinen, T., *The Philosophy of the Marquis de Sade* (Routledge, 1995)

Allison, D., M. Roberts & A. Weiss, *Sade and the Narrative of Transgression* (Cambridge University Press, 1995)

Aquinas, T., *Summa Theologica*, tr. the Fathers of the English Dominican Province (publishers and dates vary according to volume)

Aquinas, T., *Summa Theologiae: A Concise Translation*, ed. T. McDermott (Eyre & Spottiswoode, 1989)

Aquinas, T., *Summa Contra Gentiles*, tr. the Fahers of the English Dominican Province (Burns Oates & Washbourne, 1924-29)

Basinger, D., 'Evil as Evidence against God's Existence', *Modern Schoolman* 58 (1981), pp. 175-84; repr. in Peterson, 141-52

Bayer, O., 'Poetological Theology', tr. Gwen Griffith-Dickson, *International Journal of Systematic Theology* 1 (1999), 2 pp. 153-67

Berkovits, E., *Faith after the Holocaust* (Ktav, 1973)

Berkovits, E., *Major Themes in Modern Philosophies of Judaism* (Ktav, 1974)

Besdin, A.R., *Reflections of the Rav* (World Zionist Organization, Department of Torah Education and Culture in the Diaspora, 1979)

Birnbaum, D., *God and Evil: A Jewish Perspective* (Ktav, 1989)

Boër, S.E., 'The Irrelevance of the Free Will Defence,' *Analysis* 38.2 (1978), pp. 110-12

Bowker, J., *Problems of Suffering in Religions of the World* (Cambridge University Press, 1970)

Buber, M., *Between Man and Man* (Routledge & Kegan Paul, 1949)

Buber, M., *Images of Good and Evil* in M. Buber, *Good and Evil: Two Interpretations* (Scribner's, 1953).

Cohen, A., *The Tremendum: A Theological Interpretation of the Holocaust* (Crossroad, 1981)

Cohen, H., *Religion of Reason: Out of the Sources of Judaism* (F. Ungar, 1972)

Cohn-Sherbok, L. & D., *A Short History of Judaism* (Oneworld, 1994)

Conway, D.A., 'The Philosophical Problem of Evil', *International Journal for Philosophy of Religion* 24 (1988), pp. 35-66

Copleston, F., *A History of Philosophy: Medieval Philosophy*, vol 2, part II (Doubleday & Co., 1962)

Cowell, E.B. *et al.* (eds.), *Buddhist Mah-y-na Texts* (Dover Publications Inc., 1969)

Davies, B., *Thinking About God* (Geoffrey Chapman, 1985)

Davies, B., 'The Problem of Evil and Modern Philosophy I', *New Blackfriars* 63 (1982), pp. 529-39; 'The Problem of Evil and Modern Philosophy II', *New Blackfriars* 64 (1983), pp. 18-28

Davies, B., (ed.) *Philosophy of Religion: A Guide to the Subject* (Cassell, 1998)

Davis, S.T. (ed.), *Encountering Evil: Live Options in Theodicy* (T. & T. Clark, 1981)

Dilley, F., 'Is the Free Will Defence Irrelevant?' *Religious Studies* 18 (1982), pp. 355-64

Dilley, F., 'The Free-Will Defence and Worlds without Moral Evil', *International Journal for Philosophy of Religion* 27 (1990)

Efros, I., *Studies in Medieval Jewish Philosophy* (Columbia University Press, 1974)

Fackenheim, E.L., *To Mend the World* (Schocken, 1982)

Fackenheim, E.L., 'Transcendence in Contemporary Culture: Philosophical Reflections and a Jewish Theology,' in H.W. Richardson & D.R. Cutler (eds) *Transcendence* (Beacon Press, 1969)

Feldman, S., 'The Binding of Isaac: A Test-Case of Divine Foreknowledge' in T. Rudavsky (ed.), *Divine Omniscience and Omnipotence in Medieval Philosophy. Islamic, Jewish and Christian Perspectives* (Reidel, [Kluwer], 1985), pp. 105-33

Fischer, J. (ed.), *Moral Responsibility* (Cornell University Press, 1986)

Fischer, J. & M. Ravizza (eds.), *Perspectives on Moral Responsibility* (Cornell University Press, 1993)

Fleischner, E. (ed.), *Auschwitz: Beginning of a New Era* (Ktav, 1977)

Flew, A., 'Divine Omnipotence and Human Freedom' in A. Flew & A. MacIntyre (eds), *New Essays in Philosophical Theology* (London, 1955), pp. 144-69

Flew, A., 'Theology and Falsification', in A. Flew & A. MacIntyre (eds.), *New Essays in Philosophical Theology* (SCM Press, 1955), pp. 98-9

Frankfurt, H., 'Alternate Possibilities and Moral Responsibility', *Journal of Philosophy* 66 (1969), pp. 828-39

Gaon, S. ben, *Book of Theodicy: Translation and Commentary on the Book of Job*, tr. S. Rosenblatt (Yale University Press, 1988)

Glatzer, N.N. (ed.), *The Dimensions of Job: A Study and Selected Readings* (Schocken Books, 1969)

Greenberg, I, 'Cloud of Smoke, Pillar of Fire: Judaism, Christianity, and Modernity after the Holocaust', in E. Fleischner (ed.), *Auschwitz: Beginning of a New Era* (Ktav, 1977)

Griffin, D., *God, Power and Evil: A Process Theodicy* (Westminster, 1976)

Griffin, D., 'Critique of Roth' in S.T. Davis (ed.), *Encountering Evil: Live Options in Theodicy* (T. & T. Clark, 1981)

Halbfass, W., 'Karma, Apūrva, and "Natural" Causes: Observations on the Growth and Limits of the Theory of Samsara', in O'Flaherty, W.D. (ed.), *Karma and Rebirth in Classical Indian Traditions* (University of California Press, 1980), pp. 268-302

Hertz, J.H. (ed.), *Pentateuch and Haftorahs* (Soncino, 1960)

Hick, J., *Evil and the God of Love* (Harper & Row, 1966; 2nd ed. Macmillan, 1990)

Hopkins, G.M., *The Poems of Gerard Manley Hopkins*, ed. W.H. Gardner & N.H. MacKenzie (Oxford University Press, 4th ed., 1980)

Howard-Snyder, D., *The Evidential Argument from Evil* (Indiana University Press, 1996)

Hume, D., *Dialogues Concerning Natural Religion and the Posthumous Essays of the Immorality of the Soul and of Suicide* (Hackett Publishing Co., 1980)

Jaini, P., 'Karma and the Problem of Rebirth in Jainism', in W.D. O'Flaherty (ed.), *Karma and Rebirth in Classical Indian Traditions* (University of California Press, 1980), pp. 217-38

Kaplan, M., *The Meaning of God in Modern Jewish Religion* (Behrman House, 1947)

Kaplan, M., *Judaism without Supernaturalism* (Reconstructionist Press, 1958)

Keane, F., 'The day I met a mass killer – and he smirked, knowing he'd escape justice', *Independent*, Saturday, 20 June 1998

Kenny, A., *The God of the Philosophers* (Clarendon, 1979)

Kierkegaard, S., *Fear and Trembling* (Penguin, 1986)

Klossowski, Pierre, *Sade My Neighbour* (Northwestern University Press, 1991)

Kondylis, P., *Die Aufklärung im Rahmen des neuzeitlichen Rationalismus* (Ernst Klett, 1981)

Kropf, R.W., *Evil and Evolution: A Theodicy* (Fairleigh Dickinson University Press, 1984)

Kumar, Frederick, *The Philosophies of India: A New Approach* (Edwin Mellen Press, 1991)

Küng, H., *Judaism Between Yesterday and Tomorrow* (Crossroad, 1992)

Lambert, W.G., *Babylonian Wisdom Literature* (Oxford University Press, 1960)

Lamm, N., *The Face of God* (Yeshiva University, 1982)

Landau, D., *Piety and Power: The World of Jewish Fundamentalism* (Hill & Wang, 1993)

Leaman, O., *Evil and Suffering in Jewish Philosophy* (Cambridge University Press, 1995)

Long, J., 'Karma and Rebirth in the *Mahābhārata*', in W.D. O'Flaherty (ed.), *Karma and Rebirth in Classical Indian Traditions* (University of California Press, 1980), pp. 38-60

Mackie, J.L., *The Miracle of Theism* (Clarendon Press, 1982)

Mackie, J.L., 'Evil and Omnipotence' repr. Marilyn McCord Adams & Robert Merrihew Adams (eds), *The Problem of Evil*, Oxford Readings in Philosophy (Oxford University Press, 1990), pp. 25-37

Martin, M., 'Is Evil Evidence against the Existence of God?', *Mind* 87 (1987), pp. 429-32; repr. M. Peterson (ed.), pp. 135-9

Masters, B., *The Evil that Men Do* (Doubleday, 1996; Black Swan edition, 1997)

Maimonides, M., *Guide of the Perplexed*, tr. S. Pines (Chicago, 1963)

McDermott, J., 'Karma and Rebirth in Early Buddhism', W.D. O'Flaherty (ed.), *Karma and Rebirth in Classical Indian Traditions* (University of California Press, 1980), pp. 165-92

Mendelssohn, M., *Jerusalem, or On Religious Power and Judaism*, tr. A. Arkush (University Press of New England, 1983)

Mesle, C.R., *John Hick's Theodicy: A Process Humanist Critique* (Macmillan, 1991)

Moore, G., *Believing in God* (T. & T. Clark, 1988)

Müller, F.M. (ed.), *The Sacred Books of the East* vol. 34 (Motilal Banardisass, 1973)

McKim, R., 'Worlds Without Evil', *International Journal for Philosophy of Religion* 15 (1984), pp. 161-70

Nayak, G.C., *Evil, Karma and Reincarnation* (Centre of Advanced Study in Philosophy, Vivsva-Bharati, 1973)

Nayak, G.C., *Philosophical Reflections* (Motilal Banarsidass, 1987)

Nielsen, K., *Ethics Without God* (Prometheus Books, 1990)

Obeyesekere, G., 'Rebirth Eschatology and its Transformations: A Contribution to the Sociology of Early Buddhism', in W.D. O'Flaherty (ed.), *Karma and Rebirth in Classical Indian Traditions* (University of California Press, 1980), pp. 137-64

O'Flaherty, W.D. (ed.), *Karma and Rebirth in Classical Indian Traditions* (University of California Press, 1980)

Ormsby, E., *Theodicy in Islamic Thought* (Princeton University Press, 1984)

Pagels, E., *Adam, Eve and the Serpent* (Weidenfeld & Nicolson, 1988)

Peterson, M. (ed.), *The Problem of Evil: Selected Readings* (University of Notre Dame Press, 1992)

Phillips, D.Z., *Concept of Prayer* (Routledge & Kegan Paul, 1965; 2nd ed. 1968)

Philo, *De decalogo*, nos 176-8, in *Works*, ed. and tr. F. Colson, G. Whitacker & R. Marcus, 12 vols. Loeb Classical Library (Harvard University Press, 1929-62)

Plantinga, A., *God, Freedom and Evil* (Allen & Unwin, 1975, first published Harper & Row, 1974)

Plantinga, A., *The Nature of Necessity* (Clarendon Press, 1974)

Plantinga, A., 'Epistemic Probability and Evil' in D. Howard-Snyder (ed.), *The Evidential*

Argument from Evil (Indiana University Press, 1996)

Potter, K.H. (ed.), *Encyclopedia of Indian Philosophies*: *Advaita Vedānta* up to *Śankara and His Pupils* (Princeton University Press, 1981)

Potter, K.H. (ed.), 'The Karma Theory and its Interpretation in Some Indian Philosophical Systems', in W.D. O'Flaherty (ed.), *Karma and Rebirth in Classical Indian Traditions* (University of California Press, 1980), pp. 241-67

Potter, K.H. (ed.), *Presuppositions of India's Philosophies* (Prentice Hall, 1963)

Reichenbach, B., *Evil and a Good God* (Fordham University Press, 1982)

Reichenbach, B., 'Evil and a Reformed View of God', *International Journal for Philosophy of Religion* 24 (1988), pp. 67-85

Richardson, H.W. & D.R. Cutler (eds), *Transcendence* (Beacon Press, 1969)

Roth, J.K., 'A Theodicy of Protest', in S.T. Davis (ed.), *Encountering Evil*: *Live Options in Theodicy* (T. & T. Clark, 1981), pp. 7-22

Roux, G., *Ancient Iraq* (Pelican, 1980)

Rubenstein, R., *After Auschwitz*: *Radical Theology and Contemporary Judaism* (Bobbs-Merrill, 1966)

Rudavsky, T. (ed.), *Divine Omniscience and Omnipotence in Medieval Philosophy. Islamic, Jewish and Christian Perspectives* (Reidel, [Kluwer], 1985)

Sade, Marquis de, *The Passionate Philosopher*, ed. Margaret Crosland (P. Owen, 1991)

Scholem, G., 'Kabbalah', in *Encylopedia Judaica*, vol. 10, cols 588-601

Schulweis, H.M., *Evil and the Morality of God* (Hebrew Union College Press, 1984)

Sharma, I.C., *Ethical Philosophies of India* (Allen & Unwin, 1965)

Sinari, R.A., *The Structure of Indian Thought* (Charles C. Thomas, 1970)

Sontag, F., 'Anthropodicy and the Return of God', in S.T. Davis (ed.), *Encountering Evil*: *Live Options in Theodicy* (T. & T. Clark, 1981)

Staub, E., *The Roots of Evil*: *The Origins of Genocide and Other Group Violence* (Cambridge University Press, 1989)

Stcherbatsky, F. Th., *Buddhist Logic* (Dover, 1962), 2 vols

Steinsaltz, A., *The Thirteen Petalled Rose*, tr. Yehuda Hanegbi (Basic Books, 1980)

Stewart, M., *The Greater Good Defence*: *Essay on the Rationality of Faith* (Macmillan, 1992)

Stoeber, M., *Evil and the Mystics' God*: *Towards a Mystical Theodicy* (Macmillan, 1992)

Stump, E., 'Knowledge, Freedom, and the Problem of Evil' in M. Peterson (ed.), *The Problem of Evil*: *Selected Readings* (University of Notre Dame Press, 1992)

Stump, E., 'Aquinas on the Sufferings of Job', in D. Howard Snyder (ed.), *The Evidential Argument from Evil* (Indiana University Press, 1996)

Styron, W., *Sophie's Choice* (Picador, 1992)

Surin, K., *Theology and the Problem of Evil* (Basil Blackwell, 1986)

Swinburne, R., *The Existence of God* (Clarendon Press, 1979)

Tilley, T., *The Evils of Theodicy* (Georgetown University Press, 1991)

Trau, J.M., 'The Positive Value of Evil', *International Journal for Philosophy of Religion* 21 (1988), pp. 21-33

Vardy, P., *The Puzzle of Evil* (Fount/HarperCollins, 1992)

von Glasenapp, H., *Buddhism – A Non-theistic Religion,* tr. I. Schloegl (Allen & Unwin, 1970)

Watt, W., *Freewill and Predestination in Early Islam* (1948)

Wetzel, J., 'Can Theodicy be Avoided? The Claim of Unredeemed Evil', *Religious Studies* 25 (1989), pp. 1-13. Reprinted in M. Peterson (ed.), The Problem of Evil: Selected Readings (University of Notre Dame Press, 1992)

Wiesel, E., *The Oath*, tr. M. Wiesel (Random House, 1973)

Wiesel, E., *Messengers of God*, tr. M. Wiesel (Random House, 1976)

Wolpin, N., *A Path through the Ashes* (Masorah Publications, 1986)

Yandell, K.E., *The Epistemology of Religious Experience* (Cambridge University Press, 1993)

Zimmer, H., *Philosophies of India* (Routledge & Kegan Paul, 1952)

Index